Rain Forest Literatures

Cultural Studies of the Americas

Edited by George Yúdice, Jean Franco, and Juan Flores

Rain Forest Literatures

Amazonian Texts and Latin American Culture

Lúcia Sá

Cultural Studies of the Americas, Volume 16

University of Minnesota Press
Minneapolis ∾ London

The University of Minnesota Press gratefully acknowledges assistance provided for the publication of this book by the Division of Languages, Literatures and Cultures, Stanford University, Palo Alto, California.

A portion of chapter 1 appears in "*Tricksters* e Mentirosos que Abalaram a Literatura Nacional: as Narrativas de Akúli e Mayuluaípu," in *Macunaíma e Jurupari: Cosmogonias Ameríndias,* edited by Sérgio Luiz Medeiros (São Paulo: Editora Perspectiva, 2002), 245–59; reprinted with permission of the publisher. A portion of chapter 5 first appeared in "O Índio muda de voz: 'Gaspar Ilóm' e 'Meu Tio o Iauaretê,'" in *Romance Languages Annual* 4 (1992): 564–69; reprinted with the permission of Purdue University. A portion of chapter 7 appeared in "A *Lenda do Jurupari:* texto sagrado ou fruto da imaginação de *littérateurs?*" in *Macunaíma e Jurupari: Cosmogonias Ameríndias,* edited by Sérgio Luiz Medeiros (São Paulo: Editora Perspectiva, 2002), 347–58; reprinted with permission of the publisher. Chapter 11 first appeared as "Perverse Tribute: Mario Vargas Llosa's *El hablador* and Its Machiguenga Sources," in *Tesserae: Journal of Iberian and Latin American Studies* 4, no. 2 (1998): 145–64; see http://www.tandf.co.uk for more information on *Tesserae: Journal of Iberian and Latin American Studies.*

Published by the University of Minnesota Press
111 Third Avenue South, Suite 290
Minneapolis, MN 55401-2520
http://www.upress.umn.edu

Library of Congress Cataloging-in-Publication Data

Sá, Lúcia.
    Rain forest literatures : Amazonian texts and Latin American culture / Sá, Lúcia.
      p.   cm. — (Cultural studies of the Americas ; v. 16)
    Includes bibliographical references and index.
    ISBN 0-8166-4324-5 (hc : alk. paper) — ISBN 0-8166-4325-3 (pb : alk. paper)
    1. Latin American literature—Indian influences.   2. Indian literature—South America—
History and criticism.   3. Acculturation—Latin America.   I. Title.   II. Series.
    PQ7081.S2155 2004
    860.9'98—dc22

2003025854

Printed in the United States of America on acid-free paper

The University of Minnesota is an equal-opportunity educator and employer.

12 11 10 09 08 07 06 05 04   10 9 8 7 6 5 4 3 2 1

For Gordon Brotherston

Contents

Note on Translations

TITLES OF NON-ENGLISH PUBLICATIONS that appear in English refer to existing translations, cited in the bibliography. On occasion, small emendations have been made to correct obvious slips, to restore missing phrases or sentences, and to create consistency with other texts.

Unless otherwise stated, all translations of works whose titles appear in the original language are mine.

Acknowledgments

M ANY PEOPLE AND A FEW INSTITUTIONS have helped me to bring this work to a conclusion. A shorter version of it was presented as a Ph.D. dissertation to the departments of comparative literature and Spanish and Portuguese at Indiana University. As a doctoral student there, I received financial support from the Department of Spanish and Portuguese as well as a College of Arts and Sciences Dissertation Award. At Stanford, I was given grants by the Division of Literatures, Cultures, and Languages and by the Center for Latin American Studies in order to conduct further research in Brazil.

Over the years, friends have heard me talk endlessly about the subject of this book and have helped me, one way or another, to focus more clearly; among them are Vânia Castro, Ana María Ochoa, Eduardo Brondízio, Andrea Siqueira, Eduardo Góes Neves, Ana Amélia Boischio, Jean Langdon, Benito Rodriguez, and Niraldo de Farias. Claus Clüver, Edward Friedman, Betty Mindlin, Sérgio Luiz Medeiros, and Heloisa Pontes were patient enough to read the manuscript and make valuable suggestions. The Stanford study group that met on Tuesday afternoons at Paula Ebron's house gave me great support and offered helpful critiques: many thanks to her, and to Miyako Inoue, Claire Fox, and very especially to Mary Louise Pratt for her comments and friendship. Many thanks also to all my colleagues at the Department of Spanish and Portuguese for their open generosity. The current shape of this work owes a lot to the responses, criticisms, and practical help at all levels offered by them and by students at Stanford, especially Karina Hodoyan, Sara Rondinel, María Helena Rueda, Alex Lang Susman, Jessi Aaron, and Miguel Hilario, plus the many undergraduates who took and contributed to my "Reading the Rain Forest" courses in 1999, 2000, and 2001. David Treece, Marcio Souza, and Neil Whitehead sent me vital materials, and I am particularly grateful to Gerhard Baer for his generosity in mailing copies of the Machiguenga texts drawn on by Vargas Llosa, which otherwise had been impossible to find and which are indispensable for an adequate assessment of *The Storyteller.* I have benefited from conversations at conferences, with Ellen Basso in Tempe; Henry Glassie in Bloomington; and with Carmen Junqueira, João de Jesus Paes Loureiro, Mário César Leite, and many others at the magnificent meeting on the Amazon, in both senses (we sailed from Belém to Santarém and back), organized by Maria do Socorro Simões in 1999. Earlier in Brazil, I learned much from Claudia Andujar, coordinator of the Comissão pela Criação do Parque Yanomami (CCPY); from Lígia Chiappini, who introduced me to *Quarup* and *Maíra* in my early days at Universidade de São Paulo; from Flávio Wolf de Aguiar, who directed my M.A. thesis on those two novels at the same institution; and from the experience of teaching rain forest texts in courses given at the federal universities of Maceió and Belém (and repeated more recently at Oberlin). Thanks go also to my sister Cândida, for innumerable FedEx packages from Brazil of last-minute articles and books that could not be found elsewhere; to Fátima Roque for all her support; and to Clemence Jouet-Pastré and Alicia Ríos for the afternoon coffee breaks we shared.

Gordon Brotherston's contributions to this book have been so many that he deserves a paragraph of his own. He has been a guide, a careful reader and copy editor, a devastating critic, and a generous supporter. I could not possibly thank him, so I offer him the book instead.

1. Pemon
2. So'to
3. Macuxi
4. Desâna
5. Tariana
6. Tukano
7. Manao
8. Baniwa
9. Machiguenga
10. Guaraṇi

11. Tupinambá*
12. Tupiniquim*
13. Tamoio*
14. Urubu-Kaapor
15. Kamayurá
16. Kalapalo
17. Gê-Bororo

* 16th-century groups

Introduction

SHELTERING ALMOST HALF THE EARTH'S LIVING SPECIES, the rain forest and tropical lowlands of South America are also home to indigenous peoples who speak many different languages and have diverse customs. These peoples are quite defined in themselves, yet they have never been pristine units living in complete isolation from each other, as anthropologists have sometimes wanted us to believe. For millennia, they have been in contact with near and distant neighbors. They have always traveled, fought, made and broken treaties, and traded goods, shamanic knowledge, cures, songs, speeches, and narratives. This was certainly the case before the European invasion, and has continued to be since. After the invasion, however, indigenous groups throughout the tropical lowlands, as elsewhere in America, have had to deal with a more concerted and technologically efficient pressure on their lives, cultures, and land.

Nobody knows for sure how many native American lives were claimed by disease or assassination in the region during the first two centuries of invasion, but most historical accounts agree that they must amount to millions. In addition to physical violence and expropriation of land, rain forest people were (and continue to be) subject to constant attacks on their culture by religious and secular institutions and individuals convinced of their own cultural and moral superiority. The consequences of these policies, as we know, have been devastating for indigenous peoples throughout the Americas.

The imbalance of power in this confrontation is undeniable, yet the process cannot be described exclusively as the imposition of one cultural system upon another. From the first moments of contact, rain forest peoples resisted invasion. Speeches they have made record clear scepticism toward European claims to cultural superiority. When imposed, European religious and cultural practices have rarely been accepted entirely but more often have been adapted and modified in order to fit indigenous needs and beliefs. Conversely, native knowledge and ways of living have left a definite mark on the European and Europeanized worlds.

After Independence in the nineteenth century, South American authors writing in Portuguese, Spanish, and other imported languages became increasingly drawn to the idea of a rain forest literature, to songs, speeches and narratives original to their part of the world. Again and again, they delved deep into old chronicles, travelers' reports, and ethnographic journals in search of characters, plots, and ways of narrating, anxious to know more about their own countries and the peoples who had lived there longer than they had. They re-created characters, stole plots, quoted paragraphs and pages, and even structured their own works in ways that recall the structure of indigenous texts.

Yet literary historians and critics have seldom noticed these developments, largely ignoring the indigenous source texts, both as an antecedent indispensable for later writers and certainly as a literary corpus in its own right. No single history of Tupi or of Carib literature exists, for instance, nor is there any systematic study of Tupi-Guarani or Carib influence on Brazilian and Spanish American texts. In reflecting the experience of Brazil and the neighboring Spanish American lowlands, literary histories and national anthologies rarely begin by acknowledging native precedent, even in the "token" samples that sometimes represent prior culture elsewhere in the continent, like the Andes, Mesoamerica, and the English-speaking north. On the very few occasions when scholars have accepted and paid attention to the influence of rain forest texts, it has mostly been to consider them as "ethnographic material" or "raw data," that is, devoid of any inherent literary qualities. For this reason, the very notion of intertextuality, basic to all that is done here, has never been brought into play.

Going against the grain of critical traditions long-standing in Portuguese and Spanish, this book examines the impact of rain forest texts on literature that has been written over the last 150 years in Brazil and neighboring Spanish American nations, Venezuela, Colombia, Peru, Paraguay and, to a lesser degree, Argentina and Uruguay. Part of a process of cultural contact between native and non-native populations which defies such categories as "cultural imposition" or "acculturation," this impact is best described by the term "transculturation." Coined by Fernando Ortiz in 1940, the term was revitalized by Angel Rama in 1980 and by Mary Louise Pratt in 1992. Pratt's understanding of the term is especially germane: "While the imperial metropolis tends to understand itself as determining the periphery (in the emanating glow of the civilizing mission of the cash flow of development, for example), it habitually blinds itself to the ways in which the periphery determines the metropolis"(6).

The four parts of the book correspond to the four tropical lowland traditions that have had most influence on South American authors: Macro-Carib, Tupi-Guarani, the upper Rio Negro Tukano-Arawak system, and Western Arawak. In each case, the opening chapter deals with the corresponding native texts, the history of their publication, and how they may be seen to constitute a corpus—all within the geo-historical frame to which they and their authors belong. In this, given characteristics of the texts in question are examined in detail, always having in mind their impact on later writers.

"Pacaraima Texts," which opens Part I ("Roraima and the Carib"), offers a detailed analysis of Pemon narratives collected by Theodor Koch-Grünberg (1924), focusing, above all, on cosmogony and trickster tales. It also compares these Pemon narratives with Macuxi versions published, many decades before, by Richard Schomburgk, and to another set of Pemon texts published a few decades later by Cesáreo Armellada. Moreover, it examines the coherence of those texts within the Carib tradition by comparing them to *Watunna,* a stunning body of sacred narratives told by the So'to, Western neighbors of the Macuxi and the Pemon. Common to all is a geographical imaginary that centers on the Pacaraima ridge and the fabled mountain Roraima, the landmark now shared by Venezuela, Brazil, and Guyana, and the improbable hydrography that joins the Amazon and Orinoco river systems.

In "Tupi-Guarani Texts," the introductory chapter to Part II, priority is given to a long and complicated publication history. It begins with the colonial chroniclers, whose commitment to conquering and/or converting the Indians allowed little room for finer literary appreciation. Yet these early descriptions of the Tupi-Guarani are a valuable tool for understanding them as they were three or more centuries ago, in spite (and sometimes because) of their authors' racial and moral prejudices. Through these texts, we first come to sense the reference points of the Tupi-Guarani world, whose language was carried over the entire rain forest, and well beyond, south to Uruguay (a Guarani name) and Argentina: their "Great lowland territory." The native voice has to be listened for, and is usually heard in the form of short dialogues, indirect quotations, speech formulas, and more rarely, songs. After the chroniclers, we move on to the nineteenth- and early twentieth-century collections of narratives—classic texts like Couto de Magalhães's *O Selvagem*, Barbosa Rodrigues's *Poranduba Amazonense*, and above all, Curt Nimuendaju's *Die Sagen von der Erschaffung und Vernichtung der Welt*. Couto de Magalhães's and Barbosa Rodrigues's collections of native stories are the first ever to be published in Portuguese, or indeed a European language, and they exude, not surprisingly, a certain period interest in "folk." Nimuendaju foreshadows modern anthropology in Brazil with narratives that allowed a first prolonged insight into Guarani philosophy, their perceptions of *Yvy marã ey* (land without ill) and the creation of the world—principles also evident in the subsequent collection by León Cadogan, *Ayvu Rapyta*.

Having a multi-layered archaeology, the Rio Negro system is also multilingual, and it is characterized by a profusion of narratives whose publication history begins in the late nineteenth century (Part III, "Confluence in the Rio Negro"). In the main, these texts deal, one way or another, with the interconnected themes of Jurupari and the Big Snake, and the subsequent story of settlement, which ranges north from the Amazon towards the Andes on the one hand and Roraima on the other. The opening chapter "The Upper Rio Negro: Jurupari and the Big Snake," concentrates on the major cosmogonies, classics like Stradelli's *Leggenda dell' Jurupary*, Brandão do Amorim's *Lendas em Nheengatu e em Português*, and the Desâna *Antes o Mundo não Existia*—this last being the first genesis story in Brazil and South America actually to be published by a specific group in its name and language.

By contrast, in "The Arawak and the Uppermost Amazon" (Part IV), the fact that relatively few Machiguenga texts have been published makes the task of tracing their history easier. At the same time and for the same reason, the geography of the world they emerge from has been little recognized by outsiders. Hence, the introductory chapter, "The Machiguenga and Their Heritage," attempts to locate them as a people living between the western edge of the rain forest and the Andean cordillera, who are well aware of a history of invasion from both sides that dates back to the Inca and even earlier.

Despite differences among these four traditions, and indeed among groups within each, the overall coherence of rain forest culture serves as a working principle. This coherence has been attested in major anthropological statements, such as Claude Lévi-Strauss's *Mythologiques* (1964–1971), Gerardo Reichel-Dolmatoff's *Amazonian Cosmos* (1971), Peter Roe's *The Cosmic Zygote* (1982), and Lawrence Sullivan's *Icanchu's Drum* (1988), which taken together, allow us to speak of a tropical-lowland view of the world. In this view, we find emphasis placed not on a single definitive creation, like that in the Bible, but on multiple genesis, dreamings into existence, metamorphoses and ongoing transformations of the world after its usually problematic beginnings. There is also the celebration of human kinship with other species rather than our absolute difference from them, communion with the great jaguars, snakes, even plants; agriculture— Cain's calling—and harvest; means of curing; hospitality as a social priority; and the problematic nature of any who would be "heroes." Leaving aside statements directed explicitly at Western ears, this philosophy, as a mode of human understanding, is not to be found in treatises or abstract argumentation. Rather, it is embodied in the very sinews of narrative and turns of verse, inviting listeners and readers to tease out meaning, to articulate the knowledge for themselves.

These rain forest texts were gathered through several agencies, each of them having, of course, its own ideological agenda. This is obviously the case with the religious orders—Jesuits, Franciscans, and Capuchins in colonial times, Dominicans, Capuchins, and Salesians in the twentieth century. Protestant organizations such as the Summer Institute of Linguistics have also participated in the process, as have several state institutions, such as the Brazilian Instituto Histórico e Geográfico and the Serviço de Proteção ao Índio, later replaced by the Fundação Nacional de Apoio ao Índio; the Banco Central de Venezuela, which financed the Spanish translation of the Koch-Grünberg collection; the Baessler Institut in Berlin, which early in the twentieth century sponsored several scientific journeys to Latin America. The range of individuals involved includes missionaries, adventurers, soldiers, naturalists, academic ethnographers, and, of course, the Indians themselves.

Of these last: the young Pemon named Mayuluaípu and Akuli, who told and translated the stories included in Koch-Grünberg's collection, were so committed to their work that they made the long and arduous trip from Roraima to Manaus in order to deliver the manuscripts directly to the German Consulate there, even though Koch-Grünberg himself had asked them just to leave them in the nearest town. Ernesto Pinto, the Pemon who tells most of the stories published by Cesáreo Armellada, gives us a history of those texts in a preface to that collection, *Pemonton taremuru*. Marc de Civrieux took the originals of *Watunna* back to the So'to, who discussed them in detail before approving their publication. A century ago in the Rio Negro region, the Tariana Indian Maximiano José Roberto spent a good part of his life gathering stories which he wrote down in Nheengatu (modern Tupi) and translated into Portuguese, having discussed their import and structure with those who gave them to him. As is so often the case, those stories nonetheless appeared under other people's names: Barbosa Rodrigues and Ermanno Stradelli. In our day in the same region, Umusī Pārōkumu and Tōrāmū Kēhíri, representatives of the Desâna, decided to publish the cosmogony of their people, *Antes o Mundo não Existia,* because of the mistakes that they thought were being propagated by other versions. Among the Tupi-Guarani, Curt Unkel was the first foreigner (nonnative) to be told the Apapokuva creation stories, an honor bestowed on him for his loyalty, after he had become a member of the tribe and adopted the name Nimuendaju. A Portuguese translation of those stories was published only in 1984, through a process that involved the Guarani groups living on the coast of São Paulo. Finally, a few years ago, the Txucarramāe Indian Kaká Werá Jecupé, who grew up a Guarani in the city of São Paulo, wrote an autobiography that culminates in activism on behalf of Native American cultures and their survival.

These native originals have been transmitted through a range of imported languages: Portuguese, Spanish, German, French, English, Italian, and Dutch. Altogether, the mediation of different languages, agencies, and individuals complicates the process of interpreting and assessing them, to the degree indeed that many critics have considered them not worth reading as literature or intelligent self-representations of a culture. These complications are important, and will certainly be taken into consideration, yet they need not be critically paralyzing, or an excuse to stay away from a given text. After all, similar problems have affected the Homeric epics and the Bible, without in any way compromising their status or authority.

None of these native traditions is restricted to a single nation-state. The northern Carib, who gave their name to the Caribbean, today continue to occupy the borders of Brazil, Venezuela, Suriname, and Guyana. The Tupi-Guarani still inhabit regions all the way from Cayenne to southern Brazil, Paraguay, and Argentina, and from the Atlantic to Bolivia. The Rio Negro Tukano-Arawak system operates on both sides of the border that divides Brazil from Colombia. The Western Arawaks, among them the Campa and the Machiguenga, live and defend themselves in Peru, Brazil, and Colombia. Nor are all of these territories, strictly speaking, both "Amazonian" and "rain forest." Most Tupi groups mentioned by colonial chroniclers, as well as some present-day Guarani, lived and still live near or in the rain forest of the Atlantic coast, while other Guarani inhabit more temperate and drier regions toward the interior. However, anthropologists and archaeologists nowadays generally attribute to them all an Amazonian origin and hence an experience shared with the Carib, the Tukano, and the Arawak alike. Along with the philosophical and literary preferences noted earlier, this helps justify the title of the book, at least at the deeper time level.

In their texts, these peoples emphasize the specificity of the territories they have inhabited for centuries, giving the names and sacred histories of mountains, rivers, and waterfalls. They also narrate history. As anthropologists like Jonathan Hill, Ellen Basso, Terence Turner, and Alcida Ramos have pointed out, the distinction between "history" and "myth," once held to be axiomatic in Western thought, derives, most of the time, from our limited conceptions of each, and not from any necessary absence of historical discourse in the "mythical" texts. For this and other reasons, I avoid using the word "myth" in this work. More often than not, it has served the purpose of excluding native texts from the categories of "literature," "art," and "history"—an exclusion irrelevant and even inimical to the argument here. The problem is signally present in the volumes of Lévi-Strauss's *Mythologiques,* indispensable as they are, for they reduce to manipulable "mythic units" narratives that are specific with respect to territory, history, and politics, and turn extraordinary works of literature into summaries. More recently, it is true, the term has been used quite differently by the North-American ethnopoetics group—Dell Hymes, Dennis Tedlock, Jerome Rothenberg—and many other anthropologists who, following in their footsteps, have been paying close attention to the poetic structure of the native texts. Yet, the history of the term "myth," the systematic use of it to separate "indigenous texts" from "high art," and its popular meaning as "something that is not true," all point to distinctions that are not helpful to this study. As for the sacredness of "myth" and its supposedly specific functions—that is, the explanation and legitimation of cultural values—they are not necessarily separable, in my view, from the idea of "literature," as any study of Hesiod, Homer, or the Bible can show. This is not to say that I want the word "myth" and its derivatives removed from Western vocabularies, or that I wish to suggest that "literature" should replace "myth" in all contexts. Reading native texts as literature is a possibility among many: a possibility that has yet to be fully explored, especially with regard to America.

The same can be said about the differentiation between "oral" and "written" literatures, which has been used, quite profitably, to highlight specific characteristics of oral texts, in a vast amount of recent studies on performance. Yet in practice, the indigenous texts studied here have all been published, often with direct involvement of native authors, and it is in their published form that they became, for the most part, known to the writers who quote and re-create them. Above all, it is in their written form that we may compare them with each other, and with works by other South American writers. Thus, although at times I do take note of certain characteristics of "oral" literature, such as repetition and gesture, for the most part whether the texts studied here belonged or not to an "oral" tradition before they were published becomes a secondary matter.

Respecting indigenous texts and their own literary procedures, this study engages in questions about characters, plots, genre, and social and environmental context. Many characters in these texts, for example, tend to defy simplistic oppositions between "good" and "bad," "divine" and "human." Several plots deny the common Western belief that, to use the words of the anthropologist Michael Jackson, "the domains of darkness, wilderness or the Dreaming are other-worldly, super-natural, non-empirical." On the contrary, in those texts such domains are "worlds that enter experience and of which direct experience is had. They are, so to speak, dimensions of the lifeworld not ordinarily brought into consciousness, but they are integrally part of empirical reality" (15).

These and other notions learned from the indigenous texts brought about fundamental changes in South American writing, this being the focus of the subsequent chapters in each of the four parts. Where appropriate, as is the case with the Carib and the Tupi-Guarani traditions in the first and second parts, I give an historical overview of how rain forest texts have influenced Brazilian and Spanish American literature. At the same time, I have taken care throughout to bring out at length how understanding native precedent can be critical for close reading and interpreting key works. To this end, *Macunaíma, Maíra, Cobra Norato,* a pair of plays by Souza, and *The Storyteller* are allotted a whole chapter each (chapters 2, 6, 8, 9, 11).

"Penetrating the Dark Interior" (chapter 3) analyzes the importance of the Carib concept "canaima" in Rómulo Gallegos's *Canaima,* the role of Schomburgk's travelogue in Alejo Carpentier's *The Lost Steps* and, briefly, Eduardo Galeano's use of So'to cosmogony (as it appears in *Watunna*). "Romanticism and After" (chapter 5) contrasts the limited relevance, at first, of Guarani literature in Paraguay, Argentina, and Uruguay with the overwhelming impact that Tupi texts have had on Brazilian literature since the mid-nineteenth century. The careful study of colonial sources proves particularly useful for understanding the differences between the two most important Brazilian Romantic *Indianistas,* the poet Gonçalves Dias and the novelist José de Alencar. After 1922, *modernistas* of opposing ideologies combined the same colonial sources with their knowledge of recently published texts. In the process, the *antropófago* Oswald de Andrade transformed Tupi ritualistic cannibalism into a statement of postcolonial cultural appropriation; going the other way, the nationalists Plínio Salgado, Cassiano Ricardo, and Menotti del Picchia made of the supposedly "docile" Tupi a base on which to impose Brazilian nationhood. Quite another reading of the Tupi-Guarani is offered by João Guimarães Rosa in his short story "My Uncle the Iauaretê," whose protagonist avenges his native ancestors by re-entering his mother's Tupi-Guarani world, her language and shamanic beliefs.

As for the chapters dedicated to major works, chapter 2 deals with Mário de Andrade's novel *Macunaíma* (1928) and the impact of Koch-Grünberg's narratives on it, focusing particularly on its trickster protagonist and his subversions of the "language of the city." Chapter 6 examines Darcy Ribeiro's novel *Maíra* (1976) and its native sources, comparing it with the author's own anthropological works. Raul Bopp's poem *Cobra Norato* (1931) and its somewhat uneven relationship with upper Rio Negro texts are the subject of chapter 8. Chapter 9 analyzes two plays by Márcio Souza: "Dessana Dessana" and "Jurupari, a Guerra dos Sexos," linking them respectively to Umusĩ Pãrõkumu and Tõrãmũ Kẽhíri's *Antes o Mundo não Existia,* and to Stradelli's *Leggenda dell' Jurupary.* Chapter 11 concentrates on Mario Vargas Llosa's interested use of Machiguenga literature in *The Storyteller.*

Overall, the intertextuality in these cases can be seen to adhere to four basic models. The first is the journey of exploration. In this kind of narrative, the protagonist goes from an urban center into the "dark forest," in the footsteps of European invaders epitomized by the Spanish *conquistador.* In early examples of this model, Quiroga's "pioneering" short stories, *Canaima,* and the trilogy of exemplary novels *Doña Bárbara, Don Segundo Sombra,* and *Vortex,* the indigenous cultures are usually seen from the outside, and the intertextual exchange with their literatures is rather limited. The same can be said, in poetry, of Raul Bopp's *Cobra Norato.* Carpentier's *The Lost Steps* represents a change in this respect, for it allows the "dark other" to have a voice of its own, by appealing precisely to indigenous texts which include not just Carib but Meso-American cosmogonies. In the case of Posse's *Daimon,* the figure of the *conquistador* is actually domesticated and becomes a revolutionary from within, as a result of persistent exposure to philosophies and ways of life explained in the novel through quotations from Tupi and other sources. *Quarup* also describes a journey into the "dark forest," and although the Indians in it are still seen from the outside, the novel's protagonist learns from their culture things that become fundamental, later, to his revolutionary project. For its part, and at first sight surprisingly, *The Storyteller* proves to follow an earlier rather than a later version of this same journey, for the protagonist Mascarita abandons his life in Lima to join a Machiguenga community in the jungle and despite all his apparent respect for Machiguenga culture, ends up wanting to impose values and agendas of his own.

The second literary model that governs the contact with indigenous texts goes formally in the opposite direction, to incorporate Indians into the nation-states that have in practice devoured their territory, in the course of American independence. Here, the Indian is proposed as national hero, as he was above all by the Brazilian Romantics and *Indianistas* in the nineteenth century. From the start, this program was diagnosed as escapism, bourgeois bad faith, in particular a way of avoiding a more pressing and populous Afro-American presence in the nation. Only a careful reading of the sources used by the Romantics can disclose distinctions between them that would otherwise remain invisible. Such is the case of the poet Gonçalves Dias, whom critics have persistently accused of inventing medieval Indian "knights" that have no connection whatsoever with the original inhabitants of Brazil, despite their Indian names. Yet, when we compare Gonçalves Dias's works with their sources, we see that the behavior and discourse of his warrior-heroes is definitely closer to that of Tupinambá males than to European chivalry. Such a reading allows us to expose prejudices that have hampered critical analysis of *Indianismo* for nearly a century, and which circumvent primordial questions of land rights. Meanwhile in Spanish-speaking Uruguay, the main monument of Romanticism was Zorrilla de San Martín's *Tabaré*. The Guarani-named hero of this "national epic" is allowed that role only on condition that, acknowledging his racial inferiority, he vanish from the landscape.

As late as 1928, the Indian national hero was resuscitated by Mário de Andrade in *Macunaíma*. Thanks to a thoroughgoing involvement with Carib Pemon texts and their trickster-heroes, Mário actually deconstructs what had hitherto been thought heroic and creates instead "a hero without a character," a hero and an anti-hero at the same time.

In the third model, the indigenous texts become the basis of not so much national as revolutionary discourse, along lines powerfully evident in the Andes and Mesoamerica. What is at stake in this discourse is not just Indian rights to cultural and physical survival, but less destructive relationships with other species and with the environment, and a philosophical overhaul of Western notions of history and religion. Directly following the example of Asturias and Arguedas, in "My Uncle, the Iauaretê" Guimarães Rosa uses Nheengatu and native texts to ground a Tupi mestizo's capacity to resist and to battle against a surrounding society hostile to his Indian heritage and to his Indian totem animal, the jaguar. For the Peruvian novelist and critic José María Arguedas, Guimarães Rosa touched on ways of feeling he sought to bring to the fore in his own work, plumbing the depths of racial insult and exposing the limits and menace of Western universalism.

The revolutionary potential, in this sense, of native texts is drawn out more fully by the Spanish American authors Roa Bastos, Posse, and

Galeano, and by the Brazilian playwright Márcio Souza, all of whom rigorously counterpose received Western and often Christian notions of genesis with rain forest and particularly Tupi-Guarani and Rio Negro cosmogony. Exactly this situation recurs in Ribeiro's *Maíra,* where the debate between the two systems is enshrined in the very structure of the novel.

True, Ribeiro's Mairuns are a fictitious people who, though Tupi in name, also display characteristics of other Indian groups. In the novel, no attempt is made to create the illusion that one is reading "scientific data": No names of ethnographers, or of ethnographic works, are ever mentioned. When, in the central chapter, Darcy Ribeiro speaks directly to the reader, it is only to say how he met those who inspired him to create his main characters. Yet of course the author's background is not irrelevant here, and a comparison between the novel and his ethnographic works shows that the intertextual exchange is in fact intense. Indigenous texts collected in part by Ribeiro himself are quoted and re-created at length. Usually, the process of re-creation intensifies the original argument of the native texts. Thus, the Tupi-Guarani cataclysmic view of the world is intensified in Maíra's monologue, when the god of that name asks himself whether perhaps he might after all be mortal. The struggle between father and son, already present in Tupi-Guarani literature, is made into the tragic central argument of Ribeiro's novel, while for its part the binary social division of the Gê-Bororo is taken to extremes as an organizing principle. Although the Mairuns are fictitious, their cosmogony, their social life and worldview, are heavily grounded in indigenous texts. In the process of rewriting those texts, the author plays with them, modifies them, re-creates them, but never diminishes or contradicts them.

Of course, involvement with native texts does not in itself guarantee support for the native cause. Our fourth model applies to Vargas Llosa's *The Storyteller,* which represents a reaction against the forms of revolution proposed by the previous texts. *The Storyteller* resembles *Maíra* in its intense use and rewriting of indigenous texts, in order to establish a cosmogony that in principle conflicts with the Christian Genesis. However, it situates its present-day Indian subjects far more specifically in time and space. It deals with a single recognizable group, the Machiguenga, physically located in eastern Peru. Ethnographic studies of this group are frequently cited in the novel, and so are the names of almost all the anthropologists and missionaries who have ever worked among them. The readers are made to believe that what they are reading corresponds, in fact, to a "scientific" account. Quoting indigenous texts at length, Vargas Llosa most of the time stays quite close to his sources. However, he makes certain changes to their cosmogony which affect, drastically, the way we see the Machiguenga and their world. Vargas Llosa tends to make the invasion of the Machiguenga territory by non-Indians less criminal and tragic, by altering cosmogony in such a way as to suggest the Machiguenga are nomadic, of "no fixed abode," and always on the move. Moreover, the novel presents the Machiguenga as a culturally weakened and dispersed group, among whom the intrusive Mascarita with "his" narratives can allegedly come to play a central and centralizing role. As a result, the Machiguenga in the novel can survive only as pariahs, as fugitives whose sense of community and cultural cohesion must diminish with time—a fate that is not seen as something necessarily negative. Only the comparison of *The Storyteller* with its indigenous sources can alert us to Vargas Llosa's ideological maneuvers in the novel, and confirm that its message differs little from opinions that he has otherwise offered on Latin America's need for an Indian-free destiny.

Most of the Latin American texts studied here are modernist, either in the strict sense of belonging to the Brazilian cultural movement called *Modernismo*, or in the broader sense of being part of a Western political and cultural project that was interrupted in the 1980s, with the demise, at least for the moment, of most Marxist revolutionary hopes. Thus, this book can also be read as a discussion of Latin American modernist ethics and aesthetics: its indebtedness to Romanticism; its complex relationship with European adoption of "primitive" art; its contradictory links with various nationalist projects; and above all, its practice of cultural appropriation and incorporation of popular discourses. Such practice can take several forms. In the case of Mário de Andrade's *Macunaíma*, for instance, the profound intertextual relationship with native stories and ways of narrating allowed the creation of a trickster-hero that much complicates, in my view, the allegorical interpretations that most critics have made of the novel. Conversely, Raul Bopp's *Cobra Norato*, which is usually understood to be a rewriting of rain forest "myth," on close examination proves to belong more to the tradition of Western travel writing. Modernism (and its links to ideas of nationhood) can also help us understand the inherent pessimism with regard to the future of indigenous communities that marks even the most committed of these authors, as is the case with Darcy Ribeiro. For its part, though Mario Vargas Llosa's *The Storyteller* could be seen as postmodern in its deconstruction of committed ethnography and *indigenista* literature, comparison with its native sources reveals an overtly political and nationalist program, which therefore brings it closer to a reactionary latter-day modernism. This is what William Rowe has argued with respect to Vargas Llosa's later work, noting how it centers on what he calls "authoritarian enunciation" (100).

Vargas Llosa's hostility to modernist *indigenismo*, epitomized in his study of José María Arguedas, *A Utopia Arcaica,* is not unique. It is part of a larger debate that has divided Latin American writers and critics for over a century. In nineteenth-century Brazil, the protagonists of this debate were the *Indianista* writer José de Alencar (himself a conservative politician) and important political figures such as the historian Varnhagen and the great abolitionist Joaquim Nabuco. In order to criticize Alencar's use of Tupi Indians as symbols of the nascent Brazilian nation, Varnhagen went so far as to write an anti-*Indianista* novel, *Sumé.* Nabuco did not write anti-Indianist fiction, but engaged in active attacks against Alencar, stating, at one point, that "we are Brazilians, not Guaranis" (Coutinho, 109). One of the reasons for Nabuco's passionate attacks on Alencar is quite noble. In Alencar's model for Brazilian society, which relied heavily on the miscegenation between whites and Indians, there was an element missing: the black slave—an absence that could be easily explained by Alencar's anti-abolitionist tendencies. In a society that brought four million black slaves from Africa, such absence is unforgivable, and Alencar was indeed (and quite correctly) never forgiven for it.

But there is another reason for Nabuco's attacks on Alencar: In the nineteenth-century debates about whether or not Native Brazilians should be granted any rights at all to their ancestral lands, Nabuco was an active defender of the position that they should not, on the grounds that they were "nomadic hordes"—a description hostilely incorrect for almost any indigenous group in Brazil, and certainly for the highly agricultural Tupi. Nabuco's platform in both debates is the same. Alencar may not have realized it, but Nabuco certainly did: By claiming the historical importance of Indians in the formation of Brazilian society, one is dangerously close to accepting their ancestral rights to land. In other words, most debates about Indians and indigenous cultures, whether in the nineteenth century or now, have to do, one way or another, with rights to land. Nabuco's argument that the Tupis should not be granted land rights because they were "nomadic" was reproduced by Vargas Llosa when he rewrote Machiguenga cosmogony in *The Storyteller.* That argument, in turn, cannot be dissociated from Vargas Llosa's obsession with José María Arguedas and his critiques of the latter's interest in indigenous cultures. For Vargas Llosa, Arguedas's intertextual experiments with indigenous literatures were the result of personal problems, not of any particular contact with the indigenous cultures themselves. The argument is well known, for it has been at the center of post-structuralist critiques of Western meta-narratives: A non-Indian can never really get to know indigenous cultures, and her/his attempts to engage with them are always going to result in invention. This argument may have some philosophical edge, and it certainly can caution us academics in our presumed claims to authority. Yet in practical terms it has had the paralyzing effect of relegating native cultures to a frozen ahistorical otherness, denying them any possibility of voice or interference in our cultural creations. The only true Indian is the Indian we don't understand, and in order for her/him to continue to be an Indian, she/he has to remain beyond understanding. An Indian who speaks or writes, whose discourse can be understood or translated to/by us, who has incorporated part of our discourse or been incorporated by it, has no claim to "Indianness" any more, and therefore to ancestry or ancestral territory.

This attitude is, unfortunately, very widespread. In Brazil and Spanish America, indigenous cultures have been repeatedly written out of historical discourse. Their resistance, their texts, their cultural legacy have constantly been ignored or denied, and very often the attempts to highlight them have been quickly dismissed as "romantic." This is not to deny that romantic descriptions of indigenous societies exist, but the ease with which this adjective is applied to depictions of indigenous cultures, especially if they are minimally positive, is in itself a symptom of a general prejudice. Why is a negative description of an indigenous culture necessarily "truer," or "less romantic" than a positive one? And if it is, why don't we then immediately discard as "romantic" any positive description of, say, suffragist democracy, or the market economy, knowing as we do that these institutions do not always work in practice as they ought to, and that the general discourse about them is highly idealized?

For all of these reasons, this study repeatedly engages in detailed analysis of existing critical traditions. My objective is not to attack individual critics, but to denounce a general practice of ignoring indigenous texts or treating them merely as "ethnographic data," unworthy of close examination, which happen to have inspired certain writers. To demonstrate the advantages of my method, which relies on the careful study of indigenous sources, I have found it useful to draw attention to what is lost when critics ignore those sources. By doing so, I do not intend to present my readings as the only valid ones, but to confirm them as historically and ideologically no less germane, albeit based on premises different from those of the dominant critical tradition. I also hope to demonstrate in this process how much I have learned from and respect the existing critical tradition.

Although there are few literary studies of rain forest texts, and still fewer of their impact on nonindigenous literatures, those that do exist have been indispensable for the approach adopted here. Sérgio Luiz Medeiros's *O Dono dos Sonhos*, an analysis of Xavante narratives, and Ivete Camargos Walty's *Narrativa e Imaginário Social: uma Leitura das Histórias de Maloca Antigamente, de Pichuvy Cinta Larga* are among the rare examples in the first category. For the impact of indigenous texts on South American literatures, a fundamental work is Angel Rama's *Transculturación narrativa en América Latina,* which, however, focuses principally on José María Arguedas and the Andes, having less to say about the Amazon and such writers as Darcy Ribeiro. Rama's lead was taken up by Martin Lienhard, again mostly with reference to Arguedas and the Andes. In the case of Paraguay, the impact of Guarani language and texts on the works of Augusto Roa Bastos has been studied by Rubén Bareiro Saguier and Antonio Cornejo Polar. Both empha- size Roa Bastos's unique position, in this respect, in Paraguay, and they do it so well that I unashamedly have restricted myself to quoting them here, rather than engaging in further analysis. Above all, the guiding principle of this study has been Gordon Brotherston's respect for indigenous texts. His article "Gaspar Ilóm y su tierra," on Asturias's debt to Maya texts, and *Book of the Fourth World: Reading the Native Americas through Their Literature,* brought about a turning point in my way of "reading the rain forest."

Evidently, the choice of the four traditions studied here meant neglect- ing important texts that belong elsewhere. In the case of the Gê-Bororo, whose songs are quoted by Jorge de Lima in *Invenção de Orfeu,* the absence is partially corrected in the analysis of *Maíra.* The same cannot be said about the Caxinauá tradition, whose poetry has been recently studied by Claudia Neiva de Matos, and has influenced the works of the poet João das Neves. Other absences of this order will no doubt be noticed by those who read this work, it is to be hoped, with the understanding that not every last case of such intertextuality could be examined in detail.

As a book written by a literary critic, about literary texts, this study was done within the walls of libraries and apartments. Yet, the political urgency of the South American Indians' struggle to defend their land and culture was never out of my mind. In the Roraima region, the Pemon, So'to, and Macuxi are still being abused and killed by Brazilians and Venezuelans. The construction of a power line and an international highway across their territory threatens to serve as a catalyst for further mining activities. (Con- flicts with miners having been their main problem in the last twenty years.) All over Brazilian territory, Tupi and Guarani groups struggle to defend their land. In the eighties, for instance, the journalist Priscila Siqueira campaigned nationally to assure the territorial rights of Guarani groups who, migrating in search of the "land without ill," had been occupying, for decades, the mountains of Serra do Mar, less than four hours from metro- politan São Paulo. The Kaiowá Guarani of Mato Grosso do Sul, who share a crowded reservation with Terena Indians, have been witnessing suicide rates of epidemic proportions among their youth; similar problems have been faced by the Pai-Tavytera Guarani of Paraguay. In Argentina and

Bolivia, the situation of the Guarani is not much better than in Brazil and Paraguay. In Peru, the Machiguenga occupy the "last frontier" of the national territory—a frontier which, as in other South American countries, is presently being claimed by neoliberal enthusiasts in the style of Mario Vargas Llosa. The methods of destruction are the same as they were three centuries ago: purposeful contamination with diseases, false land titles, roads, mining, and armed attacks, which are conveniently ignored by the government authorities. The "conquest" of native America did not happen just in the sixteenth century: It is still happening now, as I write these pages.

The native peoples of lowland South America have been resisting these aggressions, as they always did. The last fifteen years have seen more and more of them organizing throughout Latin America, and those studied here are no exception to that trend. The general demand for land rights, for instance, is being slowly replaced by a demand for "territory"—a term that includes not only a piece of land, but also geographical and sacred markers, and a historical relationship with those markers. Intellectual rights have also taken center stage in native strategy, especially with regard to biological patents and shamanic knowledge of medicinal plants. Publication copyrights are also in question, so much so that the process of incorporation of native texts described here may not be possible in the future, at least not so cheaply, not without clear compensation for the indigenous peoples and individuals involved. Indigenous organizations themselves have become active in the publication of texts, as among the Desâna; the second edition of *Antes o Mundo não Existia* was published by FOIRN (Federation of Indigenous Organizations of Rio Negro). And the first text published by an individual Indian in Brazil, Kaká Werá Jecupé's *Oré awé roiru'a ma/Todas as Vezes que Dissemos Adeus* is, after all, the autobiography of a Guarani activist. Jecupé's text, whose analysis serves as an epilogue for this book, replaces with fine irony and an intense sense of adaptability the pessimism that characterizes most works by non-Indians studied here; and it may well be an indication of what awaits us in terms of rain forest literature in the future. It is also to be hoped that the next few years will see histories of indigenous literature written by the Indians themselves. Their value would certainly outweigh any this book may have.

Part I

Roraima and the Carib

He put his elbow on his knees
his head in his hands. He just sat
there in silence, thinking, dreaming,
dreaming. He dreamt that a woman
was born. It was his mother.

—*Watunna*

chapter 1

Pacaraima Texts

IN OCTOBER 1911, as he was about to leave Koimelemong to visit the great Mount Roraima, Theodor Koch-Grünberg was contacted by Mayuluaípu, a Taurepang Indian "dressed in a clean linen suit" (1: 138). Mayuluaípu (or José, his Brazilian name) offered the German naturalist his services, which included his wide knowledge of different Pemon dialects and a good command of Portuguese. A few weeks later, the expedition would gain yet another important member: Mõseuaípu, better known by his nickname Akuli (agouti or *cutia*, a small rodent), a young Arekuna shaman who could not speak a word of Portuguese. This encounter between the two Carib Pemon Indians and the German naturalist would later play an important part in the Brazilian literary scene: the stories that Mayuluaípu and Akuli told Koch-Grünberg, collected in the second volume of the naturalist's *Vom Roroima zum Orinoco* (1924), became the basis of Mário de Andrade's 1928 *Macunaíma*, a turning point in the history of Brazilian contemporary narrative.

Carib languages are spoken today in the Orinoco Basin region known as the Guiana shield, which includes parts of Guiana, Venezuela, and northwestern Brazil; in southeastern and northeastern Colombia; and further south in the Xingu Basin and Rondônia (Durbin, 345). Through their incursions into the islands of Central America, the Caribs strongly influenced the native Arawaks of those regions as well. But in spite of this wide territorial penetration, "the vast majority of Carib languages have always been (as they are today) in the Guianas." Located on the frontier of Brazil, Venezuela, and Guiana, this is a region of savanna, drier open areas of the forest where game is scarce, fish less abundant, and agriculture more difficult. It is also the location of the bountiful mountain Roraima, celebrated by the Caribs in songs already quoted by Richard Schomburgk in the 1840s, in the Pemon narratives collected by Koch-Grünberg, and in the So'to text *Watunna*.

The gathering of Carib texts began, then, not with Koch-Grünberg but with a compatriot of his, Richard Schomburgk, who published his *Reisen in Britisch-Guiana* in 1847/48 (widely known in Walter Roth's English translation, *Travels in British Guiana*). In this work, Schomburgk had been able directly to observe the Macuxi Carib, eastern neighbors of the Pemon, although in his report he also drew on yet earlier accounts (for example, one that had been included in Filippo Salvadore Gilii's *Saggio di storia americana, o sia storia naturale, civile, e sacra de regni, e delle provincie spagnuole di terra-ferma nell' America meridionale, sacra*, 1782). Schomburgk recorded few Macuxi narratives, but did not omit one that concerns the all-important hero-figure Makunaíma; and he transcribed some of the Roraima songs. From the first, and following Humboldt's hydrography, Schomburgk also recognized the notion of Pacaraima itself, the ridge and cultural domain that stretches between Roraima and Marahuaka, precisely the terms of Koch-Grünberg's later journey. Upon arrival there, Koch-Grünberg found that the local people still remembered Schomburgk positively, and clearly, despite the intervening seventy years. Now, in recent decades, the Carib textual corpus has been much extended, thanks to the work of the Capuchin missionary Cesáreo Armellada and the French anthropologist Marc de Civrieux. Providing Pemon originals and a close Spanish translation, Armellada has produced a two-part collection of stories, *Tauron Panton* (1964, 1973), and one of "Pemon incantations," *Pemontón Taremuru* (1972). Civrieux's *Watunna* was first published in Spanish in 1970, and translated into English (with important editorial modifications) by David Guss in 1980. Called a "Fourth World classic" by Brotherston (1992, 6), *Watunna* offers us an impressive account of the cosmogony and history of the So'to Carib, western neighbors of the Pemon. The So'to (known, too, as Makiritare, or Yekuana) were also visited by Koch-Grünberg in his journey, but he referred to them as Majonggong, their Pemon name, and took little interest in their literature.

Carib texts have had a strong impact on American literature written in Portuguese, Spanish, English, and Dutch, Andrade's *Macunaíma* offering the first and most salient case of intertextuality to date. In the other countries whose borders, like those of Brazil, touch Roraima, important examples of contact are also to be found. In Venezuela, Rómulo Gallegos's *Canaima* (1935) takes its title and theme from a Carib word; in Guyana, *Green Mansions* (1904), by the Anglo-Argentine William Henry Hudson, and *Palace of the Peacock* (1960), by the Guyanese Wilson Harris, trace the "ascent" to Roraima. In Surinam, Thea Doelwijk's *Wajono* (1969) draws on strong local awareness of the Carib which has resulted in the publication there of native-language texts (Kempen 1989, 28–38, 104–6). In the case of the Cuban Alejo Carpentier, who lived in Venezuela for some years, becoming aware of the native substrate in *The Lost Steps* (1953) is critical to an adequate reading of the novel.

Given its key importance for Andrade, the Pemon tradition here provides a first term of reference. Comparisons with the So'to text *Watunna* will also be made, especially with regard to cosmogony and notions of geography. Together, both texts offer an irrefutable demonstration of cultural coherence and wealth.

The Pemon: A History of Contact

There seems to be no controversy about the fact that Pemon is the name by which the Taurepang (called Taulipang by Koch-Grünberg), Arekuna, and Kamarakoto call themselves. Pemon means "people," those who speak the Pemon language. It also means "men who live on top of a mound," a reference to the Pemon architectural custom of building their houses on top of little man-made hills (Barcelo Sifontes, 13). The Pemon still inhabit their ancestral territory, parts of which are now integrated into the Canaima Park and the Imataca Forest Reserve, in the state of Bolívar, Venezuela. Their territory, as well as the territory of their other Carib neighbors (Macuxi and So'to), has been subject to systematic invasion by non-Indians since the eighteenth century, when it was disputed by different colonial powers: Spain, Portugal, and Holland. This dispute caused immense trauma to the local populations, who saw their movements barred, and traditional ethnic differences being replaced by new frontiers, distinctions, and antagonisms (Santilli, 9).

In a history that repeats itself throughout the continent, the Pacaraima Indians, in the first century of invasion, saw their population decimated by epidemics, slavery, or sheer massacre. This happened despite the fact that most colonial attempts to establish regular settlements in the region throughout colonial times ended in failure. It was only in the nineteenth century, with the official and meticulous introduction of cattle-raising, that such settlements began to prosper. Both cattle-raising and the extraction of rubber (the two main economic activities in the region in the nineteenth century) depended on Indian labor, and at least on the Brazilian side, enslaving was still a common practice. In their late nineteenth-century border disputes, England and Brazil produced documents that often mention violence against Indians, who tended to flee to Guyana to escape the slavers. In the 1940s the same behavior was a source of preoccupation for military border posts (Santilli, 40).

Oil prospecting led to the appropriation of Indian lands by Venezuelan authorities in the 1920s. At the same time in Brazil, land titles were being freely given to cattle ranchers. In the thirties, mining was introduced on both sides of the frontier. In spite of all this, the Pemon and Macuxi territory remained roughly the same until the 1960s, when the Venezuelan government created the Canaima Park and the Imataca Forest Reserve.

The military forces who seized power in 1964 in Brazil were the main promoters of the large-scale devastation of the Amazon that we are still witnessing. Before then, except for the short period of the rubber boom (1880–1910), generations of governments and entrepreneurs had tried to dominate the region economically, with no success. The "generals' blueprint," as Hecht and Cockburn call it (95–127), was based on major tax-breaks and incentives that were offered by the Brazilian government to cattle ranchers, wood extractors, mining companies, and all sorts of economic enterprises interested in establishing themselves in the Amazon. At the same time, the generals planned a long-term migration to the region, involving poor peasants from the drought-ridden regions of the Northeast.

As a result, miners and cattle-ranchers started to invade Indian territories in the Pacaraima region in the 1970s on a scale never seen before, and the economic pressure in the region was such that it surpassed national borders. The situation worsened in the 1980s and 1990s, with constant invasions of the Canaima Park, the Imataca Forest Reserve, and the Macuxi territory (in Brazil) by miners. In addition to that, big multinational mining companies lobbied the Venezuelan government to pass the Decree 1850, which allows mining in protected Indian territories. In recent years, the Pemon have organized several demonstrations against Decree 1850. President Hugo Chaves, who in his electoral campaign had promised to pay the centuries-long debt of Venezuela to its indigenous populations, has nevertheless supported the Decree.

The Pemon and the Macuxi have also been protesting against a series of economic initiatives that will affect their territory. The first is a high-tension power line that will cross Canaima Park, Imataca Reserve, and Macuxi land, and serve as a catalyst for further mining activities in the area. The second is the 1,600 km-long Manaus-Caracas highway, also a joint venture by the two countries, which will cross Indian territories and bring more migration to the region.

Approximately ninety years ago (1914), when Koch-Grünberg arrived in Roraima, mining and highways were not part of the reality of the region. Nevertheless, he did witness violence, as well as the results of previous abuse in the form of groups that had to migrate or be assimilated by other groups. Many Pemon were integrated in non-Indian economic activities (including, of course, serving as guides to travelers like Koch-Grünberg himself), but the group still lived in the traditional *malocas* (large collective houses) and followed their own religion. Later, the *malocas* were replaced by brick-built, nuclear-family houses, and many Pemon became Christians. The narratives Koch-Grünberg collected serve therefore, like all narratives, as testimonies to a particular historical period, and make, as we will see, active comments on that period.

Vom Roroima zum Orinoco

Using the latest technology of his day, Koch-Grünberg recorded the stories by means of a phonograph. Mayuluaípu would tell his narratives in Portuguese, and help the naturalist with cultural information and explanations of relevant native terms. Akuli would narrate in Arekuna, and his stories were then translated by Mayuluaípu, who would also add some commentaries of his own. As for the linguistic information given by Mayuluaípu to Koch-Grünberg, it is important to notice that it is still today regarded as a valuable tool for understanding the Pemon languages (Durbin, 333).

The arrangement of native materials in Koch-Grünberg's five-volume study is as follows (the last two volumes are posthumous):

1. Songs [in Travelog]; Pemon text
2. Narratives, by Mayuluaípu and Akuli; some Pemon text
3. *Tarén* or incantations [in Analysis]; Pemon text
4. German-Pemon Vocabulary
5. Photographs

The stories by Mayuluaípu and Akuli in volume two were told in informal, public performances which took place in the boat or by the camp fire, and whose main objective was to keep boredom at bay:

> The days are boring, cool and ugly. Each cloud brings with it a dense light rain. It is the true April weather. But Akuli does not let us get melancholic. . . . Most of the time we squat all together under the big tent, around the fire, and tell each other stories of Piaimá, the evil cannibal, who is finally tricked and killed by a stronger and smarter man. (1:182)

The Pemon stories, like their So'to counterparts in *Watunna*, fall into several cycles. These focus on the flood and the great events of creation; Makunaíma and his brothers; other "tricksters," among them the rabbit-like

Konewó and Kalawunseg, the liar; the sky people and astronomical phenomena; and the origins of poisons and dances. One could possibly speak
of a jaguar cycle as well, although several of the jaguar narratives belong
to the Konewó cycle. The same happens with Piaimá, the ogre: Most of
his stories are part of the Makunaíma cycle, but one of them is related to
Konewó. There is also a small group of short (probably summarized) turtle
narratives in the book, and there are quite a few miscellaneous pieces.

In introducing the corresponding So'to stories cycles as these are recorded in *Watunna,* Civrieux says of this text that

> [it] is in its essence a secret teaching restricted to the circle of men who
> undergo the initiations of the *Wanwanna* festivals. But there is another,
> popular *Watunna* which belongs to everyone regardless of sex or age, and
> this is the *Watunna* which is told daily outside the ritual dance circle. It is
> an exoteric *Watunna* told in everyday language, a profane reflection of that
> of the sacred place. (16)

This secretiveness relates directly to the So'to taboo that forbids their sacred texts being recorded and/or transcribed, a phenomenon studied by
David Guss (1986).[1] Among the Pemon, there seems to be no core body
of texts comparable to *Watunna* in terms of unchangeability and secrecy.
Apparently, the Pemon are in general more willing to tell their stories to
the foreigners than the So'to. But the distinction between ceremonial and
nonceremonial texts does apply to them. In *Pemontón Taremuru,* Cesareo
Armellada tells us about the differences between the everyday narratives
(told inside the houses or during trips, by the fire) and two other genres:
songs, usually accompanied by musical instruments, and the *tarén,* "which
are recited in a low and mysterious voice" (11).

Guss's recent account of the So'to is particularly interesting because it
makes a harsh critique of Koch-Grünberg's attitude toward these people:

> In page after page he lacerates the Yekuana in a series of denunciations
> astounding to the contemporary reader. Showing little of the cultural
> sensitivity he was to reserve for other tribes (particularly the neighboring
> Taulipang), he in turn accuses them of moodiness, undependability, rude-
> ness, lack of cleanliness, laziness, obstinacy, dishonesty, and quarrelsome-
> ness. (1986, 414)

Inquiring into the reasons which would have made Koch-Grünberg so un-
willing to accept the Yekuana or So'to, Guss arrives at the conclusion that,
unlike the Pemon and other tribes, the So'to refused "to play Indian"; and
they repeatedly resisted telling the naturalist their stories.

Guss's account has much to recommend it, not least the fact that he himself has made a major contribution to the modern understanding of the Yekuana through their own texts, in his admirable edition and translation into English of Marc de Civrieux's *Watunna. Mitología maquiritare* (1970). Yet Guss overlooks narrative elements present in Koch-Grünberg's travelogue (volume one) which refer to his So'to helper Manduca. The naturalist becomes increasingly irritated with Manduca, to the point of showing a clear contempt for the Indian's description of the So'to universe, on one of the rare occasions in which Manduca decides to speak about it:

> Nor does the Majonggong want to be left out. He tells us about his tribe's life after death. According to the belief of these Indians, who obviously think of themselves as something extraordinary, the world is a great globe with nine covers, that is, nine skies underneath and above the earth, peopled with various inhabitants of strange shapes and habits, and by spirits and gods, masters and judges of the souls of the dead. (1: 169)

This mode of discourse contrasts almost violently with the sensitivity Koch-Grünberg shows generally towards the imaginative tendencies of Carib cosmogony, and on his own admission it can hardly be thought the result of Manduca's unwillingness to "play Indian." In practice, on Koch-Grünberg's own evidence Manduca is the most helpful of all the Indians who work for him, and at moments he acknowledges this fact as such. Yet, he clearly prefers Akuli's poise in telling stories, his *buffonerie* and good humor, and his dramatic talents, to Manduca's pragmatism and pride—even though Akuli, as the naturalist describes him, is not very courageous and can often be a bit lazy and moody as well. Koch-Grünberg's irritation with Manduca is a result of his sympathy for the two Pemon. In other words, he is adopting a Pemon attitude towards the Yekuana, following local rivalry and taking sides—within what, from an ethnographical point of view, is a common Carib culture. If we trace his irritation and his increasing lack of patience towards Manduca throughout the narrative, we can easily foresee that his impression of the Yekuana when he finally arrives at their village will be negative, because it was already negative before he got there.

The Food Tree, the Flood, and the Shaping of the Earth

We begin with the Food Tree narrative, of which Koch-Grünberg provides two versions, one by Mayuluaípu and the other by Akuli. In both, Makunaíma and his brothers are starving, having only bad fruit to eat. Near Roraima, the rodent agouti (*akuli* in Pemon, like the narrator), finds Wazaká, the tree that carries all the good fruit. But he does not tell the brothers, and Makunaíma waits until the rodent has fallen asleep to check his teeth and see what he had been eating. In Akuli's version Makunaíma finds maize or corn, and in Mayuluaípu's, banana. The agouti then leads the brothers to the tree, and Makunaíma, against his older brother's advice, suggests that they cut it down. The cutting of the tree causes the great flood, forcing Makunaíma and his brother Zigé to look for shelter on top of an inajá palm tree. The tree stump becomes the mount Roraima, and the tree's branches fall across the Caroni river, forming the Wazaká-melu waterfall. As it is falling, the Wazaká tree takes with it two other trees, Yulywazaluina-yég and Elu-yég, whose stumps become the mountains Élu-tepe and Yuluwazaluimá-tepe. The branches of the trees also become waterfalls in the Caroni. All of those trees fall across the river, causing the fruit and seeds to grow on the opposite bank, i.e., towards the north, beyond Roraima.

When Wazaká falls and its branches end up on the other side of Roraima, this place becomes an earthly paradise, a kind of magic garden in contrast with the much poorer savanna. The abundance of plants in Roraima is in fact confirmed by Schomburgk, who calls the region a "botanical El Dorado":

> I believed myself transported to some fairy garden, for such a blending of colour, such a multiplicity combined within so small a space, had been a surprise to me until to-day. The border of brushwood that enclosed this botanical El Dorado consisted of the glorious *Thibaudia nutans Klotzsch,* a new and beautiful species. . . . (2: 209)

In Akuli's version of the felling of Wazaká, "All of the trees fell on the other side. That's why still today one finds there banana trees, corn, cotton, and many fruits that have not been planted, but which grow on their own in the woods" (2: 40). Mayuluaípu adds:

> If the tree had fallen on this side, we would have lots of banana trees here in the forest, but it fell on the other side of Roraima, and many bananas fell over there. That's why nowadays there are many banana orchards in those woods which have not been planted, and there is never lack of anything there. Those banana trees belong to the Mauarí. (2: 43)

This side of Roraima, the south side where the Pemon actually live, is the place where plants do not grow on their own; they have to be planted. The way toward planting is indicated by the food tree itself—the cotton and the corn which, along with the fruit, had to be brought to the ground. In this sense Wazaká, the Pemon food tree, is a concept that points in two different directions: toward the past, to a time when the wandering ancestors of the Pemon had to live off the fruit they collected from the ground; and toward the future (i.e., present-day) Pemon, who settled down in the dry, parsimonious savanna and became planters.

For its part, the flood brings fish to the region—although, as we could expect, most of them end up (according to Mayuluaípu) in the streams and rivers beyond Roraima. In order to escape the waters, in Akuli's version, the brothers plant two *inajá* palm trees and each of them "climb his own" (2: 41).[2]

This is the first post-diluvial planting, and the one that will save their lives. The planting of the inajá trunk in the water also suggests sexual fertilization: The fruits of the inajá palm acquire flavor only after Makunaíma rubs them against his penis (2: 41). It is the beginning of a transformational process that will culminate with Makunaíma's exile in the land beyond Roraima. First, there is a great fire, whose passage through the Earth, according to Mayuluaípu, can be noticed "when one finds big pieces of charcoal on the earth" (2: 43). As a geological motif, the great fire continues the transformations started by the felling of Wazaká. After the fire, Makunaíma makes two attempts to create new people, initially, with human beings made of wax, who prove to be a failure, melting completely in the sun. In his second, successful attempt, he makes clay people, who, like pots, get drier and tougher when exposed to the sun.

In Akuli's version the felling of Wazaká is preceded by the cutting of another tree—a narrative device that prefigures (for the listener/reader and for agouti, the rodent) what will happen later. And it is preceded by the story of how fire was stolen by Makunaíma and his brothers from the *mutug* bird (whose onomatopoeic name announces dawn). Mayuluaípu gives us another version of how fire was acquired by humans, through an old woman's farting, an isolated narrative that has nothing to do with the Makunaíma cycle. The order in which fire is introduced by Akuli brings a fine coherence to the series of transformations performed by the brothers. With the knowledge of fire, humans can make use of other technologies brought by the siblings, such as agriculture and ceramics.

Within the main narrative of the food tree and flood, other smaller stories are embedded. They tell us how Kalí, the squirrel, acquired his swollen eyelids and how Akuli, the rodent, had his buttocks burned and reddened by fire. The inclusion of small etiological tales within a larger narrative, itself often etiological, is a common technique in South American narratives. Here they highlight, with humor, the changing of species and the constant metamorphosis of nature.

Wazaká is not merely a temporal concept. By falling down, it defines the topography of the savanna, with its mountains, rocks, and waterfalls. It also establishes the difference between the magic and bountiful territory beyond Roraima, seen in its complete magnitude only by the shamans, and the land to the south of the sacred mountain, home of the Pemon. After the felling, Makunaíma continues to effect a series of changes in this territory. Most of these further define the region geologically. Rocks are an extremely important element in the Pemon culture: They delineate the shape of their territory, creating waterfalls and cliffs that make journeys (and the intrusion of foreigners) more difficult, and they are the home of many spirits. The pre-Cambrian rocks from the Guiana and Brazilian shield, some hundred million years old, are among the oldest geological formations in the planet (Hecht and Cockburn, 17). The Pemon know stories that explain the strange shapes of many of these rocks, and their sense of history is intimately linked to them. Makunaíma left tracks of different animals on the rocks, covered them with his own wounds so that people who walked on them would also get wounded, and transformed people, animals, plants, and artifacts into stone. Such transformations not only explain rocks shaped like animals, humans, plants, or artifacts, but are also consistent with the idea that history, in the form of fossils, can be written in stone: Stone fish are said to have been left by Makunaíma in several places. But history written in stone exists for the Pemon not only in the form of fossils; in *Tauron Panton,* Makunaíma and his siblings become "the Makunaímas," ancestors who "walked far and wide and painted rocks and things, which now give the Indians much to think about" (Armellada 1964, 57). This is a clear reference to what are called *timehri* in Carib and *itaquatiara* in Tupi, "painted rocks." A similar reference to Makunaíma as the creator of hieroglyphs is made by Schomburgk, when he comes across a rockface with "complete series" of picture writings: "When the Indians first noticed them [the glyphs], they called out in a subdued voice 'Makunaíma, Makunaíma'" (2:177).

Part of this early cosmogonical story is retold in the texts collected by Armellada (who, curiously, never mentions Koch-Grünberg), mainly at the beginning of *Tauron Panton,* where the Makunaíma concept is treated from a different angle. In that account, the Makunaíma ancestors are plural, and are openly identified as the offspring of the Sun and a woman created for him by a water nymph. Prior to the birth of their offspring, the Sun used to work alone burning trees to clear planting areas or *conucos.* This woman, made of red clay—that is, a combination of red earth (considered the most productive type of soil in the Amazon), sun, and water—is the result of the nymph's third attempt to make a companion for the sun. The first one, made of white earth, would melt easily. The second woman was made of black wax, and also melted. The third became his wife, since she could execute the tasks demanded by the sun, tasks normally performed by the Pemon women, like planting the *conuco* and preparing food. Thus, the ancestors and their Pemon descendants are the result of a contract between the Sun and a woman, which has a clear a *social* element.

The Macuxi version of this story told by Schomburgk is notable mainly for its early publication date. Much in it is readily recognizable from the Pemon account: Makunaíma's ax and the felled tree, the flood, Makunaíma's inscribing of the landmark rocks. Yet there are important variations, due perhaps less to geographical or tribal differences than to the prevailing ideology of Schomburgk's day. Perceived simply as a culture-bringer, Makunaíma is raised to the role of a supreme creator, and the story of the flood is openly identified with that of the biblical Genesis.

The food tree, the flood, and the successive creations, common themes throughout Amazonian cultures, also feature prominently in the So'to *Watunna*.[3] There, the tree, called Marahuaka, originally joins earth and sky, like an umbilical cord. Its prototype and counterpart to the east is Roraima (Dodoima, as the So'to call it), originally a tree grown from a yucca splinter that Kuchi had planted after bringing it back from a journey to the sky in search of food. It was, for the So'to, the beginning of food as they know it: "Dodoima was the first tree. Now we see it as a very tall mountain. Many wild fruits still grow there. No one plants them. They just grow as reminders" (129). Reminders, that is, of the same botanical paradise celebrated in the Pemon texts: The So'to ancestors take the plants from there, journey to Marahuaka along the Pacaraima route later followed by Koch-Grünberg, to establish their own home at Marahuaka. When it falls, Marahuaka in its turn becomes a rock massif and the source of the great Orinoco river. Even more clearly than in the Pemon tradition, the felling of the food tree is shown to be a hinge event, marking the transition from a hunter-gatherer to an agricultural society.

Paralleling *Tauron Panton* more closely than the account by Mayuluaípu or Akuli, *Watunna* also relates the successive attempts to make ancestors of colored clay and the activities of the "house-builders," named Wanadi—in some respects Makunaíma's counterparts. The third of these Wanadi goes on an epic journey to recover his first wife, the fishwoman Kaweshawa, the only one that suited him because she could perform the tasks normally performed by the So'to women. Human beings, in the same cosmogony, are created by the same Wanadi through the smoking of tobacco, singing, and maraca shaking—activities that are all ritually and socially important for the So'to.

In a highly articulated structure well analyzed by Civrieux and Guss, *Watunna* puts emphasis on the first harvest. This is the moment when, after the felling of Marahuaka, the spirit people dance and sing in tune with brilliantly colored birds, and show how manioc should be collected and planted. Observing all this from below is the anaconda Huiio (Keyeme in Pemon), a dread aquatic monster who heaves her great body into the air to join the birds, growing feathers and exclaiming: "I want my crown" (137). A key concept in the evolutionary story developed more explicitly and at greater length in the *Popol Vuh* and the Quetzalcoatl legends of Meso-America (Brotherston 1992, 269), this brightly colored feathered snake, or "plumed serpent," is also present in Akuli's "Origin of the Poisons" story, where the birds are said to take the colors of their feathers from the scaly skin of a huge aquatic snake.

Comparing these various Carib accounts of the food tree and the harvest sharpens our focus on an intriguing difference between Mayuluaípu's and Akuli's stories of Wazaká, which for the former bears bananas, and for the latter, maize. These foods represent, respectively, two different kinds of plant reproduction, vegetative and cross-fertilized, which are clearly defined in the American context by Eric Wolf and in the creation stories of Meso-America, where they are explicitly contrasted in functional and ideological terms. The plants most often associated with the rain forest, above all manioc, are of the vegetative type. Yet there is now archaeological evidence of the early and effective presence of maize agriculture in the region, which has major implications for the circum-Caribbean area and the larger map of early America.

In *Watunna,* maize is never mentioned, while manioc is repeatedly. As Brotherston says of Marahuaka: "Identified with the prime crop manioc, it bears a multitude of other foods, yet those actually specified—manioc, two types of palm nuts, and gourds plus the plantains and rubber-tree fruit mentioned in other texts—strongly represent vegetative as opposed to seed reproduction" (1992, 262). Manioc tuber reproduction also supplies the model for Attawanadi's exchanged head, the grafting back of his wife's severed limbs, and Wlaha's seven outgrowths of himself (Brotherston 1992, 263). Conversely, though a dietary staple among the Pemon, manioc is scarcely mentioned by Akuli or Mayuluaípu. Among the things that Makunaíma transforms into rocks on his way beyond Roraima are a gourd and a basket for squeezing manioc; and just before that, the fisherman prepares some manioc *beijus* to take on his trip. Yet these are the only references to that root. Akuli's assigning of maize, and not manioc, to the Wazaká tree, specifies a preference also hinted at among the Macuxi, for whom maize is the food first found after the flood.[4]

In the Pemon narratives, Akuli's maize is also highlighted by Mayuluaípu in another context, in the story "The Visit to the Sky." Here, Mayuluaípu tells how maize appeared among the Pemon when Maitxaúle, a white termite ant, marries the daughter of the black vulture (*urubu* or *zamuro*), and goes with her to visit her family in the sky. There, he cannot drink or eat what is prepared by his wife's family, which usually consists of rotten meat, so he has his meals in the house of the parrot Oro'wé, who offers him maize-beer or *caxiri*. In the process, he hides a maize kernel in his mouth and brings it to his relatives, upon returning to the Earth, and teaches them how to plant (2:85). While the two versions of the Wazaká story establish the culture of planters without distinguishing seeds from other modes of reproduction, the Maitxaúle story celebrates the introduction of seeds into a society that already had the garden, that is, a society that already knew how to plant. Further, instead of *giving* his people maize, Maitxaúle barters it, in a world familiar not just with agriculture but with commerce. Overall, this would affirm the notion that maize was introduced into rain forest culture after the development of root crops.

In these stories, Carib interest in maize is complemented by the fact that the one who fetches it for the ancestors is an ant. This is precisely the Meso-American model: In order to fetch the first maize, the epic Quetzalcoatl becomes an ant. All this reinforces the cosmogonical links intimated above in the story of the plumed serpent, links which Schomburgk ([2: 264] again following Humboldt) proposed in relation to jade-working and which come to play a key role in the work of Alejo Carpentier.[5]

Be it maize or manioc, the harvest itself everywhere emerges as a fundamental event. As Brotherston shows in his reading of *Watunna*, the felling of Marahuaka marks the end of a period in which human beings were simply hunters and fruit collectors, and the consequent beginning of agriculture (1992, 306). After all, in the Wazaká episode, the emphasis lies on the importance of agriculture as such, not on specific types of crops. Moreover, as a display of plants that humans will be able to cultivate (a display that includes "new" imported plants like oranges), Wazaká is part of another philosophical statement, also common to many Native American texts: The creation of men has not just a biological, but a social meaning as well. The Pemon can only exist as Pemon (i.e., be *created*) after the features that characterize their culture (planting, weaving, ceramics, and socially significant geographical markers) come into existence. According to this way of thinking, you are not only what you eat; you are, i.e., exist, only so long as you exist socially—create, transform, work, sing, smoke. Thus, those who do not participate in the process, those who refuse to join in and work—like the jaguar and the tapir alone among the animals in *Watunna*—are excluded from society.

The flood that accompanies the felling of the food tree, together with the very notion of the garden that is an earthly paradise, have insistently suggested a comparison between the Carib genesis and the biblical story of Eden, and some have claimed direct derivation (a note in the Schomburgk translation reads: "the correspondence of this with the biblical story only too clearly establishes the influence of indirect missioneering or rather Christian enterprise" [2: 253]). Striking as the similarities may seem, the Carib story may be more aptly compared with the Flood present in most American cosmogonies, and actually depicted in the pre-Cortesian books of Mexico.

While the Carib are nostalgic for Roraima's bounty, they are not negative in this, unlike Adam and Eve who eat from the tree of knowledge and end up, as a result, expelled from Paradise. The cutting down of the tree is by no means a punishment imposed by a superior god intent on complete and blind obedience. On the contrary, it announces human achievement in agriculture and the capacity to feed oneself within the natural environment. Also, the Earth was by no means a paradise *before* the tree was cut down. There was starvation, and even after Wazaká/Marahuaka was found, it was so tall that people had to be content with the fruit they found on the ground: When Kalí, the squirrel, tried to climb the tree to pick the better fruit, the wasps bit him and deformed his eyes. Thus, if the felling of the tree is actually lamented, it is more due to the great flood it caused than to the loss of the fruit:

> Akuli, who was very intelligent and knew everything beforehand, said:
> —No, let's not cut it down. Let's just get the fruit. If you cut down the tree there will be a big water. (Koch-Grünberg 2: 42)

Further, even though it is a disaster, the flood has the advantage of bringing fish to the rivers.

Again, for the first Carib, manual labor is not the curse it was for Cain and Abel. Rather, it serves another end; the task of the first Caribs, performed with a lot of humor and in concert with the animals (who are the teachers, a total impossibility in the Bible), is to prepare the ground so that future generations may continue, in their daily round, the work of transforming and being transformed by nature. In this sense, the concept of planting revealed in these narratives does not necessarily separate forest from garden *(conuco/roça)*. After the tree is cut down, fruit will be grown as well as seed-plants and tubers. Plants growing on their own, i.e., the *untouched* forest, is a concept that belongs to the spirits, the *waiurá*, and to sanctuaries like Roraima. Only in recent years has Western science grasped the idea of a constantly changing forest, and of a forest created to a large degree by the intervention of humans (Hecht and Cockburn, 29; Moran).

Above all, these intercessions are not unilateral, or simply another chapter in the history of human domination over nature, *Kultur* over *Natur*. Rather, they are just one factor in the intense process of change that goes on constantly in the Amazon—an area that concentrates half of the species existing on the planet:

> Here is an evolutionary environment inflected by forces great and small, from geological upheaval and climatic catastrophe to the chance fall of a single tree which may bridge a stream, open up the forest floor to light. In this world of calamities, the diversity of species in the forest reflects the constant "fine grain" disruptions of falling trees creating light gaps and new environments, randomly killing trees and thus creating a landscape of patches of different ages where such events constantly changed the rules of the game, and where competitive exclusion could never entirely hold sway. This is no primeval forest where species and communities evolve at a stately pace, but rather one in which rapid change takes place. (Hecht and Cockburn, 25)

Makunaíma and the Trickster Narratives

After telling us about Makunaíma's making of new human beings, his sub-sequent transformations, and his final exile in the land beyond Roraima, Akuli and Mayuluaípu take us back to the time of his childhood. As a young boy, this Pemon hero would change into an adult in order to have sex with his older brother's wife. When beaten cruelly by the jealous brother, he "got tired of this life" and used his magical powers to move the house, with his mother in it, to the top of a mountain. His brother's family remained below, starving. Later, after bringing him to the mountain, Makunaíma laughed at his brother for being so thin and feeble that he could not dance. Makunaíma is easily the most charismatic of the Carib "epic" heroes, and embodies, as one, traits and roles assigned to separate figures in *Watunna* and other sources.

Makunaíma can be cruel, selfish, lustful, and readily bored. But he can also be smart and sensitive, and above all he is creative, the culture hero of the Pemon, the one who defined their land, gave them tools and fire, and made them what they are. He prepares the way for agriculture and hence human society, according to the Native American norm, and introduced knowledge of poisons, one of the defining features of tropical America in world history. The contradictions in Makunaíma force us to consider him in the light of a definition stemming from a North American indigenous char-acter, but now applied to different literatures around the world: the *trickster*. Interest in this character began with the first steps of North American an-thropology, and as Ellen Basso points out in her book *In Favor of Deceit*:

Writers were impressed then, as now, by the contradictions in Trickster's moral character, by what Boas called the "troublesome psychological discrepancy" between the apparently incongruous attributes of the "culture hero" (who makes the world safe and secure for human life) and the "selfish buffoon" (who ludicrously attempts the inappropriate). (4)

Paul Radin's classic study of the trickster considers the "culture hero" aspect of the trickster stories as intrusive (167), and his/her divinity, when it occurs, as secondary and "largely a construction of the priest-thinker, of a remodeller" (164). For Carl Jung, the trickster represents the shadow aspect of humanity (211). More recently Michael P. Carroll has defined the trickster as an attempt to recast "Freudian reality" through the "psychological association between the two things—the immediate gratification of sexual desires and 'culture'—that all human beings would like to have associated" (115).

As Ellen Basso points out, such works derive from "very general theories about human psychology, and about myths and their symbolic functions" (6). The fact that a character can be at the same time a culture hero and a "selfish buffoon" is taken as a universal anomaly, and not enough effort is spent on relating tricksters to the cultures that gave birth to them.

After studying several trickster stories narrated by the Carib speaking Kalapalo of the Xingu, and the cultural context in which they were produced, Basso arrives at a very different conclusion:

> if the idea of fixed psychic structure is questioned (and some psychologists have questioned it), then the contradictions in the patterns of a trickster's action need not be viewed as anomalous or paradoxical. In fact, to the Kalapalo, those characters whose action is stable and falls into a general pattern, whose goals and modes of orientation to them seem not to vary, are regarded as excessively compulsive and inflexible, and ultimately, as failures of imagination. Pragmatic creativity and flexibility, the ability to conceive of more than a single kind of relation with other people, and the ability to fashion or invent a variety of thoughts about one's capacity as an agent, is, on the other hand, entirely human. (356–7)

Looking at Makunaíma's cycle, one can see that the Pemon culture hero, in spite of being terribly lustful and selfish, is less a "buffoon" than some of his fellow tricksters in North America. There are no episodes in the cycle that resemble the one in which the Winnebago trickster, for instance, helplessly watches a fight between his two hands; nor do we see a solitary Makunaíma surprised at the size of his own *phallus erectus*. Actually, Makunaíma is never presented in these stories as a loner. His adventures generally emphasize the relationship between him and his brothers, and it is in the context of that relationship that his "tricksterness" has to be analyzed.

In the Food Tree episode, for example, Makunaíma is usually the one who makes the most important decisions, the one who operates the key transformations in the life of the Pemon. He decides to look for signs of food in agouti's teeth, and he is also the one who sends his older brother after the rodent in order to find out where the food is coming from. In Akuli's version, the felling of the tree is Makunaíma's responsibility, and the Great Flood happens because Makunaíma uncovers the hole in the fallen tree trunk so as to let more fish come out. On the other hand, he is also the one who saves them from the Flood, by planting the inajá palm trees on the ground. That Makunaíma, the youngest brother, should be the one to make all those decisions is thus explained by Akuli: "Makunaíma, the youngest of the brothers, was still a boy, but he was 'más zafado' than all the others" (2: 40). The expression "más zafado" comes from the Portuguese *mais safado,* used by Mayuluaípu, the translator (Koch-Grünberg, who employs the term *verschlagener,* feels the need to supply his readers, in a footnote, with the Portuguese expression). The first meaning given to *safado* in the *Novo Michaelis* Portuguese/English dictionary is *trickster.*

This extraordinary power held by the youngest child over his siblings is acquired, as we are told later, during his early years. The little boy, who used to ask his sister-in-law to take him for a walk, and after they were far enough from the house, would transform into an adult and have sex with her, one day asked his brother to make him a hunting loop. The brother at first refused to do it, but under the daily insistence of the youngest sibling, finally gave him the rope, which was placed by Makunaíma on an old path, where no tapirs were seen anymore. The brother was himself trying to hunt a tapir whose recent tracks were found on a different route. When the mother told the older brother that a tapir had fallen into Makunaíma's trap, she had to give the information twice. Totally perplexed, her son exclaimed: "—I am much older and no tapir falls into my trap. How come there is a tapir in this boy's trap?" (2: 46). Makunaíma wanted to distribute the meat after the hunt, but the older brother not only did not allow it, as he also "did not want to give him any of the meat, because he was still too young. He took all the meat to his house and left the tripes to the boy" (2: 47). Soon after this (as we have seen above) the older brother beats Makunaíma, who then moves the house to the top of the mountain and all but starves his brother and his family to death. After this episode, Makunaíma goes back to having sex with his sister-in-law, but the older brother protests no longer "because he remembered the hunger he had suffered, and because he could not live without his younger brother" (2: 48).

While some of Makunaíma's actions could certainly be called gratuitous tricks, others, such as in the episodes just mentioned, reveal a clear,
well-planned, and conscious struggle for power. According to the Pemon
hierarchy, Makunaíma, as the youngest brother, owes the older ones respect
(Thomas 55–6)—a respect that he is not willing to show. His domination
over the older brothers, on the contrary, demonstrates the subversive tone
of these narratives insofar as the Pemon sibling hierarchy is concerned. It
is not that Makunaíma replaces the older brothers, or that he simply shows
he knows more and therefore deserves respect as if he were in fact older;
in some stories the culture hero is still depicted as a spoiled child who
gets into trouble for his excessive curiosity or lack of obedience, and has
to be saved (from death, even) by the older brothers. But the fact that the
Pemon culture hero—i.e., the one who caused the Flood and created new
human beings, the one who brought them fire, defined their territory and
taught them how to live in a society—should be portrayed as the youngest
brother, and a rebel, shows that in the Pemon history of social organization the definition of rules and the possibility of subverting them are seen
as the creation of the same being. This is not simply a matter of dialectics:
Makunaíma, like the Kalapalo tricksters mentioned by Basso, is averse to
any kind of rigidity.

In fact, if we were to look for a characteristic of Makunaíma's present in most, if not all of his stories, we would probably find it to be his
adaptability—what Ellen Basso calls the "pragmatic creativity and flexi-
bility" of the Kalapalo tricksters and culture. If as we read those stories
we stay away from fixed categories such as good and evil, we will see that
Makunaíma is simply more adaptable and more creative than his brothers or the other characters around him. He is the one who has the idea of
following the agouti in order to find out what this rodent has been eating,
and it is because he pretends to be asleep that they can actually scour the
agouti's mouth for hints of food. It is also Makunaíma who ties the rope to
the *mutug* bird's tail with the purpose of discovering where fire is hidden,
and according to Akuli's version of the Wazaká narrative, he is also responsible for the decision to cut down the tree. As with "pragmatic creativity" at
any level, while some of his solutions work, others do not. And it is exactly
when the solutions do not work that we can see Makunaíma's creativity and
adaptability at their best. After cutting down the tree, for instance, he does
not let Zigé and Akuli cover the stump immediately: "—Let some more fish
come out for these streams. Then we will cover the stump" (2: 41). It is this
decision that causes the Great Flood. But faced with this new and serious
problem, Makunaíma immediately finds a solution, by planting the *inajá*
palm tree in the ground. Here, another problem arises: The fruit has no

flavor. But as we have seen, Makunaíma does not give up, rubbing the fruit against his penis so as to give it a better taste. Similarly, when the rivers and lakes were low in water and fish were abundant, Makunaíma created a wax fishing hook, which for obvious reasons did not work. He then saw a man fishing with a metal hook and tried to steal it, by transforming himself into a huge *aimará* fish. But once again the plan did not work; Makunaíma opened his mouth after being caught, letting the hook go. He then turned into another *aimará*, and the same happened. Finally, he went into the water as a piranha, and was able to take away the fisherman's hook, which was eventually captured by the *aimará*. "What are we going to do now?" he asked his brother after losing the hook. But the solution this time was not to be found locally. He and his brother transformed themselves into crickets, got into the fisherman's basket, and followed him to the other side of Roraima (then British Guyana), where the man was going to work in order to acquire a new hook.

This story can be read as a satire of the Pemon's own historical experience of trading metal tools with Europeans or South American nationals—a process which eventually resulted in the need to emigrate in order to sell their labor. And as a satire, it speaks of the incredible adaptability of these people, who have been facing invasions of their land and their way of living for about two centuries, but have nevertheless managed to continue being Pemon.

A similar account of the trade for metal is given in *Watunna*. The twins Iureke and Shikiémona steal metal hooks from Ahisha, a white fisherman, and enter the man's basket (disguised as cockroaches) in order to follow him to his house. Later, Iureke, the youngest brother, changes into a bird and accompanies Ahisha to Amenadiña (Kijkoveral, once a Dutch outpost), the city where he buys iron and fabric. The journey represents, for the So'to, the discovery of this important center of trade, and the historical shift toward their alliance with the Dutch (Guss 1986, 421).

The trickster Makunaíma is not a problem solver, but a restless transformer, who often creates the problems he will then have to solve. There are several reasons for his doing so. Sometimes he wants power, as in the dispute for his brother's wife and hunting status. Sometimes he wants revenge, as in the story in which a man who stole some *urucu* from him is cut into pieces and transformed into stone. And sometimes he is just bored, as when he "gets tired of this life" and decides to move his house to the top of the mountain, or when he covers his own body with wounds and then decides to get rid of them.

Neither is Makunaíma above good and evil. Quite the contrary: in the *tarén*, for instance, he and his brothers are often held responsible for diseases and problems the Pemon have to deal with in their daily life, and those texts do not omit any complaints about "Makunaíma, the evil one." But "being evil" and "being a culture hero" do not have to result in a contradiction, as in so many studies about tricksters. As Makunaíma's restlessness and creativity seem to suggest, for the Pemon, adaptability and capacity for transformation are more important attributes of a culture hero than rigid conceptions of bad and good.

Thomas sees the same lack of rigidity in several aspects of Pemon society, such as family relations, trade partnerships, and social leadership: "the Pemon social system cannot be encompassed by any strict dualism which splits the world into 'us' and 'them.' Just as the continuously rolling savanna spreads far and wide, so the continuous Pemon social field spreads over it" (234). The consequence, according to him, is an acute sense of the ever-changing order of things—a sense that clearly defies, I would add, Lévi-Strauss's definition of *hot* and *cold* societies.

Diffuseness and fluidity mark yet other aspects of these narratives, which do not establish rigid rules dividing Makunaíma, the trickster, from the rest of the characters. Thus, the rodent agouti, although wiser than the siblings, is also a type of trickster: He deceives Makunaíma and his brothers in order to keep all the food for himself. And Makunaíma's brothers also play the role of tricksters in relation to the ogre Piaimá, performing several tricks so as to deceive him and save their little brother's life. Piaimá himself will also be given a more positive role in another story, as the one who taught the shamans how to do their job.

As constructions of a fictional "self," the Makunaíma stories told by Mayuluaípu and Akuli reveal this same fluidity, this same lack of rigidly defined traits. Makunaíma can be extremely brave on certain occasions, and a perfect coward on others; he can solve problems brilliantly and later be deceived in the most stupid way; he is a hero and, at the same time, a villain. These incongruities would cause no surprise if used to describe most human beings, but they seem to go against certain received expectations with respect to traditional narratives, according to which heroes and villains should be depicted as such, as truly good or truly bad characters. In the Native American case, such expectations derive from the imposition of models normally used in the study of traditional European oral tales. A trickster like Makunaíma, however, is closer to the contradictory and decentered characters of twentieth-century fiction than to traditional models of heroism.

As a culturally defined study of human nature, Makunaíma depicts several of its impulses—from the most quotidian needs such as sexual pleasure and the satisfaction of hunger, to more complex feelings such as boredom and sadomasochism. Like a latter-day Gilgamesh, he is prompted to action through being "bored with life" ("des Lebens überdrüssig" in Koch-Grünberg's German), and he tends to sadomasochism when, in an attempt to seduce his sister-in-law, he covers his own body with wounds to amuse her. It also offers elements that help us understand the mechanisms of power among the Pemon: hierarchichal definition of family and possibilities of its subversion; redefinition through knowledge (it is Makunaíma's knowledge, that is, his "practical creativity," that grants him power over his brother); pragmatic significance (through power Makunaíma can have sex with the woman he wants and can distribute as he pleases the meat he has hunted); and constant redefinition in situations in which Makunaíma reassumes his role as the younger brother who has to be protected by the older and wiser ones.

Makunaíma's is not the only trickster cycle narrated by Mayuluaípu and Akuli. Koch-Grünberg also collected stories about Konewó and Kalawunseg the liar, all of which contribute to Mário de Andrade's protagonist. Besides these, the group of stories about the jaguar comprises another trickster cycle, and several isolated trickster-like characters can be found throughout the whole collection.

Konewó

The stories Mayuluaípu tells about Konewó form a well-structured cycle and appear in two versions, with and without interlinear translations. Unlike Makunaíma, Konewó is not a culture hero; that is, he did not participate in the process of creating the world. We meet him *mediis rebus* as he is about to play his first trick, against his favorite victim, a jaguar. By breaking a nut between his legs, he makes the jaguar believe that he is eating his own testicles. After trying some of the nut, the jaguar is convinced by Konewó to break his own testicles as well, and dies.

We are not given a description of Konewó, and Koch-Grünberg does not offer an explanation for his name. However, Cesareo Armellada's dictionary lists the word *keneuo* as meaning both *rabbit* and *one who deceives*. Thus, Konewó, as a trickster, is close to rabbit counterparts in North America. After this first episode, we follow him in his lonely journey through the forest—a journey in which he deceives several victims, most of them jaguars but also a caiman, a few humans, and Piaimá, our well known ogre. Hostile toward jaguars and some human beings, he nevertheless is summoned to protect the lives of other humans, who are threatened by a fierce caiman. He seems to have no other objective in life, at least from the moment we meet him until his death, at the end of the cycle, than to deceive his victims. He goes on playing his tricks until he is actually killed by a small beetle who gets into his anus and devours his intestines, as a consequence of what becomes his last trick. For Konewó, the natural course of life lies in the interplay be-tween deceiving and being deceived.

Konewó is never portrayed as a fool. He is smart, creative, and uses his creativity to deceive others. But his power of deceit does not always work in the same way. If it is true, for instance, that he deceives all the jaguars, and kills most of them, some still escape and swear revenge. Moreover, in his stories jaguars may also try to play the role of deceivers, as happens in the second episode, against the monkey, in which there is no winner: The jaguar, the monkey, and Konewó all run away, in different directions. And in his last fight against Piaimá, Konewó makes the cannibal believe he is dead by showing him the bones of a tapir while telling him they are his own bones. We also are convinced that the trick worked until the very end, when Piaimá reveals to have known the truth all the time. Konewó, the trickster, becomes then the one who is tricked. Since that episode does not have a definitive closure (Konewó simply runs away after hearing Piaimá's words), we are again left without a clear winner or loser.

Movement is a key element in this narrative. A refrain repeated at the end of almost every episode says: "Oh, Konewó went away," and it may be accompanied by sentences indicating that other characters also went away: "Oh, the jaguar went away. / Konewó went away." Konewó plays tricks and leaves, and so do the other characters if they can. Only death, the final trick, will stop them.

As in the case of Makunaíma, there is in the stories of Konewó a valida-tion of movement and deception, a fight against static essences. But Maku-naíma is a transformer. His pragmatic imagination finds expression, most of the time, in acts of metamorphosis or change, such as cutting trees, turn-ing people into rocks, or transforming himself into a fish. Konewó, on the other hand, is a verbal trickster; his main mode of deception is language. As a culture hero, the god-like Makunaíma can create change and trans-formation that is impossible for mortal beings such as Konewó. Together, Makunaíma and Konewó set the stage for the Pemon to continue "favoring deceit," as Basso's title so well puts it, through movement, transformation, and language—a capacity that will be socially represented at its best by the shaman and by the storyteller.

Shamans are in contact with the changing nature of things. They know the power of plants that can make illnesses go away; they can communicate with the spirits; and when in trance they make their own souls travel to experience marvellous things. Pemon shamans, as in so many Amazonian cultures, can also change into jaguars (Koch-Grünberg 3: 174). For the Pemon Ernesto Pinto, the powerful shamans are actually similar to the

Makunaímas themselves: "But there are Indians of very live intelligence, similar to the Makunaímas, and these have found out many things, which helps them prepare cures and see many things" (25).

Telling a story, on the other hand, is for the Pemon a theatrical experience. The narrator transforms him/herself into the characters he/she represents, and this capacity for deceiving is deeply enjoyed by the audience:

> Little by little the narrator raises his voice, until it reaches a falsetto. All of a sudden he incorporates the character, gesticulating with arms and legs. In quiet tension, the audience listens. For a moment, everything is silent. Then, all of a sudden, a burst of noisy laughter. The joke was strong. The members of the audience spit several times with pleasure. (Koch-Grünberg 3: 107)

Among the Pemon there are no storytellers as such, that is, persons who are considered by the society as having the function of performing narratives. Stories are told by different people on various occasions, but some people are regarded as being specially talented in such a role, and that, Cesareo Armellada tells us, is a highly admired quality:

> The one who has the stories is called *sak*, owner or holder, just like those who know about bone-setting or have useful tools. The Indians never find it an imposition to give hospitality to anyone who tells them stories, brings them news or passes on new songs. They consider themselves well paid. (1964, 10)

The shaman is often a good storyteller as well. Akuli, one of Koch-Grünberg's narrators, is himself a shaman, and Mayuluaípu wants to study to become one when he returns to his village. Not only that, but shamans are specially known for their theatrical skills, as Koch-Grünberg points out: "Also, the talent for imitating is highly pronounced among many Indians. Such skill is particularly found among shamans, for it is part of their profession" (3: 109). In fact, David Guss, elaborating on Rothenberg's definition of the shaman as a proto-poet, describes the shamanic journey as being, above all, linguistic (1985, xi).

Thus, the different modes of metamorphosis and deceit expressed by the Pemon tricksters will find continuity in the actions of storytellers and shamans. Deceiving and transforming, far from being gratuitous activities, play important roles in Pemon society. That is certainly the case with the shaman and the storyteller, and has already been discussed with regard to Makunaíma, whose actions define society and territory. But even Konewó's tricks can be described as having social justification: As a hunter, the trickster Konewó is smart and courageous, astute and artful rather than strong, and in his hunting tales he defies the most feared animal in South American forests. Moreover, Konewó's stories should probably also be con-sidered shamanic tales, since among the Pemon the jaguar cannot be killed, except by the shaman (Koch-Grünberg 3: 165).

Kalawunseg, the Liar, and Other Trickster-like Characters

Another Pemon trickster, Kalawunseg, plays no such role. His name means "a man who cries a lot" (*chorão* in Portuguese). He is a liar, yet within the stories his lies have no positive consequences—actually no consequences other than the irritation of those to whom he tells them. As a deceiver, he can only make his victims believe him, if they believe him at all, for a lim-ited time. And since he is not able to hunt, his "hunting tales" are nothing but lies. In one of the episodes, for instance, he tells his brothers-in-law that he found tracks of a tapir, but when they go to look for them, no tracks can be seen. "The tapir hid his tracks," he says, making his brothers-in-law totally furious. In another one, he claims to have killed two deer, when he had actually hunted two rats burned by fire. But maybe the most interesting of Kalawunseg's lies is the one that he tells his people after his return from the "Englishmen Country" (Guyana). In this tale, the liar describes how he bought goods from an Englishman, claiming that all the products (rifles, fuses, partridges, and gunpowder) grew on trees. Koch-Grünberg reads this story as a satire of the lies told by those Pemon who return to their land after working temporarily in Guyana. Such lies, he adds, are also told among neighboring tribes (2: 134), and indeed might be considered to be-long to a traveler-tale mode found more widely in Native American litera-ture. (Koch-Grünberg actually compares Kalawunseg to Munchhausen.)

Kalawunseg's stories are entertaining: They make the Pemon, and oth-ers, laugh. But in his interaction with the other characters, the liar is treated with irritation, or ridiculed, since the others always become aware that he is lying. Not only that, but his lies do not help him hunt, transform the world, or protect the lives of other people: they have no immediate function in the Pemon society. In this sense, he is different from Makunaíma and Konewó, and maybe should not even be considered a trickster, since his attempts to deceive are unfruitful and therefore basically negative—a fact reinforced by Akuli in performance, who pronounces the words as would a mentally retarded person. In that sense, Kalawunseg's tales can be read as a satire of deceit, a satire of "tricksterness": The liar is an unsuccessful deceiver, a trickster who cannot transform or create illusion.

Another character with certain trickster traits is Akalapijeima, the protagonist of Akuli's "Akalapizeima and the Sun." This isolated story tells us how this "father of all the Indians" was thrown onto a desert island by

Walo'ma, the frog, whom he was trying to catch. Lonely, exposed to cold and to the excrement of the vultures, he asks the morning star and the moon for help, but ends up being rescued by Wei, the Sun, who decides to marry him to one of his daughters, as long as he does not have sex with any other woman. But Akalapizeima falls in love with one of the daughters of the vulture, and is thus punished by the Sun, who tells him: "If you had followed my advice and had married one of my daughters, you would have been always young and handsome as I am. Now you will be young and beautiful only for a short time. Soon you will be old and ugly" (2: 54). Akalapizeima then married the vulture and "settled down" (2: 54).

This ancestor of the Pemon cannot be properly called a trickster, since he does not demonstrate any desire to deceive his fellow human beings. If it is true that one could compare his lust to Makunaíma's, the fact that he is so clearly punished for it by another character demonstrates that "Akalapizeima and the Sun" is closer to a moral tale than to a trickster story. Moreover, Akalapizeima's behavior is not so much characterized by an uncontrollable lust, but rather by his attraction for the young daughters of the vulture, whom "the man found very beautiful and he fell in love with them" (2: 53). Instead of remaining faithful to the daughter of the Sun, the principle of life, Akalapizeima feels attracted to those of the vulture, an animal clearly linked to death. His punishment therefore could not be any other than the loss of perennial youth, i.e., the condemnation of his descendants to an unavoidable death. But such condemnation is not necessarily tragic; Akalapizeima gets used to life, and to the fact that life, at least as the Pemon see it, is inextricably connected (and attracted) to death.

Some trickster traits can also be found in Etetó's brother-in-law, one of the protagonists of Mayuluaípu's "Etetó: How Kasana-Podole, the Vulture-King, Got his Second Head." An unlucky hunter and fisherman, Etetó one days steals from the otter a magic *totuma* that makes him catch many fish. His brother-in-law follows him, discovers the *totuma*, tries to use it but ends up losing the precious object. The same thing happens with several magic objects that Etetó finds, until he cannot find them any more. In order to punish his brother-in-law, Etetó makes a fishing hook and instructs it to get into his brother-in-law's hand. The hook enters the man's body and kills him. In revenge, the brother-in-law's mother instructs the ghost of her son to change into different types of food and poison Etetó. Etetó at first realizes the trick, but later eats some of the food and becomes prisoner of a spell: He cannot stop eating; he becomes "Wewé, the father of the gluttons." He eats his own wife, his mother-in-law, the rest of the family, and everything he sees, until he becomes the second head of the vulture-king.

Like many tricksters, Etetó's brother-in-law is smart enough to steal the magic objects, but fool enough to lose them quickly. However, the brother-in-law's tricks have less importance in the story than the subsequent disputes between Etetó and his mother-in-law and Etetó's final transformation into a malignant ghost. "Etetó" is a shamanic tale, which tells the Pemon that the use of magical objects should be restricted to those who have the necessary competence. Moreover, the protagonist's transformation into a ghost shows that a powerful shaman who helps the community to get a lot of food may become a venomous threat when power disputes place him against his own people.

In their various ways, all these Koch-Grünberg narratives confirm how tricksters as diverse as Makunaíma and Konewó, and partial-trickster characters like Akalapizeima and Etetó's brother-in-law, may share the "pragmatic creativity" identified by Basso, at the same time that they refine, in a Pemon way, our notions of trickster.

The *Tarén* and the Songs

Two other types of Pemon texts—*tarén*, or incantations, and songs—are included in the first and third of the Koch-Grünberg volumes. Described as *Zaubersprüche* by Koch-Grünberg, the incantations are known as *tarén* among the Pemon, the term used by Armellada as a title for his collection of them. The priest himself confesses that he became aware of the existence of the *tarén* as a literary genre only after living a long time among the Pemon. Until then, he had heard just of smaller, abbreviated versions (1972, 11). Koch-Grünberg, who stayed only a few weeks among the Pemon, noticed the existence of shorter and longer versions of *tarén*, but he also observed that those texts

> hardly attract the foreigner's notice, because they are rarely pronounced in public. In general they are said within the intimacy of the family, as a whisper. Also, the Indians do not reveal them easily to the Europeans, probably because they are afraid of lessening their magical power or of losing them. (3: 189)

The *tarén* are used for healing as well as spells, and they normally start with a narrative, whose characters may be human beings, animals, plants, or natural phenomena. For the most part, they appeal to the cosmogony and beliefs narrated at length in the creation stories, a pattern found among the Maya, Cherokee, Cuna, Navajo, and proper to the Native American tradition generally.

In *Pemontón Taremuru* (1972), Cesareo Armellada divides the *tarén* into four parts:

(a) a narrative of how a wrong or sickness began

(b) a presentation of the one who opposes this wrong

(c) a formula with which the opponent becomes the cure

(d) the name or names which it used to identify itself on that occasion (14)

The most striking formal characteristics of the *tarén* are repetition and enumeration, which were accompanied, according to Koch-Grünberg, by monotonous pronunciation (3: 190). The lines or stanzas to be repeated are the ones which have direct relationship with the problem to be caused or cured by the formula. For example, in a text used to cause or heal acne on teenagers, Makunaíma and his brothers want to have sex with a beautiful young girl, who refuses them. Each one of the brothers tries to sleep with her, and each of them is repelled in the same way: she bites them and strikes them on the face. Even though we already know at the beginning of the story that the girl "didn't want any of them," for each attempt the action of refusal is repeated in the same way. In revenge, Makunaíma then decides to make the girl ugly, using fish eggs to give her acne: "I am Makunaíma. I make this ancestor girl ugly, with eggs of *padzidzi*, with eggs of *padzidzi-podole*." A long enumeration of twenty-four types of fish follows, and for each fish the expression "with eggs of" is repeated. The other three brothers also decide to use fish eggs to give her acne, and each of them repeats the formula in exactly the same way. But the young woman meets five kinds of rain, each born of a different constellation, and three different types of pepper—and to every one of them she tells her sad story. As a result, every variety of rain and pepper will repeat the healing formula (there is one formula for the rain and another one for the peppers) and help cure her. For any person trying to treat acne it is necessary to repeat the rain formula six or seven times and wash the patient's face six or seven times with lukewarm water. Then one must repeat the pepper formula six or seven times while spreading crushed pepper the same number of times over the affected area.

As a frequent Native American literary resource, repetition has drawn the attention of many critics. Several of them consider it a memory tool, and some, like Margot Astrov, go so far as to think it a childish device (Allen, 181–2). Paula Gunn Allen considers the "entrancing effect" of repetition the most important formal aspect of ceremonial literature: "The most significant and noticeable structural device is repetition, which serves to entrance and to unify—both the participants and the ceremony" (179). In the Pemon *tarén* collected by Koch-Grünberg, we can see two types of repetition: an internal repetition that obeys principles dictated by the narrative itself and an external repetition, i.e., the repetition of the complete formula performed during the ritual of cure. The entrancing effect mentioned by Allen refers more directly to the latter, and it depends on the different steps of the healing process; the person performing the cure will repeat the text as many times as he/she has to carry out certain actions. The internal textual repetitions depend usually on the number of characters involved. Thus, in the acne formula, the action that makes Makunaíma and his brothers upset—the girl's refusal—is repeated to each one of the brothers, who then repeat the formula that will make her ugly. Later, the girl narrates her story to every one of the elements that will help cure her, and all of them will repeat the healing formula as well. In the case of the peppers, the number of repetitions depends on the actual types of pepper that are necessary for the cure. This is not, however, the case of the cultural heroes involved—three in some texts and four in others—nor is it the case of characters in other formulas, which have no direct relation to remedies used in the healing ritual. In the text to convert enemies into friends, for instance, two armadillos set the example of how to make the enemies laugh, each repeating the complete formula, which must be said six times while moving a stick in the direction of the enemy's house.

Without denying the entrancing effects that such repetitions certainly have, we need to notice that one of their main characteristics is that they are pronounced either by different characters, or by one character to several others. There is not one single narrative among those reproduced by Koch-Grünberg in which the magic formula is repeated by and to the same character. In the case of a text to avoid tumors transmitted by the meat of large animals, for example, the curing formula has to be pronounced by various kinds of jaguar, because jaguars eat all types of meat and do not get ill. In the narrative to clear the throat, the text has to be said by different species of monkeys, and in the one to ease birth, by different fish. In two of the texts there is no repetition of the formula, the ones used to heal the effects caused by the poison of the ray and the snake (these are the only cases in which the creatures who teach others how to say the formulas are human beings). In all the other texts, repetition is used to put humans in contact with the natural world in its different manifestations. More than mere repetition, the successive sayings of the same formula by or to different characters represent a pluralization of voices. In order to avoid tumors, the Pemon have to appeal not to "the jaguar," an abstract entity, but to the black jaguar, the tapir-jaguar, the puma, the spotted jaguar, and the red jaguar. Once the text has been said by all of them, a sense of community has been established, and human beings can then take part in it. Repetition, therefore, is closely related to enumeration in these texts, both of them having taxonomic functions. Through repetition and enumeration, the Pemon can reaffirm their knowledge of nature—a knowledge used not to exclude them from it, but to constantly reintegrate them in it. And since for the Pemon the concept of nature is more comprehensive, this knowledge makes human beings part of a larger cosmic order that incorporates not only the animals easily found in the forest or the savanna, but also spirit jaguars and monkeys seen only by the shamans, and the Pemons' cultural heroes and ancestors.

The ancestors play a very significant role in these texts. In the acne formula, the girl whom Makunaíma and his brothers desire is called "ancestor girl" *(Pia-bazi)*, while a young man suffering from worms is called "ancestor boy" *(Pia-moínele)*. Having experienced just the problem which the healing ritual is supposed to cure, they set the example of what to do in such a situation. The temporal interplay is particularly remarkable here, and quite different from what we find in the cosmogonical narratives. There, the story of what happened to the ancestors is narrated in the past tense, and considered throughout the story as a historical, finished action: "Once upon a time there was among our ancestors a very beautiful girl called Pia ama riemo. Makunaíma wanted to marry her, and also Maanape and also Zigé. Makunaíma went to sleep with her" (199). But in the dialogues, when the characters make use of repetition to tell each other what happened, or when they repeat the healing or spell formulas, the ancestors and the present-day Pemon occupy a concomitant time frame: "I have acne caused by Makunaíma, by Maanape, by Zigé. The people of today, the sons, have to suffer from it as I do, when others have caused it to them" (201). The expressions "the sons" *(mule-san)* and "the people of today" *(amenan-gon)* are formulaic elements used in all these texts to refer to the present day Pemon, mentioned here by the "ancestor girl" when she tells the rains and peppers about what happened to her. This co-existence of the ancestor girl and the people of today does not imply, however, any kind of atemporal quality. On the contrary, the constant references in these texts to "ancestor" and "people of today" assert the importance of temporal difference. But through ritual, the Pemon can reaffirm their historical knowledge— what they have learned from and about their ancestors—and make it present in their lives. Just as a detailed taxonomy of nature is invoked through repetition in order to establish a sense of community (by repeating parts of a text ritually, different types of rain, jaguars, etc., come into being), so historical knowledge is revived in ritual to make man part of a cosmic order that includes different levels of time, but without attempting to eliminate the distinctions between them.

Another genre transcribed by Koch-Grünberg is what he calls "little innocent songs," usually sung informally at parties and often improvised

(3: 145). Lyrical, these songs mostly consist of a single stanza plus refrain, and they generally express a feeling of nostalgia for the paradise of Roraima, as in the following example:

> kinatoli poítene-pe kómeme-tana azike loloíme
> haí-a ha-ha-ha haí-a
> (while the japú stays as a servant, come here Roraima
> haí-a ha-ha-ha haí-a). (3: 145)

The japu is a playful, easily domesticated bird, prized by native peoples for its black and yellow feathers. The period in which the japu works as a servant indicates therefore a time in which one is at home, away from Roraima. The Pemon are great travelers: their *conuco* garden is often a two-hour walk away from their houses, and they do not mind walking several days to pay a visit to a relative or a friend (Thomas, 35). Moreover, they are known for their trading activities—a tradition which is many centuries old and integrates a complex system of commercial and cultural interdependence known as the "Orinoco System" (Arvello-Jiménez and Biord, 57). Roraima is a sacred place, where the spirits known as Mawari live. The nostalgic invocation of the sacred mountain brings it home, calming down the urge to visit Roraima, to travel again, to set foot on the road once more. But Roraima is also the bountiful place, the land where there are plenty of animals and fish, where trees and crops grow more easily than on the dry savanna. The presence of the domesticated japu at home brings Roraima's bounty back—a bounty invoked in another lyric poem translated by Mayuluaípu and Koch-Grünberg:

> When I go to Roraima I want to eat bananas
> haí-a ha-ha-ha haí-a. (3: 147)

The lamenting refrain, a characteristic of all these songs, sets the tone of the poem. It is not just the expression of a desire (I want to eat fruit when I go to Roraima), but rather the realization that this desire cannot be fulfilled, at least for the moment. But going to Roraima is not the only way of experiencing the bounty of the sacred mount. In another poem, one's only wish is to dream about it:

> While I sleep come here Roraima
> haí-a ha-ha-ha haí-a

Similar songs about Roraima had already been described by Schomburgk:

> For the most part it was the wonders of Roraima, although this extra-
> ordinary mountain lay a hundred miles distant, that were glorified.

'Roraima, the red crag wrapped in clouds, the ever-fruitful mother of the streams,' or 'I sing about the red rocks of Roraima on which dark night reigns even by day' were refrains of the songs that we were to hear so often, especially among the Arekuna in the neighbordhood of the mountain." (2: 151)

Koch-Grünberg also mentions war narratives, but he does not transcribe any. In the travelogue (first volume) he recognizes that they play an important part in the Pemons' lives, and actually compares them to Homer: "Among other things, José tells me also about a war that the Taulipang fought a long time ago against the Pischaukó, their ancestral enemies. These live descriptions of old fights, which still today in the Indian *malocas,* or by the fire in the fields, are the main subject of conversation, sometimes give me a Homeric impression" (1: 220). Schomburgk also comments on the importance of these war narratives: "With a trifling modulation of the voice they sing about all their deeds in war and in the chase, and at times give way to an almost inexhaustible flow of sarcastic humor and biting satire to which it would seem Indians are unfortunately inclined" (2: 152). Although critical for our historical knowledge of the northern Amazonian savanna, such stories have never been published.

From creation stories, to trickster narratives, curing formulas, lyric songs, and war-stories: Koch-Grünberg's collection is a striking demonstration, in a variety of genres, of the wealth of Pemon literature, which has its equivalent in the So'to text *Watunna.*

chapter 2
Macunaíma (1928)

ELEVEN YEARS AFTER THE ENCOUNTER between Koch-Grünberg and the two
Pemon Indians, in February 1922, a group of (mostly) young men
and women from São Paulo organized a series of presentations in the
Municipal Theater of this city—the bastion of high culture for the *paulista*
elite of the time. The presentations included performances of avant-garde
music by the composer Heitor Villa-Lobos; exhibitions of paintings; conferences on avant-garde poetry and art; and readings of poetry by Oswald
de Andrade, Manuel Bandeira (who sent the poem "The Frogs" from Rio to
be read for the occasion), Menotti del Picchia, and Mário de Andrade, author of *Macunaíma* (1928). The event was called *Semana de Arte Moderna*
(Modern Art Week), and its participants became known as *modernistas*
(modernists). For many critics and historians, 1922 became, so to speak,
the birth date of modern art in Brazil, although, needless to say, avant-
garde art had been published, performed, and exhibited before 1922 in
several parts of the country.[1]

The first years of *modernista* literature (1922–24) were characterized
by a celebration of urban modernity, epitomized in most cases by the city
of São Paulo. The links with European movements, such as Futurism and
Dada were clear, and so was the need to break with formal constrictions
(especially in poetry) imposed by a rhetorical tradition still dominated
by Parnassianism. The exemplary work of this phase is perhaps Mário de

Andrade's *Paulicea Desvairada* (1922), a collection of poems inspired by the city of São Paulo.

In the second phase of the movement (1924–31), the *modernistas* began a search for popular, and often nonurban, Brazilian culture; in so doing they focused on the nation's indigenous antecedents, notably three of the traditions explored here: Carib, Tupi-Guarani, and Rio Negro. It is in this phase that Mário de Andrade intensified the practice of incorporating popular rhythms into his poetry, a strong tendency, for instance, of his 1927 collection, *Clã do Jabuti*. He also published studies on popular music and culture in *Revista de Antropofagia,* and wrote the most important novel of the time, *Macunaíma,* heavily indebted as it is to Carib texts. Together with *Leyendas de Guatemala* (1930) by Miguel Angel Asturias, *Macunaíma* marks a watershed in Latin American literature, both Brazilian and Spanish American, in terms of its interaction with native texts, as Gerald Martin has observed (1989). Oswald de Andrade's "Manifesto Antropófago" (Cannibalist Manifesto 1928) and Raul Bopp's *Snake Norato* (1931) also belong to this phase.

Macunaíma is the biography, so to speak, of its eponymous protagonist, "a hero with no character" *(sem nenhum caráter),* as the subtitle has it. He is born in the region of Roraima, near the Uraricoera river, into the Tapanhumas, a native Amazonian tribe with a Carib name yet unusually dark skin, which was described by the German traveler von den Steinen. The hero reveals his special nature from birth and in childhood adventures with his mother, brothers, and sisters-in-law, setting up sibling rivalries that run through the novel. He marries Ci, the Mother of the Forest, who dies of sadness upon losing their only son. Before dying, Ci gives him a green stone amulet or *muiraquitã,* which brings him power as "Emperor of the Forest" as well as luck, but the amulet then falls into the river to be swallowed by a turtle. Macunaíma and his brothers then embark on a journey south to São Paulo (chapter 5) in order to recover the amulet, which had fallen into the hands of the Peruvian (with an Italian name) Wenceslau Pietro Pietra, also known as the ogre Piaimã. After many adventures in the metropolis, with its strange language and customs, they recover the amulet and go back north to the Amazon (chapter 15). Back home, Macunaíma finds his people gone, gets into a new dispute with his brother Jiguê, who changes into the vulture-king, and destroys all members of the family, except for Macunaíma. Plagued by Vei, the sun, for having spurned one of her daughters, he loses his right leg and is badly mutilated. The amulet is again swallowed by a water beast, this time for good. Lonely, and "tired of this life," he decides to become a star, but not before telling his life story to a parrot, who tells it to the author of the book (chapter 17).

This summary alone cannot do justice to *Macunaíma,* which was called by its author not a novel, but a rhapsody, and could be better described as a complicated net of plots and subplots, etiological narratives, and multiple encounters between the protagonist and myriad other characters. The majority of these plots and subplots were taken from previous sources, most of them native, which are then combined with popular sayings and songs, data from Mário's[2] own life and, of course, the author's own inventions. All this, plus the hero's remarkable inconsistencies, have provoked, from the time of publication, quite contrasting reactions. *Antropófagos,* like Oswald de Andrade, liked the novel so much that they immediately incorporated it, against Mário's own will, into their literary movement. Others, however, disagreed. Nestor Victor, for instance, called it "lamentable" (Lopez 1988, 344), and João Ribeiro considered it the product of a "a guest in a mad house" (Lopez 1988, 346).

With time, most debates about the novel came to concentrate on whether or not it is an allegory of Brazilian society and, within that, the role played in possible allegorical readings by its inconsistent hero. For if Macunaíma was born from an indigenous tribe, it is a tribe that has unusually dark skin. In other words, he is an Indian, but he looks like a Black. And if this were not enough, he later takes a miraculous bath that transforms him into a "beautiful white prince." Most readers have thus seen this tri-colored hero, quite reasonably, as a representation of Brazil's three formative races. This reading is reinforced by the fact that Macunaíma is called "the hero of our people" in the very first sentence of the novel.

Yet, all allegorical readings of the novel become difficult to sustain beyond these initial steps, due to the hero's unusual shifts in behavior. Mário himself did not help the debate by defending, throughout his life, quite contrasting views about *Macunaíma* and its polemical hero. The author's insecurities about the novel predate the publication, as we can see in the following letter to Alceu Amoroso Lima: "Faced with *Macunaíma,* I'm absolutely incapable of judging anything. Sometimes I have the impression that it is the only work-of-art, truly artistic, ergo, disinterested, that I did in my life"[3] (Lopez 1988, 400). Also before publication, Mário wrote to Augusto Meyer about his fears: "This one indeed, a book that I am scared with the idea of publishing. It is actually a scary thing" (Lopez 1988, 401); and to Alceu Amoroso Lima, in another letter, he once more revealed his insecurities about the work : "There are moments in which I find it terrible. There are moments in which I think it is damn good"(Lopez 1988, 403).

He often denied any intention of turning Macunaíma, the character, into a symbol of Brazilian society: "On the one hand I had no intention of making Macunaíma a symbol of the Brazilian. Yet if he is not *the* Brazilian no one can deny that he is *a* Brazilian and quite Brazilian at that" (Lopez

1988, 403). On the other hand, "the lack of character" of his protagonist is said by Mário to represent the "lack of character" of the Brazilians—a people, according to him, still in the process of formation (Lopez 1988, 395). On some occasions, he will see the hero of the novel as a satire of Brazilian society: "Now he seems to me a perverse satire. Even more perverse because I don't believe you can correct people's behavior through satire" (Lopez 1988, 403). On other occasions, he strongly denies his intentions of satirizing (letter to Alceu Amoroso Lima, 1928): "And it's not [a satire]. Not even when I made such fun of Brazilian sensuality and pornography did I intend to produce satire. I'm incapable of satire since the world seems to me so much as it actually is!" (Lopez 1988, 401). In 1929, soon after the publication, he confessed his own confusion in a letter to Augusto Meyer: "because frankly, I'm not at all sure what my rogue-hero is. I *knew*, but no longer know. The critics got me; and since the symbolic vagueness of Uraricoera's son is quite elastic, each one featured his own Macunaíma" (Lopez 1988, 412). By 1942, however, Mário had become so convinced of the allegorical vocation of his character that he wrote this embittered description of him in a letter to Álvaro Lins:

> it's true I failed. If the whole book is a satire, a rebellious non-conforming with what is, with what I feel and see Brazilians are, the funny side won. It's true I failed. Because it does nothing for me to turn the blame on the Brazilians, the fault must be mine, because the one who wrote the book was me. Look at the book to see the introduction they gave me! For those people, as for the modernistas of my generation, *Macunaíma* is 'the lyric projection of Brazilian feeling, it is the soul of a virgin and unknown Brazil'! Virgin, never! unknown, never! Virgin, my God! Much more likely a Nazi dog! I failed! (Lopez 1988, 471)

Alfredo Bosi aptly observed that these changes in Mário's own view of the novel and the different reactions it has provoked are related to the author's "two motivations" in the composition of the work. First, the desire to "tell and sing episodes about a legendary figure who had fascinated him for the most diverse reasons and who bore in himself the attributes of the *hero*, understood in the broadest possible sense of a being both human and mythical, who has certain roles, goes in search of a basic good, risks dangers, undergoes extraordinary changes, in short wins or loses. . . ." Second, the need to "think the Brazilian people, *our people*, following the crossed or superimposed tracks of our existence, savage, colonial and modern, in search of an identity which being so plural borders on surprise and indetermination; hence the hero with no character." For Bosi, in order to understand *Macunaíma* one has to pursue both motivations, "that of narrating, which is playful and aesthetic; and that of interpreting, which is historical and ideological" (1988, 171).

These opposing motivations have helped to feed a critical debate that has also tended to polarize between various allegorical readings of *Macunaíma* and those readings that refuse allegory altogether. The major players in this debate are Haroldo de Campos's *Morfologia de Macunaíma* (1973), a structural reading of the novel based on its popular sources, which eschews allegory; and Gilda de Mello e Souza's harsh critique of Campos in *O Tupi e o Alaúde* (1979)—an ingenious allegorical rendition of Mário's work.

Brilliant and different as they are, these and basically all other studies of the novel have one thing in common: a refusal to engage in detailed interpretive comparisons with *Macunaíma*'s indigenous sources. Not that these sources have not been recognized. Campos himself recognized them, as did the Amazonian folklorist Raimundo de Moraes soon after the publication of the novel, in an entry dedicated to Koch-Grünberg in *Dicionário de Cousas da Amazônia,* reportedly written to "defend" Mário from accusations of plagiarism. (The "defense" was, of course, a way of exposing Mário's use of native sources as plagiarist.) Mário's response to Moraes, published in *Diário Nacional* in 1931 makes no secret of his use of sources:

> Yes, I copied, my dear defender. What shocks me—and I find this supremely generous—is that my detractors forgot all they know, restricting my copying to Koch-Grünberg, when I copied them all. And even you, in the Boiúna scene. I confess I copied, and copied sometimes verbatim. You really want to know? Not only did I copy the ethnographers and the Amerindian texts, but further, in the Carta pras Icamiabas, I took whole sentences from Rui Barbosa, Mário Barreto, and the Portuguese colonial chroniclers, and I tore apart the ever so precious and solemn language used by the contributers to the Revista de Língua Portuguesa.[4] (Lopez 1974, 99–100)

By defining his literary creation as re-creation, as copying, Mário aligns himself with several writers and theorists of the twentieth century—from Brecht and Borges to Kristeva and Derrida—who see literature as an intertextual practice. Unlike them, however, he is less concerned with intertextuality as such than with the possibilities of intercultural relations opened by the intertextual dialogue.

Cavalcanti Proença's *Roteiro de Macunaíma* (1955) carefully mapped the sources of Mário's novel. This important study allowed readers to visualize more clearly Mário's monumental project: to bring Brazilian *belles lettres* into a fruitful, dynamic contact with heterogeneous and diverse forms of popular culture. And as we can see in the *Roteiro,* from the complicated fabric of texts that compose *Macunaíma*, the indigenous ones ("Amerindian text" in the words of Mário) stand out, providing the novel with its main characters and the great majority of its plots. Most of these plots were taken from Koch-Grünberg, but some also came from Capistrano de Abreu, Barbosa Rodrigues, Brandão do Amorim, Couto de Magalhães, and others. In *Macunaíma: a Margem e o Texto* (1974), Telê Porto Ancona Lopez went on to discuss Mário's marginalia in his own copy of Koch-Grünberg's *Vom Roroima zum Orinoco*. And she suggested that after Proença's *Roteiro,* and her own work, there was little else left to do with regard to the indigenous sources of the novel (3).

We need, however, to consider the aesthetic and cultural implications of this intertextuality, to relate *Macunaíma* closely to the indigenous texts that informed it, going beyond the first (and extremely important) step taken by both Proença and Lopez, of locating the specific intertextual dialogues at play. For if the influence of the indigenous texts on *Macunaíma* is not usually denied, the engagement with them is most often considered superfluous, given their status as "raw data," or "ethnographic material." My objective in this chapter is to question the economic discourse of a critical tradition that tends to see indigenous texts as unworked raw material that only becomes manufactured in the hands of nonindigenous intellectuals. That Mário himself disagreed with these assumptions we can see in the following letter to the poet Carlos Drummond de Andrade (1928):

> You say that there is no interest in the Indians . . . From the artistic point of view, I imagine. I really don't know how to make myself clear, really not. I have an artistic interest in them. Now and again they do amazing things. Certain ceramic bowls from the North, certain Marajoara vases, certain linear designs, certain music and above all certain legends and tales are stupendous, Carlos . . . I believe this propensity of mine is not just of the moment or the result of fashion. I always had it and for me these great traditional legends of the tribal peoples are the finest histories, tales and novels there can be. (Lopez 1988, 394–95)

Thus, this chapter makes a double move: It attempts to offer a reading of *Macunaíma* based on close attention to its indigenous sources at the same time that it engages in discussions with the existing critical discourse about the novel. I hope to show not only what one gains by taking the indigenous sources seriously but also what one loses by not doing so. Needless to say, my reading could not and certainly does not intend to invalidate the readings it engages with. At most, I hope to complement them, offering a contribution to what has been a rich and fruitful debate.

A Trickster Hero

Macunaíma's debt to the Pemon narratives published by Koch-Grünberg begins, of course, with the protagonist, whose name and ways of behaving are most strongly related to the trickster-hero of the Pemon studied in the previous chapter. Macunaíma's relation to his antecedent is above all aesthetic, as the author himself says in a letter to Alceu Amoroso Lima the year the novel was published:

> In general, my acts and my work are far too deliberate to be artistic. But not *Macunaíma*. I decided to write then because I was overcome with lyric emotion when upon reading Koch-Grünberg I realized that Macunaíma was a hero without any character either moral or psychological, I found this hugely moving, I don't know why, surely because of the newness of the fact, or because he so fully suited to our times, I don't know. (Lopez 1988, 400–1)

The similarities between the actions and behavior of the two characters can be more fully appreciated, in the first instance, if we compare excerpts from the texts. Here the novel describes, in the first chapter, how Macunaíma goes with his sister-in-law to the forest:

> The next day he [Macunaíma] waited, watching with half an eye for his mother to start work, then he begged her to stop weaving split cane into a basket, so she asked her daughter-in-law, Jiguê's wife, to take the little boy. Jiguê's wife was a nice girl called Sofará who came rather apprehensively; but Macunaíma was behaving himself; and didn't try to put his hand where he oughtn't. Sofará gave the lad a piggyback till she came to a place where a giant arum lily was growing on the riverbank. . . . The girl put Macunaíma down on the bank but he began to whine—too many ants there, he said— and he begged her to carry him to the crest of a ridge hidden behind the trees. Sofará did this, but as soon as she laid the child down on the litter of dry leaves carpeting the forest floor among the sedges, eddoes and creeping spiderwort, he transformed himself into a comely prince. There they made love . . . many times. (5)

The same sequence of events was narrated by Akuli, as we can see in Koch-Grünberg's text:

> When Makunaíma[5] was still a boy, he would cry all night long and would ask his oldest brother's wife to take him outside of the house. There he wanted to secure her and force her. His mom wanted to take him out, but he didn't want her to. Then his mom told his sister-in-law to take him. She carried him out, for quite a distance, but he asked her to take him even farther. Then the woman took him even farther, until they were behind a

wall. Makunaíma was still a boy. But when they arrived there, he turned
into a man and he forced her. It was then always like that with the woman,
and he would use her every time his brother went out to hunt. The brother,
however, knew nothing of this. At home, Makunaíma was a child. When
outside, right away he would turn into a man. (2: 46)

The novel goes on to tell us how the boy Macunaíma tried to convince his
brother to make him a trap:

Jiguê suspected nothing and began plaiting some fiber drawn from the
leaves of the wild pineapple to make a cord. He had come accross the fresh
tracks of a tapir and wanted a noose to trap it. Macunaíma asked for some
of the cord for himself, but Jiguê said it wasn't a baby's toy, which caused
him to start blubbering again and giving them all a sleepless night.

Macunaíma then begged again for some of the fiber. Jiguê eyed him with
distaste but sent his wife to fetch some yarn for the boy, which she did.
Dawn had barely climbed above the treetops on the following day when
Macunaíma woke everyone with hideous bawling. (6)

Once again, the text closely resembles Koch-Grünberg's:

The oldest brother went to look for caroa fibers in order to make a trap for
a tapir. He said that he had found fresh tapir tracks and he wanted to make
himself a trap. Makunaíma also asked for a trap, but the brother told him
no, saying: "What do you want it for? Traps aren't for children to play with.
This is only for those who know how to handle it." But the boy insisted and
he absolutely wanted to have it. He asked for it every day. Then the oldest
brother gave him a few caroa fibers and asked the mother: "What does the
boy want the trap for?" (46)

But the boy is more successful in his hunt than the brother expected, as we
can see in both the novel and in Koch-Grünberg's text:

"Hey! Someone go down to the waterhole! There's a beast caught in my
trap!" But no one believed him, and they all started their day's work.
Macunaíma, really miffed, begged Sofará to make a quick visit to the
drinking place just to have a look. She did so and came racing back shout-
ing to everyone that there was indeed a huge tapir in the trap, already dead.
The whole tribe turned out to fetch the animal, dumfounded by the brat's
cunning. Jiguê, with nothing in his own noose, met them all carrying the
carcass and lent them a hand. As he cut it up and shared out the flesh he
didn't give Macunaíma any of the meat, only the innards. The hero swore
he'd take revenge. (M. Andrade 1984, 7)

The next day, Makunaíma sent his mother to go see if any tapir had fallen into the trap. One really had. The mother returned and said that the tapir was already dead. Then the boy told his mom to go let his oldest brother know, so that he would take out the tapir and distribute it. She had to repeat herself two times, because the oldest brother didn't want to believe her and said: "I'm much older; no tapir fell into my trap, how is it possible that there is one in the little one's trap?" Makunaíma said to the mother: "Tell him to take his wife, so that she can carry the meat!" When the brother and his wife had gone, Makunaíma told the mom not to go there. When the brother had already cut up the tapir, Makunaíma sent the mother to tell him to bring the tapir back home whole, because he wanted to distribute the meat himself. But the oldest brother didn't want to give him a portion of the meat, saying that he was still too young. He carried all of the meat home and left only the intestines for the boy. Makunaíma was furious. (Koch-Grünberg 1984: 2, 47)

In the novel, Jiguê finally suspects that his wife was having sex with his younger brother:

The Evening Star was already bright in the sky when the girl returned, pretending to be tired out from carrying the child on her back. However, though Jiguê was a witless sort of chap, he had become suspicious and had followed the couple into the forest where he saw the transformation and all that followed. He was hopping mad with fury when they arrived, and snatching up a thong he plaided rawhide called an armadillo's tail, he walloped the hero until his arse was skinned. (M. Andrade 1984, 7)

Jiguê's realization is also based on Akuli's story:

The oldest brother figured out that Makunaíma was sleeping with his wife. He went out to hunt, but he came back after going halfway, to spy on the boy. He waited close to the place where the woman would always go with Makunaíma. She came with the little one in her arms. When she got behind the wall, she sat the child on the floor. Then Makunaíma turned into a man. He grew bigger and bigger. (The boy was very fat.) He lay down with the woman and he possessed her. The brother saw everything. He took a stick and beat Makunaíma terribly. (Koch-Grünberg 1984:2, 47)

Comparing both texts, we can see that Macunaíma's basic qualities, as they are defined in the first chapter of the novel, are already present in the native text: his childish behavior and capacity to transform into an adult, his lust, his ability to deceive, his innate talents (for hunting), and his dispute with the older brother. In the novel's next chapter, the family is suffering from hunger, and Macunaíma asks the mother to imagine that their house is on the other side of the river. The house is then magically transported, and they have plenty to eat. However, Macunaíma's mother cuts some bananas to give to Jiguê and his wife, who remained on the other side of the river, hungry. Macunaíma gets angry and transports the house back again to its original place. The same sequence is found in Koch-Grünberg's narratives, with the difference that the house is transported not to the other side of the river, but to the top of the mountain. Many other examples of close intertextuality with the adventures of Makunaíma, the Pemon hero, could still be described. Besides Makunaíma, other Pemon characters from Koch-Grünberg's collection, studied in the first chapter, influenced Mário de Andrade in the creation of his protagonist, suggesting not only modes of behavior, but story lines to be enacted by the "hero of our people" as well: Konewó, from whom Macunaíma inherited his capacity as a verbal deceiver, as an illusionist; Kalawunseg, who made him a gratuitous liar; Akalapizeima, who, as we saw in the first chapter, could also be considered a trickster for his excessive lust, although his story resembles more a moral tale; and Etetó's brother-in-law, perfectly classifiable as a trickster for his laziness, his envy, and his excessive curiosity, but whose positive qualities and heroism are harder to see. However, it is the Pemon Makunaíma who gives Mário de Andrade's protagonist his most important qualities: his name, his ability to transform into other beings, a good portion of his malice and mischief, his capacity for boredom, and his status as a hero. And since he is a hero, a Pemon type of hero (i.e., a trickster), he can accumulate good and bad qualities, as long as he maintains his ability to change, to create problems and find good (and bad) solutions for them; as long as he maintains his "pragmatic creativity."

A Folk-Tale Morphology?

The question of how to define *Macunaíma*'s characters, specifically with respect to the novel's structure, was taken up by Haroldo de Campos in *Morfologia do Macunaíma* (1973), the most detailed analysis of the relationship between the novel and the narratives in Koch-Grünberg's second volume. This impressive scholarly work understood, as only Cavalcanti Proença and Telê Ancona Lopez had done until then, the great respect felt by Mário for the indigenous texts that inspired him. Campos refers to letters written by the novelist, in which he defended the logic of certain passages of the novel, found illogical by others, as being that of the indigenous texts:

> This logic of "being without logic," as well as the "psychological link" that
> results from a psychological "non-definition," may be attributed to the
> contradictory character of the hero, which *already appears as such in the*

Koch-Grünberg legends. Moreover, when he has to justify a chain of events, rather than give us a psychological explanation of the characters or a novel-like argument about prior motivation, Mário doesn't fail to warn us: THIS HAPPENED, BECAUSE IT IS SO IN THE LEGEND. The Arekuna legend is the "authoritative argument." The touchstone. Thanks to an impulse of workman-like conviction, spontaneous and deep, Mário extends loyalty to the logic of semiological linkage, to the concrete logic of the fable, which justifies and absolves whatever other apparent illogicalities, identifiable as such only beyond the intrinsic domain of the story. (68–69)[6]

For all that, Campos makes very little use of Koch-Grünberg's narratives themselves, since his perspective, as the title of his book intimates, is tied to Vladimir Propp's model, created by the Russian formalist to analyze his country's folk tales. The applicability of such a model to the Pemon stories, and consequently to *Macunaíma,* is questionable. In using it, Campos often restricts his analysis to exceptions to the model, or to the least common cases described by Propp. The usage of such a theoretical framework forces him to concentrate on what he calls the *backbone syntagma* of *Macunaíma:* the protagonist's search for the lost *muiraquitã.* It is in connection with this theme that he defines the basic functions of the novel, according to the Proppian model. The other plots, the several adventures that Macunaíma has throughout the novel, are described as mechanisms for postponing the epic effect *(retardamento épico).* But the importance of those plots in *Macunaíma* is such that any attempt to describe the novel as "the adventures of a hero who loses, and after several adventures, recovers the *muiraquitã*" would, as we saw, completely miss the point. As far as the plot is concerned, what attracts attention in *Macunaíma,* what made it innovative and has turned it into one of Brazil's main works of fiction, is the complex net of stories that compose it. Campos is certainly aware of that: describing the plot of *Macunaíma* as an arch between two distinct moments—the moment of the loss of the muiraquitã and the moment of its recovery—he adds:

> The taking to extremes of these two tenses, the dividing up of this functional temporality into current tenses—micro-times punctuated by suspended events and by the resolution (or overcoming) of these events, constitutes the true aesthetic or semiological *tempus* of Mário's narrative, the "cronia" of his most special chronicle. (59)

However, his analysis concentrates on the "two ends of the arch," that is, he privileges the actions that facilitate or complicate the recovery of the lost magical stone. He misses, therefore, what he describes on the one hand as "the true aesthetic *tempus*" of the narrative, and on the other as a "permanently effective medium for coloring the fundamental action" (59). If the application of an analytical model presupposes the separation between the "fundamental action" and "the true aesthetic *tempus*" of a text, it seems to me that it creates distortions, and is thus questionable.

Moreover, Campos considers the intricate net of stories that mediate the loss and the recovery of the *muiraquitã* as a consequence of *Macunaíma*'s "high art" status: "If this can be seen with respect to the folktale, it will be even more so in the case of a work of art, sophisticated in nature, which works the legend with far more liberty" (59).

A careful reading of the novel in the light of the Carib stories that informed it shows that the constant movement of digressing from what Campos considers the "central plot"—the search for the *muiraquitã*—is actually closer to the Pemon way of telling stories than the "central plot" itself. The basic assumption of *Morfologia do Macunaíma* is that Pemon narratives are structurally identical to Russian tales. Thus *Macunaíma*, through its intertextual dialogue with the Pemon narratives, would be structurally identical to the Russian tales as well. But that assumption is not based on an actual comparison between the European and Carib tales. Rather, its point of departure is a presupposed idea about the "universality of structural man" (17).

This is not the place to question the applicability of Propp's method to the very tales that generated it: years of post-structuralism have dealt with that problem. The point is to show that the Pemon stories, rather than being similar to the European tales, have a clearly distinct way of relating to the world, and to the act of narrating—a difference that will have profound consequences for Mário's use of them in *Macunaíma*.

Recognizing the lack of adaptability of certain aspects of Native American literature to the scheme proposed by Propp, Campos makes use of an additional text: Alan Dundes's *The Morphology of North American Indian Folktales* (1962). As he tries to fit North American Indian tales into the list of functions described by Propp, Dundes acknowledges that the "Russian fairy tales, like most Indo-European tales, do contain elements of the traditional dualism between good and evil, hero and villain. This dualism as such does not appear in American Indian tales as a rule" (131). Despite that difference, Dundes continues to use Propp's model to analyze Native American texts. However, the nonexistence of a strict dualism between good and evil seems to me much more than a simple detail: it is a basic difference in the way of conceiving a story, a difference that upsets the elementary division of roles between the characters. If, in the episode of Macunaíma's fight against the giant Piaimã, for instance, the protagonist of Mário de Andrade's novel can be considered mostly a good hero, that is not the case in several of his other adventures, such as when he kills his own mother, when he is punished by Vei, or when he is mercilessly fooled by the merchant Tequeteque—to mention just a few cases. How can such disparate roles, played by the same character, be conflated into categories that assume, rather unproblematically, the existence of villains and heroes, or that at least assume that certain functions are always going to be played by a certain type of character?

According to the model developed by Propp, "The names of the dramatis personae change (as well as the attributes of each), but neither their actions nor functions change. From this we can draw the inference that a tale often attributes identical actions to various characters" (20). We can change the names of the dramatis personae only because their functions are identical; that is, the role they play is completely fixed. Thus, thinking about European tales, the name (social rank, species, etc.) of the hero doesn't matter, because the hero is the one who is going to overcome a series of obstacles in order to repair an initial lack, or an initial misdoing. And the hero is going to fight against a villain, who can be a dragon, a person, a giant, etc. Also, this hero will probably help somebody else, who can be a princess, a simple girl, another kind of being. So, if the hero in some of the stories studied by Propp decided to change into a dragon and eat the princess, the functions of those stories could obviously not be classifiable in the same way. And that is exactly what happens in *Macunaíma,* whose hero saves the life of his family from an initial lack (of food), but immediately after that starves his brother and sister-in-law almost to death. Similarly, after having saved a princess who has been transformed into a carambola tree, he tells her to climb a banana tree, throw him the ripe bananas and eat the green ones. The princess eats the green bananas and "dances with cramps" for the hero's enjoyment. Or worse: after having stolen the "beautiful Iriqui" from his brother, Macunaíma causes her death, by exchanging her for the princess, the same princess he has just saved in the episode mentioned above. In Proppian terms, Macunaíma could be classified as a hero as well as a "dragon"—or even a "princess," if we consider his naive helplessness in the episode in which he is caught by Piaimã and has to be saved by his brothers. In other words, structure is inseparable from moral scheme.

If it is questionable how much the model developed by Propp can help us understand the European tales, it is clear that its application to a novel such as *Macunaíma* will only be possible if we restrict ourselves (as Campos did) to the story line of the *muiraquitã.* Otherwise, the model would have to be used in such abstract terms that it would completely lose its meaning. For Propp, as for Campos (who quotes him on the matter) the secondary plots are structurally similar to the central plot: "If a cell of the fable organism becomes a fable on a small scale within it, it follows in its constitution the same laws as any other fable" (125). But is that really so?

The several small plots that constitute *Macunaíma* are very distinct in nature, and often have little to do, structurally, with the "central plot," i.e., with the search for the *muiraquitã*. While the quest for the magical stone is, from the point of view of a traditional European story, unproblematic (the initial villainy—the stealing of the stone by Piaimã—is repaired after the hero and his helpers have gone through several obstacles), those other plots could not be easily defined as problem-solving tales. Moreover, the relationship between Macunaíma and Piaimã in this "central plot" is clearly defined: Macunaíma is, within this specific episode, a true hero, and Piaimã (unlike the indigenous, more complicated character that inspired him) an unquestionable villain.

The same is not true with the other plots. In the long passage from the beginning of the novel, quoted above, for instance, we see that the child Macunaíma creates a problem by transforming into an adult and having sex with his brother's wife. (In the second chapter, he also has sex with Jiguê's second wife, Iriqui.) But he also solves, twice, their problem of starvation: once by hunting a tapir and another time by moving the house, with his mother in it, to the other side of the river. In the continuation of that sequence, Macunaíma, back at the original site of their house, manages to bring food to whole family, and although he again has sex with his brother's wife, his brother does not mind it, because the younger brother has become a food provider.[7]

This episode of *Macunaíma*, like the Pemon story that inspired it, is not a problem-solving tale in which heroes are made to win battles against villains. Rather, both the novel and the narratives are complex discussions of power. Power, a necessary condition for both the cultural hero of the Pemon and the hero of the novel, is acquired through mischievous acts, initiated by the hero himself. One cannot clearly define who is the hero, and who the villain.

In another story, narrated in the beginning of chapter 6, we are told how the three brothers were trying to make a *papiri* (a leafy shelter). Macunaíma gets upset with Maanape and Jiguê because the first would spend most of the time drinking coffee and the latter would sleep all day. He then decides to take revenge, sending an insect to sting Maanape's tongue, and a caterpillar to suck Jiguê's blood. The brothers, on the other hand, looking for their own revenge, create a "hard leather ball" to hit the little brother without killing him. Macunaíma, as a result, decides to stop the construction of the *papiri*. From the point of view of a traditional European tale, this story is absolutely noncanonical: the "initial lack" (the need for shelter) is never solved, and we are left with no loser or winner. The "objective" of the story is to reveal the origin of the three "national plagues": the coffee worm, the pink caterpillar, and soccer. The story is a re-creation, very faithful to the original, of Mayuluaípu's narration of how Makunaíma and his brother Zigé invented the poisonous snake and the stingray (Koch-Grünberg 2: 48), an etiological tale.

Recognizing that the "explanatory motif," which appears often in Native American literature, does not fit the scheme proposed by Propp, Campos appeals once more to Dundes: "The explanatory motif is a non-structural, optional element in folkore. Its usual function is to mark the end of a tale or segment in a longer tale. The overall structure of the tale is *not* affected by its presence or absence" (253).

Mário's use of etiological narratives mimics the Pemons'. As we saw, the great majority of the stories told by Akuli and Mayuluaípu are etiological narratives, the cycles of Konewó and of Kalawunseg being among the few exceptions. Moreover, several stories also include little explanatory tales which, rather than being disregarded as unimportant, should be analyzed as a main structural characteristic not only of Pemon stories, but of a great part of Native American literature as well. In *Macunaíma,* the explanation sometimes derives from an indigenous narrative, as when we are told how the *guaraná* tree came into existence, in chapter 4 ("Ci, mãe do mato"): the story is, according to Teshauer, a Maué tradition (Proença, 135). At other times, Mário uses the structure of a native narrative in order to explain the appearance of a nonnative object, or institution. For example, in the story that Macunaíma tells the chauffeur and his girlfriend (which will be discussed later) Mário takes the structure of a jaguar story from Koch-Grünberg's collection and uses it to explain not the existence of the jaguar's beautiful eyes (as in the original), but of the automobile. In addition, Mário also invents explanations, using the techniques that he found in the native tradition: in chapter 5, for instance, after being told by the prostitutes that the machine was not a god, but was made by men and moved by electricity, wind, smoke, etc., Macunaíma invents the obscene gesture called *banana* in Brazil:

> He rose from the bed, and with a sweeping gesture of disdain—bah!—he struck his right arm, bent at the elbow, with his left forearm and jerked his right fist rudely at the three trollops. It was at that instant, they say, that he invented the famously offensive gesture—the banana! (35)

Also, in chapter 16 ("Muiraquitã") a little explanatory note is given for the behavior of the ticks (*carrapato,* an expression used to refer to insistent people as well):

These ticks were once people just like us. Once a tick set up a stall on the
sidewalk and did a booming trade because he didn't mind selling on tick.
He sold so much on tick, and so many Brazilians never paid up that in the
end it was over all for the tick and he went out of business. He sticks so close
to us because he wants to settle his bills. (120–21)

Etiological narratives explain the origin of things, and as such, they
often have sacred meaning in Pemon literature; several of these stories are
also very funny, so that an additional function is to provide an amusing,
humorous explanation for the existence of things.[8] But the fact that an explanation is amusing and the fact that it may be sacred are not mutually exclusive. Thus, the shaman Akuli is also the entertainer of Koch-Grünberg's
expedition, narrating, among other things, etiological tales:

Akuli is a lovely and happy trickster *(bufón)*. Most of the time all of us
would sit together near the fire, under a tent, and tell each other stories
about Piaimã, the evil cannibal who was finally tricked and killed by a
courageous and smarter man. These tales describe how the mutuns and
jacamis fight and how the jacami received the grey spot he has on his back,
and also his black head. Also, how the mutun got his feather crest, and
finally, a funny tale that made us cry with laughter, about how the animals
and the humans received their anuses. (Koch-Grünberg 1: 182)

Moreover, etiological stories have the function of reaffirming the importance given to *metamorphosis* in the Pemon culture, and in the case of the
least comic stories, the explanatory element—which often appears only at
the end—seems to lend significance to misfortune, making it fecund. The
beautiful narrative, told by Akuli, of how the poisons *aza* and *ineg* came into
existence, for example, tells us how the boy Aza (son of a female tapir and a
man) was killed by the great snake Keyemé, the rainbow. At the end of the
narrative we see the desolate grandmother singing and carrying a basket on
her back with the remains of the boy. The blood, genitalia, and bones of Aza,
falling to the ground, gave origin to three types of the fish poison, *timbó*.

Evidently the etiological stories that form such an important part of
Macunaíma have no sacred meaning, but they share with the Pemon narratives their humor, their amusing way of explaining how things came into
existence. Moreover, they also serve to depict a world in which things are
always being created, re-created, and changed, and Macunaíma, the hero
and transformer, is responsible for many of these changes.

By carefully reading those stories, we can find parallel narrative lines
that would remain invisible if we considered, as Dundes and Campos seem
to propose, the etiological and intercalated tales as unimportant.

Siblings

The dispute between the protagonist and his brother Jiguê for women and for the position of main hunter and provider begins in the initial chapters and is continued at the end of the novel, causing the whole family, except for Macunaíma, to die. This dispute has likewise intrigued critics, among them Campos, and is based on two Pemon stories: the first, the adventures of Makunaíma told by Akuli, by now familiar, and the second, Mayuluaípu's "Etetó. How Kasana-Podole, the Vulture King, acquired his second head (see "Kalawunseg, the Liar and Other Trickster-like Characters," in chapter 1)." Mário de Andrade's rewriting of the Etetó episode in *Macunaíma* makes full use of its plot, emphasizing the absence of heroes or villains in the dispute. Etetó is replaced by Macunaíma, and his brother-in-law by Macunaíma's brother Jiguê. It is Jiguê's moment of glory in the novel: The middle brother, after being replaced by Macunaíma in the beginning of the narrative, had spent almost the rest of it crushed between the older Maanape, a mighty but rather discreet sorcerer, and Macunaíma, the trickster. Suddenly, he is in control of magical powers which urge him into a position of leadership among the brothers: He becomes the main food provider and is then able to be the lover of Macunaíma's wife, the princess. The position is symmetrically opposite to the initial dispute between the brothers, in which Macunaíma controls the knowledge of magical forces that allow him to become the one responsible for supporting the family, and thus be the lover of Jiguê's wives. So, Jiguê goes from a relative position of victim (relative because, as we have seen, he was quite mischievous as the older and powerful brother in his relationship with Macunaíma) to a position of hero. Macunaíma, in all this, plays the role not so much of a villain, but of a stupid trickster, a fool. Here Mário de Andrade makes an inversion in regard to the original story: Instead of having Jiguê wound his brother with the poisonous hook, it is Macunaíma who does it, driven by a desire for revenge. Macunaíma becomes, at this moment, clearly a villain, placing his brother in the position of a victim. But when the princess transforms the dead Jiguê into a ghost who wants to destroy Macunaíma, the roles are inverted again. As Macunaíma escapes, Jiguê is touched by the siblings' intelligence and is filled with desire to return to the family: "The spirit of Jiguê confirmed that the hero was very intelligent, and desperately wanted to join his family again" (153). However, this emotional Jiguê cannot help but swallow the members of the family as he tries to get close to them. Like the shaman who inspired him, Jiguê becomes, in spite of his own desires, a threat to his people. Who is the victim, who the hero? Macunaíma manages to escape the danger of being devoured by the shadow, but the outcome is

not necessarily heroic: His whole family has been destroyed, and the protagonist will spend the rest of his days sad and lonely.

In Campos's analysis of this episode, Jiguê is seen as an unsuccessful opponent of Macunaíma. Both disputes of the protagonist after the recovery of
the *muiraquitã* (against Jiguê and against Vei) are included in what the critic
calls, in Proppian terms, "the second movement" of the narrative line. In the
first movement, Macunaíma fights against Piaimã and wins. In the second,
he fights against Jiguê and also wins; but he then fights against Vei, and loses
his life. In spite of Campos's excellent analyses of both episodes, I suggest
another classification of them. Jiguê's rivalry with his youngest brother is
not related to the search for the *muiraquitã*; therefore, it should not be considered a second movement to that story line. Instead, the fight between the
two brothers is a parallel dispute, a "movement" that starts in the beginning
of the narrative and ends in this final fight between the two siblings. It is
debatable, also, whether Jiguê is really an "unsuccessful opponent," as the
critic calls him (223): because of their dispute (in which the roles of victim and villain are, as we have seen, juggled between the two brothers) the
family is destroyed and Macunaíma is left completely alone, ready to die.
Macunaíma's death, that is, his decision to go to the sky and become a star, is
not a sudden occurrence, caused by his dispute with Vei and the mutilation
he suffers from the Uiara. It is actually a slow, gradual process of depres-
sion that began with the recovery of the *muiraquitã* and his return from São
Paulo, and that had been prefigured in his initial dispute against Vei, as a
result of which she told him he would become old and ugly.

Mário de Andrade respects the Pemon story's complex relations of power,
and its lack of resolution in terms of good and evil, as he does with respect
to the overall structure of the novel.

The Quest

Responding to Campos in *O Tupi e o Alaúde* (1979, thought by many to
be the best study of *Macunaíma*[9]), Gilda de Mello e Souza also censures
him for concentrating on the dispute between the protagonist and Piaimã.
According to her:

> Were we to try, from now on, to put the analogy with the Russian folk-
> tale in parenthesis, allowing, in a relatively innocent reading, the deep
> morphology of the Brazilian rhapsody to emerge, we should see that it is
> governed not by *one* but by *two* great antagonistic syntagmas: the first is
> represented by Macunaíma's encounter with the giant Piaimã, from which
> the hero emerges *victorious*, recovering the muiraquitã; the second is rep-
> resented by Macunaíma's encounter with Vei, the Sun, an episode divided

into two complementary sequences, which we shall call *fateful choice* and *vengeance*—and from it the hero emerges defeated, losing the magic stone forever. (53–54)

Souza's discussion of the alternative syntagma privileges what she calls its second sequence: the loss of the magical stone. In so doing, she limits her analysis of "Vei, the Sun" to those aspects of the story that fit into the overall *muiraquitã* theme. As a result, the dispute between Vei and Macunaíma loses importance, being significant only as part of the larger syntagma, privileged to the extent of allowing her to read the novel within the context of a specifically European genre: the Arthurian romance, which, in its turn "elaborates one of the most widespread archetypes of world folk literature: the quest for a miraculous object, in this case, the Grail" (74).

"Vei, the Sun" is based on the Pemon episode discussed in the first chapter, "Akalapijeima and the Sun," in which Akalapizeima is punished by the Sun for being unfaithful to his wives-to-be, daughters of the Sun. Souza's reading of the episode is largely supported by an allegory proposed by Mário de Andrade in 1943, which, as the author himself confessed, he had forgotten:

> I had already forgotten the allegory of this that I included in *Macunaíma* . . . But it all came back to me vividly now, when I read the sentence: "It was mischief wrought by the vengeful one (the old woman Vei, the Sun), just because the hero did not take a wife from among the daughters of light," that is, the great tropical civilizations, China, India, Peru, Mexico, Egypt, daughters of heat. The allegory is developed in the chapter entitled "Vei, the Sun." Macunaíma agrees to marry one of the solar daughters, but no sooner than the future mother-in-law leaves he no longer bothers about his promise, and goes off in search of another. He takes up with a Portuguese woman, the Portugal that endowed us with European Christian principles. And, for this reason, at the end of the book, in the final chapter, Vei avenges herself on the hero and wants to kill him. (Lopez 1988, 427–28)

But, as Campos had observed, such unidirectional allegorical reading is reductive, for it does not take into consideration several factors that contribute to make the episode more ambiguous (1973, 239). Moreover, it has the disadvantage of enclosing Macunaíma within the limits of a nationalist, or tropicalist, role—a role that Mário de Andrade himself openly refused to attribute to his character on many occasions, as we have seen. If we look at the Pemon "Akalapizeima and the Sun," we will see that the "solar" idea is already there (Campos 1973, 240), but linked to perennial life and youth. As I have shown, by choosing the daughter of the vulture, Akalapizeima, "the father of all the Indians," made a pact with death, and refused, there-fore, perennial youth: "that's why we still live in this condition: we are young and beautiful only for a short time, and then we become old and ugly" (Koch-Grünberg 2: 54). The sentence is repeated by Vei in the novel when she punishes Macunaíma, prefiguring his death.

My point is not so much that *Macunaíma* should not be read as an Ar-thurian romance, or as a carnivalization of the Arthurian tradition, as Souza proposes. Such a reading is possible, but only if we concentrate on the search for the *muiraquitã*—a limited aspect of the novel, as we have seen. Thus, although apparently proposing the existence of *two* opposing syn-tagmas (instead of just *one*), Souza actually concentrates again (as Campos had done before her) on a single syntagma: the search for the *muiraquitã*.

Souza does recognize that "*Macunaíma* relies on two different referen-tial systems, one at times being superimposed on the other" (74): one in-digenous and the other European. Neither of these referential systems can be taken, I would add, as an unchangeable, timeless essence; Rather, they have to be seen as historical entities which have been mutually influenced by each other. Nor is the epic (which informs the central narrative line of *Macunaíma*) an exclusively European creation: Native American litera-ture has several epic narratives, and among the Pemon stories collected by Koch-Grünberg we can find at least one epic journey: Maitxaúle's (white termite's) visit to the sky. But as a linear narrative of a journey that starts with a well-defined objective, and in which, if we do not have a conven-tional hero we have at least a very conventional villain, Piaimã, the tale of the search for the *muiraquitã* can be associated with a more tradition-ally European type of tale. Against that, Mário de Andrade places, as we have seen, alternative plots, subplots, individual stories and substories very diverse in nature but most of them matching native—Pemon and other— ways of narrating. These stories are told with the help of popular sayings, songs, quotations from diaries and books, characters extracted from Black, indigenous, and European folklore, etc. In the words of Souza: "The inter-est of the book thus derives, in large part, from this 'simultaneous adhesion to entirely heterogeneous terms'" (75).

For Souza, however, this heterogeneity is still defined as "a curious sa-tirical game that continuously oscillates between adopting the European model and celebrating national variation" (75). A hierarchical delimitation is clear in the definition, separating the European "model" and the national "variation" of that model. Similarly, when referring to the two referential systems that gave birth to Mário de Andrade's novel, Souza adds that "the former, overt and contentious, points to the national reality, based on its varied repertoire of legends and popular culture; subterranean, the second invokes the centenary European heritage" (75). Thus, although combative and obvious, popular culture in *Macunaíma* remains, according to her, on the surface, being also shallow in time; while the European heritage, although subterranean, is long-lived and lends solidity and substance to the narrative.

Such hierarchization is in line with Souza's objective in *O Tupi e o Alaúde,* namely, to show that *Macunaíma,* in spite of its relation (in her view superficial) to native culture, is actually a European masterpiece: "independently of the successive maskings which lend the narrative a savage aspect, the central nucleus remains *firmly European*" (74). The native elements of *Macunaíma* are treated as masking, as appearance (savage aspect); unlike the centrality (central nucleus) and solidity (firmly European) of the European elements. The same hierarchization is present, evidently, in the adjectives used to qualify, respectively, the native and the European aspects of the text: *savage* and centenary. And it is present throughout the critic's work, when she calls popular culture, for instance, the "colorful background of the Brazilian hero's adventure" (9); or when she embarrassedly tries to justify, within the Arthurian reading of the novel, the comparisons between the Holy Grail and the *muiraquitã*:

> How to reduce, to a green stone in the shape of a lizard, the Grail, the
> Liturgy, the 'chalice of the Last Supper, in which Jesus celebrated Passover
> in the house of Simon and Joseph of Arimathea,' and which caught at
> Calvary the blood that dropped from the divine body. (90)

And a justification is found: in some versions of the Arthurian saga, Souza observes, the sacred object is described as a green stone fallen from the sky (90). No references are made to the fact that as early as 1848, Schomburgk described the green Amazon stones (negotiated in great amounts by the Carib) as coming, according to most indigenous accounts, from the tribes of the Amazons—the warrior women who inspired Mário in the creation of Ci.[10]

For Souza, the hybridity of Mário de Andrade's novel is manifest in the protagonist's appearance, defined by the bath given to him by the agouti—a bath in which his body grew into adult dimensions, but his head remained forever small: "The hero is thus defined from without as a hybrid, whose body has already reached the fullness of adulthood, while the brain remains immature, subject to the logical schemes of *pensée sauvage*" (43). This evolutionary assumption underlies the hierarchization of European versus native elements in Mello e Souza's reading of the novel.

On the one hand, a clear intention of Souza's work is "to bring out in the Brazilian rhapsody those features which precisely define it as a literary work, hence emphasizing the distance between it and the framework of norms and traditions which served as a stimulus" (49). She does this by reaffirming Jakobson's definition of folklore as *langue* and literature as *parole*—a definition rejected by Campos (Souza, 64). She criticizes Campos for having reduced "an admirable fact of *parole* to the banality of *langue*" (50). But while supposedly emphasizing the mechanisms through which *Macunaíma*, which she sees as a superior literary work, distances itself from folklore, she is actually emphasizing only those elements that, in her opinion, distance Mário's novel from *non-European* folklore.

Thus, the traditional dance *Bumba meu boi* (structurally similar to a European suite, as she emphasizes) still defines, for the critic, the structure of the novel, even though it is not very clear why this definition should be better than the other ones she discards, such as *mosaic* or *bricollage*: neither is the creation of a mosaic simply the "juxtaposition of borrowings from different systems" (10), as she says—it does involve the disarticulation of the pieces from a previous environment and their acquisition of a new meaning in the new one; nor can one actually believe that there is no intentionality in the activity of a bricolleur, or, conversely, no ludic abandonment to the demands created by the native stories themselves on the part of Mário de Andrade. *Macunaíma* could be described, as it has been by Mello e Souza, as a combination of suite and musical variation; but it could as well be described as a mosaic, bricollage, or, following Mário de Andrade's own description of the novel, a "rhapsody." Above all, *Macunaíma* uses techniques, common in native Amazonian (and other) traditional literatures, of incorporating new stories into old stories; of inserting small etiological tales into larger ones. Also, Mello e Souza is willing to approximate *Macunaíma* to the Arthurian saga, revealing that her objective is not to show how the novel deviates from its popular models, but to write off, instead, the importance of indigenous culture for the composition of the text and definitions of quest.

Subverting the Language of the Metropolis

Reading Macunaíma's quest in the terms defined by his Carib predecessor leads to a last major consideration: how his time in the metropolis affects him as an Indian from the forest. Certainly his origins distinguish him from those "ingenuous" observers from afar used by satirists in the European tradition. Prompting repeated subversions, above all in the realm of language, Macunaíma's culturally specific background gives him a quite distinctive point of view and, indeed, in this he continues to follow his indigenous prototypes. For the Carib tricksters can be travelers, exploring environments other than their own, and they may register the effects of such experience on themselves and those around them. Of particular interest are those accounts of journeys made to sites of Western economy and customs, in the Guyanas for instance. As we have seen, this experience may even lead to a kind of self-parody, on the part of the traveler Kalawunseg, who claims guns grow on trees. This process of exchange may include not just material but intellectual products, like European national anthems, which could make good songs. Koch-Grünberg says he heard the Dutch national anthem sung by the Pemon—a reference that also caught Mário's attention: in 1931 he published an article on the subject entitled "As Canções Migram" ("Songs migrate") in a Recife newspaper (Lopez 1974, 7).

Hitherto, when treated at all, this dimension of Macunaíma's experience has been seen in terms popularized in Western criticism, notably by the Russian Bakhtin, who provides the premises of Susana Camargo's work *Macunaíma, Ruptura e Tradição.* Unfortunately, Camargo's apparent lack of interest in the novel's native antecedents causes her, from the start, to overlook key advice offered by her model Bakhtin, with respect to his subject Rabelais. For Bakhtin, Rabelais's images "remain an enigma" that "can be solved only by means of a deep study of Rabelais' popular sources" (3). Instead of looking at Mário de Andrade's popular sources, however, Camargo simply goes through the exercise of comparing *Macunaíma* to the works of Rabelais. For her, just as *Les Grandes Cronicques* is considered by Bakhtin as having had a limited, external influence on Rabelais, the indigenous narratives *(lendário indígena)* had "just an external influence on *Macunaíma,* providing only the basic axis (the large syntagma of the narrative) and some borrowed situations, but not the fundamental aesthetic proposition" (107). But what is the novel's "basic aesthetic proposition," when so many of the elements she chooses in order to link *Macunaíma* to Rabelais can already be found in the indigenous texts? If it is true that Rabelais's intense usage of popular culture in his works finds a parallel in *Macunaíma,* and that the most aesthetically revolutionary aspects of those texts reside exactly in this usage, one has to be careful when locating them within a given literary tradition. For Rabelais, popular culture meant basically the medieval marketplace, whose importance rested on the fact that it was a "second world and a second life outside officialdom" (Bakhtin, 6). Mário de Andrade's sources, on the other hand, have very heterogeneous origins. The Pemon stories, which provide the novel with most of its plots and the majority of its main characters, do not work as a second world or second life in relation to the culture they represent: Unlike the marketplace laughter, as described by Bakhtin, these stories are at the same time comic and "official," or sacred, among the Pemon. In relation to the rest of Brazilian society, these stories cannot easily be considered a "second world" either, at least in Bakhtinian terms of class and hierarchy. Within Brazil's mosaic of cultures, what is "sacred" and "official" can vary a great deal. These stories are not, in this sense, the inversion of an official culture, and therefore cannot be taken as carnivalization, in the Bakhtinian sense, of that culture. Gilda de Mello e Souza, who also appeals to the idea of "carnivalization," accepts its limitation when applied to the character Macunaíma, for, according to her, he

> represents a far more ambiguous and contradictory character: he is a defeated victor, who makes of weakness a strength, of fear a weapon, of cunning a shield; who, living in a hostile world, pursued, harrassed, deeply into adversity, always ends up cheating misfortune . . . Close kin of Charlie Chaplin and even Buster Keaton, in silent film, it is however Cantinflas— that admirable hero of the Third World—whom he most resembles. (89–90)

Yet nor does Macunaíma resemble Cantinflas or Charlie Chaplin, as Souza claims, since for him the surrounding world is never so hostile; nor can we define him as a victim who ends up being victorious. Mário de Andrade's protagonist is capable of truly mischievous acts, which might upset Cantinflas of Chaplin fans, because they follow another logic. It is to the Native American, more specifically to the Pemon trickster, that we have to relate the protagonist of *Macunaíma*.

As with any trickster-hero, his job is to transform the world he sees. His most significant transformation, one could argue, is to the language of the metropolis. At the moment when Macunaíma arrives in São Paulo, looking at all the things that he had never seen before (automobiles, skyscrapers, elevators, etc.), he explains them in terms of his own culture, and has therefore to be taught, by the prostitutes, a new, powerful word:

> The women told him laughing that the sagüi monkey wasn't a monkey at all, it was called an elevator and was a machine. From first light they told him that all those whistles shrieks sighs roars grunts were not that at all, but were rather bells klaxons hooters buzzers sirens, everything was a machine. The brown jaguars were not brown jaguars, they were called fords hupmobiles chevrolets dodges and were machines. The anteaters the will-o-the wisps the inajá palms plumed with smoke were really trucks trams trolley-buses illuminated billboards clocks headlights radios motorcycles telephones mailboxes chimneys . . . they were machines and everything in the city was just a machine! (34)

The machine, the prostitutes also explain to the hero, is not a god nor a woman: It is made by humans and moved by energy. Macunaíma, however, does not accept the explanation, and after a week of abstinence from food and sex, a week in which the only thing he does is to think (*maquinar* is the expression used in Portuguese) about the "bootless struggle of the children of manioc against the machine," he starts to feel:

> that the machine must be a god over which humans had no true control since they had made no explainable Uiara[11] of it, but just a world reality. In all this turmoil, his mind found a ray of light: "Humans were machines and machines were humans!" Macunaíma gave a great guffaw. He realized he was free again, and this gave him a huge lift. (36)

In other words, Macunaíma discovers that the only way to dominate the machine is by telling an etiological tale about it—to transform it into "an explainable Uiara." Free, Macunaíma can then have his first experience dominating the machine: As he had always done in the region of the Uraricoera, where he was born as a hero and had become the "Emperor of the Forest," he is able to dominate things by transforming them. Thus he turns his brother Jiguê into the "telephone-machine" and makes a phone call.

This narrative line continues in the chapter "Carta pras Icamiabas," the first attempt by the hero to show a command of written Portuguese. This chapter is a parody of the conservative way of writing that was cultivated by intellectuals such as Rui Barbosa, Mário Barreto, and "those who wrote for *Revista de Língua Portuguesa*" (Lopez 1988, 427), as the author himself explains in the letter to Raimundo de Moraes quoted above. In his letter, Macunaíma describes São Paulo for the benefit of the warrior women back home, the Amazons, or *Icamiabas,* of the tribe of his dead wife Ci. He touches on its geography, fauna, flora, and people, adopting the colonialist tone used by the chroniclers who wrote about Brazil. São Paulo, "the strange place," is described in terms of "the known place," Amazonia. Thus, the odd habits of the inhabitants of the big city have to be explained to the Icamiabas through comparisons with things and habits that they already know. Part of the humor of the letter resides in the fact that it parodies the chronicles by inverting several of their references. Thus, some of the daily habits of the *paulistas* appear in the text in a new light, strange and surprising. The "Imperador do Mato Virgem" (Emperor of the Virgin Forest, as Macunaíma is often called in the novel) is depicted in the text as the colonizer, the one who describes the absurdities found in the "new world." But the "colonizer" writes in the language of the "colonized," creating a relationship that is in itself absurd, and for that very reason, comic. And it becomes yet more comic because, as an outsider, Macunaíma is able to see that such absurdity reproduces itself in the "two languages" used by the urban Brazilians as they try to express themselves—that is, the language of the colonizer (*Português de Camões,* i.e., European Portuguese) and that of the colonized (*língua bárbara*, i.e., Barbarian language). As he describes it, *Português de Camões*, the written language, is committed to its own desire for separation from the *língua bárbara*, the oral language. Macunaíma tries in the letter to master the *Português de Camões*; he tries to reaffirm the separation that he sees as a strange cultural fact. Fortunately, however, he is not successful. Another source of humor in the letter is the fact that while exaggerating the *Português de Camões*, he also makes mistakes: misused words, wrong agreements, bad spelling, etc. Not only that: *língua bárbara* invades the text all the time, through the presence of Tupi, as the hero tries to explain to the *Icamiabas* some facts and things about São Paulo.[12]

Macunaíma's next attempt to master the languages of the metropolis happens in the chapter that follows "Carta pras Icamiabas," "Pauí-Pódole." While waiting for the villain to return to the city, Macunaíma "took advantage of the delay mastering the two languages of the land, spoken Brazilian and written Portuguese. He now had all the vocabulary" (87). But one day, as he was invited to buy a flower on the street, he realized he did not know the word for "button hole" *(botoeira)*. Ashamed of showing his ignorance to the girl who sold the flower, he introduced into Portuguese a word from his own language: *puíto* (anus). The word became current in the language, and Macunaíma realized he had been smart in creating it and had scored a point over the language he was struggling to learn: "At first, our hero was overwhelmed and was about to take it badly, but then realised he was in fact quite smart. Macunaíma gave a great guffaw" (82). But the victory will never be recognized by the scientists, the practitioners of the *Língua de Camões*:

> The fact is that "puíto" had already appeared in those learned journals that dealt with both the spoken and the written idiom, with much display of erudition. There was now a measure of agreement that by the laws of catalepsy ellipsis syncope metonymy metaphony metathesis proclesis prothesis aphaerresis apocope hapology popular etymology, by virtue of all these laws, the word "buttonhole" had been transmuted into the word "puíto" via an intermediary Latin word "rabanitius" (buttonhole-rabanitius-puíto). Although "rabanitius" had never actually been found in any medieval document, the experts swore it had certainly existed and had been current in vulgar speech. (82–83)

The passage strongly satirizes etymology as it was practiced by the writers of *Revista de Língua Portuguesa*. The false origin attributed by etymologists to the word *puíto* confirms the Eurocentric tendencies of those who practiced the *Língua de Camões*, and curiously foreshadows the same tendencies in later critics of the novel: Eneida Maria de Souza, in *A Pedra*

Mágica do Discurso (1988), completely ignores the Pemon origin of the term *puíto*,[13] and describes it as as a neologism created by the protagonist of the novel to replace the gallicism *boutonnière*.

Still in the same chapter, Macunaíma makes his first public speech, in which he passionately redefines the constellation Southern Cross (which appears on the Brazilian national flag) by giving it a Pemon name, and by narrating the Pemon story of its origin. Thus, *Cruzeiro do Sul* becomes *Pauí Pódole*, or *Pai do Mutum* (Father of Mutum, a bird), exactly as it is in the Pemon text. The audience was entranced, completely moved by the discovery that each star, or constellation, was the father of a living species:

> Macunaíma stopped, exhausted. From the crowd there rose a long blissful murmur which seemed to reinforce the scintillation of those beings, those fathers-of-birds fathers-of-fishes fathers-of-insects fathers-of-trees, all those familiar folk up there in the sky. Great was the satisfaction of that crowd of Paulistas gazing with wonder at those people, those fathers of the living that dwelt shining in the sky . . .
>
> The people left the park deeply impressed, happy in their hearts, full of enlightenment and full of living stars. No one was bothering any more about the day of the Southern Cross or about the fountain machines combined with the electric light machine. (86)

By learning with Macunaíma how to look at the stars in a native way, the people from São Paulo become less aware of certain city technologies, such as the water fountain and the electric light, that is, they become a bit less dominated by the machine. In the words of Renata Mautner Wasserman:

> The anarchy that is his [Macunaíma's] medium cannot realistically be raised to a principle of government and interpretation, an ordering of political and epistemological meanings, but it can at least remind its readers that the arrangements they take for granted are not facts of nature, and that differences are imaginable. (113)

After telling the story, Macunaíma hears a bird that sounds like a train but that is actually a bird, and all the lights of the park go out. This scene inverts the one previously described, in which the prostitutes explain to the hero that the "animals" he hears and sees are actually machines. Here, what is initially thought to be a machine, is actually an animal.

In the beginning of the next chapter Macunaíma, despite having a cold, is still very happy about the results of his speech on the previous day, and decides to tell more stories to the people. But he cannot tell them during the day (quem conta história de dia cria rabo de cotia"/"who tells a story by day grows a cotia tail") and, instead, he invites his brothers to hunt. Then, repeating one of Kalawunseg's stories, the hero, unable to hunt deer as he had planned, eats just two rats, but calls all of his neighbors to tell them he had hunted a deer. After finding out the truth from Macunaíma's brothers, the neighbors come to ask the hero what he had hunted. "Two deer *(dois viados mateiros),*" he says, but the neighbors immediately start to laugh, uncovering the truth. Part of the humor in this story comes from the fact that Macunaíma's lies are discovered, and the hero is unmasked as a liar, exactly as it happens in Kalawunseg's narratives, seen in the first chapter.[14] But Mário de Andrade makes the story even more comical by adding the following dialogue between the landlady and the hero, based on a personal anecdote (Lopez 1988, 424):

> "Well, my darling, why do you speak of two deer when nothing but two singed rats came out?"
>
> Macunaíma was brought up short by this, and looking her straight in the eye, said, "I made it all up!" (89)

The brothers are envious of Macunaíma's intelligence, and he in his turn confesses that has no intention to lie, but "I just wanted to tell them what had happened and then noticed I was lying" (89). As he does on the occasions when he wants to fight physically against Piaimã, Macunaíma in this episode seems to be testing his strength, but with words; he seems to be trying his ability to verbally deceive in the new environment. There is no winner or loser in this small battle: Macunaíma lies, is discovered, but comes out of the situation elegantly and admired by his brothers.

The next day, trying to take revenge on Maanape and Jiguê for having told the truth to the neighbors, Macunaíma (in a story once more re-created, quite closely, from one of Akuli's Kalawunseg tales) tells them another lie: He claims to have found tapir tracks in front of the *Bolsa de Mercadorias* (Board of Trade).[15] The brothers go hunt, and the people that are around the building start to imitate them. Incapable of finding any tapir, however, they ask Macunaíma where he had seen the tracks. The hero answers in Arekuna: "Tetápe, dzónanei pemonéite hêhê zeténe netataíte" (97), a phrase taken from the original narrative.[16] After receiving the same answer twice, the frustrated multitude of hunters ask him for the meaning of the phrase, and Macunaíma replies: "I don't know. I learned those words back home when I was young" (91). The crowd gets furious, and the hero is forced to give the people an explanation for the tracks that could not be found: "All right, all right! Tetápe hêhê! I didn't say there are tapir tracks, no, I said there were! Now there aren't any more" (91). The answer is actually the translation of the Arekuna phrase Macunaíma claims not to know. What follows is massive confusion: The crowd wants to beat the hero, but he accuses his brothers of having started the hunt. A student then makes a speech against Maanape and Jiguê and somebody in the crowd starts to suggest that they should be lynched. Macunaíma tries to defend his brothers, and the multitude turns once more against him, starting a real fight. A policeman comes to resolve the situation; Macunaíma hits him and is arrested. With the arrival of other policemen, the crowd starts a riot to defend the hero. The policemen, however, all have blond hair and blue eyes, and talk in a foreign language that does not allow them to understand or be understood by the rest of the people. Macunaíma then takes advantage of the situation and escapes.

As in the "Father of the *Mutum*" episode, Macunaíma's actions have a subversive effect on the city crowd. Through his lie, he is able to make a large number of people search for a tapir in front of the *Bolsa de Mercadorias*; that is, he makes them look for a concrete *mercadoria* (commodity) in a place where the word has a purely abstract meaning. He also (and once more) brings an indigenous expression into a Portuguese-speaking context. This time, however, the expression is not assimilated by the crowd, as had happened before with the word *puíto* or the new name of the Southern Cross. Although the people are actually told what it means, they are not conscious of that, and *Tetápe, dzónanei pemonéite hêhê zeténe netaíte* remains undeciphered: Macunaíma, who has the power to reveal its meaning, manipulates the knowledge and the crowd. Subsequently, the Arekuna phrase is matched with other non-Portuguese expressions, whose meanings are not revealed in the novel: the German words spoken by the policemen in front of the irritated crowd. At that time, the policemen (according to Cavalcanti Proença *grilo* means "civil police, in São Paulo" [267]; for Telê Porto Ancona Lopez it refers to "traffic police") were mostly from Santa Catarina, and therefore of German descent (Lopez 1988, 447). Thus, through its series of misunderstandings and fights, this scene puts Portuguese face-to-face with the plurality of languages actually spoken in Brazil. Macunaíma, the hero, is responsible for exposing such plurality, and what the exposition reveals is by no means a melting pot: in the confusion caused by lack of communication, the German-speaking policemen are clearly on the side of the repressive, official power. But the crowd is not passive before the situation, and it immediately transforms Macunaíma from villain into victim. The hero, however, does not accept such a role, and in very trickster fashion Macunaíma, the subverter of order, the creator of confusion, abandons his own defenders, and flees.

The next adventure in our story line likewise takes its plot from a Pemon story, Mayuluaípu's "Cacaos y Kong" ("The Jaguar and the Rain"). Macunaíma disputes with Drizzle (Chuvisco) about which of the two could make Piaimã and his family more scared. The hero tries to frighten the cannibal's family with his collection of dirty words. The results, however, are rather disappointing: "So Macunaima flung his entire repertoire of smut at them, ten thousand times ten thousand curses. Venceslau Pietro Pietra remarked very quietly to his old woman Ceiuci, "There were a few we didn't know before, save them for our girls" (95).

Drizzle then climbs on top of a cloud and pees on the giant and his family, making them look for refuge inside the house. Macunaíma, this time, loses the battle: His offensive words are not able to harm his enemy, nor do they prove to be stronger than his rival Drizzle, i.e., nature. Humiliated, the hero swears at Chuvisco, but does so in a way that the other would not understand: Playing the children's game *língua do pê*,[17] he encodes the expression *vá à merda* (roughly equivalent to "go to hell") into *vá-pá-à-pá mer-per-da-pá*. Thus, through another act of language manipulation and deceit, Macunaíma is able to achieve, if not a victory, at least a small revenge against his rival Chuvisco.

In the next chapter, two episodes closely re-created from stories taken from Mayuluaípu's Konewó cycle place Macunaíma in the position of a victim, who is deceived first by Tequeteque, the merchant, and then by the monkey, who kills the hero by convincing him to eat his own testicles. (He revives.) In the case of these two tricks, Macunaíma is deceived visually as well as orally.

Visually, the hero will be tricked yet once more before killing Piaimã. This occurs through the *mirage* created by Uiara, the indigenous Mother of the Waters, to make Macunaíma think he was seeing a ship that could take him to Europe, where he believes his prey Piaimã has fled. Orally, Macunaíma finally becomes the one who prevails. As he tells the chauffeur and his girlfriend the story about how the car came into existence, his discourse will finally allow him to explain, and therefore dominate the machine and "become its true owner." The argument is actually based on Mayuluaípu's narrative "The Game of the Eyes,"[18] about how the jaguar acquired his beautiful eyes: The jaguar sees the shrimp sending his eyes to the sea (*palauá-kupe*, sea lake) and asking for them back. "Send my eyes, too," he asks the shrimp, but the latter does not want to do it because he sees that the trahira fish is approaching, ready to eat the eyes. The jaguar insists, and the shrimp finally does it. The trahira fish eats the jaguar's eyes, and the shrimp leaves. Later, the vulture helps the jaguar to acquire new eyes, through a medicine made with milk. In Mário's version, the brown jaguar (*onça parda*) sends the black jaguar's (*onça preta*) eyes to the sea. They never come back and the blind black jaguar pursues the brown one who, desperately trying to escape, gets on top of four wheels when passing by an abandoned steel mill. Little by little, she acquires different elements that end up transforming her into a car, until she can finally avoid the pursuit. As such, the mode of explanation is the same as it was with Uiara, i.e., an etiological narrative, but now he controls it. And the hero knows well how to choose his audience, telling the story just to a chauffeur, a man who is professionally dominated by the "car-machine." The chauffeur and his girlfriend cry with emotion:

> Emotion poured from the mouths of the young couple. From across the water the breeze floated belly up. The boy ducked his head to hide his tears and came up with the flapping tail of a tambiú fish between his teeth. Then at the door of the house, a fiat-jaguar opened its throat and howled at the moon—a-honk-a! a-honk-a!—[and a choking stink filled the air]. (126–27)

As soon as Macunaíma ends his account of the origin of cars, Piaimã's Fiat arrives at the house, and the hero can finally kill the cannibal. It is the end of one phase of the hero's attempt to command and subvert the language of the metropolis.

But as with most native narratives, this one does not have a neat, happy ending. After killing Piaimã, the hero goes back to his birthplace. Before leaving, he converts São Paulo into a stone sloth, matching an act of his predecessor Makunaíma. But does he really? São Paulo goes back with him, in the form of a Smith-Wesson rifle and a Patek watch (besides the pair of leghorn chickens, imported birds). His attempts to dominate the machine thus seem to have backfired; he takes two machines back to the Amazon, and quite significant ones: the rifle (symbol of the white colonizers and their power to kill) and the watch, i.e., the time of the metropolis. He cannot forget São Paulo, and like so many people who have lived in a foreign place, he has become divided; he is incapable of deciding between the two cultures.

At first, he and his brothers are enthusiastic about their return to the Amazon. They sing and celebrate their land of origin, and at their approach, Macunaíma is again followed by the court of parrots and macaws that characterized his reign as Emperor of the Virgin Forest. He can even control the birds, make them silent so as to hear, still far away, the subtle noise of the Uraricoera river. But at night, looking at Capei, the moon, the hero misses São Paulo and its white women, daughters of manioc. Although at this stage he is still able to have adventures and meet the princess who will be his last lover, by the time he reaches the Uraricoera the hero has contracted malaria and is still coughing because of the laryngitis, "the sore throat that everyone brings from São Paulo" (143). The trickster-hero has been irremediably modified by the time he spent in the metropolis. In other words, the transformer has been transformed. Once again, this process is not strange to most native Amazonian tricksters. Macunaíma's Pemon antecedent and his brother Zigué, for instance, after having lost the metal hook they had taken from a fisherman, transform themselves into crickets to get inside the man's basket and follow him to Guyana, where they still live. Similarly, as we will see (chapter 4), the Apapokuva-Guarani transformer makes a long journey in search of his father, creator of the world, only to get into a fight with him—a fight that lasts to this day. Native Amazonian creators and transformers are far from omnipotent: Not only do they often lose disputes with their opponents, but they are also (and sometimes fatally) affected by them.

Thus, slow and lazy because of the disease, the hero finds no more energy to have sex, and his hunting talents are replaced by those of his brother Jiguê, to whom Macunaíma also loses his lover, the princess. The disputes between the two brothers end up destroying all the members of the family, except for Macunaíma himself. Completely alone, the hero, who had learned to dominate the language of the metropolis, "was deeply upset because he could not fathom the silence. He lay like a dead man, dry-eyed, in total apathy" (155). The expression "like a dead man" *(morto-vivo)* indicates his state as a zombie, a dead/alive being. He has no energy to build himself a house, and the parrots and macaws, except for one, all have left him. To this single parrot Macunaíma starts telling the adventures of his life. And one day, attracted into the river by the Uiara, Macunaíma has his body badly mutilated, and loses the *muiraquitã* again.

The formula used by Macunaíma to dominate the machine had been, as we saw, the act of creating an etiological narrative, the transformation of the machine into a "explainable Uiara." The hero was successful in this transformation: He was capable of telling a story about the origin of the car and then killing the giant Piaimã who had just arrived in a Fiat. Yet, it was precisely the Uiara who mutilated him and ultimately caused his death. Macunaíma's transformations and etiological stories are thus pragmatic solutions for certain problems. They can change the world, but they do not give him power over the things or beings he explains, nor do they save his life.

So, after losing the *muiraquitã*, Macunaíma decides to die, to go up to the sky and transform himself into the "useless shine of a star."[19] The Uraricoera becomes silent. All of the members of the Tapanhuma tribe have died, and "everything was the solitude of the desert" (167). Nobody else knows how to speak the language of those people, and the stories would be forever silenced:

> No one on earth could speak the language of the tribe, or recount those
> juicy episodes. Who could know of the hero? [His brothers, transformed

into a leprous ghostly shadow, have become the second head of the Father of the King Vultures; and Macunaíma became the constellation of the Great Bear] No one could any longer know that wealth of pretty stories and the speech of the extinct Tapanhumas. An immense silence slumbered on the banks of the Uraricoera. (167)

But one day a man comes to the region and finds the parrot, who starts telling him the stories of Macunaíma, the hero. The language in which the bird tells those stories is described as a "a gentle tongue, something new, completely new! that was song and was cassiri sweetened with wild honey, and had the lovely fickle flavor of unknown forest fruit" (168). This new language, with the "lovely fickle flavor of unknown forest fruit," is the language used by the man, the narrator: "And that man was me, dear reader, and I stayed to tell you the story" (168). It is the "impure tongue" created by Macunaíma, the hero of our people.

In a quest and narrative line parallel to the story of the loss and recovery of the *muiraquitā*, Macunaíma learns, as we have seen, how to dominate the language of the metropolis by exposing its hybridization and by hybridizing it even more through incorporating his own language into it. It is the narrative of Macunaíma, the storyteller, the trickster-hero who narrates to the *paulistas* stories that tell the indigenous names of things and indigenous ways of looking at the world. And by doing so, Macunaíma creates a new, "lovely and fickle" way of narrating, impure because it is Indian, while also being white, and black.[20] In the words of Wasserman:

> The legacy of the parrot is the innovative, revolutionary language Mário de Andrade invents for his work, incorporating the vocabularies of the many nations that form Brazil, respecting a popular, native syntax and, cultivated man that he never denied being, transforming it into a new, flexible, expressive, recognizably Brazilian literary language. (114)

If we now return to Bosi's description of the "two motivations" that led Mário to write *Macunaíma*, we can perhaps say that the "playful and aesthetic" motivation proves to be the strongest *ideological* achievement of the novel: Mário/Macunaíma's transformation in the language of the metropolis. This "language" quest in *Macunaíma* can only be understood if we carefully read those stories that others have considered unimportant in the narrative structure or have disregarded in favor of supposed European prototypes. Rather than being mere "raw data" or "on the surface," the Pemon narratives gave Mário the idea of the novel's basic aesthetic proposition, which is to tell the story of a "hero without any character," a hero who cannot be defined through the use of categories such as good or evil, but rather through what Ellen Basso calls "pragmatic creativity," in other words, a hero whose behavior changes from situation to situation, and whose unpredictability could represent, in the author's opinion, modernity itself. Thus, Macunaíma is not "the anti-hero, transposed into the primitive mode" (Wassermann, 108), but a Pemon hero interacting with and changing modern Brazilian society. And he is Pemon not so much because he was born in the Pemon territory, but because he acts and reacts as a Pemon hero is supposed to act and react. Indian, black, and white, Macunaíma remains, above all, faithful to the behavior of the Pemon trickster.

chapter 3

Penetrating the Dark Interior

T HE IMPACT OF PACARAIMA CARIB LITERATURE on Spanish American writing occurs later and is less radical than in Brazil. It dates back to the novels
of the Venezuelan Rómulo Gallegos and comes through principally in
the works of the Cuban Alejo Carpentier,[1] midway through the twentieth
century. More recently, Eduardo Galeano chose to begin his *Genesis,* the
first volume of the trilogy *Memory of Fire,* with the *Watunna* creation story,
which is followed by passages from the literature of the Macuxi and other
Caribs of the region.

Both Gallegos's *Canaima* (1935) and Carpentier's *The Lost Steps* (1953)
take place in the same geographical area that gave birth to the character
Macunaíma. There appears, however, to be nothing like the intense intertextual relationship found in Mário de Andrade's 1928 novel. To a certain
extent, *Canaima* and *The Lost Steps* have more points of contact with earlier "forest" novels in Portuguese, such as Inglez de Souza's *O Missionário*
(1888) and the Portuguese José María Ferreira de Castro's *A Selva* (1930).
These works deal with journeys of outsiders into the forest—as such, they
contrast exemplarily with that of *Macunaíma*'s insider protagonist, who
goes out from Amazonia to southern Brazil (and back again). At the same
time, as a sequel to his *Doña Bárbara* (1929), Gallegos's *Canaima* can be put
together with the other South American novels from the twenties that deal

with exploration of inner South America, these being José Eustasio Rivera's *Vortex* (1924) and Ricardo Güiraldes's *Don Segundo Sombra* (1926).

As Tieko Miyazaki points out, in most of these "forest" novels the journey into the interior is deeply related to processes of self-knowledge and self-discovery, and/or to a search for the specificity of the Latin American culture (76). The first of these processes represents, for many critics, a more "universal" tendency, which could bring these works closer to other world masterpieces. A fine example of this line of criticism can be found in the works of Roberto González Echevarría, who has produced what is probably the most comprehensive and consistent study of Alejo Carpentier's works, and has written detailed comparisons between *The Lost Steps* and Gallegos's *Canaima*.

González Echevarría's erudition has provided a valuable basis for much of the criticism that followed him,[2] including my own. Yet his critical project is similar to the tendency we have seen in studies of *Macunaíma*—namely, to write out the impact of native cultures and texts on Latin American literature. In the beginning of *The Pilgrim at Home* (1977), this project is spelled out quite clearly:

> Contemporary Latin American literature is, with few exceptions, a bourgeois, post-Romantic literature, not the direct descendant of an autochthonous tradition going all the way back to a primal birth in the colonial period. As a post-Romantic literature, it draws its thematics from the late eighteenth and early nineteenth centuries, the period when, coincidentally (but not accidentally), most of Latin America became politically independent from Europe. . . . Being bourgeois and post-Romantic, Latin American literature centers around a lack, and absence of organic connectedness, and its mainspring is a desire for communion, or, in a Hegelian sense, for totality through reintegration with a lost unity. That lack leads Latin American writers to invoke "culture" as the ontological and historical entity from which their works have sprung and to which they must return. But the lack is never overcome, for culture becomes in their works an entelechy (in its etymological sense of a finished teleology), a static, reified end product lacking a temporal dimension. (20–21)

In *Myth and Archive* (1990), a theory of the Latin American novel, he goes even further, stating that "Latin America is part of the Western world, not a colonized other, except in founding fictions and constitutive idealizations" (41–42). In this book, González Echevarría defends the thesis that Latin American literature owes more to nonfictional texts, such as historical documents and anthropological studies, than to a literary tradition that can be traced back, as in the case of European novel, to epic poetry. Attractive as this thesis may be and, indeed, useful as it is in its reading of Domingo Faustino Sarmiento's *Life in the Argentine Republic in the Days of the Tyrants; or Civilization and Barbarism* and Euclides da Cunha's *Rebellion in the Backlands,* the fact is that it leaves out key elements in Latin American literature. Moreover, the emphasis on the connection of Latin American literature with legal documents and scientific Western discourse plays down its strong indebtedness not only to European literary models, but also to non-European literary traditions. Thus, novels like José María Arguedas's *Deep Rivers,* Miguel Angel Asturias's *Men of Maize,* and Augusto Roa Bastos's *I, the Supreme* are seen in *Myth and Archive* as mere products of anthropology's fascination with the "other." In other words, it is the scientific discourse of anthropology that, according to Echevarría, influenced those works, and not the stories and songs heard or read by their authors. The point is not to deny the importance of anthropology as a mediating discourse, but to emphasize that in spite of all mediation, these novels drew from literary sources that cannot be made to fit cosily into entirely European models or scientific Western discourse.

In "Canaima and the Jungle Books," González Echevarría places Gallegos's novel and *The Lost Steps* together in the context of the "jungle books," which would include such works as

> *Tristes tropiques* by Claude Lévi-Strauss, *The Lost Steps* (of course),
> Conrad's *Heart of Darkness* (doubtless the best), *The Lost World* by Arthur
> Conan Doyle, *King Salomon's Mines* by H. Rider Haggard, *The Vortex* by
> José Eustasio Rivera, *Green Mansions* by W.H. Hudson, *The Story Teller* by
> Mario Vargas Llosa, *Colibrí* by Severo Sarduy, and *The Royal Way* by André
> Malraux. And *Canaima*, it goes without saying. (340–41)

Related to children's literature and popular culture, the story of the "jungle books," according to González Echevarría, "takes the form of the adventure journey, or a quest romance. The quest romance combines adventurous wanderings with a love story, which are typical components of the jungle books" (336). The reductiveness and generality of such a definition make its use for the analysis of any of the works involved rather questionable.

As a "jungle book," *The Lost Steps* is, still according to González Echevarría, closer to *Canaima* than its author and all the writers of the so-called Latin American "Boom" would be ready to accept. What brings them closer is not Carpentier's links to any form of regionalism, but, on the contrary, Gallego's unsuspected "modernity" or "universality."

> Carpentier, but more especially Fuentes, feels the need to distance himself
> from Gallegos to clear ground for the foundations of his own works, for
> their claim to difference and originality. . . .

Fuentes and his colleagues of the Boom are the heirs of international modernismo, not of embarrassing "South American" local color. I am interested in showing how *Canaima,* on the contrary, belongs to a "universal" and modern tradition—that it does not manage, after all, to escape from its historical moment—and that only by reading it in that broader context can one perceive its deeper meanings and discover its values, which are much more than being a mere inventory of great descriptive passages. (334)

In passing, may we recall Chinua Achebe's comment on the term *universal*: "I should like to see the word universal banned altogether from discussions of African literature until such a time as people cease to use it as a synonym for the narrow, self-serving parochialism of Europe" (13).

González Echevarría's "universalist" reading of Latin American literature would indeed be more appropriately called "Europeanist." In the case of *Canaima* and *The Lost Steps,* this reading goes so far as to omit the name of the "jungle" that links both works. The Amazon is reduced (or "broadened," as the critic would probably say) to a generic jungle, hardly distinguishable from the African *Heart of Darkness.*

Many aspects of *Canaima* and *The Lost Steps* indeed bring to mind Joseph Conrad's novel. The same can be said of other "forest novels" already mentioned, including Inglez de Souza's *The Missionary,* published before *The Heart of Darkness.* The dazzling multiplicity of life forms in constant process of movement and transformation, a characteristic of the Amazon forest, is seen in those works as a fearful and dangerous prospect, a "heart of darkness" that puts us in contact with the less controllable aspects of life. Thus, the protagonist of *O Missionário* loses the pious convictions that brought him to the forest, succumbing to long-repressed sexual instincts. The Portuguese Alberto in *A Selva* is destroyed by the jungle when pursuing the dream of becoming rich; and *Vortex*'s last sentence tells us that its main character, Arturo Cova, was "devoured by the jungle." In the words of Clemente Silva, another character in Rivera's novel, "the jungle dazes humans, developing in them the most inhuman instincts: cruelty invades souls like a twisted thorn, and greed burns like fever" (79).

Kanaima

At the beginning of *Canaima,* having lost two sons to the nearby forest, the mother of the protagonist Marcos Vargas sends him to Trinidad, hoping that the education in a British school will keep him away from the dangerous attractions of the Amazon. But the boy was already charmed by the stories told to him by a So'to Indian, and after returning from boarding school he follows the steps of his older siblings, going into the forest in search of riches. Like his Colombian predecessor Arturo Cova, Marcos Vargas ends up "swallowed by the jungle."

On the one hand, with the striking exception of *The Lost Steps,* all of these "forest" novels can, to different degrees, be considered social narratives. They strive to denounce the brutal exploitation of human labor, of mestizos and Indians in particular, that takes place in the race for enrichment in the Amazon. In that respect, one further text should be added to the list: Alberto Rangel's 1907 collection of stories *Inferno Verde,*[3] whose similarity to *Canaima* can be seen in the heavily metaphorical descriptions of the forest, clearly inspired in this case by Euclides da Cunha (Bosi 1970, 350). Euclides himself wrote a preface to the collection, also reproduced in the Spanish translation (1932).[4] Even Rangel's expression "green hell" (inferno verde) is echoed by Gallegos: "The green hell where those who have lost their bearings wander in desperate circles retracing their own footsteps over and over again" (179). In the work of Alberto Rangel, the expression is also the title of the last story in the collection, which puts forth the author's thoughts about how the Amazon should be explored by educated men, so as to guarantee a just division of land, hard and honest work, and a respectful treatment of Indians and mestizos—a treatment that would properly instruct them toward the "natural path of civilization." That is also the thesis of *Canaima,* which ends with a comparison between the decadent Tumeremo, a village whose main activity is the exploration of gold and rubber, and the prosperous farm Tupuquén where the mestizo son of Marcos Vargas is going to be raised, a ranch that derives its wealth from imported herds of cattle. Despite its indigenous name, Tupuquén boasts the ethic of the "enlightened" Santos Luzardo (hero of the better-known novel *Doña Barbara*), which Gallegos himself endeavored to put into practice as Venezuelan president in 1948.

On the other hand, if as social narratives these "forest" novels attempt to explain the Amazonian "problem" and perhaps find a solution for it, they also share another, less explanatory feature: All of them attribute to the forest a mysterious force, an incomprehensible power of attraction (the vortex), which drives human beings to violence and self-destruction. In the words of *Canaima*'s narrator:

> This was the fabulous jungle from whose influence Marcos Vargas would now never again be free. The abyssal world wherein lie millenarian secrets. The inhuman jungle. Those who ever penetrate it begin to be something more, or something less, than men. (177)

In this context, however, *Canaima* holds a special position among these works: Rather than just accepting the mysteriousness of this force, it uses an indigenous explanation for it, more in line with the appeal to Guarani and Upper Amazonian texts in other members of the "exemplary trilogy." This is how the novel defines the Carib concept *canaima*, a Carib word that has also served to entitle works by Wilson Harris (Guyana) and Thea Doelwijk (Surinam):

> The malign one, the dark divinity of the Waikas and the Makiritares, the frantic god, principle of evil and cause of all ills, disputes the world with Cajuña, the good. Demon with no form of its own and able to assume any appearance, ancient Ahriman reborn in America. (252)[5]

In fact, as Jaime Tello, one of the English translators of the novel, points out, "Gallegos identifies [canaima] with the Devil, [and] adopts the Makiritare term *Cajuña*, meaning Heaven, as his counterpart" (181)—a binary relation that does not exist in the Carib. The confusion is comprehensible, since *canaima*, which appeals to the notions of world change and homicidal madness, is in fact quite a complex concept that seriously exercised the minds of the first travelers to describe the cultures of the region. According to Schomburgk:

> In the demonology of the Macusis, Akawais, Wapisianas, and Arekunas, this Kanaima plays quite a peculiar part. It appears to be not only the personified desire of man's revenge but in general the author and source of all evil, yet without developing into a distinct individual Evil Spirit—to put it shortly, it is a Proteus without definite shape and fixed conception. . . . Who and what Kanaima is they could never tell us, but they explained every death as his effect, his doing. (1: 288)

Koch-Grünberg gives a similar, yet more detailed, impression:

> In the concept of Kanaimé a lot is still undefined, even for the Indian. . . . Thus, Kanaimé is always the secret enemy, something unforeseen, often inexplicable, spectral, from which we cannot protect ourselves. For the Indians, Kanaimé is at the same time the tragedy that threatens him and his own need for revenge, which comes to him suddenly, takes hold of him, and drives him into a fatal action. (3: 187)

But he also goes beyond, defining it within the relationship between cultural groups:

> Entire tribes can be Kanaimé. Hostile neighbor tribes, tribes whose previous enmity has become a doubtful friendship, are openly or secretly considered Kanaimé. A tribe always calls another one by that name. The Yekuana say that there are many Kanaimé among the Arekuná, the Taulipáng and

the Makushí and, naturally, not a single one in their own tribe. Among the Makushí and the Taulipáng, on the other hand, the Ingarikó and Seregóng are considered evil Kanaimé. . . . Specially the Ingarikó who live in the jungle, the once mortal enemies of the Taulipang and Arekuná, are feared as Kanaimé by their neighbors. That could be seen many times a bit before and during our trip to Roraima. It is thus with good reason that the legend calls their protofather Piaimá, an evil witch and cannibal. (3:186)

Ultimately a cause of death, *canaima* is related to revengeful and negative feelings, to people who convey those feelings, and to the malignant power of the shaman. In recent ethnographic work among the Macuxi, for instance, Neil Whitehead described *canaima* as violent assassination and mutilation related to shamanic practices (2002). Walter Roth, who in 1915 related *canaima* to the name of a tree, also called it "the expression of the law of retaliation" (354). But *canaima* is also related to intra-cultural relationships, to the struggle for power between different cultural groups. Thus, the worst Kanaimé, Koch-Grünberg was told, were the Pischaukó, a group that in the opinion of the German naturalist existed only in the fantasies of the local Indians: "The most disturbing Kanaimé are the Pischaukó because, apparently, they exist only in the fantasy of the Indians. Everybody talks about them, but when one wants to check the subject more profoundly nobody has seen them" (3: 186). The Pemon Ernesto Pinto, however, explains that the Pischaukó used to live in the region many years ago (23). According to Pemon belief, the shamans of this powerful group still inhabit the region. Walter Roth also used the term *canaima* to describe "the blood-thirsty tribes of Rio Branco" (355), and Henri Coudreau referred to the wild tribes that lived in the mountains as *canaémés* (Farage, 108).

Hence, the term can be used to define the relationship between invaders and invaded: Not only is *canaima* the destruction brought by the invaders, but it refers as well to the self-destructive forces that drive the invaders to act as they do. It carries in itself all the past and present histories of invasions. Along these lines, the So'to define it as an evil passed to them by the Kariña in the process of negotiating for guns and iron (Civrieux, 165–73). In his *Genesis*, Eduardo Galeano cites another native reading, that of a demon created by the defeated to destroy the victorious Carib (Kariña):

The phantom lay in wait for them behind the trees. He broke their bridges and placed in their paths tangled lianas. He traveled by night. To throw them off the track, he walked backward. He was on the slope from which rocks broke off, in the mud that sank beneath their feet, in the leaf of the poisonous plant, in the touch of the spider. He knocked them down with a breath, injected fever through their ears, and robbed them of shade.

> He was not pain, but he hurt. He was not death, but he killed. His name was Kanaima, and he was born among the conquerors to avenge the conquered. (44–45)

And Alejo Carpentier, in "Visión de América," says that for the Arekuna, Canaima (who inhabits the mountain Ayuán) "punishes those who let themselves be convinced by the missionaries" (282), which makes of him a guardian of native belief.

The term *canaima* in Rómulo Gallegos's novel conveys all of those meanings, and, in fact, in the narrative itself goes far beyond the definition given by the narrator, quoted above. It is at the same time a mysterious force that attracts individuals to their own destruction, and the exploitation process that enslaves and destroys Indians and mestizos, on the one hand, and their very destroyers, on the other. This complex indigenous concept gives coherence to *Canaima,* linking the social narrative to the psychological quest of the protagonist.

The Steps of the Journey

Exiled in Venezuela, in part during Gallegos's presidency, Alejo Carpentier developed a deep interest in the region, as the journalism he wrote at the time shows. This was the moment of the great Franco-Venezuelan expedition to the So'to and the headwaters of the Orinoco, which generated widespread public interest, and of which Marc de Civrieux was a member. Carpentier himself traveled to, and read widely about, Venezuela's "Amazonian territory," and demonstrably learned a great deal from Schomburgk's *Travels,* not least the concept of Pacaraima itself.

As far as is known, Alejo Carpentier never read *Macunaíma.* A strange fact, when we recall that his novel *The Lost Steps* displays, quite proudly (albeit ironically), a wide bibliographical knowledge about the Roraima region and culture. As near-contemporary Latin American novelists, he and Mário had a lot in common. They were strongly drawn to music, and indeed were both musicologists. Mário defined *Macunaíma* as a rhapsody, and *The Lost Steps* not only has a musicologist as its protagonist, but follows, according to several critics, a musical structure as well.[6] Mário de Andrade and Alejo Carpentier were both concerned with the specificity of Latin American culture—a specificity which their respective novels attempt to define. In Paris, Carpentier met a friend of Mário's: the Brazilian composer Heitor Villa-Lobos, admired by both authors as a characteristically "Brazilian" musician.[7] Above all, *Macunaíma* and *The Lost Steps* are strongly connected to Pacaraima, the Roraima-Orinoco region generally defined as "Guyanas," the borderlands of Brazil, Venezuela, and Guyana, inhabited by the Carib-speaking peoples to whose culture the two novels are, to different degrees, indebted.

In *The Pilgrim at Home,* González Echevarría points to the close relations between *The Lost Steps* and "Visión de América," a collection of three articles originally written by Carpentier as part of the unfinished *Libro de la Gran Sabana,* a project that was later replaced, also according to González Echevarría, by *The Lost Steps.* The three articles in *Visión de América* describe Carpentier's journey through the Sabana region.

In *The Lost Steps* an unnamed first person narrator tells us, in diary form, of his journey to the Orinoco region in search of an ancient musical instrument that could help him explain the origins of music. The journey is described as a journey to the past—first, the past of human race, as they encounter ever more primitive societies:

> At dusk we stumbled upon the habitat of people of a culture much earlier than that of the men with whom we had been living the day before. We had emerged from the Paleolithic. . . . to enter a state that pushed the limits of human life back to the darkest murk of the night of ages. (182)

Second, it is a journey to his personal past, marked by the memories of his Spanish-speaking mother and a childhood spent in Latin America. The perspective is boldly male, and it could hardly be otherwise, as a first-person diary account of a journey made by a man. The three main female characters in the novel have highly allegorical functions: Ruth, the protagonist's actress wife represents the coldness and mechanization of the United States and of modern urban life in general; Mouche, his French mistress, stands for the French and the surrealists, with whom Carpentier himself had been connected and had recently fallen out (the title of the novel is an obvious reference to André Breton's homonymous book); and Rosario, the woman he falls in love with during the journey represents both indigenous Amazonia and popular Latin America.

In "Visión de América" Carpentier actually mentions Makunaíma, the Carib divinity that became the hero of Mário de Andrade's novel: "In the beginning there was not the word. There was the axe. The axe of Macunaíma, whose flint edge—blow after blow, cut after cut—went slicing off pieces of bark from the Great Tree" (Carpentier 1990, 291). Contrary to what Raúl Antelo says in the excellent article "Macunaíma: Apropriação e Originalidade" (260), Carpentier came across the creation story he quotes not in Koch-Grünberg's collection, but in Richard Schomburgk's earlier *Travels*: "climbing a tall tree, [Makunaíma] cut away with his mighty stone axe some pieces off the bark" (2: 253). This earlier version differs considerably from Koch-Grünberg's, and in it Makunaíma appears less a trickster than a culture hero, a supreme creator, who becomes resentful toward his creatures when they forget him. All but paraphrasing Schomburgk (save for the odd colloquial interjection), Carpentier continues:

> Then Macunaima, the highest being, let the axe rest and created mankind. Man began by sleeping deeply. When he awoke, he saw that woman was lying beside him, and it was the law thereafter that woman should be at man's side. But what next, the Bad Spirit, the counterpart of the Good Spirit, gained much sway among mankind. Ungrateful, mankind had forgotten Macunaima and no longer worshiped with due praise. (Carpentier 1990, 292)

Seen here as entirely good, this Macunaíma is nonetheless the same as the rather more ambiguous culture hero who created the world by cutting down the food tree, according to the cosmogony shared by the Macuxi, Pemon, So'to, and other Carib groups of the region. This cosmogony goes on to explain and name in detail the rocky, mountainous, difficult geography of Pacaraima, which greatly impressed Humboldt, Schomburgk, Koch-Grünberg, and Carpentier. Furious at his creatures, this Macunaíma personally sends them the great Flood:

> And so Macunaima sent down the great waters, and the whole earth was covered by the great waters, and only one man escaped from them, in a corial. After a long while, imagining that Macunaima must now be tiring of so much flood, the man in the corial dispatched a rat, to see if the waters had subsided. Then the man in the corial threw stones behind him, and the Arekuna were born, who, as everyone knows, are the people preferred by the Creator. (Carpentier 1990, 292)

Schomburgk had reported this event ("Makunaima sent great floods: one solitary man escaped in a corial from which he dispatched a rat to see if the waters had subsided, and it came back with a maize cob." [2: 253]); and it is reproduced again by Carpentier in *The Lost Steps,* with a remark from the protagonist about how appropriate it was to the fauna and flora of the region:

> Reflecting on the Noahs of so many religions, it struck me that the Indian Noah was better adapted to the reality of these lands, with his ear of maize, than the dove with its olive branch, here in the jungle where nobody had ever seen an olive tree. (196)

If Mário de Andrade's *Macunaíma* is largely indebted to Koch-Grünberg, *The Lost Steps,* as González Echevarría also pointed out, owes a lot to Schomburgk: "The echoes of Schomburgk's book in Carpentier's novel are too many to cite: the Sturm und Drang of the *Lost Steps* derives from *Travels in British Guiana,* as do the descriptions of the heart of the jungle" (1977, 177). In a romantic fashion, Schomburgk, like Carpentier in "Visión de América" and the protagonist of *The Lost Steps* after him, feels small and insignificant before the grandiosity of the rock formations in the region—a Romantic revelation of the *sublime.* Schomburgk compares several of those formations to European constructions and landscapes. In the Pacaraima mountain chain, the mount Pausing, for instance, reminds him of "the crumbling masonry of an old feudal castle" (2: 144). And in the case of the Twasinki range, two large boulders "looked exactly like the large watch-towers of an old castle ruin [which] lent that mountain a quite peculiarly romantic charm, and reminded me of the happy hours spent on my trip down the Rhine" (1: 293). In "Visión de América," Carpentier comments ironically on such comparisons:

> The imaginative habits of my Western culture make me invoke, straight-away, Macbeth's castle or Klingsor castle. But no. Such fancies are inadmissable, since so limited, in this corner of virgin America (276).

Yet, after all, *The Lost Steps* is a novel precisely about the conflict between the "imaginative habits" of Western culture and the specificity of Latin America. Hence, the protagonist will describe a group of rocks as "piles of basalt rock, near-rectangular monoliths, thrown down amid sparse and scanty vegetation, which seemed to be the ruins of most archaic temples, of menhirs and dolmens"(199). Such descriptions, it is true, can be said to derive from Schomburgk's romanticism. In the words of González Echevarría, the apparent human origin of certain landscapes, frequently mentioned by Schomburgk and Carpentier, has its source in

> Goethe's theory of Urformen (Shelley's "thoughts and forms, which else senseless and shapeless were," Neruda's "shape of potter's earth") and ultimately of Romantic monism—the emergence of master forms from the desired communion of Mind and Nature. Spengler's theory of the materialization of master cultural symbols in man derived from the observation of landscape is a part of this Romantic doctrine, as is Surrealism. This is also the basis of Carpentier's "marvelous American reality" and the narrator-protagonist's mimetic theory of the origins of music in *The Lost Steps* (the field of allusions in the novel—Schiller, Shelley, and Beethoven—is decidedly Romantic). (1977, 180–81)

But neither Schomburgk's text nor Carpentier's novel can be satisfactorily described within an exclusively Romantic field of allusions. When traveling through a rocky region, for instance, Schomburgk clearly refers to the fact that for their part the "Indians had some special name for, or some special legend about, every peculiarly shaped rock" (2: 161). Thus, at the same time that Schomburgk's travel book explains what Echevarría calls the novel's "Sturm und Drang," it also brings it into contact with the indigenous cultures and literatures of the region. The naturalist's naming of American plants after European princesses, for instance (which so much amused Carpentier in "Visión de América") proves to be overshadowed by his more general respect for the native geography and toponymy, as in the following example:

> Closely connected with it is the Wayaka-piapa, the 'felled tree,' which, according to Indian tradition, the good spirit Makunaima cut down on his journey overland and changed into stone to leave behind as a memento of his wanderings among the human race: it very much resembles an obelisk. (2: 205)

Such literary geography marks the course of Carpentier's trip through Pacaraima and the Gran Sabana region, as he describes it in "Visión de América," and gives coherence to the places mentioned in *The Lost Steps,* as he explains in a note at the end of the novel:

> The river in question, which, earlier in the book, might be any great river of America, specifically becomes the Orinoco in its upper reaches. The location of the Greeks' mine might be not far from its confluence with the Vichada . . .
>
> The Capital of the Forms is Mount Autana, outlined like a Gothic cathedral. From this point on, the landscape becomes that of the Gran Sabana, a vision of which is to be found in different portions of Chapters III and IV. (xv–xvi)

González Echevarría, however, considers the journey described in the note absurd, by claiming it involves a "detour":

> By making the action of the novel take this geographically impossible détour, Carpentier may be underscoring the fictionality of the text and the relationship between the narrator-protagonist's quest and those of the many explorers who set out to find the lake with the golden sands and the king whose body was painted gold. (1977, 169)

In fact, Carpentier himself makes no mention of a detour in his note. Rather than affirming that his protagonist made a journey "westward" from the Orinoco to the Gran Sabana, as Luis Harss claims (quoted in González Echevarría 1977, 169), he simply states that the upper Orinoco and the Gran Sabana are the two areas which can be associated with the landscape description and cultural references made in chapters 3 and 4 of his novel. And these two areas, far from being too distant or disconnected, in Amazonian terms, have actually a geographical and cultural coherence given to them by the indigenous cultures of the region (mostly Carib), and by the geographical presence of the Pacaraima range (Brotherston 1993, 163). In fact, Schomburgk himself recognizes such coherence, by saying that "With Roraima there stood before me the watershed of the three large river areas of Guiana, that of the Amazon, the Orinoco and the Essequibo" (2: 204). For being the source of several rivers, which flow in different directions, the mountain range, according to Schomburgk, is called by the Indians the "ever fruitful mother of the torrents" (2: 206). And Schomburgk claims to be entering the Orinoco watershed when, traveling through the Gran Sabana, near Roraima, he witnesses that the rivers start flowing north:

> With the new plant region [the "botanical El Dorado" of the Pemon] we had at the same time entered a new watershed, that of the Orinoco, divided off from the Amazon basin by the steep wall: because to the west of us all the streams flowed, like the Yarawira, northwards to the Orinoco." (2: 171)

Moreover, it was journeying from the upper Orinoco to the Great Savanna (eastward, evidently) that a group of Maiongkongs (So'to) who were going to Georgetown to trade goods met the Schomburgk brothers on their way:

> It was a long string of Maiongkongs, a tribe occupying the watershed of the upper Orinoco and its tributary, the Parima. My brother no sooner discovered amongst them some acquaintances he had made on his journey to the sources of the Orinoco in the years 1838 and 1839 than he was recognized by them with the heartiest manifestations of delight. (1: 357)

Of the three articles included in "Visión de América," the third, entitled "La Biblia y la ogiva en el ámbito del Roraima," is the one that most specifically deals with the journey of the German naturalists through the Gran Sabana, and it is not always kind to its subject:

> the great Romantic travelers in Guyana. Romantic in the style of Chateaubriand—never dismayed by the landscape, contemplating it in half-profile, their hands well placed on their waistcoats, as if a devout pencil would fix their noble posture for posterity. Even so, the Schomburgk brothers are entertained by their journey as if they were living in a story by Jean-Paul. (289)

Yet, much in the Schomburgk brothers' work belies this assessment of Carpentier's. Indeed, quite apart from the fact that Chateaubriand never traveled to the territory he wrote about, that of the Natchez, Richard Schomburgk often ridicules his own Romantic impulses, describing "fairy-like" landscapes that all of a sudden are invaded by mosquitoes, oases that reveal themselves to be much less than promising, and so on:

> The whole of Nature was wrapped in the most impressive silence which was only occasionally broken by the Indian fishers when they hauled in their catch, or by the mournful cry of a goatsucker. But this fairy landscape brought us no enjoyment because the mosquitoes were present in swarms so awful as to make a bitter torment of the beautiful moonlight night. (2: 122)

Also, the account of his journey to Roraima begins with the description of an Indian village which had been destroyed by the Brazilians. The historical awareness shown at this point by Schomburgk and his group—most of whom were Indians—bears no resemblance at all to Echevarría's description of Schomburgk's idea of nature as "the maternal world, the moment of immersion into the formlessness and form-giving pre-natal existence, which is anterior to a fixed, historical past, one in which signs have yet to acquire a set meaning" (González Echevarría 1977, 178). According to Schomburgk

> As soon as our party reached the ruins, they stood still and burst into loud lamentation crying "Caraiba, Caraiba." A lawless gang of manhunters from the Rio Branco had some three years previously set fire to the peaceful homes and driven off their occupants to die in slavery far from their native country. . . .
> Our party was greatly depressed. (2: 118)

On another occasion, Schomburgk addresses the question even more clearly, with a description in which the idea of "the silence of the forest," used both by himself elsewhere and by the narrator-protagonist of *The Lost Steps*, is firmly demystified:

> The formerly happy village of five houses had been visited by a Brazilian Descimento (Slave Expedition), surprised at night, and set on fire, with the object of carrying its inhabitants—men and women, old people and youngsters—into slavery. . . . While with inward indignation in the midst of this obvious testimony of human wickedness, we were regarding all the misery that European Culture had brought to the peaceful hearths of fellow brothers entitled to the same rights as ourselves, and each of us was picturing to himself, from the confusion in which shattered cooking utensils, broken weapons and half-charred firebrands lay scattered around, the scene that only the tranquilly murmuring trees had been witness of. (2: 40)[8]

Carpentier's representation of Schomburgk in "Visión de América" as an exclusively Romantic character anticipates his invention of the protagonist-narrator of *The Lost Steps*; and this is the view strongly developed, in turn, by critics such as González Echevarría. At the same time, by appealing to native texts mediated or not by Schomburgk, Carpentier establishes, in "Visión," a validity for the Carib world of Makunaíma and further intimates the link between "Guianas" and "Anahuac," or Mesoamerica. This connection, as we will see, plays a key role in *The Lost Steps*, whose cultural reference, in spite of the protagonist's Romantic tendencies, certainly touches a domain very different from that of Goethe, Schiller, and Beethoven.

In order to understand the role played in the novel by this cultural domain, the reader must take the step to differentiate, more than most critics have found convenient, Alejo Carpentier from his unnamed protagonist. The temptations not to do so are many. The biographical similarities between the author and his character were emphatically pointed out by González Echevarría and other critics before him:

> The anecdotal parallels between *The Lost Steps* and Carpentier's own life are numerous and many of them well known, for Carpentier himself has often drawn them, first and foremost by adding a note to the novel suggesting that some of the adventures in the book were experienced by the author. (González Echevarría 1977, 162)

Yet, even González Echevarría finds a need to discredit claims for total identification between the novel and Carpentier's biography: "However, if the novel were autobiographical in the direct and almost literal way in which critics (and recently Carpentier himself) would have us believe, what can be made of the ending? The protagonist's quest ends in failure" (1977, 164). This question remains unresolved in González Echevarría's study. In the preamble, for instance, he still calls *The Lost Steps* an "autobiographical novel," and references to the "Carpentier implied in his stories" abound throughout the book. His problem is not only how to reconcile this auto-biographical approach with the failure in the protagonist's project, but also how to explain, under the category of autobiography, the contradictions in the protagonist's behavior. To make things even more complicated, he also points to an "error" in the novel's diary structure: the omission of a Monday, which makes the dating illogical. His conclusion is thus that the novel is "unfinished":

> The missing Monday suggests that the novel is "discordant," an "unfin-ished" text. The fact that some sections are dated while others are not, the presence of unassimilated essayistic passages, and the blatant contradictions

in what the narrator-protagonist says about others and what he says about himself (his scorn of Mouche for faults that he shares with her, for example) reinforce this suggestion of incompleteness. Is the text a travel journal in the process of becoming a novel, or is it an unfinished novel that will imitate a travel journal? (1977, 186)

If, on the other hand, we look at the protagonist with the suspicion usually recommended when approaching any first-person narrator, we will regard the novel as quite a "finished" work: an ironic account of an irremediably Europeanized white male's contact with tropical America. "Errors" and contradictions are, after all, commonly used techniques that authors employ to make us doubt, suspect, and even dislike first-person narrators. Autobiographical data should not stand in the way of such a basic reading principle.

Furthermore, the separation between Alejo Carpentier and his protagonist-narrator is a critic's decision that might ultimately impinge on the novel's readability, at least to contemporary women. How else could we go on reading it after the protagonist's misogynist brutality against Mouche, whose only fault, as González Echevarría correctly pointed out in the quote above, is to be culturally as European as the narrator-protagonist himself—one of the great ironies of the novel?

It is precisely the women characters, especially Mouche and Rosario, who gain most when we keep Carpentier and his protagonist-narrator apart. Mouche reemerges as a double of the protagonist, and her European insensitivity, so harshly criticized by him, ironically mirrors his own. Rosario is able to escape the timeless present she is cast into by the protagonist as an allegory of the tropical jungle; he often describes her as the essential (i.e., timeless) woman: "*Your woman* was an affirmation that preceded all agreement, all sacraments. It had the pristine truth of that *womb* which prudish translators of the Bible render as *bowels,* muting the thunder of certain prophetic implications"(180). When the protagonist leaves Santa Mónica de los Venados in search of paper to continue the writing of his symphony, he assumes rather unproblematically that upon his return she would still be there waiting for him, and is surprised to find her pregnant and married to another man when he comes back. "She no Penelope," says Yannes, an ironic reference to the protagonist's tendency to project European myths onto the jungle.

It is also by respecting the difference between Carpentier and his narrator-protagonist that Gordon Brotherston is able to analyze Rosario's time:

> . . . it is through Rosario's time that the strongest challenge is made to the temporal models inherited and more or less unconsciously reproduced by

the hero. And from the start it should be seen that this alternative time is not just the mindless present of the old anthropology's "savage". . . , as has sometimes been assumed, but a complex mechanism that articulates cosmogony and political history no less than, and within, the moments of the present. (1993, 170)

First of all, Rosario's is the time of days lived one by one, a time that teaches the protagonist to enjoy "a new intensity in the present moment, a new rhythm in days and nights, and the immediacy even of a remote gene-sial time" (Brotherston 1993, 170). It is also the time of her own needs and necessities, and the lunar cycle of her menstruation, which keeps her apart from him: "I didn't even have the consolation of Rosario's embraces: she 'couldn't,' and when this happened she became nervous, morose, as though every sign of affection annoyed her" (212). Incapable of understanding Rosario's time, the protagonist projects over her his European expecta-tions: urged by the priest, he unwillingly asks her if she would like to marry him, and is negatively surprised by her denial:

> I finally made up my mind to ask her, in a voice that did not come out very steady, if she thought it would be a good thing for us to get married. And when I thought that she was going to snatch at the opportunity to assign me a role in an edifying Sunday chromo for the use of the new converts, to my amazement she answered that marriage was the last thing she wanted.
> Like lightning, my surprise turned to jealous indignation. (225)

Unlike the priest's Christian idea of eternal marriage, and the protago-nist's own view of it as an official institution, Rosario believes in a com-mitment that has a specific type of temporality: It will last only while the woman feels she is being well treated by the man. According to this con-tract, the woman will "serve" the man in his domestic needs, while he will provide the family with food and guarantee his wife's sexual happiness: ". . . and there was a man to serve as mold and measure, with the compensa-tion of what she called 'the body's pleasure,' she was fulfilling a destiny . . ." (180). Apparently identical to the patriarchal notion of marriage, this idea of relationship differs from it insofar as it assumes unproblematically the sexual pleasure of the woman and the possibility of her decision to separate. Of course the "women of the people's" natural approach to sex is a white male phantasy common in the literature of the 40s and 50s, often accompa-nied by the pleasure with which these women are glad to "serve" their men (Jorge Amado's Gabriela is perhaps its best-known example). Nevertheless, the disregard for Catholic rulings about sexual behavior among unedu-cated women from certain regions of Latin America was indeed a common practice much before the sixties, and probably traceable to non-Christian roots. The protagonist's lasting disappointment with Rosario's refusal to marry him shows how much this notion differs profoundly from a traditionally European point of view on the matter.

Although some cultural traits of the mestiza Rosario certainly link her to medieval notions of Christianity, much of her behavior connect her to Native American roots. About her notion of time, Gordon Brotherston comments that:

> It stems from the pronouncements on calendar cycles which form the backbone of the books in the Chilam Balam tradition. There time periods are literally borne for their duration, loads to be carried and shed along the road of life—a concept graphically conveyed in the hieroglyphic inscriptions of the Classic Period, and echoed in the sky and earth cycles of Pacaraima narratives. It is precisely this act of unloading which the hero wishes but fails to perform. In his words he remains burdened with his own Epoch and "the tremendous load of its rules, taboos, aspirations and intransigence." (Brotherston 1993, 177)

The critical link between the cosmogony and cultural history of Pacaraima and Mesoamerica can be found in the Carib texts studied in chapter 1. Such links had been suspected by Humboldt on the basis of mathematics (vigesimal counting) and by Schomburgk because of Olmec-like jade work. In *The Lost Steps,* this grand vision comes through, for instance, in the following passage:

> Just as other cultures were branded with the sign of the horse or the bull, the Indian with his bird profile place his culture under the sign of the bird. The flying god, the bird god, the plumed serpent were the nucleus of his mythologies, and everything beautiful was adorned with feathers. The tiaras of the emperors of Tenochtitlán were made of feathers, as were the decorations of the flutes, the toys, the festive and ritual vestments I had seen here.
>
> Struck by the discovery that I was now living in the Lands of the Bird, I remarked somewhat superficially that it would probably be difficult to find in the cosmogonies of these peoples myths that paralleled ours. Fray Pedro inquired if I had read a book called the *Popol-Vuh,* of which I did not know even the name. (203–4)

And it is geographically outlined by the protagonist when, drawing acutely on versions of the food tree story, he proposes a Carib maize saga which extends northwestwards over the Caribbean islands:

One afternoon I learned with surprise that the Indians here preserved the memory of an arcane epic, which Fray Pedro was reconstructing bit by bit. It was the account of a Carib migration moving northward, laying waste everything in its path, and filling its victorious march with prodigious feats. It told of mountains moved by the hand of fabulous heroes, of rivers deflected from their courses, of singular combats in which the planets intervened. (210)

Carpentier's appeal to cultural connections between the Amazon and Mesoamerica begins already in "Visión de América," where, expressly putting the Bible in second place, the author can find no better words to describe the dramatic landscape of the Roraima region than the ones he transcribes from the beginning of *Popol Vuh*: "It is the world of Genesis, which is better expressed in the American language of the *Popol vuh* than in the Hebraic verses of the Bible" (277). And the giants from the Chilam Balam books seem to him to have been the authors of the strangely shaped rocks that he sees in the Gran Sabana. These textual references in "Visión" are far more fully developed in the novel.

Besides providing epigraphs for the central rain forest chapters (3 & 4), Mesoamerican literature supports the whole concept of native cosmogony and worldview. The sheer geological processes of rock formation, like the subsequent evolution of the vertebrates—the metamorphoses that involve fish, the plumed serpent and bird-reptiles, and monkeys—take place within a larger scheme and philosophy of world-ages that is decidedly Native American (Brotherston 1993). The Chilam Balam books and the *Popol Vuh* in particular (quoted in Asturias's translation) offer definitions of work and time as "a load" to be carried, as in the case of Rosario, and authoritatively warn against just the order of dehumanized automation that plagues the protagonist (Brotherston 1993). All this has the effect of corroborating the Carib stories as products of a tropical world which exists in its own right, with no need for European taxonomy or reason, and which strongly exemplifies Carpentier's ideas of cultural ontology and "marvelous American reality." Indeed, in the larger perspective, it is this definite and sourced Native American factor which best comes to serve as the diagnostic of "marvelous reality" in Carpentier's writing, firmly distinguishing this key concept from the less-specific and less-rooted notion of "magic realism." "Marvelous reality" is better defined and becomes more serviceable as a literary critical term precisely when it has included in it an idea of textual evidence and precedent, native (or African) rather than Western in origin, which may radically affect and direct our reading of the novel.

As for the *Popol Vuh* warning against ill-used time, this is a recurrent theme in the novel, and one of its main preoccupations. It comes in the world-age story quoted above, told to the protagonist by Fray Pedro and qualified by him, despite the fact he is a Christian missionary, as "the only cosmogony that has foreseen the threat of the machine and the tragedy of the sorcerer's apprentice" (204). It details how the domestic animals and even the house objects rise up against their robot-like masters during the great eclipse, and reveals the danger of "the unfeeling technology that has marred the hero's own life" (Brotherston 1993, 172). Thus, not only does the protagonist describe the people in the big city as having become slaves of their own technology, of their own lifestyles, but the fate of Ruth, his wife, reveals also the similar tragedy of an actress who became a slave of the roles she plays. And the hero himself cannot escape that destiny even after his journey, for he becomes dominated by a musical composition that alienates him from the very people he had chosen to live with. Like the robot people in the *Popol Vuh,* the Europeanized contemporary artist is, in the words of the protagonist, "the calling of a scion of the race."

The contradiction between the protagonist's desire to become part of a nonurban Latin American society and his incapacity to do so is not a sign of the novel's unfinished state: It is the main problem it poses. The protagonist is indeed a Romantic hero, who believes that the people in the jungle are more spontaneous and true to themselves at the same time that he is incapable of recognizing the congruity and historicity of their cultures. Above all, he cannot, for the most part, see how far he is from being like them. We readers are forced to watch, with a somewhat irritated smile, the way he criticizes Mouche for her reliance on written sources at the same time that he moves painfully through a labyrinthine jungle of quotations. We see how his insistence on writing a symphony about the origins of music keeps him away from Rosario's world and from the popular music that Marcos, Rosario's future husband, is more capable of producing. And we can observe the irony of his reliance on a European epic, the *Odyssey,* for the composition of his American symphony, when Fray Pedro and the very epigraphs of the novel point to American epics he could have used.

Whether or not the novel proclaims that the protagonist's robot-like alienation is a destiny irremediably shared by all contemporary artists, including Carpentier, is a question I prefer to leave open. The strength of the novel lies precisely in its lack of definite responses, in the cracks opened by the ironic distance that keeps author and narrator apart, allowing us to gaze simultaneously at the protagonist's limitations and the world that native literature helped Carpentier intuit, Rosario's world.

Part II

The Great Lowland Territory of the Tupi-Guarani

Having himself fostered the origin of future speech,
having himself fostered a minimum of love,
having himself fostered a minimum chant,
he prospected who
should share the origin of speech,
should share the minimum love,
should share the thread of the chant
—Ayvu-Rapyta
(translated by Ed Dorn and Gordon Brotherston)

chapter 4

Tupi-Guarani Texts

A MONG NATIVE LITERARY TRADITIONS of South America, that of the Tupi-Guarani is one of the best known and most widely studied. Tupi-Guarani texts have had a recent but powerful effect on Spanish American writing, while they have been a feature of Brazilian literature ever since colonial times and the Romantic period, and they have exerted a major influence on the *Modernismo* of the 1920s, and on novels and short stories published after the sixties.

Approximately forty Tupi-Guarani languages and dialects are spoken by indigenous groups all the way from northern Amazonia to Río de la Plata, and from the Atlantic coast to the Andes. The Tupi-Guarani are characterized by their tendency to migrate, moving over long distances within this vast territory. Most studies place their origin in the south Amazon some thousand years ago. For reasons that are still debated—and which some scholars relate to the religious search for *Ivy marã ey,* (the place without ill)—they migrated toward the east and south a few centuries before the arrival of the Europeans.[1] The migration routes followed two paths, known as "Brochado's fork": the eastern route took the Tupi to the coast; the southern route led both to the interior and to the coast. The Tupi groups living on the coast of Brazil (mostly Tupinambá) were the first natives to face the invasion of the Portuguese in 1500.

Nheengatu or Língua Geral, a Tupi dialect with some Portuguese influence (also called modern Tupi), was so widely spoken in Brazil in the first centuries of colonization that it was forbidden by an edict promulgated in 1757 by the governor of Grão Pará, Francisco Xavier de Mendonça Furtado, brother of the Marquis de Pombal.[2] Yet, it was still being used for letter-writing in 1875. Since 1967, Guarani has been one of the two national languages of Paraguay, and was subsequently acknowledged by Mercosur (the South American free-trade organzation). In spite of differences and enmities, a notable cultural unity seems to have characterized the distinct Tupi groups at the time the Europeans arrived (Tupinambá, Tupiniquim, Tapirapé, Tabajara, and Timbira, among others). Similarities between those Tupi cultures and the ones of today, as well as between the Tupi and the Guarani of the interior, can be verified not only in language, but also in cosmology and religion.

Tupi-Guarani texts have been transcribed and published in three main phases. The first covers the colonial and early Independence periods; the second, the latter half of the nineteenth and the first decades of the twentieth centuries; and the third, modern ethnology, from the 1930s onward.

Landmarks and First Encounters

The first text to describe the territory that later became Brazil is Pero Vaz de Caminha's "Carta a el Rey Dom Manuel."[3] Caminha was the official scribe in Pedro Álvares Cabral's fleet, which brought the first Portuguese to South America. The people they met at the coast, probably Tupinambás, are described as "good people, good and simple, on whom may be easily imprinted whatever belief it is wished to give them"(105). This first depiction of the Tupinambás sets the tone, so to speak, of the first thirty years of colonization, which were characterized by a relationship of relatively peaceful economic exchange. The main product exploited by the Portuguese was Brazil wood, a source of red dye, which was exchanged by the Indians for metal tools. In addition, as Mário Maestri explains: "They [the Indians] taught them [the Europeans] how to hunt and fish in these regions; to plant maize, tobacco, sweet-potatoes, and manioc; to know the plants and the animals of the land. They revealed to the Europeans the complex process of transforming poisonous manioc into a versatile food staple" (10).

In 1530, the Portuguese Crown sent 400 heavily armed men to Brazil, led by Martim Afonso de Souza, with instructions to expel the French from the coast and found villages. They also brought sugar plants with them, and very soon this crop became the Crown's main source of income from the colony. Indians were taken as slaves for the plantations, and not surprisingly, they started to revolt. In the 1500s there were several conflicts between Portuguese and Indians, the best known being the "Tamoio Confederation"—an alliance between Tupinambás, Goitacás, Guaianás, Tamoios, and Aimorés—which offered resistance to the Portuguese from 1554 to 1567. By the beginning of the next century, thousands of coastal Tupinambás had been killed, enslaved, or had fled to the interior.

Descriptions of the Tupinambá and other groups in this period vary a lot in tone, according to the origin and ideology of the writer. The first European to describe in detail a Tupi society was Hans Staden, a captive among the Tupinambá on the northern coast of São Paulo for nine months. Staden's *Warhaftige Historia und beschreibung eyner Landtschafft der wilden nacketen grimmigen Menschfresser-Leuthen in der Newenwelt America gelegen* was first published in 1557. In the detailed description of his captivity, the German soldier shows the Tupinambá already engaged in complicated treaties and warfare with the French and Portuguese. In Staden's text, the bellicosity of the Tupinambá stands out, as they fought to resist the Portuguese and the Tupiniquim, their long-term enemies. He also discusses Tupinambá cannibalism in detail.[4] Staden registers, for example, the set dialogue that was usually exchanged between the prisoner who was about to be killed and ritually devoured, and his killer. The killer would say "Yes, here I am, I want to kill you, because your people killed and devoured many of our people." The victim would reply: "When I am dead, I will still have many friends who will come and avenge me" (182).[5] Notwithstanding the probable exaggerations of a man in constant fear of being killed, Staden's text also allows us to savor the black humor of the Tupi, who mocked their own ritualistic cannibalism in order to scare the fearful German even more—since among them fear of death could never be shown. When he was being brought into the Tupinambá village, for instance, Staden was forced to say, in Tupi: "Aju ne xé peê reiurama" (I am arriving and I am your food).

In Staden's captivity accounts we also find Tupi toponyms and the Tupi geographical definition of the region—which ranged from São Vicente on the coast of São Paulo, the oldest European settlement in Brazil, to Rio de Janeiro (or, as the Indians called it, Niterói), passing through the whole northern coast of the state of São Paulo, where place names like Guarujá, Bertioga, Ubatuba, Mambucaba, and Parati can still be recognized today as names of towns and summer resorts in the region.

The most eloquent Portuguese travelers who came to the region in the sixteenth century were committed to the Crown's colonial objectives and were interested in proving preconceived ideas about the Tupi's lack of belief in any divinity—what Pero de Magalhães Gandavo in his *Tratado da Terra do Brasil e História da Província de Santa Cruz* (1576) and Gabriel Soares de Sousa in *Tratado Descritivo do Brasil em 1587* referred to as the "lack of the letters 'f' (for *fé*: faith), 'l' (for *lei*: law) and 'r' (for *rei*: king) in their language." Gandavo's aim was to promote the new Portuguese territory so that the poorest subjects of the Crown could find a place to live and work there. After all, according to him, in spite of the Jesuits it was still easy to find Indian slaves who could support themselves and their masters in the "new land." Gandavo describes several different tribes but considers them "all the same," and thanks God for having made the Indians enemies to each other, since otherwise it would be impossible for the Portuguese to inhabit the land. The traveler gives detailed descriptions of Tupi everyday life and, like Staden, emphasizes their bellicosity and ritual cannibalism. He describes in some detail the ceremonial tearful greeting and the prisoner's aggressive reproach to his captors before dying.

Like Gandavo, Soares de Sousa does not feel any sympathy or respect for the Indians he describes in minutiae. Though he focuses on the distinctions between different tribes, the emphasis lies once again on the Tupinambá, and he spends a lot of time portraying their bellicosity, their "depraved sexuality," and their "ignorance of any religion." Yet he acknowledges that, because of the habit of community property, those Indians "could be Franciscans," and recognizes the importance of music in their society: "Among these people, musicians are highly thought of, and wherever they go they are well received, and many have crossed the sertão and the land of their enemies without harm being done to them" (316). The ceremonial greeting of guests is described in detail:

> When a guest enters a Tupinambá house, the lance-lord in the house he has come to gives him his hammock, and his wife sets food before him, never asking who he is or whence he comes, nor what he wants; and when the guest is eating, they ask him in their own language: "You arrived then?" and he answers "Yes"; this is the welcome which is given him by all who wish to, and then they converse most slowly. (316)

A great contrast to these mostly negative views of the Tupi presented by Gandavo and Soares de Sousa is Jean de Léry's positive depiction of them in *History of a Voyage to the Land of Brazil, Otherwise Called America* (1578). In this text, the Calvinist Léry gives voice in the original language to a Tupi Indian, in a sample dialogue meant to serve partly as a language lesson. According to Manuela Carneiro da Cunha in "Imagens de Índios do Brasil: o Século XVI," the dialogue "is, however, a rhetorical figure, a positive counterpoint to all the horror that the hunted Hugonaut wants to denounce in the land of his birth" (165). Yet, Léry's dialogue offers us not only clear examples of the Tupi language at work, but also territorial definitions of the tribes who inhabited the Rio de Janeiro area (then part of

France Antarctique), besides Tupi questions about life in Europe. Moreover, the dialogue opens with the Tupi ceremonial welcome, presented in terms almost identical to those found in Gabriel Soares de Sousa:

TUPINAMBÁ: *Ere-ioubé?* You arrived?

FRENCHMAN: Yes, I arrived.

TUPINAMBÁ: *Teh! augé-ni-po.* Very well. *Mara-pé-déréré?* What's your name?

FRENCHMAN: *Léry-oussou.* A great oyster.

TUPINAMBÁ: *Ere-iacassopienc?* Have you left your country to come and live here?

FRENCHMAN: *Pa.* Yes

TUPINAMBÁ: *Eori-deretani ouani répiac.* Come then and see the place where you'll stay.

FRENCHMAN: *Augé-bé.* Very well.

TUPINAMBÁ: *I-endé-répiac? aout i-eudérépiac aout é éhéraire. Teh! ouéreté Kenois Léry-oussou ymeen!* Here he has come then, my son, having us in his memory, alas! (236–37)

Léry also included in his travel book a few Tupinambá songs, and like Gabriel Soares de Sousa, he was impressed by the Tupinambás's talent for music, as we can see in this description of a religious dance:

These ceremonies went on for nearly two hours, with the five or six hundred men dancing and singing incessantly; such was their melody that— although they do not know what music is—those who have not heard them would never believe that they could make such harmony. At the beginning of this witches' sabbath, when I was in the women's house I had been somewhat afraid; now I received in recompense such joy, hearing the measured harmonies of such a multitude, and especially in the cadence and refrain of the song, when at every verse all of them would let their voices trail, saying *Heu, heuaure, heura, heuraure, heura, oueh*—I stood there transported with delight. Whenever I remember it, my heart trembles, and it seems their voices are still in my ears. (142–44)

And he transcribed the exhortation speech made by the elders to convince the young ones to go to war:

"What!" they will say, speaking each in turn, without interrupting each other by a single word, "have our ancestors, who have not only so valiantly fought, but also subjugated, killed, and eaten so many enemies, left us their example so that we should stay at home, effeminate and cowardly of heart? In the past our nation was so greatly feared and dreaded by all the others that they could not stand their ground before us; must our enemies, to our great shame and confusion, now have the honor of coming to seek us out at our very hearths? Will our cowardice give the Margaia and the Peros-engaipa, those two worthless allied nations, the occasion to attack us first? Then the speaker, slapping his shoulders and his buttocks, will exclaim: *Erima, erima, Toüpinambaoults, conomi ouassou tan tan,* and so forth, that is, "No, no, my countrymen, strong and valiant young men, we must not do this; we must prepare ourselves to go and find them, and either let ourselves all be killed and eaten, or avenge our own." (113)

Léry played an important role in shaping the ideas that Montaigne was developing about the inhabitants of the Americas (A. Franco, 238), thanks in part to conversations he had with Tupi Indians he had met at Rouen, one of whom lived with him for ten years. It is through Montaigne that Tupi literature achieves its first European recognition, with the inclusion of two native poems in his essay "On the Cannibals" (1580, first version).[6] The poems were given to him by a "simple, rough man" who stayed "some ten or twelve years" among the Tupinambá. The first one is a war song—the type of song, mentioned by Staden, Gandavo, and Soares de Sousa, that was recited by the prisoner before he was killed and ritually eaten in a cannibalistic ceremony. The captive cries: "These sinews, this flesh and these veins—poor fools that you are—are your very own: you do not realize that they still contain the very substance of the limbs of your forbears: savor them well, for you will find that they taste of your very own flesh" (239).

The second one is a love poem, described by the essayist as "thoroughly anacreontic":

> O Adder, stay: stay O Adder! From your colors
> let my sister take the pattern for a girdle
> she will make for me to offer to my love;
> So may your beauty and your speckled hues be for
> ever honored above all other snakes. (240)

Among the sixteenth-century travelers who left us their impressions of the Tupi, the Franciscan André Thevet (accused by many of being the worst liar of all the travelers[7]), was the only one to reproduce Tupinambá cosmogonical stories, which were narrated to him by an old shaman. In these stories we can read for the first time the names of the Tupi cultural heroes Monan and Maíra, the latter being correctly identified by the Franciscan as a "transformer" (*Cosmographie Universelle*, reproduced in Métraux 1950b). Thevet also translated a Tupinambá Flood narrative, in which the brothers Aricute and Tamendonare saved themselves and their wives by climbing up a palm tree and an *urucum* (achiote) tree, respectively. This story inspired the final scene of the novel *O Guarani* (1857) by the Romantic novelist José de Alencar.

The fleet that brought the first General-Governor of Brazil, Tomé de Sousa in 1549, also brought the first Jesuits, who soon would become active players in the process of colonization of Brazil, Paraguay, Argentina, and Uruguay. Father Manuel da Nóbrega was the leader of the five Jesuits that arrived in Brazil in 1549. Another group of Jesuits arrived in 1553, among them the legendary José de Anchieta, beatified by the Catholic Church in 1980. Initially, the Jesuits were optimistic about the prospect of converting the Indians, whom they saw as malleable and good-spirited. By 1556, such positive ideas had been replaced by a cautious, if not bitter view of conversion. In his *Diálogo sobre a Conversão dos Gentios* (1558?) Nóbrega laments that Indians who appeared to have converted to Catholicism often went back to their original religious practices.

These perceived difficulties led to a change in the attitude of the Jesuits, some of whom became open defenders of force in the process of conversion. Anchieta, for instance, stated in a letter to Loyola in 1555 that

> one cannot expect nor obtain anything in this land with regard to the conversion of the Indians unless many Christians are sent here. By living according to the will of God, these Christians can subject the Indians to slavery and oblige them to shelter under the banner of Christ. (quoted in Monteiro, 41)

Not necessarily opposed to slavery, as the above quote shows, the Jesuits served nevertheless as a buffer between colonizers and Indians. By establishing a system of *aldeamentos* ("villagization"), they hoped to be the sole controllers of Indian labor—the ones responsible, in other words, for educating and training the Indians to become, in European terms, "productive."

The system, however, failed for several reasons. First, several epidemics of contagious diseases brought from Europe killed thousands of Indians. Second, the Indians themselves revolted and organized resistance. And third, the relationship between Jesuits and colonizers deteriorated, since the latter resented the Jesuits' control over their access to workers. While colonizers were still allowed to enslave Indians captured in "just wars"— that is, those accused of making war against the Portuguese or their allies, or of committing cannibalism—they were particularly interested in the Indians that could not be legally enslaved, that is, the Guarani. The reason was clear: The Guarani were experienced agriculturalists (Monteiro, 70).

Slave-hunting expeditions (or *bandeiras*) led by *paulistas* attacked not only free Guarani villages, but, at a growing rate, the missions themselves. These expeditions moved westward all the way to the Spanish possessions, and were particularly active in the disputed region of Guairá, home to thousands of Guarani. In 1609, the Jesuits Cataldino and Maceta had received authorization from the Spanish Crown to establish the first "reductions" in the area. According to the Jesuit Antonio Ruiz de Montoya, the objective of the reductions was to "reduce"—that is, concentrate—the Indians into large villages where they would be made to follow a strict routine, with set hours for working, praying, and leisure (6). Thus, the Fathers believed, the Indians would abandon their dispersed and idle life. By 1628, there were eighteen reductions in the Guairá, where more than fifty thousand Guarani lived.[8]

The reductions were constantly raided by the *bandeiras.* Between 1628 and 1630, the *bandeirantes,* among them the infamous Raposo Tavares (still studied in Brazilian schools as a hero for his role in conquering the Brazilian West), attacked eleven missions, and destroyed most of the Guarani villages of the region. Forced to abandon most of their missions in the Guairá, and suffering continuous attacks on the missions in the adjacent regions, the Jesuits obtained, in 1639, an authorization from the Spanish Crown to arm the Guarani. The wars of 1640 and 1641 managed to repel the *paulistas.*

From then on, the Jesuit reductions, which occupied mostly the region between the Paraná and Uruguay rivers, flourished. Described by many authors as "utopian" societies,[9] the reductions were urbanized villages of rectangular blocks of houses and some monumental architecture. Their economy was based on egalitarian production and distribution of goods— a system that had, according to Meliá, Guarani origins:

> One can point out that the division of labor and the provision of means of subsistence from the part of the *caciques* was an ethnographic reality which the priests intuitively took advantage of for the social organization of the reductions. (120)

The highly ritualized daily life, still according to Meliá, seemed to owe as much to Guarani spirituality as to the Christian religion (121). And Guarani, not Spanish or Portuguese, was the language spoken and written in the reductions.

However, if in general terms the reductions represented an alternative to the violent behavior of the colonizers, they were also a repressive force that tried to change the Guarani way of being. It is the Jesuit Meliá who tells us that

> The reduction has a totalizing character and its consequences will be irreversible at all levels. The reduction disturbs traditional ecology, brings

in a new morphology, organizes urban space according to very precise intentions, changes family relations. In the reductions Guarani religion was attacked, ridiculed, suppressed, and finally replaced. The shamans were prosecuted and harassed; expelled or domesticated. There is no doubt that the reduction wanted to change the Guarani way-of-being. (178)

For all their impact on the lives of Tupis and Guaranis in colonial times, the Jesuit missions recorded little native literature. They became known for having produced important language books in Tupi and Guarani, and for having translated into those languages parts of the Bible, religious songs, "Christian doctrines," prayers, and plays. José de Anchieta, author of the *Arte de gramática da língua mais usada na costa do Brasil* (1595), wrote poems, dialogues, and plays in Tupi. His *autos* often make use of the theatrical expertise of the Tupis, combining it with medieval drama techniques.

In the seventeenth century, the Jesuit Fernão Cardim published the *Tratados da Terra e da Gente do Brasil* (published first in English in 1625). Cardim is not an admirer of the indigenous cultures, whose everyday life he nevertheless describes in detail. The chapter dedicated to Tupi warfare contains rich information about those practices, including (in indirect speech), a prisoner's song similar to the one reproduced by Montaigne in his essay:

> and the savagery of these people is such that, having no ill other than that before them, they are so together as if it were nothing, both in speaking and in testing their strength, since after bidding farewell to life saying *even though they die, many have their dead, and besides, their brothers and kin remain here to avenge them.* (99)

Without exhibiting the quality of José de Anchieta's works, Christian poems in Tupi or Guarani were written by several Jesuit priests, including Antonio Ruiz de Montoya, who published, also in the seventeenth century, an important history of the Jesuit missions in Paraguay, which bears the emblematic title *La Conquista espiritual* (1639). In the words of Hélène Clastres, however, the Jesuits of Paraguay were, in general,

> less concerned with describing the customs of the natives than with relating in full detail the progress of evangelization. Here we have nothing comparable to the great chronicles of Brazil, so that our knowledge of the Guarani during the early days of the Conquest cannot compete in any way with that which we have of the Tupi.[10] (11–12)

Perhaps the Jesuit documents that open the widest windows into Guarani ways of thinking are the collections of letters, a few of which include speeches by Guarani Indians—mostly shamans—who resisted conversion and life in the reductions. In the following example, we see a keen perception of the "dissimulated captivity" of the reductions, as well as of the serious changes that Christianity was bringing to Guarani way of life:

> Was the patrimony that our Fathers left us any other than freedom? The same Nature which kept us from the burden of serving others, has it not made us men bound to a place? Has our common house up to now not been this region surrounded by hills, so that we never went off in the valleys and thickets? So, why do you allow, through our example, our Indians, and what is worse, our descendants, to be subject to this dissimulated captivity of the reductions, which Nature itself never forced us into? (quoted in Meliá, 177)

The most significant accounts of Tupi culture in the seventeenth century were published not by Jesuits, but by priests from other orders. Claude d'Abbeville's *Histoire de la mission des pères capucins en l'isle de maragnan et terres circunvoisines* (1614); and Yves d'Evreux's *Voyage dans le nord du Brésil fait durant les années 1613 et 1614 par le père Yves d'Evreux* (Ferdinand Dénis's edition, which made it more popular, dates from 1864). All of these works give detailed descriptions of the lives, beliefs, and habits of the Brazilian Indians, above all the Tupi groups.

Abbeville cannot disguise his admiration for the Indians' generosity and communal life, for their physical beauty and lack of preoccupations. His book includes a speech made in Tupi by the Indian Itapucú to King Louis XIII and his wife, Marie de Médicis, in the Louvre, in 1614,[11] and another speech by an old Tupi man in Maranhão, which reveals a profound understanding of colonial history. With irony, the old Tupi explains to the French priest how the Portuguese, at first, had not wanted to come and live in Tupi territory, but with time, they saw the need to build forts and villages and to bring the *paí* (priests), who in turn demanded slaves. Comparing the French to the Portuguese, he proclaims: "For the moment we are happy with you French, but then again so were we once with the Portuguese" (115).[12]

Abbeville also gives the names of many Tupi villages in the northern region of Maranhão, plus valuable information about the astronomical knowledge of the Tupinambá, including the names (and meaning) of several constellations. Moreover, the Capuchin reproduces some comments made by the Indians who accompanied him to Europe after his trip: "as the traders sometimes failed to deliver the goods for the stated price, they became averse to this nation (the English) whom they called *tapuitim* (white barbarian). In their language they said: *tapuitim scateim atupave,* these white foes are worthless, mean and greedy" (236).

Yves d'Evreux's work is less sympathetic toward the Indians, concentrating more on the importance of doing missionary work among them. Yet, since the priest makes wide use of direct and indirect dialogues, we can sense, at times, Indian criticism of European customs and religion (Gonzalez; Brotherston, 1979). By reinforcing Léry's and Montaigne's positive depiction of the indigenous societies, seventeenth-century works such as Abbeville's and, in a minor degree, Evreux's, would later help to define enlightened views of the "noble savage," in a period (the eighteenth century) which itself produced no collection of Tupi or Guarani texts, nor any major description of their life and beliefs.

Only recently resurrected by writers and critics, one further early account of the Guarani deserves note here. It is the Archdeacon Martín del Barco Centenera's astounding verse narrative *The Argentine and the Conquest of the River Plate*. Published in Lisbon in 1602, this work was written as much as twenty years before, to record the author's journey across Guarani lands, from the island of Santa Catarina on the Atlantic coast of Brazil, west through what is now Uruguay and Paraguay, up towards Peru. It offers insight into Guarani politics, language, and history at a date and from an area where little else has survived in alphabetic documents. In stanzas that admittedly have their prosaic moments, Centenera shows considerable understanding of how various Guarani groups related to each other and the philosophies that held them together; he also takes time to record etiological and other legends of origin which draw out the semantics of their language. Reduced as it was compared with what happened in Portuguese-speaking Brazil, the literary contact that the Spanish had with the Guarani in nineteenth-century Argentina and Uruguay came mainly via Centenera.

In the nineteenth century, the works of missionaries and adventurers tended to be replaced by texts of an emergent scientific kind. *Travelers* became *naturalists,* and, in the case of Brazil, the previous centuries' interest in the different Tupi nations (allies of the French or the Portuguese) was mostly replaced by a focus on the *botocudos*—a word used both to refer to specific Gê groups and to describe, at the time, those Indians who did not want any contact with the whites (from the word *botoque,* the lower lip stone insertion used by some tribes). In the words of Manuela Carneiro da Cunha:

> From the end of the eighteenth century to the middle of the 19th, there was a debate about whether to exterminate the 'hostile' Indians (índios "bravos"), cleaning out the backlands—a solution generally favored by the settlers—or whether to try civilizing them so as to include them in civil society—a solution generally proposed by politicians, which presupposed their incorporation as a work-force. (Cunha 1992, 134)

This new scientific approach brought into question even the human status of the natives:

> ... it is in the nineteenth century that the question of the Indians' being human was in effect first posed. In the 16th century—contrary to what might be supposed from the 1532 papal declaration which affirmed that the Indians really did have souls—there was never any doubt that they were men and women. But the scientism of the 19th century became concerned to make a clean break between anthropoids and humans, a controversial demarcation line. (Cunha 1992, 134)

But it also brought a renewed interest in the *folk,* and some naturalists from early nineteenth century were beginning to collect songs and narratives authored by the natives themselves. This is the case with Spix and Martius, whose third volume of *Reise in Brasilien* (1823–1831, 4 volumes) included in the footnotes two indigenous songs in Nheengatu. The first song is an example of black humor:

Chamanú ramê curí	When one day I die
Tejerru iaschió	and you stay dry-eyed
Aiqué caracaraí	there is the *caracaraí*
Serapiró arumu curí	ready to devour me.
Cha manu ramae curí.	When one day I die
Se mombôre caá puterpi,	and you toss me in the thicket
Aiqué tatú memboca	there is the armadillo
Se jutú ma aramú curí.	ready to bury me. (141)[13]

According to Martius, the *caracaraí* is a small eagle, who pursues the big mammals in order to eat the larvae that nest in them. The armadillo *(tatu),* on the other hand, has a bad reputation for digging up graves in order to eat corpses. The second song is also humorous:

Nitio xa potar cunhang	I dislike a lady
Setuma sacaí waá	with legs too slender
Curumú ce mama-mamane	she could coil round me
Baia sacaí majaué.	just like a snake.
Nitio xa potar cunhang	I dislike a lady
Sakiva-açú	with hair too long
Curumú monto-monto-que	she could cut me
Tiririca-tyva majaué	like brambles and grass (294)

Translations by Joaquim Norberto appeared in the *Revista Popular* in 1859.

Over these centuries of first encounters, under colonial and then the national regimes of Brazil and the Spanish American republics, few actual texts in Tupi-Guarani were transcribed or published. On the one hand, the emphasis was practical, instructions on how to behave and speak in the company of natives (typified by the model dialogues of Léry). On the other, the natives were appreciated for their exotic qualities of newness and difference, precisely the bravery and sensibility, and even humor, exemplified in the songs featured by Montaigne. There are glimpses of cosmogony in references to the shaping of the earth and the flood, and to the thunderous Tupã later equated with the Christian God; and from the start the *Ivy marã ey*, or land without ill, becomes a concept, along with more fanciful stories of culture-bringers like Zumé, who arrive from afar (harbingers, clearly, of the European invaders themselves). Yet remarkably few texts, as such, are transcribed or published. Curiously this situation persists well after Independence in Brazil (1822) and Spanish America.

The First Collections

In Brazil, after the middle of the nineteenth century, an interest in the *folk* led to significant collections of native texts, the first being Couto de Magalhães's *O Selvagem* (1876). Printed by the Brazilian Imperial Government for display at the 1876 Universal Exhibition in Philadelphia, and dedicated (in Tupi) to the Emperor D. Pedro II, the work is described by the author as a "A preparatory work for the exploitation of the savages and of the land occupied by them in Brazil." The stories, collected from the Tupi by Couto de Magalhães and accompanied by interlinear translation,[14] constitute, at this early date, an important document in the Tupi literary tradition. They include the narrative "Como a Noite Apareceu" ("How Night Appeared"), described by Couto de Magalhães as "probably a fragment of the Genesis of the ancient South American savages" (217), and several trickster stories focusing on the tortoise *(jabuti)* and the jaguar. The author also reproduces a song in Guarani, sung by the inhabitants of Asunción, Paraguay, and of Corrientes, Argentina, as well as invocations of *Rudá* (the "god of Love"), *Cairé* (full moon), and *Caitití* (new moon). Such texts were promptly noticed by writers: Machado de Assis, for instance, refers to *O Selvagem* in the poem "Lua Nova" (Treece, 237),[15] and the original in question is in fact the invocation to *Caititi* (new moon). The intertextual connections of *O Selvagem* with Brazilian literature are not limited to this poem: Several decades later Mário de Andrade would also use some of the stories in *Macunaíma*. The story that tells how night came into existence (*O Selvagem* 215–17), along with some tortoise narratives, play an important role in Antonio Callado's *Quarup* (1967).

O Selvagem is one of several late nineteenth-century collections of Tupi and Guarani stories, among them Charles Frederick Hartt's *Amazon Tortoise Myths* (1875)[16] and Filiberto de Oliveira-Cézar's *Leyendas de los indios guaraníes* (1892). At this same time, the first publications were made of texts in Nheengatu. These include Barbosa Rodrigues's *Poranduba Amazonense ou Kochiyma uára porandúb* (1890), stories and songs in Nheengatu collected in the Amazon region; Ermanno Stradelli's publication of the Tariana (an Arawak/Tukano group) *La Leggenda dell' Jurupary* (1890), in Italian (based on an original in Nheengatu given to him by the Indian Maximiano José Roberto); and Brandão do Amorim's *Lendas em Nheengatú e em Português* (which were gathered jointly with Maximiano José Roberto in Nheengatu and published posthumously only in 1926). Although based on Nheengatu originals, these texts will be discussed later, along with other Rio Negro texts and collections.

Isolated stories and songs also appeared in periodicals, and include Barbosa Rodrigues's "Lendas, Crenças e Superstições" (1881), and "Curupira,"[17] a publication in Nheengatu by Cunha Mendes which appears as an appendix to Raimundo Ulisses de Pennafort's *Brasil Prehistórico* (1900). Several of these stories were also reproduced, in translation, in anthologies of popular literature, such as Silvio Romero's *Estudos sobre a Poesia Popular do Brasil* (1888), F. J. de Santa-Anna Nery's *Folk-lore brésilien* (1889); and Clemens Brandenburger's *Lendas dos nossos índios* (1923),[18] among others.

By far the most important of all collections in this period is Curt Nimuendaju's "Die Sagen von der Erschaffung und Vernichtung der Welt als Grundlagen der Religion der Apapocuva-Guarani" (1914), with texts in Guarani and German. The German Curt Unkel, named Nimuendaju after being adopted by the Apapocuva-Guarani from the interior of São Paulo, lived so closely involved with the people he studied and defended, that his name became, in the words of Eduardo Viveiros de Castro, a legend. "Die Sagen" reproduces the narratives of Earth creation and Flood, both amply commented on by Nimuendaju. The stories were told to him by the shaman Joguyrovyjú, and also by Guyrapaijú (described by the ethnologist as "old and conservative") and by the "well traveled" Tupãjú. Nimuendaju's collection brings us into contact, for the first time, with the complex eschatology of the Guarani, with the division of the human spirit into the celestial soulword and the terrestrial soul-animal. Those texts were also the first published works substantially to evidence the theme of the Guarani migrations in search of the *Ivy marã ey* ("Place without ill").

The Apapokuva-Guarani creation story begins with the striking image of Ñanderuvuçú (Our Great Lord) discovering himself alone amidst darkness, with the Sun on his chest. Initially, only the Eternal Bats populate such darkness, but Ñanderuvuçú soon finds Ñanderú Mbaecuaá beside him. Ñanderuvuçú asks Mbaecuaá to look for a woman. Ñandecy, the woman, is found in a clay pot, and soon becomes pregnant by both Ñanderuvuçú and Mbaecuaá. Mbaecuaá disappears, leaving Ñanderuvuçú and Ñandecy living as a couple. After a conjugal fight, Ñanderuvuçú retires to the brace that supports the Earth, where he makes his house. The pregnant Ñandecy then starts a journey in search of her husband, communicating with her unborn child during the trip:

> Then she walked a little and her son asked for a flower. She picked the flower for the child and walked a bit more. She tapped on the place where her child was, and asked him: "Where did your father go?" "He went that way!" She then walked a little more and her son asked for another flower. She picked the other flower, and a wasp stung her. And she said to her son: "Why do you want flowers when you are not (in the world) yet, letting me be stung by a wasp?" Her son got angry. (144)[19]

Both humorous and moving, this passage focuses on the unique relationship between mother and child—a relationship that starts while the child is still in the womb and that unites them in their search for the absent father. The quest for Ñanderuvuçú eventually drives Ñandecy to the house of the Eternal Jaguar, where she is killed. Her sons Ñanderyquey and Tyvyry are raised by the Jaguar-Grandmother, but after discovering that the jaguars had eaten Ñandecy, the two brothers decide to avenge her, killing the animals one by one.

Like other twins in the native tradition, these two, defined in the text as "older" and "younger," show trickster-like traits. Tyvyry resembles the Carib Makunaíma in his combination of childish attitudes and destructive power: For example, after the two brothers find and resuscitate the bones of their mother, the younger one wants to suck at her breasts and ends up killing the woman again as a result. Their jaguar-killing exploits much resemble the tricks of the Carib Pemon Konewó: They build a trap and tell the jaguars that it does not work, so that the felines, one by one, are finally convinced to enter it. The only jaguars to survive are the unborn male and female cubs of the Jaguar-Grandmother, who become parents to all the jaguars that exist today. Moreover, the brothers play several tricks on the spirit Añay, and some of those tricks resemble Konewó's adventures. Like Makunaíma, the two brothers transform the world through their tricks, creating several animals and stealing fire from the vultures. Tyvyry, the younger brother, particularly resembles the Pemon hero in the way that he often appears to be helpless, but is, at the same time, capable of resuscitating his older sibling when the latter, on two different occasions, dies.

From birth, the two brothers are saddened by the absence of their parents—a sadness that is clearly voiced when the parrot tells them that Ñandecy was killed by the jaguars: "And he cried with his little brother: 'While we were still being formed, we lost the one who had been our mother'" (145). Their task, from then on, is to recover contact with their mother and father, which they do by avenging her death, and by undertaking the epic journey that will finally lead them to Ñanderuvuçú and their resuscitated mother. In order to get there, they have to fight the jaguars and the spirit Añay, and they also have to be good shamans so that they can bring Ñanderuvuçú back into contact with them: "And he [Ñanderyquey] prepared (carved) a *maracá* and wanted to follow the tracks of his father. He called the *Añay* so that these spirits would dance, and taught the *Añay* how to dance. After four months the father came to them. Ñanderuvuçú took his son with him" (150).

After meeting his parents, the little brother goes to his mother's breast to suckle from it, while Ñanderyquey, the older one, tries to persuade his father into letting him use his equipment in order to rule the world. As is so often the case with native tradition, in this story the fact that the twins find their parents does not necessarily bring their journey to a happy, unproblematic ending, for there is still latent tension between Ñanderuvuçú and his son Ñanderyquey. In fact, this creation story then goes on to tell us about the imminent destruction of the world:

> And he [Ñanderuvuçu] gave the equipment to his son. And he hid again from his son and went to stop the ruin (of the world) and only the Blue Jaguar watches him.
>
> Ñanderyquey is above us (in the zenith). He now watches the Earth and looks after its supporting brace, because, if he leaves, the Earth will fall. Nowadays the Earth is old, our tribe does not want to multiply anymore. We shall see all the dead ones; darkness will fall, the bat will come down and all of us who are here on Earth will have an end. The Blue Jaguar will come down and devour us. (150)

This cataclysmic view of the world is behind the Guarani migrations toward *Ivy mará ey*, the place without ill. Nimuendaju himself encountered several Apapokuva groups who were migrating toward the Atlantic Ocean where, according to their cosmogony, *Ivy mará ey* is located:

> We dance all year long, and then the direction comes (is revealed) to the shaman. When time is up, the direction comes. Then we go with him toward the East and we arrive at the eternal water. And our father (the shaman) crosses it, his children then go through the earth and the water is dry for them. (150–51)

The possibility of reaching this earthly paradise is linked to the Apapokuva-Guarani division of the soul into *ayvucué* (breath-soul) and *acyiguá* (violent-soul). While *ayvucué* is the same in most human beings, *acyiguá* is variable, determining the person's most evident characteristics. Thus, in the opinion of the Apapokuva-Guarani, the Kaingang Indians, their traditional enemies, have the *acyiguá* of jaguars. And the Kaingang themselves, according to Nimuendaju, believe that certain mental states may drive some men to fall in love with the daughter of the Lord of the Jaguars, and change into actual jaguars—an idea that becomes the central argument of João Guimarães Rosa's "Meu Tio o Iauaretê," as we will see.

In 1915, Curt Nimuendaju published, in German, another small collection of Tupi-Guarani stories, this time from the Tembé (Tupi) of Maranhão, in northern Brazil. The adventures of the twins Maíra and Mycura (skunk) bear great similarity with the Apapokuva-Guarani stories he published a year earlier, including the prenatal communication between mother and son that will reappear in Darcy Ribeiro's 1976 novel *Maíra*.

In this second phase in the story of Tupi-Guarani texts, which coincides with the international emergence of folklore (Völkerkunde) as a discipline, much weight is put on the native *folk* of America as the source of "tales" and songs, inherently interesting in themselves and evidence of the larger evolution of humankind.

Word-Souls of the Forest

Nimuendaju's "Die Sagen" is frequently described as foreshadowing modern ethnography in Brazil. After the thirties, when systematic studies of lowland South American indigenous groups began to appear, other important collections and studies of Tupi-Guarani texts came out. In 1940, Nunes Pereira, for instance, edited a few adventure tales concerning the Maué (Tupi) hero Bahira, also a trickster character; he went on to publish a study of the Maué, which included a series of stories, in Portuguese (*Os Índios Maués*, 1954). Between 1949 and 1951, the ethnologist Darcy Ribeiro made two expeditions to the area of the Urubu-Kaapor Indians, a Tupi group from Maranhão. During this trip he collected creation stories and stories about the twins Maíra and Micura; a summarized version came out in 1957 under the title "Uirá sai à procura de Deus" (Uirá goes in search of God). In the same article, the author presents the information he gathered about Uirá, an Urubu Indian who, accompanied by his wife and child, attempted an expedition in search of *Ivy marã ey*.

The most important collection of Tupi-Guarani literature was published in 1959 by León Cadogan: *Ayvu Rapyta*, esoteric poetry of the Mbyá-Guarani, from Paraguay. Published in São Paulo in Guarani and Spanish, the volume includes aspects of Mbyá cosmogony never before revealed to outsiders. The stories were told to the Paraguayan León Cadogan in an act of appreciation for favors received from him in his capacity as their legal defender in several cases; Cadogan was asked to use his influence to release from prison the Mbyá Mario Higinio. Mario then asked the *Cacique* Pablo Vera to discuss the Mbyá esoteric texts with Cadogan.

> Mario . . . went to the Cacique and asked him if he had already conversed with me—guero ayvu—on the origin of human language—Ayvu Rapyta. When the Cacique said he had not, Mario again asked me whether he had divulged the sacred hymns concerning the "bones of the one who bears the rod *yvyra'ikaga.*" The Cacique again said he had not and Mario told him I was now deserving of having divulged to me the *Ñe'e Porã Tenonde,* the first beautiful words; indeed, he said, the favors that the Mbyá owed me made me worthy of being considered a member of the tribe. (9)

As evidenced by Cadogan's account of how he got to know these texts, the Mbyá-Guarani religious literature, like the So'to's, can be divided into two categories, or genres: sacred and everyday texts. As Cadogan himself says:

> The religious annals of the Mbyá—and in this they are like those of the Apapokuvá, according to Nimuendaju—may be divided into two catego- ries: the common, accessible to anyone who wants to set about copying them, and the sacred, called Ñe'e or Ayvu Porã Tenonde, the first beautiful words, these being divulged only between members of the tribes and to those who enjoy the complete confidence of the Indians. (8)

The publication of *Ayvu Rapyta* threw a new light on our knowledge of Tupi-Guarani eschatology, generating, in the following years, a rich series of stud-ies about this people's philosophy and religion, among them Egon Schaden's *Aspectos Fundamentais da Cultura Guarani* (1962), Hélène Clastres's *The Land without Evil: Tupi-Guarani Prophetism* (1975), and Eduardo Viveiros de Castro's *Araweté: os deuses canibais* (1986). It also made available one of the most astounding texts in South American literature.

In *Ayvu Rapyta,* we find the adventures of the two brothers Kuaray (Sun) and Jachyrã (moon), who are not twins, since the younger was cre-ated by the older one. Like other Tupi-Guarani sets of brothers, particu-larly Ñanderyquey and Tyvyry in Nimuendaju's collection, and Maíra and Micura in the Tembé and Urubu-Kaapor traditions, Kuaray and Jachyrã play tricks on the jaguars (primitive beings) who had killed Kuaray's mother, with whom the hero had also (like the other Guarani ancestors) communicated before birth. All of these Tupi-Guarani stories emphasize the strong relationship between these cosmogonical children and their parents—a relationship that is, for the most part, deeply desired but quite difficult (in the case of Maíra and Micura in the Urubu-Kaapor texts, father and son get to the point of actually declaring war on each other), and as such they can account for the Tupi-Guarani philosophy about family relations, and about the conflicts between older and younger generations with regard to changes and transformations.

If the adventures of the brothers resemble texts from other native traditions in the Americas, the search for *Ivy mará ey* is a unique characteristic of the Tupi-Guarani culture. The belief in the place without ill was in fact reported by several of the chroniclers who wrote about the Tupinambá, and considering the religious commitment of most of those writers, it is surprising that they did not pay more attention to it. For Hélène Clastres, the missionaries had perhaps a "deeper reason" for their "curious disdain" for the idea of *Ivy mará ey*: The belief that it could be reached before death "would have appeared scandalous or pure folly, a religion in which men themselves try to become equal to the gods, immortal like them" (23–24).

According to Léry, the coastal Tupi located the land without ill to the west, beyond the mountains (the Andes, perhaps?). And indeed, Huxley refers to the presence of Guaranis in the ancient city of Chachapoyas in 1549 (10). For the Apapokuva and Mbyá (Guarani of the interior), such a land is located beyond the ocean. Accounts of migrations of Mbyá and Apapokuva Guarani from Paraguay and the countryside of Paraná, São Paulo, and Mato Grosso do Sul to the coast started to appear in the beginning of the nineteenth century (Ladeira and Azanha). The sea, according to Nimuendaju, has an ambivalent meaning for these Guarani. On the one hand, it represents the proximity to *Ivy mará ey,* being therefore central to their religion. On the other hand, it is an obstacle to their arrival at the desired land, and, as such, it seems hostile to the Guarani of the interior, who prefer to live at a safe distance from it.

As in the case of the Apapokuva, the Mbyá-Guarani belief in *Ivy mará ey* is closely related to their division of the human spirit into soul-words and animal souls. The soul-words are the essence of the divine origin of the Guarani. As we can read in the first lines of *Ayvu Rapyta* (very similar, in that respect, to the Apapokuva-Guarani creation story), the creator of the world made himself amid darkness:

> Our father, our very first and last, created the eldest darkness for his own body.
> The divine soles of his feet, the small round seat, he created them amid the eldest darkness, in the course of his evolution.
> The reflection of divine wisdom (the organ of sight), the divine

hears-all (the organ of hearing), the divine palms of hands with flowering branches (fingers and nails), Ñamandú created them, in the course of his evolution, amid the eldest darkness. (13)

Delicately described, the Mbyá-Guarani creator gives himself, little by little, a corporeal existence. This divine creature is fed by the hummingbird, and though living amidst darkness, he is illuminated by the Sun generated out of his own wisdom:

> He did not see the darkness: with no sun, he existed brightened by the reflection of his own heart; he made the wisdom held within his own spirit serve as sun. (14)

The original winds, amidst which Ñamanduí lived before creating his own house, come back every winter—a time-space identifiable as the original chaos that precedes, every year, the arrival of Spring:

> the original wind in which our father existed is experienced again with each return of the original space-time (winter), each time the original space-time arises (winter, in religious terms).
> As soon as the eldest age ends, when the Palacho flowers, the winds shift to the new space-time: the new winds rise now, the new space; the resurrection of space-time happens (spring). (15)

Before the existence of the Earth, Ñamanduí created "the origin of human speech," love, and the first sacred hymn:

> Having stood (assumed human shape), from the knowledge in his spirit, having his engendering knowledge, he conceived the origin of future speech. From the knowledge in his spirit, having his engendering knowledge, our father fostered the origin of speech, made it of his spirit
>
> Having conceived the origin of future speech, from the knowledge in his spirit, having his engendering knowledge, he conceived the root of love (for others)
>
> Having fostered the root of human speech, having fostered a small measure of love, from the knowledge in his spirit, having his engendering knowledge, he made the origin of a minimal chant, in his aloneness. (19–20)

As in *Watunna*, and in the Pemon texts we have seen, the Mbyá creation of the world is a creation of physical as well as of social elements: the Mbyá can exist as Mbyá only when they share a language, are able to love each other, and have a common religion and poetry.

The first sacred hymn is taught by Ñamanduí to the gods (the parents of the soul-words of his future numerous children), making them conscious of their own divinity. And these gods will be responsible for the incarnation of these soul-words in the bones of human beings. A good shaman, after a lot of preparation, should know where somebody's soul-word came from—which god, in other words, is its parent. The soul-word is the divine origin of the Mbyá, to which each individual should remain faithful by knowing the sacred hymns and the sacred stories, and by living entirely as a Mbyá, avoiding, by all possible means, any ambivalence. But true divinity can be reached only when one travels the path of suffering and pain to *Ivy marã ey*.

Nimuendaju saw the migration to *Ivy marã ey* as sign of an intrinsic melancholy and pessimism of the Guarani—traits that antedated, in his opinion, the arrival of the Europeans. Eduardo Viveiros de Castro disagrees:

> Perhaps he [Nimuendaju] and his followers may have confused what seems to us to be a tragic conception of life with its counterfeit look-alike: pessimism. Perhaps, having analyzed it thoroughly, Nimuendajú failed to perceive that behind Guarani cataclysmology there lies a highly subtle blend of hope and dejection, passion and action, and that its negative appearance masks a powerful affirmative force: amid their misery, humans are gods. (1987, xxiv)

Ayvu Rapyta includes several sacred hymns; a list of rules dictated by the divine fathers, which tell the Mbyá how to behave in regard to agriculture, marriage laws, and general health; healing formulas, animal narratives, and children's songs. Its general precepts, hymns, and prayers, are still followed and sung by the Mbyá of today. As an anthology, *Ayvu Rapyta* demonstrates the richness of Mbyá-Guarani literature, and the intense religiosity of these people, helping us understand the beliefs of other Tupi-Guarani as well. Both Hélène Clastres and Eduardo Viveiros de Castro, for instance, emphasize the similarities between the eschatology of the Mbyá-Guarani and that of other contemporary groups (such as Apapokuva, Jeguakáva, Araweté, and Urubu-Kaapor, among others), also comparing their beliefs with those of the colonial Tupinambá.

The Guarani groups who presently live on the coast of São Paulo and Santa Catarina,[20] and those who inhabit villages on the periphery of the city of São Paulo, are descendants of the same Indians who journeyed, at the end of the nineteenth century, in search of *Ivy marã ey*. Until the 1960s, most of these groups who lived in the Atlantic forest near the coast were able to stay in their villages without being disturbed by non-Indians. Speculators who acquired land in the region in the 1940s and 1950s "allowed" the Guaranis to maintain their lifestyle as long as the Indians witnessed in their favor for legal possession of land. Since the Guaranis were not interested in ownership, they readily agreed. After the 1970s, with the construction of the Rio-Santos tourist highway, prices of land soared, and the Guaranis were threatened with expulsion. With the help of activists, most groups managed to have their territories, or parts of them, demarcated in the 1980s (Ladeira and Azanha). Today, the villages on the coast and the ones on the periphery of São Paulo function as a network for mutual help and marriages. The selling of handcrafts, the Guarani's main economic activity, is done mostly in the city of São Paulo. Moreover, the two city villages (Morro da Saudade and Pico do Jaraguá) are an obligatory stop for Guarani individuals or families who travel from the coast of São Paulo to visit relatives in Santa Catarina, Paraguay, and Argentina, as well as for Guaranis from these places who travel to the coast.

As all recent studies about the Guarani emphasize, the *Ñandereko*—the Guarani way of being—is the most important concept in their philosophy and everyday life. Without land, the Guarani are not able to keep their *Ñandereko*. In order to maintain it, they need a bit of forest to hunt, rivers to fish, and a garden where they can plant maize, gourds, beans, and medicinal plants. Thus, if a Guarani group is threatened, they join other Guaranis, or they go back to walking, until they find a spot that has all of these characteristics. In many places, however, this second option is not available anymore. In the state of Mato Grosso do Sul, near the city of Dourados, the Kaiowá-Guarani share a reservation with a few Kandevá (Apapokuva) Guarani and a larger number of Terena. The reservation was demarcated in the 1930s, but in the 1950s, under the leadership of a Terena, the land was divided among the Indians themselves into private lots. This, plus the outside pressure of farmers and missionaries, and the super-population inside the reservation, has led to a desperate situation for the Kaiowá-Guarani. As a result, the suicide rate among them has reached epidemic proportions in the last ten years. In an attempt to alleviate the problem, some Kaiowá have brought shamans from Paraguay to teach them traditional songs and prayers.[21]

Still today, texts in Tupi and Guarani are being collected in Bolivia (Riester), Argentina (Vargas), and the Guianas (Grenand), as well as in Brazil (Mindlin; Castro, 1986) and Paraguay. At the same time, Indian activism among Tupi and Guarani groups has generated another kind of literature, signed by the Indians themselves with or without the mediation of non-Indians. An example is the rewriting of the historic episode known as "Tamoio Confederation" by the Tapirapé in 1984, in the form of cartoons, published by Eunice Dias de Paula. The most important text along these lines is *Oré Awé Roiru'a ma: Todas as Vezes que Dissemos Adeus*, by Kaka Werá Jecupé (no date, but after 1992). As the first literary work to be published in Brazil under the name of an individual native author, it points to a future of native literatures in that country, and will be analyzed in the epilogue of this book.

chapter 5
Romanticism and After

I
T IS IMPOSSIBLE TO DISCUSS THE IMPACT of Tupi-Guarani texts on South American literature in Spanish and Portuguese without first making some
reference to Romanticism. In Spanish America, it is precisely the dearth
of texts during a period by definition attuned to native America that is of
interest, and which now in modern times is being powerfully compensated
for. In Brazil, by contrast, the Tupi occupied the center of the discussions
about identity after Independence, and the key role then attributed to
them, along with the ensuing negative reaction, has ever since affected
writing about Indians in American Portuguese.

Southern Approaches

The Spanish American countries whose native populations include or have
included Tupi-Guarani speakers lie in and around the southern part of the
lowland territory, in Uruguay and Paraguay (whose very names are Guarani),
Argentina, and even parts of Bolivia. Here, as Gordon Brotherston observes:
"At this same early stage of events, nothing on quite the scale of the Brazilian
Indianist enterprise can be found . . . , perhaps because of the more powerful
legacy there of a church and crown committed to converting and reducing the
American heathen" (1987, 62). The main source for those Spanish-speaking
writers who did turn to native sources was Barco Centenera's *The Argentine*
(1602), among whom pride of place is taken by Juan María Gutiérrez. In the

1870s, Gutiérrez made a lengthy study of Centenera's work, having drawn heavily on it when composing Guarani verse legends of his own, "Caicobé" and "Irupeya" (1843). The former alludes to ideas of metamorphosis, in this case of a woman into a tree. The stories derive directly from Guarani, as Gutiérrez himself makes clear to his reader by quoting his source stanza in *The Argentine* as an epigraph and in a note that demonstrates how the very syllables of the title denote a life force shared by humans, other species, and even plants. "Irupeya" recalls the story of Liropeya and Yandubayu told in *The Argentine*. This episode was also echoed in Uruguay, in the poetry of Adolfo Berro (1819–41) and in Zorrilla de San Martín's far better known *Tabaré*.

With a notable lack of bibliographical honesty towards Centenera and, in any case, the Guarani, Juan Zorrilla de San Martín composed *Tabaré* (1888) with the typically Romantic idea of its becoming a national epic. The name of the eponymous hero, like that of Uruguay itself, could be felt to indicate a cultural precedent that would distinguish the newborn nation from Europe. In fact, travelers' accounts provide *Tabaré*'s very few effective links with the Guarani, through the names of the hero and other leading characters, and of many trees and birds—not least the *sabiá* immortalized by the Brazilian Gonçalves Dias. The plot unfolds among the Charrúa Indians, whose territory is however never actually named except for one or two rivers, despite the massive legacy of Guarani toponymy in the Republic of Uruguay. The Indians are silenced and dematerialized, according to a logic that hideously combines "progress" with Spanish Counter-Reformation principles of "honor." Doris Sommer, who includes *Tabaré* in her list of "foundational fictions," comments that the story of the "blue-eyed" mestizo Tabaré represents an *indigenismo* that was very different, indeed, from its counterpart of the time in Brazil, where quite other views on *mestiçagem* were expressed by Alencar:

> Instead of Alencar's casting of Iberian racial hygienists as the prehistoric and now absent causes of a new mestizo nation, Zorrilla's latter-day indigenism gave that vanishing role to Indians. And his mestizos were hardly a racial improvement but rather a self-destructing, sterile hybrid, rather like sentimental donkeys. Tabaré is half Indian and half "human" (Zorrilla, 1259), as Zorrilla writes in a candidly racist moment that survived four corrected editions. (245)

As a foundational statement, *Tabaré* was later echoed in national epic poetry produced in twentieth-century Uruguay, notably Sara de Ibáñez's *Canto a Montevideo* (1942), which makes good, as if deliberately, the territorial vagueness of its predecessor, relishing the sounds and meanings of Guarani place names in Uruguay.

At the start of the twentieth century, a quite different line of connection was established in the short stories of Horacio Quiroga, the Uruguayan who became a "pioneer" in the subtropical northern forests of Argentina, in Misiones. Critics have correctly diagnosed Quiroga's ideology and perception of the "jungle" as hostile and threatening; yet as Bareiro Saguier has carefully shown (1990), the culture of the Guarani-speakers in Misiones has had a palpable impact on several of the stories. As their titles indicate, "La vuelta de Anaconda," "Yasy-yataré," and "En el Yabebirí" take the reader into the world beyond individualist fantasy or terror, where the sacred Guarani animals converse and become protoganists; through the references to death as *aguara* in the last of these stories, there are even hints of *Ayvu Rapyta* eschatology.

Quiroga's adoption of Guarani animal lore was taken up by his Argentinian near-contemporary Ricardo Güiraldes, in a little-noticed chapter of *Don Segundo Sombra* (1924), like Gallegos's *Doña Bárbara* one of the "exemplary novels" of Spanish American regional narratives. Güiraldes's pagan Guarani tale is told around the gaucho campfire (chapter xii) and as such is matched and cancelled later in the novel by a folktale that is heavily Christian in its cultural reference (chapter xxi). It concerns the recovery of a young woman who lived on the banks of the Parana and who, like several of her kind, has been bewitched by the Añang, a bird-like shaman or "devil" who turns these prizes into flamingos and other birds. Often neglected in criticism, this tale inset into *Don Segundo Sombra* is important in exemplifying, vividly, the native part of the mestizo gaucho's origins, even though (or just because) the novel goes on to cancel out this heritage.

In the River Plate tradition common to Uruguay and Argentina, all this has been profoundly changed in quite recent years, as a result of the work of Eduardo Galeano (*Genesis,* 1982) and of Abel Posse (*Daimón,* 1987, the first of an unfinished trilogy of novels), who share both a continental scope and profound interest in native origins. After the powerful political diagnosis of *The Open Veins of Latin America* (1971), Galeano cast deeper in his search for the roots of his continent's reality. The first section of *Genesis* is entirely devoted to native texts, which provide the platform and premise on which all succeeding history rests. Opening with the So'to Carib creation story, Galeano here turns most frequently to passages from Tupi-Guarani cosmogony, as it had been made available by Nimuendaju and Cadogan: "The First Father of the Guaranis rose in darkness lit by reflections from his own heart and created flames and thin mist. He created love and had nobody to give it to. He created language and had no one to listen to him" (11). For his part, Posse appeals to native America as the only effective antidote and cure for the "demon" behavior of the invading Europeans. Quoting songs and legends from the *Ivy marã ey* doctrine, he focuses on the pilgrimage west to the Andes, precisely to the remote city of Chachapoyas reached by the Tupi in 1549: there, representatives from native groups all over the continent assess their predicament on the eve of 1992 (when such a conference was in fact held nearby in Quito), in the company of the animals and the plants who, in line with Tupi-Guarani and Native American lore generally, are able to communicate and be communicated with:

> Not just humans, animals as well. Groups of jaguars, delegates of the Becacinas, pumas from the pampas, owners of traditional estates, families of monkeys, delegations of gaucho mastiffs, pamiperrunos; with the discretion characteristic of the animal kingdom they marauded the outskirts of the Circular Cities. (232)

Certain scholars in Argentina and Uruguay have compared Posse's perspective on America with that of Centenera's early seventeenth-century epic *Argentina* (Vittori, 103; Giorgi, 135).

Of the three southern-rim countries, Uruguay, Argentina, and Paraguay, this last presents the most unusual model with regard to Guarani texts; Guarani has always been widely spoken there, and is nowadays one of the country's two official languages. After the experience of the Jesuit Missions, it was used in proclamations issued by General Belgrano and other heroes of the Independence; today it continues to enjoy social and political acceptance and is used by poets and in the theater. Yet the effective contact with the older and pagan Guarani tradition—for example the doctrines of creation and of language itself—has been minimal and is still less felt in literature written in Spanish with native pretensions. In Paraguay, we can hardly talk about a Romantic movement, thanks, in the first place, to the long Francia dictatorship, and, later, the war against Argentina, Brazil, and Uruguay. During that war, a vast amount of nationalist poetry was certainly written in Guarani, yet none of it refers to the indigenous cultures, or makes any intertextual contact with them. This peculiar characteristic of Paraguayan literature in Guarani has been exhaustively analyzed by Rubén Bareiro Saguier, whose works I will quote at length. According to him, it is the result of "the dynamic of the colonial process" (1980), which has continued well into this century, deeply restricting the range of literary reference and the effective contact with non-Western ideology. The "indigenist generation" from the first half of the twentieth century, for instance, in spite of having access to Nimuendaju's collection, rehearses the colonialist distortions of the Jesuit priests, who converted Tupã into the monotheistic god of the Guarani. This is the case with Narciso Colmán (Rosicrán), who wrote long poems in Guarani, including a "cosmogony" called *Ñande Ypykuéra* (1929), considered by the Paraguayan *indigenistas* as "the most representative work in Guarani and on Guarani culture" (1990, 119). According to Bareiro Saguier "In this work the author bows servilely to all the conditionings of the colonial missions" and presents Tupã as "the Supreme God of the Guarani" (1990, 118). For this critic:

> Indigenist self-contradiction goes far in the work of Narciso R. Colmán. In some cases it takes the grotesque form of colonial contempt for the native: hence when he defines the Yvyjaú he says: "A nocturnal bird of Paraguay, famous for its sloth . . . It is like the Indians in its laziness or slovenliness."
> (1990, 119)

The most important theoretician of this nationalist/indigenist group is the poet and essayst Natalicio González, who was for six months (1948/49) president of Paraguay. González confirms, in *Proceso y formación de la cultura paraguaya* (1938), that Tupã is "the greatest of the Guarani gods, or rather the only god, since the other spirits are mere creative forces who contribute by their actions to the constructive process of the world, but have no divine essence" (quoted in Bareiro Saguier 1990, 121). The same idea is repeated in his poem "Credo" (Creed):

> Pale Christ, I am not a Christian.
> In our heaven, the great Tupang dwells.
>
> I believe in Tupang, my strong native God,
> and in his power to defeat the wicked.
> (quoted in Bareiro Saguier 1990, 120)

Natalicio González's ideas continued to influence Paraguayan literature at least until the seventies, as is evidenced by a group of poets whom Bareiro Saguier calls "courtly" (1990, 107), and who used generic concepts such as *raza guaraní* (Guarani race) in order to support Alfredo Stroessner's dictatorship: "To march united along burning paths/ In quest of its ideals, facing the future,/ Of a noble nation, the Guarani fatherland" (Angel Peralta Arellano's *La epopeya de la selva*, quoted in Bareiro Saguier 1990, 108).

The ideas and practices of the "nationalist generation" were definitely superseded in the work of intellectuals and dramatists like Rudi Torga, the novelist Roa Bastos, and critics like Bareiro Saguier himself. An early challenge was issued by Augusto Roa Bastos who, besides translating and editing native texts in the fashion of José María Arguedas, has incorporated them intricately into his own work. The poems gathered in *El naranjal ardiente (Nocturno paraguayo) 1947–49* reveal how native values may foster not official dogmas of nationhood but resistance to decades of savage dictatorship, among them, a set of seven poems written in Guarani, "Ñane ñe'ême," and another set of five "Yñypyru," which switches between Guarani and Spanish. The dedications to Nimuendaju, Cadogan, and Meliá indicate the Guarani source texts Roa Bastos drew upon here.

In his novel *Son of Man* (1960), the presence of Guarani language and beliefs disturbs the massive use of biblical imagery, in ways thoroughly studied by Bareiro Saguier. As he demonstrates, the struggle between the two belief systems, Christian and Guarani, is already present in the two epigraphs of the novel, one taken from the Bible (Ezekiel), and the other from *Ayvu Rapyta*: "I have to make the voice flow again through the bones . . . And I shall again make speech incarnate . . . After this time is lost and a new time dawns." Thus, the character María Rosa, "in the crucial moment when she regains the lucidity of madness, she invokes the notion of Guarani reincarnation, the new flowering of the bones, and the continuity of life in the territory of death" (Bareiro Saguier 1990, 138). The very notion of death in the novel is Guarani rather than Christian: True to the epigraph quoted above, the novel often invokes the "Himno de los muertos" (Hymn of the Dead) from *Ayvu Rapyta*: "Ho'áta che ári keraná pukú" ("An intense and long dream will fall over me," 318). This dream, as Bareiro Saguier explains, "is described with concrete characteristics, in firmly material detail" which comes from a Guarani notion of death: "Far from the sadness that normally surrounds Christian death, it is defined by sensorial, even sensual expressions. Hence the Guarani idea of death and resurrection is imposed on that of Catholicism" (1990, 145).

The search for *Ivy marã ey* is also a recurrent theme in *Son of Man*. When the characters Casiano, Natí, and the baby are trying to escape from the *yerbal,* for instance, "they dragged themselves towards the setting sun" (138), as in the Guarani migrations to the west (Bareiro Saguier 1990, 146). Moreover, these same three characters are saved thanks to the intervention of a *jaguarate'i,* the Guarani sacred animal.

In the novel *I, the Supreme* (1974), Roa Bastos subverts the morphology of the Spanish language by drawing on the structure of Guarani, "its polysynthetic or agglutinative nature, which allows—with great ease— for the construction of semic units on the basis of a central, or radical element, that is modified by the multiple addition of prefixes and suffixes" (Bareiro Saguier 1990, 69–70). Guarani texts and beliefs influence, as well, the very structure of the novel. The protagonist The Supremo, for instance, internally divides into several manifestations of himself—a device that owes a lot, according to Martin Lienhard, to the Guarani notion of "word-souls":

One of the above-mentioned mythological elements—the 'word-soul'—may, it seems, explain some of the specific features of the dictator. The Supremo—a literary specter—has a soul that could be called a 'text-soul,' a term related to 'word-soul' . . . In the case of the Supremo, two souls appear to differentiate themselves, folding out: the soul turned into a specter (the image in the mirror) and the 'word-soul' (the 'voice'), bestowed on the character by the compiler. (1978, 8)

Linked to that, the multiplication of the narrative voice in the novel derives from the Guarani notion of "double":

We conclude that the division of the character into I/HE (above all due to narrative necessity) and that of the text/intertext (which reflects the conditions of its production), finds its equivalent in the division of all beings and objects in mythology . . . We intuit that one of the achievements of *I, the Supreme* is to have made certain narrative needs (the division of a character with a view to producing a kind of dialogue) or consequences of intertextuality (the affirming of autogenesis on the part of the Supremo) coincide with features of the mythological substratum of America: this shows us a possible solution to the problem which working with an imported bourgeois genre poses for the Latin American novelist. (Lienhard 1978, 8)

That notion is explained in the novel by the chief *nivaklé*:

All beings have doubles. But the double of a human being is one and triple at the same time. Sometimes more. Each one of these souls is different from the others, but despite their differences they form a single one. I tell the interpreter to ask the Nivaklé if that is like the mystery of Christianity: a single God in three different Persons. The sorcerer laughs dryly, without parting his lips puckered with tatoos. No, No! That's not how it is with us, the men-of-the-forest! (169)

As a whole, the dictator Francia's court in *I, the Supreme* becomes the arena for prolonged and brilliant debates between Christians on the one hand, and on the other, philosophers true to older notions of duality, autogenesis, and the electric presence of the blue jaguar (who guards the Guarani sky in the Apapokuva-Guarani creation story published by Nimuendaju) as in the following example:

The Twins were not born of a mother; the so-called Mother-of-Mothers, so the indigenous payés who know their cosmogonies say, was devoured by the Blue-Jaguar that sleeps beneath the hammock of Ñanderuvasú, the First-Great-Father. The twins were born of themselves and engendered their mother. They inverted the idea of maternity, mistakenly considered to be the exclusive gift of women. They canceled out the difference between the sexes, so dear and so indispensable to Western thought, which can operate only by pairs. They conceived, or rediscovered the possibility, not only of two, but of many, of innumerable sexes. (132)

The Warrior Hero of Brazil

Although Brazilian nineteenth-century *Indianismo* lasted over fifty years and produced more than thirty works, it is usually identified with Gonçalves Dias's "Americanas" (1846), with José de Alencar's novels *O Guarani* (1857), *Iracema* (1865), and *Ubirajara* (1874), and, to a much lesser degree, with Gonçalves de Magalhães's epic poem *A Confederação dos Tamoios* (1856). Given the importance of these works for Brazilian literature and literary historiography, my focus will also be on them. More specifically, I shall concentrate on Gonçalves Dias's "Americanas," for its unique use of colonial and (indirectly) native sources.[1]

While nineteenth-century scientists were mostly interested in the Indians as *Botocudos,* writers continued to devote their attention to the Tupis. As Manuela Carneiro da Cunha says: "What the Tupi-Guarani are to nationality, the Botocudos are to science" (1992, 136). By concentrating on the *Botocudos,* scientists tried to answer questions related to a segment of the Brazilian population that had not been incorporated by the newborn nation in its process of self-definition. The Botocudos were the "wild Indians," as opposed to the Tupi ("gentle Indians"). They were the "strange Indians"—or, to use a term overemployed by recent anthropology, the *other.*[2] Literature, on the other hand, was not concerned with otherness in those terms. Its main preoccupation was how to explain and incorporate the pre-European past into the history of the country, forging a national culture and a "truly Brazilian" national history. With that in mind, those writers examined the historical documents available to them, or which they recognized to be such: chronicles, Jesuit letters and documents, and travelogues. In order to understand *Indianismo,* we have to understand the Romantics' dependence on these colonial sources—a voluntary dependence, explained by those writers' intentions: They wanted to create heroes of the past and make them go through the epic adventures that came to constitute, from then on, the legendary past of Brazil. Within that context, we can understand—not justify—the lack of interest that most of those writers had in contemporary Indians.

If the sources used by the Romantic *Indianistas* were mainly colonial, their inspiration, as it were, came mostly from such contemporaries as René de Chateaubriand (*Atala,* 1801, and *The Natchez,* 1826) and James Fenimore

Cooper (*The Leatherstocking Tales*, 1823–41). The French Luso-Brazilianist critic and writer Ferdinand Dénis (himself the author of an Indianist novel, *The Matchakalis*, 1823) also had a crucial influence, by suggesting, in his widely read *Résumé de l'Histoire Littéraire du Portugal, suivi du Résumé de l'Histoire Littéraire du Brésil* (1826) that:

> The New World could not be without notable traditions; in a few centu-
> ries hence, the present age, in which its independence was established,
> will inspire noble and moving evocations. Its age of mysterious and poetic
> fables is the centuries when there lived the peoples we are exterminating
> and which surprise us by their courage, and who maybe have tempered the
> nations who came from the Old World: remembering their wild majesty
> fills the soul with pride, their religious beliefs enliven the deserts; the poetic
> songs preserved by some nations will enhance the forests. The marvel-
> ous, so necessary to poetry, can be found in the ancient customs of these
> peoples, as in the incomprehensible strength of a nature whose phenomena
> are constantly in flux: if this American nature is more splendid than that
> of Europe, why then should its peoples be inferior to the heroes of Greece's
> fabled past, these men who could never be made to groan even once under
> the most horrible torture, and who would ask their enemies to torture them
> further, because the suffering made their glory the greater? (31)

Even the Emperor D. Pedro II agreed with Dénis's suggestions, giving his imperial blessing to Gonçalves de Magalhães's epic *A Confederação dos Tamoios,* published in 1856 as the Brazilian "national poem."

A Confederação dos Tamoios celebrates in ten long cantos the historical confederation that united Tupinambás, Goitacás, Guaianás, and Tamoios against the Portuguese invaders from 1554 to 1557. But Magalhães was not the most talented of the *Indianistas*. His poem is a failed epic: As Antônio Cândido de Mello e Souza observes, the hero Aimbirê has too many un-resolvable contradictions to be considered a true epic hero (65). Also, if it is true that *A Confederação dos Tamoios* takes the side of the Tamoios, the only solution it presents for the Indians is to embrace the Catholic religion. In that sense, the Jesuits José de Anchieta and Manuel da Nóbrega are, more than the Indians, the true heroes of the poem. São Sebastião, the patron-saint of Rio de Janeiro, reveals to Aimbirê in a dream that the Indians' fight is useless, and that their true time of opposing the Portuguese will come later, as members of the independence-seeking Brazilian nation.

José de Alencar is considered the most important novelist of Romanti-cism and *Indianismo* in Brazil. He began his career publishing articles under the pseudonym Ig, in *Diário do Rio de Janeiro*, criticizing Gonçalves de Magalhães's *A Confederação dos Tamoios*. He complains that Magalhães neglected the prettiest idea of painting: the historical sketch of these extinct races, the origin of these unknown peoples, the primitive traditions of the Indians, gave in themselves alone material for a great poem, which perhaps one day someone will produce quietly and simply, as the modest fruit of his labors. (quoted in Castello 6)

Alencar himself tried to write a better epic, "Os Filhos de Tupã," but left it unfinished. He became, instead, a prolific novelist and a conservative politician. Of his three Indianist novels, O Guarani and Iracema can be considered foundational fictions (to borrow Doris Sommer's terminology)—that is, texts which, by being read widely and taught at primary schools, come to represent a certain idea of nationhood:

These romances have been practically sacralized through frequent editions, adoption in school curricula, Carlos Gomes's opera Il Guaraní (1870; in Italian, naturally), multiple movie versions (the only examples on record of a novel being filmed four or five separate times), and the countless Brazilian children named for Alencar's artificial Indians. (Sommer 140–41)

As foundational fictions, they set up the racial pattern of the country, accepting and justifying Indian-white racial miscegenation: Peri, the protagonist of O Guarani, ends the novel holding the white woman Ceci in his arms; and the Tabajara Indian Iracema (an anagram of America) dies after giving birth to the mestizo boy Moacir (whose name means "son of suffering"), a child of the Portuguese Martim.

O Guarani was heavily criticized by Alencar's contemporaries for having made the Brazilian Indians act like medieval Europeans. As a response to this criticism, Alencar argues, in an open letter published as a post-face to the second novel, that the poetic language of Iracema was based on literal translations from Tupi. In the same letter, the writer asserts that

Knowledge of the native language is the best criterion for the nationality of literature. That is what gives not just true style but the Indian's poetic images, his ways of thinking, the bent of his spirit and even the minute details of his life.

It is in this fountain that the Brazilian poet should drink; and this is the source from which the truly national poem, as I imagine it, will arise. (2000, 141)

And in fact, Alencar did study Tupi: In Iracema and Ubirajara he makes abundant use of Tupi words, or of literal translations of Tupi words, as in the example above. He also read the chroniclers, as he is eager to demonstrate in the footnotes appended to both novels, which constitute half the text in the case of *Ubirajara*. The title of this novel, for instance, is justified through a quote of Gabriel Soares de Sousa's *Tratado Descritivo do Brasil em 1587* (123). In *Iracema*, after the heroine tells Martim that, as a guest of her tribe, he can have its most beautiful women, we read the following note: "This custom of American hospitality is attested by the chroniclers" (217). The same novel reproduces the Tupi-Guarani welcome dialogue transcribed by various chroniclers:

> "You came?"
> "I came," the stranger responded.
> "May you be welcome. The stranger is lord in the cabins of Araquém." (92)

The dialogue is followed by a note giving the Tupi words: "The normal welcome was this: *Ere iobê,* you came? *Pa-aiotu,* Yes, I came. *Augebe,* welcome. See Léry, p. 286" (216).

In *O Guarani*, Alencar actually incorporates an indigenous narrative: Peri and Ceci escape the flooding waters of the Paraíba river by climbing on a palm tree, exactly as in the Guarani Flood story published by André Thevet. Yet Alencar's desire to set the foundations of Brazilian culture on conservative premises kept a rigid control over which aspects of the indigenous societies could appear in his works. The difficult subject of Tupi anthropophagy, for instance, is astutely discussed in *Ubirajara* in terms of Christian communion—a daring comparison for his time: "The remains of the enemy became, then, like a sacred host that strengthened the warriors: women and children received just a small portion. It was not revenge, but a kind of communion of the flesh, through which heroism was transferred" (139). And, when necessary, he can disagree with the chroniclers, especially if they appear to be "disrespecting" the Indians, in other words, making them too different from the European ideal. After describing the *tapacorá*, the red garter removed as soon as the young women had their first sexual intercourse, Alencar dismisses his sources and presents us with a patriarchal explanation for the custom, which includes concepts such as "fallen women," completely alien to Tupi morality:

> This simple detail is enough to give an idea of Tupi morality, and to vindicate it against the lies of the chroniclers who, failing to understand their customs, freely attributed to them everything that ill-informed and ill-prepared explorers made up about them.
>
> In what civilized society may we observe such profound respect for the conjugal bond, to the extent of not allowing the fallen woman to keep the secret of her fall, and hoodwink the man who would wed her? (125)

In spite of the novelist's frequent comments on the natives' "natural religiosity," his novels show, most of the time, a clear disrespect for the concrete ways in which such religiosity is manifest: In *Iracema,* the actions of the shaman Araquém (the heroine's father) are unmasked as a cunning way of deceiving the other Indians. And in *O Guarani,* he describes in some detail the "barbarous rituals" of the "bad" Aimoré Indians.

Stripped of any cultural behavior that could seem embarrassing to European eyes, the hero-Indians created by José de Alencar could be described as an improved version of the Europeans themselves. In other words, they are Europeans who have not yet been corrupted by civilization. The European character chosen by Alencar as a term of comparison for his proto-European Indian is the medieval knight. In *O Guarani,* the parallels between medieval Europe and colonial Brazil are abundant: the room of D. Antonio de Mariz (Ceci's father) is decorated with heraldic symbols, and his own house "served as a feudal castle from the Middle Ages." He is described as a *fidalgo* (nobleman), a "nobleman who was bound to give protection and shelter to his vassals," and when he meets Peri, he gives the Indian a "fraternal embrace sanctioned by the statutes of ancient chivalry, of which by then just a few vague traditions remained," and so on.

Alencar's "Indian knight" has become, in literary criticism, a synonym of *Indianismo* itself. Differences between Alencar and his contemporaries are often ignored by critics anxious to perpetuate what is perhaps one of the most pervasive clichés of Brazilian literary historiography: All the Indians created by the *Indianistas* are simply colorful, exotic versions of European medieval heroes. Except for their gear and a few token behavioral traits, the Romantics' Indians are said to have little or no connection with the Brazilian Indians. In other words, they are simply another version of traditional European characters.

Yet if we take a careful look at Gonçalves Dias's poems, especially the earlier ones published under the heading "Poesias Americanas" (1846), we will find that even though his sources may be the same as Alencar's, his way of using them, and the results he obtains, are dramatically different. First of all, Gonçalves Dias's poems do not present Alencar's desire to justify, on any grounds, racial miscegenation. Son of a white man and a woman who has been described as a Carajá Indian (Lúcia Miguel-Pereira), a Black (Darcy Ribeiro in Sá, 1993) and a *cafusa,* or Black and Indian mestizo (Treece), Gonçalves Dias suffered, as many biographers and critics have said, the consequences of racial and social prejudices. In the prose work "Meditação" (1849), he wrote about the situation faced by the *caboclo* (white and Indian mestizo) population, and about the life of detribalized Indians in the urban centers, as well as of African slaves.[3] Years later he became truly committed to the subject, publishing several articles expressing opinions and giving information about the native cultures. And as a member of a "Scientific Expedition" he went to the Amazonian region of Rio Negro. In Europe, he compiled a Tupi dictionary in 1858, and in 1867 he published the book *O Brasil e a Oceânia,* comparing the Brazilian Indians to the aborigines of Australia and presenting some theories about migration routes followed by the Tupi prior to the arrival of the Portuguese. This book, along with some of his articles on the subject, are a confessed attempt to trace the history of Brazil before the arrival of the Portuguese.

Also, unlike Alencar's conciliatory view of the conquest, the poems of Gonçalves Dias often refer to the destruction of Indians by the white colonizers. In fact, if we read eight of the ten Indian poems included in the series "Americanas" in the order in which they appear, we will see that they offer us a chronological description of the colonization process. The first poem, "O Canto do Guerreiro" (The Warrior Song), is the boasting of an Indian man before going to war:

> Who took in war
> as many foes?
> Who sings his deeds
> with more verve?
> Who strikes fatal
> blows, as I do?
> –Warriors, hear me
> –Warriors, who can compare with me?[4] (97)

It is similar to the Tupinambá prewar boasting songs described by the chroniclers. Abbeville, for instance, reports that before a war the Tupinambás

> choose for a chief the one they judge the ablest and bravest, and he goes from hut to hut rousing the men, telling them with great shouts how they should get ready for war. He shows them as well that it is important to come across as courageous, since they would lose through cowardice, to their dishonor, the warrior fame of the nation that their forefathers had won. (229–30)

The Europeans are not mentioned in the poem, and it could be said to describe the Tupi before the arrival of the colonizers.

In the second poem, "O Canto do Piaga" (The Sorcerer's Song), the coming of the white people—men who will arrive from the sea bringing much suffering to the Indians—is already announced to the shaman:

> Ah! who came from the water's depth
> sniffs and seeks out our lands
> —that monster, what brings it here?
>
> You wonder what the monster wants?
> You wonder why it comes, what it desires?
> It comes to kill your brave warriors
> It comes to rob you of daughter and wife!
> (101)

As Florestan Fernandes points out, the shamanic foreseeing of enemy attacks was already described by the *cronistas*:

> The rites for interpreting dreams constituted the other way of foreseeing
> the course of war. The telling of dreams was done in public, the shaman
> being responsible for their interpretation. The content of dreams would in
> fact denote the chain of events, this being beyond doubt for the Tupinambá.
> Thanks to dreams, they knew beforehand whether they would win the war
> or be defeated by their enemies. When the evidence pointed to the latter
> outcome, they gave up the projected campaign. (1970, 77)

In the third poem, "O Canto do Índio" (The Indian's Song), we see how the fascination with the white culture, represented by a blonde woman, may drive the Indians to slavery:

> I loathe your kin as I love you;
> Yet should you wish to be mine, I promise
> to overcome my old hate for your love;
> to trade the heavy mace for tools
> and, enjoying you, to be their slave. (104)

In "Deprecação" (Insult), an Indian invokes Tupã, the Tupi-Guarani thunder deity, who was given the status of monotheistic God by the Missionaries, about the punishment he is imposing on the Indians by sending them the whites:

> Pitiless Anhangá brought from afar
> the men who shoot bloody lightning
> who live homeless, wander senseless
> panting after gold
>
> And the land they tread, and the fields and the rivers
> they injure, are ours; you are our God:

why do you grant them such power
if the deadly rays that they aim are yours? (105)

"Tabira," the following poem, is a chant sung by enslaved Indians, telling the blacks, with whom they share the *senzala* (slave quarters), how the whites had betrayed their chief Tabira:

Their force shrunk, the invaders
sign a treacherous peace with him
and he sleeps trusting unscathed in the treaty,
for Tabira is brave and loyal.
Without Tabira, what would the invaders' fate have been?
Without Tabira, who keeps and defends them,
who perhaps regrets the accord
splintered already to his loss. (109)

A dramatic dialogue, "I-Juca-Pirama," the best known of the series, narrates the humiliation suffered by the last two representatives of a Tupi nation, who become prisoners of the Timbiras. Although dealing with the conflict between Tupis and Timbiras, the destruction brought by the whites is, once again, a theme of the poem:

And the fields razed
and the bows broken
and the sorcerers glum
rattle-less
and the mild singers
in the fief of lords
who came, crookedly,
with signs of peace. (126)

"I-Juca-Pirama" starts with the prisoner being prepared to be killed and ritually devoured, in a description that closely follows the chronicles:

They pile up the wood in the huge blaze
they tighten the rope of the cage-net
they deck the clubs with fine feathers

while the women tread eagerly
used to the wild rite
anxious to finish the captive (122).

This slow, chronicle-like description is soon replaced by a faster rhythm, which corresponds to the drinking of the *cauim* (manioc beer):

> In deep bowls of whitish clay
> the *cauim* seethes
> the cups fill, merriment begins
> the orgy is on
>
> the captive whose death they crave
> sits there
> the captive who will never see the setting
> of another sun. (123)

The *cauim* and its ritualistic drinking before killing a prisoner are also described by the chroniclers. So is the location of the place without ill, seen in Abbeville:

> What do you feel, captive? Beyond the Andes
> the strong quicken anew
> having known to face the chill
> fear of death. (124)

The only element ingeniously added by Gonçalves Dias is the dramatic argument of the poem: The prisoner asks not to be killed because his blind father has no one to look after him, since all the other members of his tribe have been killed or enslaved by the whites.

In "Marabá," a woman cries because her mestizo condition makes her despised by the rest of the tribe. Finally, in "Canção do Tamoio" (The Tamoio's Song) the heroic tone of "The Warrior's Song" is recovered, in the voice of the father who encourages his newborn son never to give up fighting:

> Weep not, my son
> weep not, life is
> a keen struggle.
> To live is to strive
> life is a fight
> that brings down the weak
> that can only exalt
> the strong and the brave. (139)

The poem is based on the chroniclers' transcriptions of the words pronounced by the Tupinambá fathers to their newborn sons. Jean de Léry, for instance, explains that the father

> makes him a little wooden sword, a little bow, and little arrows feathered
> with parrot plumes; then, placing it all beside the infant, and kissing him,
> he will say to him, his face beaming, "My son, when you come of age, be

skilled in arms, strong, valiant, and warlike, so that you can take vengeance on your enemies." (154)

As we can see, Gonçalves Dias's use of the colonial sources goes much further than Alencar's descriptions of indigenous rituals and literal translations from Tupi. Gonçalves Dias incorporates in his poems genres described by the chroniclers: boasts, shamanic dreams, songs to the newborn. Also, exactly like the chroniclers' texts, his poems emphasize the courage and bellicosity of the Tupinambá and their enemies. Yet this bellicosity has often been attributed by critics to the poet's desire to equate, as Alencar would do later, native Brazilians with medieval Europeans. Antônio Cândido de Mello e Souza, for instance, talks about the poet's "Coimbra medievalism" (83), and, more recently, Cláudia Neiva de Matos presented the same argument in *Gentis Guerreiros* (1988). Given the recent date of this book, and the fact that it is one of the most important works ever written about Gonçalves Dias's poetry, I will concentrate on it in reviewing Gonçalves Dias's "medievalism." My comments should be seen not as an attempt to invalidate the critic's analysis, but as an alternative reading to hers, based on entirely different premises.

In *Gentis Guerreiros,* Gonçalves Dias's depiction of war activities among the Indians is said to have been based primarily on Montaigne:

> Hence in Gonçalves Dias's poetry Montaigne's vision prevails, and not the research of the travelers. Even in *O Brasil e a Oceania* there are passages that emphasize, as an explanation of tribal conflict, the affirmation of moral value based in both impulse and institution, rather than simple vindictive antagonism. (25–26)

And as an example of Gonçalves Dias's "Montaignian" view of the indigenous culture, Matos, who does not quote the chroniclers themselves, mentions the poet's depiction of *Ibaque,* the Tupi paradise:

> Yet what never ceases to be highlighted is that Ibaque is exclusively the domain of the strong, the reward of mystical virtue. This is how barbaric custom is justified; violence, cannibalism and war find their place in the ideological scheme of Gonçalves Dias's work as positive categories, confirmed within the very mystical-religious order in which the characters act. War is holy, is just, is natural, is at the core of life: "to live is battle endured," "to live is to fight." (27)

Yet in his 480-page *A Função Social da Guerra na Sociedade Tupinambá,* entirely based on chronicle texts, Florestan Fernandes arrived at conclusions that differ little from Gonçalves Dias's view:

for an individual to satisfy the demands inherent in the tribal system of
"social promotions" and to acquire sufficient "powers" or charismatic
qualities, if only in order to affirm his position in the *tujuaé* group, he
would have not only to carry out various warrior feats: he would have
himself to be a *warrior,* capable of acting as a "strongman" in all foreseeable
circumstance of armed combat with the enemy. This expectation was so
clear-cut, that it was mirrored even in the ritualized behavior of killer and
victim in the course of sacrifice. Those individuals whose personality was
too little grounded in bellicosity were condemned to a contemptible life on
earth, subject to being scornfully designated *cuave eim,* and to a problematic afterlife, since it would be most hard for them to gain access the company
of the forefathers. (Fernandes, 161)

Another sign of medievalism in Gonçalves Dias's poetry, according to
Matos, comes from the fact that the warriors' virtues were inherited from
their ancestors:

And whence does the courage, the merit of the famed warrior come?
Above all, from blood: "the weak do not descend from the strong," says
I Juca Pirama's aged father. Lineage, nobility, family crests: the whole
imaginative-ideological package brings Gonçalves Dias's Indianism close
to the aristocratic values comprised in the figure of the hidalgo in the
courtly ethic, or more precisely the way in which the courtly ethic was
poetically constructed by European Romanticism (27–28).

But as Florestan Fernandes observes, in the Tupinambá society described
by the chroniclers, bravery was actually passed from a man to his descendants, through a connection that was more complex than mere blood ties:
The descendants had the responsibility of maintaining the same level of
bravery of their ancestors—exactly what the father, in "I-Juca-Pirama"
demands from his son:

On the one hand, a *tujuaé* would never consider himself exempt from
having to "set an example," to young men in general, but of particular
significance for his own descendants. These last had to keep up the "level"
of the traditions concerning the ancestors and deceased kin, into which the
"examples"of those living were incorporated at once as norms of action.
(Fernandes 1970, 157)

In fact, nothing could be stranger to a medieval European logic than the
blind father's reaction in "I-Juca-Pirama," who curses his son because the
latter, putting filial love above courage, did not remain a prisoner among
the Timbira:

May the sky, like a roof in flames,
ever scorch and rack your wretched limbs
May the ocean of dark dust
be the land of this low Tupi!
Mean, needy and vile,
may the maracas not speak to you in dreams.

And may this coward be ever shadowed
by dread specters of terror
May you never have a kind friend
to embalm your body in the earth
carefully placing in a clay bowl
bow and arrow and club at your feet
Be cursed and lone on earth
for you sank so low
as to weep before death.
You, coward, are not my son. (134)

The medieval chivalric code is a Christian code, in which Christian values such as compassion and generosity are highly praised. In "I-Juca-Pirama," the Tupi hero is sacrificed by the Timbira even after he has shown the tribe that he does have a blind father for whom he is the only support, and only after he has demonstrated his courage by fighting against the whole group. The father, in his turn, applauds the killing:

The warrior got up, then fell into the arms
of his aged father, who held him to his breast
braying with tears of joy:
Yes, this is my dearly loved son
and since I find him, at last, as ever I had him,
may my tears flow freely
these indeed are tears that do no dishonor. (135–36)

Rather than displaying nobility in the medieval sense, the episode is in agreement with the description that the chroniclers make of the Tupi. According to Abbeville:

Although they could escape, given the freedom they enjoy, they never do despite knowing that they shortly will be killed and eaten. And this is because, if a captive flees, he would be considered at home a *cuave eim,* that is, a coward, and be killed by his own, insulted a thousand times for not having suffered torture and death at the hands of this enemy, as if his own nation were not powerful and brave enough to avenge him. (230–31)

The "beautiful death," attributed by Matos to the survival of chivalric codes in Gonçalves Dias's poetry (64–65), can be found not only in Abbeville, but in most colonial sources. Léry, for instance, observes that "although these barbarian nations feared natural death, their prisoners felt happy dying publicly among their enemies" (177).

The values in question bear no relation to Christianity. Instead, they refer to a religion in which, in the words of Florestan Fernandes, war played a key role:

> War was a substrate of tribal religion, being one of its determinations or, in other words, an *instrumentum religionis*; but thanks to this connection it became, reciprocally, one of the determinations of tribal religion. (160)

And if war had, in fact, the function of avenging the ancestors, the dynamics of the process were such that each act of revenge created the need for new acts of revenge, and so on—a circular movement that fulfilled a great part of the masculine life of the Tupi:

> In the confines of earthly life, the system of age categories held the social signs relevant to the stages passed through by individuals in this development, in which the *motus perpetuus* was the dead. The obligations of the living to them had a *circular character,* and the very act of "revenge" involved a holy pledge: in making their incisions, the killers exposed themselves anew to the "protest of revenge," rather than freeing themselves from it. (Fernandes, 153–54)

War was so important that "the Tupinamba system of 'social promotion' worked in such a way that those who had failed in a military undertaking could never place their ambitions and aspirations on the level of normal expectation" (Fernandes, 160). The same words could be used, undoubtedly, to describe Gonçalves Dias's heroes. In such a world, nobility and courage were, evidently, to be expected, and are not necessarily, as Matos and other critics desire, medieval values.

The Indians in Gonçalves Dias's poems belong to a complex warrior culture, similar to the one emphatically described by most chroniclers and studied by Florestan Fernandes in his work. Rather than contradicting his sources, Gonçalves Dias shows in his poems that he has carefully studied them. His idea was to write the history of Brazil, as he explicitly pointed out in an article in *Anais Históricos do Maranhão*.

> Certainly, the enslaving of the Indians was and would be a great mistake, and destroying them was and would be a great catastrophe. It is fitting that someone reveal to us to what degree that mistake was unjust and mon-

strous, and how far those catastrophes went in the past and how far they would go in the future: this is history.

It is also fitting that someone describe for us their customs, instruct us about their habits and their religion, reassemble for us that whole lost world, initiate us in the mysteries of the past and the road of the future, so that we may know where we came from and where we are going; it is fitting in sum that poets remember all this, since all this is poetry. And poetry is the life of the people, just as politics are its anatomy. (L. Pereira, 121)

In writing that history, he did not want to offer a conciliatory view of colonial violence, as Alencar would do later by defending miscegenation as a solution for the conflicts between Indians and whites. Yet in commenting on Gonçalves Dias's description of the enslavement of the Indians as a "calamity," Matos strays even further from native Brazil by proposing that, for the Indians, the consequences of the white invasion correspond to a biblical "Fall from Paradise" (her phrase):

Wrong-doing brings about calamity, and punishment: man driven from paradise. What was lost in this exile? A human order, a culture which the ethnologist describes revealing the other side of its utopia: a sensitive language (like that of poets), a religion indestructible in faith and in ritual, a strong monarchic government, all contributing to the maintaining of the manly values of courage and honor. If we exclude the first element, we note that the other three belong in common to an extremely closed value system, which is that of every conservative ideology, stuffed full of its truth and its absolutes. As I said earlier, this circle can suffer no breaks, and any break leads to explosion. An ethnocentrism well transferred and well defended, clearly. (41)

For those reasons, she sees the arrival of the whites in Gonçalves Dias's poems as the introduction of "Difference," and consequent destruction of the poet's "utopian view" of the Indians: "The White element is that Difference which identifies and/or provokes the rupture of a harmony based in Sameness; held in common are the unity of the tribe, the unanimity of the moral code, and the purity of the language" (35).

Yet for the Tupi nations of the coast of Brazil, the destruction represented by the arrival of the whites is an unquestionable fact. Millions of people died in the first years of colonization. Many were subject to slavery. Women and children were taken away. Land was irrecoverably stolen, religions and belief systems were ferociously attacked. To call this process a "fall from Paradise" is equivalent to describing the Holocaust as a "Jewish fall from Paradise": No ideas of Paradise are needed to contrast certain levels of violence and destruction. Whether or not those societies were paradisiacal or utopian (a claim that Gonçalves Dias never makes) does not change the fact that massive acts of violence were perpetrated against them.

Moreover, while José de Alencar never tried to establish connections between the Indians of the past and those who were still alive (and being killed) in his day, Gonçalves Dias, as Treece argues, does not avoid explicit references to those elements of the population that had been left at the margins of the Brazilian Empire. In "Meditação," for instance, we read:

> And the men of Indian blood and those of mixed race said aloud "And what shall we do?"
> What will be our place among the men who are masters, and the men who are slaves?
> We do not wish to share the bread of the slave, and we cannot sit at the table of the rich and powerful.
> And yet this blessed soil produces delicious fruits in all the seasons of the year—its forests abound with game—and its rivers are teeming.
> The whites govern—the blacks serve—it is right that we should be free.
> (quoted in English by Treece, 116)

And if the unfinished epic "Os Timbiras" begins by saying that he will sing the past glories of the "American people, now extinct," the poet goes on to describe an episode that is quite recent in the history of his own province, Maranhão:

> in addition to the now familiar historical pattern of Conquest and enslavement, the poem includes a lengthy denunciation of the legacy of annihilation and slavery bequeathed to the modern, "progressive" era of the nineteenth century. Futhermore, the poet's particular choice of subject matter, a war between the Timbiras and Gamelas, suggests that he wished to remind his readers that the nightmare of Conquest, the white man's persecution of the Indians and seizure of their lands, did not end in 1600 or even in 1755 but had continued on into their own century. (Treece, 123)

If denouncing the *Indianistas'* neglect of their contemporary Indians is correct with respect to José de Alencar, it is basically unfair when the target is the poetry of Gonçalves Dias. Similar affirmations can be made about the *Indianistas'* so-called avoidance of the theme of black slavery in their works. True enough, Iracema's son Moacir can then be read as a mestizo who occupies the place of another kind of mestizo: the "mulatto," on whose behalf the pro-slavery Alencar did not want to speak. But if Gonçalves Dias did not write abolitionist poetry in the style of later poets, such as Luiz Gama or Castro Alves, he often refers to black slaves, as in the poem "Tabira," in which Indians and blacks share their captive condition in the slave quarters (the poem opens with an unsigned epigraph, in French, saying that the blacks will sooner or later become free, but the Indians die when made into slaves); or in "Meditation," whose first pages describe Brazil as a beautiful country which is made ugly by its reliance on slavery.

Denouncing the Indianists' neglect of the question of slavery was undoubtedly a necessary step, duly taken by most critics who have treated the subject since at least the turn of the twentieth century. But in its name, *Indianismo* has been indiscriminately relegated to a category of less serious literature, or of a simple imitation of European models, without any connection, whatsoever, with the indigenous cultures of Brazil. Such generic classifications do not help us understand important differences between the authors, or the complexity that characterizes a movement which, with all its flaws, tried to face problems as complicated as cultural contact and identity, legitimacy of history, and the necessity of opening Brazilian culture to a new aesthetic sensitivity.

Moreover, if we can indeed accuse some Romantics of having no interest in the Indians who were still alive at their time, we can also say that most of their critics have gone even further by denying the indigenous cultures the very right to history. *Indianismo,* most of the time, is described as an Europeanized movement that owes very little, if anything at all, to the Brazilian Indians. Once more the Indians are written out of (literary) history. They gave nothing. Nothing was derived from them. They did not, as far as Brazilian culture is concerned, exist. Sílvio Romero, the nineteenth-century founding father of Brazilian literary criticism, is eloquent in this respect:

> A people that fled could not easily leave even its most marked characteristics imprinted on the body of those who took its place. The Indian is not a Brazilian. What the latter feels, seeks, hopes for and believes is not what the former felt, sought or believed. (239)

Altogether, the attitudes of most Romantics and their critics alike has had a baleful consequence, not often discussed: the avoidance of questions related to land ownership. By writing the Indians out of history, and by denying the *caboclos* and detribalized Indians any cultural connection with the indigenous cultures, we also deny them any claim to the land of their ancestors. The elimination of the Indians—physical or symbolic—solves the land disputes between the original inhabitants of the country and the big landowners, a problem that black slavery certainly did not pose, at least not in the same way. The abolitionist Joaquim Nabuco, a fierce critic of Alencar's *Indianismo,* is a good example of that. In his opinion, "the savage

dialects, the rudimentary religion, the confused myths, and the coarse customs" of the Indians did not deserve to be the focus of Brazilian literature
(Coutinho 190). Such intellectual contempt for the Indians and *Indianistas*
had also a very practical justification: In a diplomatic document defending
the Brazilian Government's policies against the Indians, Nabuco says:

> It is not a question of independent Indians but of rights over the territory.
> These wandering hordes do not constitute sovereign, independent nations
> according to right of peoples. They are subject to the jurisdiction and
> authority of the civilized nations and regular, recognized governments, to
> which the territory occupied by those hordes belong. (quoted in Treece, 218)

A less contemptuous post-Romantic view of the indigenous cultures in
nineteenth-century Brazil is given in Sousândrade's (Joaquim de Sousa
Andrade's) *O Guesa* (1888). This long and complex poem, impossible to
classify within any literary movement, has elements from several indigenous cultures and a continental scope. Tupi vocabulary plays an important
part in a satirical episode in Canto II, which is referred to as "Tatuturema"
by the critics Augusto and Haroldo de Campos (Campos and Campos,
1982). Although the episode does satirize *Indianismo,* it also incorporates
the spirit of that movement, insofar as the main focus of its critique is
the colonization process that Christianizes and corrupts the Indians. By
contrast, Lima Barreto's *The Patriot* (1911; 1915) satirizes this interest in
indigenous culture in the figure of its crazy "romantic" protagonist, a bu-
reaucrat who writes official documents in Tupi.

Antropofagia: Declarations of the 1920s

Joaquim Nabuco's motto ("We are Brazilians, not Guaranis")[5] echoes
strongly throughout the first decades of the twentieth century, provoking
debate and outright rejection, especially among the *modernistas.* As we saw
in chapter 2, the second phase of the São Paulo *Modernismo* replaced the
movement's original focus on the city with an increasing interest in nonurban popular culture; several writers and artists looked deeper, towards
indigenous cultures, thereby taking up the discussion about Brazilian
identity where the *Indianists* had left it. Among the native groups, the
Tupi became a main center of attention for these authors, especially the
Antropófagos (cannibalists) and their enemies, the *Verdeamarelistas* (from
verde [green] and *amarelo* [yellow], Brazil's national colors).

According to the *Antropófago* Raul Bopp (whose poem *Cobra Norato* is
discussed later), the concept was first used by the painter Tarsila do Amaral
when she and her husband, Oswald de Andrade, were having dinner with a
group of friends at a restaurant in São Paulo. On the menu: frogs.

When, amidst applause, the expected dish arrived, Oswald got up and
started to make an eulogy of the frog. He explained, with a good dose
of irony, the doctrine of the evolution of species. He quoted imaginary
authors, the Dutch "eggists," the "theory of the homunculus," in order to
prove that man's biological evolutionary line, in its long pre-anthropoid
phase, had included the frog—the same frog we were eating now between
sips of a chilled Chablis.

Tarsila interrupted:

—According to this argument, we arrive theoretically at the conclusion
that we are now acting like . . . semi-anthropophagists.

The thesis, in its joking tone, grew, generating a great play with ideas. We
quoted old Hans Staden and other scholars of antropophagy. (Bopp 1977, 40)

A few days later, still according to Bopp, the same group that had met in the
restaurant saw each other again at Tarsila's mansion, in order to "baptize"
a painting by her entitled "O Antropófago" (The Cannibal). In the irrev-
erence that had marked the beginnings of São Paulo *Modernismo* lay the
seeds for the *Antropofagia* movement.

At the core of the movement were those who started to publish the
Revista de Antropofagia in May 1928, first as a monthly independent magazine and later as a weekly page in *Diário de São Paulo,* a São Paulo daily.
The journal was first directed by Antonio de Alcântara Machado and
managed by Raul Bopp. Oswald's "Anthropophagite Manifesto" (hereafter
"Manifesto"), the most famous creation of the movement, was published in
the first number of this phase. In its second phase (or "teething," in the anthropophagite idiom), the *Revista* was directed alternatively by Raul Bopp
and Adour da Câmara.

The *Antropófagos* met frequently at Tarsila's and Oswald's house in order
to discuss new plans, and kept close contact with modernist publications
from other parts of Brazil. With time, verbal play gave way to more systematic attempts to discuss the "anthropophagic doctrines," and to a committed study of Brazilian history, re-posing Hamlet's question as "Tupi or not
Tupi." They also planned to form the "little anthropophagite library" *(bib-
liotequinha antropofágica),* which would include *Macunaíma* and "classics
of *Antropofagia*" chosen by the group: colonial travelers like Thevet, Jean de
Léry, Hans Staden, Claude d'Abbeville, and Yves d'Evreux; and more recent
ethnographic accounts and collections of native texts, such as those published by Couto de Magalhães, Barbosa Rodrigues, Koch-Grünberg, Karl
von den Steinen, and Brandão do Amorim.

The main ideological thrust of the *Antropófagos* was their critique of the
triumphalist West. The foundational moment that incorporated Brazilian

territory into the Western world (the arrival of the Portuguese) is seen by them as the repression of a preferable way of life: "Before the Portuguese discovered Brazil, Brazil had discovered happiness" (O. Andrade 1998, 538). The influence of Montaigne and Rousseau is evident here, and for that reason the modernists have been justifiably compared with the Romantics. Yet their main mode of discourse was parody (and self-parody), which kept them at a good distance from the Romantics's straight idealism. For the *Antropófagos,* it was important not to deny "barbarity," but to reaffirm it. "Barbarity," here in the form of anthropophagy and the Tupi goddesses Guaraci and Jaci, were the antidote to Christian patriarchal morality and to most failures of Western civilization:

> Against the truth of missionary peoples, defined by the sagacity of an anthropophagite, the Viscount of Cairu:—It is the often repeated lie.

> If God is the consciousness of the Uncreated Universe, Guaraci is the mother of the living. Jaci is the mother of plants. (O. Andrade 1998, 538)

Following the anti-Catholic tendencies of anthropophagy, the painter Flávio de Carvalho held his "Experiment number 2," a psychological study of crowds, in the middle of a Corpus Christi procession, and was almost lynched as a result.[6] In the *Revista,* we find repeated attacks on Catholicism. The violent trajectory of the Church, for instance, is the subject of the following text, signed with the pseudonym Japy Mirim:

> We know that the Church is an instrument of political domination. No more. From submission to authority, by Paul, to Athenagoras's Supplication to Marcus Aurelius and Commodus, to the crusades and the inquisition. Then we had the Pio VII's Bull. And now the "spiritual alliance" with fascism. The caraib nation, holding the club, watches its food approaching, dancing. The *cauim* is boiling. The mouth waters. (A. Campos 1975, 2nd teething, no. 2)

The expression "watches its food approaching, dancing" is a parodied quotation of Hans Staden's earlier captivity account.

The support from *Diário de São Paulo* came to an end when too many copies of the newspaper were returned by readers offended by the anti-Christian tone of *Revista de Antropofagia:*

> On a Thursday, the anthropophagite page of *Diário de São Paulo* published a quote from the New Testament: 'In truth, if you do what I tell you, in the Judgement Day you will be with me in Paradise.' The quote received the following title: BRIBE. Rubens do Amaral lost his patience. He asked for the page to be eliminated. (Bopp 1966, 78)

The group had also planned an anthropophagite conference in which they would discuss their "classics" and several anthropophagite doctrines. The conference, which never took place, was supposed to happen on 11 October, the "last day of free America" (i.e., the last before Columbus, who arrived on the twelfth).

It is in Oswald's "Manifesto" that *Antropofagia*'s philosophies are expressed more openly, if enigmatically. In its most famous sentence, Nabuco's motto ("We are Brazilians, not Guaranis") is recast in Shakespeare's English: "Tupi, or not Tupi, that is the question." The sentence satirically cannibalizes the English language, at the same time as it subverts Brazilian discourse through the use of English. It wants to bring the autochthonous Tupi to the center of the discussions about Brazilian culture, but it does so in English, an imported language, and via Shakespeare, a European author. In other words, it defends Brazilian cultural originality (through the Tupi) at the same time as it denies (through the use of English) the possibility of its full realization.

For the philosopher Benedito Nunes, Oswald's *Antropofagia* cannot be understood straightforwardly: "As a symbol of devouring, *Antropofagia* is at the same time a metaphor, a diagnosis, and a therapy" (1972, xxv, xxvi). As a metaphor of cultural colonization, *Antropofagia* is usually described as the act of devouring the colonizing culture, extracting all of its useful elements in the process, and spitting out the rest. And just as the Tupi admired their most hated enemies, in the never-ending struggle for cultural identity, the colonized countries have also an inextricable desire to savor the European cultures that they want to kill. As a diagnosis, *Antropofagia* allows us to look at colonization as a process of repressing what the Europeans and white Brazilians saw as our most barbaric sides, those sides that the Brazilian intelligentsia from the beginning of the century had also tried to eliminate in its desperate attempt to civilize—i.e., Europeanize— the country. As a therapy, Oswald's cannibalism asks us to take those "barbaric" sides out of the closet, exposing and assuming our "barbaric" (non-European) religions, our "barbaric" foods, our "barbaric" sexuality—in other words: our "barbaric" way of being.

Much has been said about the *modernistas*' links with European avant-garde movements. Alfredo Bosi points out, quite correctly, that in general terms:

> The surfeit of brilliant and affected stylizations found in the Belle Epoque scene has as its correlation an immersion into the individual dream world and, on the broader scale, an enchanted encounter with images and rhythms of non-European cultures. This is the moment of Africa, of *art nègre,* and, later, of Afro-American jazz. In Latin America, the time is that of rediscovering pre-Columbian sources. (1988, 173)

For Heitor Martins the issue is even clearer, as he finds an automatic connection between *Antropofagia* and Picabia's *Cannibale*:

> One cannot deny, however, the way in which Brazilian *Antropofagia* de-
> pended on the metaphor and the concept expressed by Picabia's group. The
> smoke-screen (Montaigne and his "De cannibalis") is too transparent for
> us not to see it the way it is. (33)

But as Benedito Nunes pointed out, "the image of the cannibal was in the
air. For that reason, those who attempt to point out its privileged literary
antecedents will have to look further and further back for previous authors,
indefinitely" (1979, 15). And more importantly: "The Oswaldian image of
the anthropophagite and the respective concept of assimilation depend,
therefore, on a way of conceiving that the various literary cannibalisms of
the time cannot fulfil" (1979, 36). The point is not to deny that the *modernistas'* fascination with the Tupi ritual is part of a more general Western
avant-garde interest for the "primitive" and "primitive art." However, as
Augusto de Campos also pointed out, the ideological thrust of the *modernistas'* choice is radically different from everything that the European
avant-garde experienced with respect to the cannibal image: "A nihilism
that has nothing to do with the generous utopia of our *Antropofagia*" (1975,
n/p.). The "primitives" invoked by the *modernistas* were, after all, part of
their own country. By studying Brazilian indigenous cultures, and the cultures transposed to Brazil with the African slave system,[7] the *modernistas*
hoped to understand, and change, their own national culture, or at least the
"lettered" culture produced by the Brazilian elites.

Further, unlike most of the European avant-garde, the *modernistas* were
interested in rewriting Brazilian history in a way that questioned the uni-
directionality of colonial influence. Oswald's "Manifesto" attacks the very
idea of cultural originality: On the one hand, it is prepared to accept (or, to
use their idiom, "devour") European influence. On the other, it wishes to
highlight the (unrecognized) influence that the American natives had on
European modernity.

> Without us Europe would not even have its poor declaration of the rights
> of man.
>
> The Golden Age proclaimed by America. The golden age. And all the girls.

> Descent. The contact with the Carahiban Brazil. *Où Villegaignon print terre.*
> Montaigne. The natural man. Rousseau. From the French Revolution to
> Romanticism, to the Bolshevik Revolution, to the surrealist Revolution and
> Keyserling's technicized barbarian. We walk. (O. Andrade 1998, 536)

São Paulo is called by its Tupi name: Piratininga, and as in the French Revolution, the "Manifesto" proposed a new calendrical beginning for the colonized nation: The manifesto is dated "Year 374 of the swallowing of Bishop Sardinha"—the date when Sardinha (whose name means "sardine"), the first bishop to come to Brazil, was killed by Tupinambás. As a revolutionary document, "Manifesto" proposes the "*caraíba* revolution," *caraíba* being used in its double meaning of Indian (Carib) and "white seen by the Indian," since it was the word the Tupis used for the white invaders: "We want the Caraiba revolution. Bigger than the French Revolution. The unification of all efficacious rebellions in the direction of man. Without us, Europe would not even have its poor declaration of the rights of man" (536). Oswald's manifesto also satirized Romantic *Indianismo*: "We were never catechized. What we really did was Carnival. Indian dressed as a Senator of the Empire. Pretending to be Pitt. Or featuring in Alencar's operas, full of good Portuguese feelings" (537).

Oswald's main interest was to develop a theory of cultural identity, so that he had little time for intertextual experiments with indigenous texts in the style of *Macunaíma*. As a theorist, he turned to the indigenous cultures in search of concepts rather than stories. The poem "New Moon" (originally published in Couto de Magalhães's *O Selvagem*) is quoted, for instance, as an example of a pre-European surrealist language:

> We already had communism. We already had surrealist language.
>   The golden age.

> Catiti Catiti
> Imara Notiá
> Notiá Imara
> Ipejú. (537)[8]

From the same source (Couto de Magalhães's *O Selvagem*), he extracts the trickster tortoise *(jabuti)*, which appears in the "Manifesto" as a symbol of cultural resistance: "But they who came were not crusaders. They were fugitives from a civilization that we are still eating, because we are strong and vengeful as a Jabuti" (538).

The first issues of *Revista de Antropofagia* included works by a group that would later go its own way: the Tapir *(Anta)* group, or *Verdeamarelistas*, a nationalist faction. Plínio Salgado, who had contributed articles on the Tupi language to the first numbers of *Revista*, became the *Verdeamarelistas*' most vehement champion; he later led the fascist Partido Integralista Brasileiro, whose members greeted each other in a Hitlerian fashion with the Tupi term *anauê*. By 1929, the *Verdeamarelistas* had left the journal, and in that same year Plínio Salgado, along with Cassiano Ricardo and Menotti del Picchia published "Manifesto Nheengaçu Verde Amarelo," in response to what they considered the xenophobic and dangerous tendencies of the *Antropófagos*: "This expression of Tupi nationalism, which was discovered by the Anta movement (and which resulted in an exaggerated and dangerous sectarianism), is evident in all aspects of Brazilian social and political life"(Salgado, 235). The group chose the Tapir as their totem, because, as they explain, this mammal represented the "docility of the Tupi," who were, in their view, destined to be colonized and integrated into the Brazilian race:

> The Tupi went down [towards the ocean] in order to be absorbed. In order to dilute themselves in the blood of the new people. In order to live subjectively and transform into a prodigious force and into the kindness and great human feelings of the Brazilian people. (Salgado, Ricardo, and Picchia, 233)

For the *Verdeamarelistas*, the invasion of the Portuguese was the mere realization of a predetermined Fate. All traces of violence and resistence were erased from their nationalist construction, which used a much-tamed image of the Tupi in order to define Brazilians as being inherently docile and amicable.

Shamanic Image and Social Defense

Despite the decisive impact that indigenous texts had on their works, *modernistas* of all ideological colors showed no more concern than most of their Romantic predecessors for the survival of the indigenous cultures, for the place actually occupied by Indians and their descendants in Brazilian society. In the second half of the twentieth century, however, three key narratives emerged which combine involvement in indigenous literature with such a concern. They are João Guimarães Rosa's short story "My Uncle, the Iauaretê" (1961), Antonio Callado's *Quarup* (1967), and Darcy Ribeiro's *Maíra* (1976), a major text analyzed at length in the next chapter.

Published in 1961, "My Uncle, the Iauaretê"[9] was written, according to Guimarães Rosa, in 1955, just before the publication of his most famous work, the novel *The Devil to Pay in the Backlands* (1956). It tells the story of an Indian-white mestizo who is hired to kill jaguars. At first he accomplishes his task with competence, but later he starts to change periodically into a jaguar himself. He falls in love with a female jaguar and ends up killing most of the humans in the area where he lives. After metamorphosing into a jaguar for the last time, he is killed by the person to whom he is telling his story.

The importance of Tupi language in the short story was thorougly analyzed by Haroldo de Campos:

His speech is marked by a repeated and near-subliminal 'Nhem?,' which incorporates an interrogative-expletive 'Hein?,' but which, as becomes clear, is rather a "Nhenhem" (from the Tupi *Nhenhê* or *nhenheng,* listed by Couto de Magalhães in his *Curso* de língua tupi viva ou *nhenhengatu*), meaning simply 'to speak.' Rosa even invents, in support of this line of interpretation, the verb 'nheengar' ('on nights with a murky moon he would shout nonsense, he would shout, he would *nheengar.*'), pure acclimatised Tupi; and by adding the verbal sound "nhenhém" to "jaguaretê" (Tupi for jaguar) he forms "jaguanhenhém," jaguanhém," to express jaguar ways of speaking . . . So we see that in this text, besides his usual practices of oral deformation and lexical renovation . . . Rosa favors a procedure that has a narrative as well as a stylistic function: the persistent Tupifying of language. As a result, the text is spattered with nheengatu, and the traces of it which appear prepare for and announce the moment of metamorphosis, which gives the narrative its nub, and the story its very being. (1983, 576)

But there are further connections between this short story and the Tupis. The plot of "My Uncle, the Iauaretê" is itself derived from the beliefs, common throughout South American lowlands, about men who change into jaguars. Alfred Métraux, for instance, observes that:

It is a common belief in the Amazon region that sorcerers wander by night as jaguars to attack their victims. It is not always clear, however, whether the belief is that the sorcerer transforms himself into a jaguar or whether he sends forth his soul to incite and lead some actual jaguar against his victims. The belief in jaguar-men was especially strong among the ancient Abipón. In Paraguay this superstition is still shared by Indians and mestizos alike. (1950a, 538)[10]

Also a collector of stories, João Guimarães Rosa could have heard the plot of "My Uncle, the Iauaretê" as an oral narrative. But it is also possible that he read it in Nimuendaju's "Die Sagen," since he could read German very well, and Nimuendaju was, already at that time, a well-known, almost legendary figure.[11] Moreover, Nimuendaju's text presents striking similarities with the plot of "My Uncle, the Iauaretê":

The Kaingyng are jaguars; not just in the opinion of the Guarani—they themselves use this name and boast of their kinship (literally understood) with that animal predator. When they paint their skin yellow with black

spots or stripes in readiness for battle, they believe that likewise in appearance they become fairly like jaguars, and the howl they utter in attack
sounds almost like the dull roar of the jaguar standing over prey. None
of this is at all symbolic; they take their kinship with jaguar so seriously
that, in the case of those of who call themselves *mi-ve* "the one who sees
jaguars," these ideas degenerate into a peculiar form of mental disturbance.
These seers, who start by being *mi-nanti* "the one who dreams of jaguars,"
believe themselves inspired by the "daughter of the lord of jaguars" *(mi-g-
tan-fi)*, cut themselves off from relatives and friends, and wander wild and
alone throught the forest until they have a hallucination in which a jaguar
points them to the path that leads to a young female jaguar. (118)

The Kaingang are a Gê group, enemies of the Apapokuva-Guarani. The
jaguar-metamorphosis, however, is also a Tupi-Guarani belief, as Hélène
Clastres shows:

> We have some information collected among the Mbyá concerning this. The
> *tupichua* is *'choo pyrygua ñe'eng'*: the soul, the vital principle of raw meat . . .
> *Tupichua* comes from raw meat in general, and is something that can find
> a home in human flesh and blood; it then produces a deadly ill that may
> bring about a transformation of the sick person into a jaguar. To avoid this
> taint, two practices are condemned. Raw meat must never be consumed;
> the *tupichua* immediately becomes incarnate in the person who eats raw
> meat and possesses him completely. Cooking and eating meat in the forest
> must be avoided as rigorously; the person who roasts and eats meat in the
> forest irresistibly attracts *tupichua* and is deceived by it. In this case, *tupi-
> chua* even likes to take on the appearance of a beautiful woman, attractively
> adorned with paint, who causes the victim to lose his mind; she says, "We
> are going to do something together." If they do it (that is, if they copulate),
> spots begin to cover her body and she soon appears quite different from a
> woman; she starts to scratch the ground and growl; her victim, too, starts
> to scratch the ground and growl. (80–81)

The jaguar with whom Guimarães Rosa's protagonist falls in love is
called Maria-Maria, a variation of his mother's name: Mar'Iara-Maria (a
combination of Maria and Iara [or Uiara], the Tupi Mother of Waters).
By falling in love with a jaguar and changing into a jaguar himself, the
Iauaretê's nephew is identifying with the culture of his Indian mother: "But
I'm a wildcat. Jaguar my uncle, my sister's brother, *tutira* . . . My kinsfolk!
My kinsfolk!" (69). The jaguars are the ancestors of the Kaingang and of
the Mbyá-Guarani and other lowland groups.

Being a mestizo, he is despised by the non-Indians:

> That Pedro Pampolino said I's no good. Tiaguim said I's a loafer, a lazy
> deadbeat. Killed heaps a' wildcat. Mas'r Johnny Guede brought me up here,
> didn't no-one wanna let me work 'longside others . . . On account of I's no
> good. Just stay here on my own, whole time. Just weren't no good, didn't
> know how to work right, didn't like it. Only knew 'bout killin' wildcat. Oh,
> they didn't oughta! Didn't no-one wanna see me, didn't like me, everyone
> cussin' me. (75–76)

At the same time, ever since his mother died he has lost ties with his Indian
ancestors. His mother was a Tacunapéua Indian, but for reasons that are
not explained, he also lived among the Caraó, whom he considers cowards
because they are afraid of jaguars. The Caraó, or Kraó, according to Darcy
Ribeiro in *Os Índios e a Civilização*, became known for having sold out to
the whites, i.e., for having betrayed the other Indians:

> But I know why you're askin'. Hmm. Ah ha, on account of my hair being
> this way, eyes real small . . . Yep. Not my pa. He was white, weren't no
> indian man. Ah right, my ma she was, she real good. Not Craô indian.
> Pewa, my ma, Tacunapewa heathen, long way's away. Not Craô: Craô real
> scared, near all them was scared of wildcat. My ma was called Mar'Iara
> Maria, she's a breed. Afterwards it was I lived with Craô, lived with them.
> Ma good, pretty, she fed me, fed me real good, plenty, heaps . . . (67)

He was sent to the region where he lives now by Nhô-Nhuão Guede and
forced to live in isolation:

> When I first came here, I's left on my own. Bein' on your own, that's real
> bad, nothin' but torment. Mas'r Johnny Guede a real bad man, brought us
> here and left us all alone. Huh! Missed my ma, she died, *sassyara*. Aaahn . . .
> Jus' me . . . —all alone . . . Didn't have no help or protection . . . (51)

The isolation drives him to the state described by both Nimuendaju and
Hélène Clastres: He becomes *mi-ve*, or *tupichua*.

But being *mi-ve* in the story is also a state of resistance: By offering
human victims to the jaguars, he can release himself from the guilt of having killed so many of those felines, and he can avenge the death of his own
Indian ancestors. His victims represent, for that reason, the antithesis of
the Indianness that he is anxious to recover. His first victim, for instance, is
a horse, the animal-symbol of European colonization in America:

> Uhnn, well I walked out of there on all fours, off I went. Got so mad, felt
> like killin' everything, tearin' everything apart, tooth and nail . . . I roared.
> Eh, I—growled! Next day, white horse of mine, one I brought with me, that
> they gave me, horse was torn to shreds, half eaten up, dead, I woke up all

caked in dried blood . . . Ehn? No harm, don't like horses, me . . . Horse was
lame in the leg, no good any more . . . (77)

The second victims, Mr. Rauremiro and his family, despised him because
he was an Indian:

> Mister Rauremiro, he's honest farming folk, decent man, but he used to
> whistle at yah, like you was a dog. Am I a dog, eh? Mister Rauremiro used
> to say:—"You ain't coming into our room, stay out there, you's a breed . . ."
> Mister Rauremiro used to talk to that black boy Tiodoro, he'd chat to him.
> He'd feed me, but he wouldn't talk to me. (82)

Rioporo also despised him and offended his mother, i.e., his indigenous ancestors. Preto Bijibo treated him well, but he was afraid of everything and
ate too much. The food he ate was needed by the jaguars, the protagonist's
relatives, and that went against the Tupi-Guarani sense of social justice:
A unanimous comment on the Tupi-Guarani, if not all the natives in the
lowlands, is that they never fail to share their food. Tiodoro was sent to the
region by the protagonist's former employer, Nhô Nhuão Guede, and took
possession of the protagonist's house; he repeated, therefore, the process of
land invasion perpetrated by the colonizers against the Indians. Gugué, in
spite of being a good man and treating the protagonist well, was lazy, and
did not perform any of the activities that for the Tupi-Guarani are syn-
onymous with being human: He did not hunt, fish, or plant. Antunias was
marked by the worst of human flaws: He was a miser. As Jean de Léry commented already in 1578, "I can assure the mean and greedy, those who hog
the trough, that they would not be welcome among the Tupinamba, since
they loathe that sort of person" (166).

The only exception to this list is Maria Quirinéia, the only victim he does
not kill. She tried to seduce him, and that became a problem not so much
because she was married, but, above all, because it repeated, in inverted
terms, the seduction of Indian women by white men. The episode should
be connected to another episode in the short story, told by the protagonist,
the killing of the Indian Caraó Curiã by the whites because he had fallen in
love with a white woman and had asked her to go to bed with him. Curiã was
considered foolish by the protagonist: "Craoh only ever talked bull" (74).

In all these cases, the violence perpetrated by the protagonist against his
victims is the inversion of the violence committed by the colonizers against
the Indians. It is, therefore, an act of revenge. Thus, it is not fortuitous that
the protagonist always claims not to dislike his victims. He is repeating,
once again, the behavior of the colonizers, who often described the Indians
in a positive way, but killed them anyway. The first example of that was

perhaps Columbus himself, who in his diary commented extensively on the Indians's generosity and good faith, assuring the king, nevertheless, that it would be easy to enslave them because "with fifty men they will have them all in their power and will make them do anything they desire" (94).

By avenging his ancestors, the protagonist of "My Uncle, the Iauaretê" recovers the land stolen from the Indians, as well as his lost dignity: "Hey, these wide open ranges, goin' on and on, that's my country, hey, this here— all mine. My ma would've liked it here . . . I want 'em all to be scared of me" (53).

But he is killed, at the end of the story, by the person to whom he is narrating the events. Before dying, he changes once more into a jaguar, and one of the last words he speaks is a name given to him years before, Macuncozo. He had, before coming to the region, several names: Bacuriquirepa, his Indian name; Beró, another Indian name, which stands for *peró*—the word used by the Tupinambá to indicate the Portuguese, and which referred, in the context of the short story, to his condition as a mestizo; his Christian name: Antonho de Eiesús (Anthony of Jesus); the name given to him by Nhô Nhuão Guede: Tonho Tigreiro (Tony Jaguar-Hunter); and Macuncozo, "that was the name of a farmstead that used to belong to some other fella, yeah—a farmstead they call Macuncozo" (68). The origin of this name is explained by Haroldo de Campos, who received the information in a letter from Guimarães Rosa himself: "macuncozo is an African note, thrown at the end of the story. A counter-note" (Campos 1983, 75). Macuncozo is, therefore, a false identity, a way by which other people denied his Indian ancestrality, calling him black. Since many of his victims are blacks, we can say that he is trying to erase, by killing blacks and whites, the false identities that kept him away from his Indian ancestors.

In the letter to Haroldo de Campos, Guimarães Rosa says that the word *macuncozo,* at the end of the story, could indicate that the character was, astutely or remorsefully, identifying with the dead blacks. Such identification shows, perhaps, a recognition, on the protagonist's part, that he had attacked the wrong people, that he and the blacks were in fact partners, all of them marginal in a society whose rules are always dictated by the "Johny Guedes." The false re-Africanization of the protagonist at the end of the story points also to a frequent theme in the Brazilian intellectual scene: the marginalization of blacks by those who, like the *Indianistas,* were interested in recovering their indigenous heritage, and the converse, equally perverse elimination of Indians from history by those who claim to be defending the blacks.

Antonio Callado's *Quarup* (1967), like Carpentier's *The Lost Steps,* is a quest narrative. As with Carpentier, the journey of the protagonist Nando to the interior of Brazil corresponds to an immersion in Latin American reality, after years spent outside or beyond. Callado, who worked as a BBC journalist in London in the forties, describes the Latin American writer's impulse to leave his or her country, and then the "lost steps" of the remorseful return:

> The second journey undertaken by Latin American writers is the contrite, remorseful return, to the heart of their own countries. They swim against the current, conquering rivers and rapids, seeking out the mixed-bloods (caboclos, cholos, peones) and the Indians. Like Alejo Carpentier, they leave Paris one day to retrace lost steps, in the jungle, in search of some musical instrument that is ancient, uncouth and forgotten. (1978, 94)

Nando, *Quarup*'s missionary protagonist, goes to the Amazon in order to convert Indians to Christianity and in order to erect, in the middle of the jungle, a new version of the seventeenth-century Jesuit Guarani Republic. At the beginning of the novel, before going to the Amazon, Nando has an idealized image of the condition of the Indians in the jungle, an image created by his extensive reading of works by missionaries, chroniclers, and ethnographers. He believed that the Indians lived in pristine, isolated societies, which had not yet been "corrupted" by the relationship with the whites. After his arrival, he discovers societies assailed by diseases and changing fast as a result of their contact with the rest of Brazil. Disappointed, and having experienced physical contact with women for the first time in his life, he abandons the religious order, but continues to work with the Indians. Later, he joins an expedition to the geographic center of Brazil, going to more inhospitable regions of the Amazon, where, to his surprise, they find rubber tappers and Indians already suffering from diseases brought by the whites. After reaching the center, Nando leaves the Amazon, and in the next chapters we find him in the northeastern state of Pernambuco working with the Peasant Leagues and supporting the socialist governor Miguel Arraes. But the 1964 military coup, which deposed the leftist president João Goulart, brought those social movements to an end. Nando is imprisoned and tortured, and later, at the end of the novel, he joins the guerrilla movement and goes underground.

It is in the first four parts of the novel that we have most of our contact with the Indians. In general terms, we are allowed only to see them as outsiders do: We visit their villages and observe their habits, and listen, though rarely, to the few words they say. The descriptions are based on von der Steinen's *Unter den Naturvölkern Zentral-Brasiliens* (1894), Ramiro Noronha's *Exploração e Levantamento do Rio Culuene, Principal Formador do Rio Xingu* (1952), Adrian Cowell's *The Heart of the Forest* (1960), and Ayres Câmara Cunha's *Entre os Índios do Xingu* (1960), among others.

The occurrences in the first half of the novel have a decisive impact on what happens in the second part. Nando's life among the Indians greatly influences his revolutionary project, and that influence can be detected, above all, in the intertextual dialogue between the novel and certain indigenous narratives. First among those texts are Couto de Magalhães's *O Selvagem* and Hartt's *Amazon Tortoise Myths*. The Tupi tortoise stories transcribed in both collections are often recited, during the expedition to the Center, by the folklorist Lauro, as in this dialogue between him and Nando:

> "There aren't any books at the post, except maybe some novels."
>
> "That's hard to believe. I should have brought my Couto de Magalhães, at least, or Hartt. He has some stories about the *jabuti*."
>
> "Yes, that would have been a good idea." (263)

Lauro's reliance on indigenous texts, which in practice corresponds to an inability to experience personal relations or to face day-to-day problems during the journey through the forest, is despised and laughed at by the rest of the group. Yet, later, as part of Nando's revolutionary project, Lauro's stories about the tortoise *(jabuti)* become instrumental in teaching him that the trickster-like cunning of this creature, also praised in Oswald's "Manifesto," is the only effective force against the military regime.

But the strongest indigenous image in Callado's text is the *quarup* itself, which gives the novel its title. *Quarup* is a ceremony Nando observed among the Xingu Indians in the first part of the novel. This Kamayurá (Tupi) ritual marks the death of a *tuxaua* and the arrival of a new *tuxaua* to power. The dead bodies are represented by decorated tree trunks, the *quarups*. During the celebration, the Indians gather and prepare enormous amounts of food, and invite all the neighboring tribes for a feast. At the end of the novel, under the severe gaze of Colonel Ibiratinga's helpers, Nando and his friends organize a dinner, the only way in which they could protest against the reactionary forces of the military regime. The communal preparation of the dinner resembles the organization of the *quarup*. And, above all, as the central metaphor of the novel, the *quarup* represents the old, dead, Brazil, which is going to replaced by the new Brazil, brought about by the guerrilla movements.[12]

chapter 6

Maíra (1976)

L IKE THE PERUVIAN JOSÉ MARÍA ARGUEDAS, Darcy Ribeiro was both an ethnographer and a novelist. Several of his ethnographic works had been published and translated into diverse languages by the time *Maíra* (1976) came out. In this novel, his first, Ribeiro creates the fictitious tribe "Mairum," which, as he explained in an interview, combines characteristics of distinct cultural groups:

> Homer took the whole of pre-Hellenic literature and created Greek mytholo-gy, that marvel, that beauty. What I do is the same: I take the whole of native mythology and create a mythology that is probable. Any Indian would accept that, just because they are less fanatic than we are they don't accept that truth is single—they accept the words of each one. (Sá 1993, 85)

Maíra is organized partly as a detective story: the first chapter, set in a police station in Brasília, presents a "mystery" that will have to be solved. As in many detective stories, the mystery comes in the form of a dead body, which in the case of this novel belongs to a blonde, pregnant young woman found dead by a Swiss entomologist on a beach of the river Iparann, in the Amazon. Within this initial frame, most of the novel will then be set along the banks of the Iparann river, home of the Mairuns, Epexãs, and Xaepes.

The novel is divided into four parts, identified with the four parts of the Christian Mass. The first three follow a ternary rhythm: for each two chapters narrated by non-Indians, or by Indians who have lived among whites, there is one chapter in which the point of view is exclusively indigenous. The fourth part does not follow any particular rhythm, but of its eleven chapters, four have an exclusively indigenous point of view, and one is mixed.

Maíra is a nonlinear and multifocal text. It alternates diverse narrative voices, and diverse times of narration. In some chapters, for instance, we travel along the Iparanã river, following the federal agent who is designated to investigate the death of the young woman. At the same time, in other chapters, we accompany this young woman, Alma, on her trip to the region, two years before her death. We also follow the Mairum Isaías, as he leaves a Catholic seminar in Rome, where he was about to be ordained, and returns to his Mairum village in the Iparanã, meeting Alma on the way. At the village, we are given the point of view of several Indian characters: Remuí, Jaguar, Teidju, and the gods Maíra and Micura, among others. As Walnice Nogueira Galvão observes, *Maíra* has much in common with "My Uncle, the Iauaretê,"

> but the author had to find another solution to the problem, so well solved by Guimarães Rosa, of developing a narrative constructed from the point of view of the Indian. Why not find it, if the book overflows with love for the Indian? Here, the solution is found in the fragmenting of the narrative focus and the multiplying of the narrators, each one with his own diction. (42)

This multiplicity of points of view is a very important element in *Maíra*, for it gives us a sense of the complexity of the questions raised by the novel, all of them connected to the relationship between indigenous societies and the rest of Brazil. The multiplicity of voices is matched by the novel's intense intertextual dialogue with indigenous sources.

Os Índios e a Civilização Revisited

A map of the intricate net of these intertextual relationships can be traced once we have taken into account Darcy Ribeiro's *Os Índios e a Civilização* (1970).[1] In this earlier work, we can find the origin of most of *Maíra*'s indigenous references. In fact, it is *Maíra*'s closest source.

The theme of both books is the same: the contact between Indians and whites. In order to describe the ways in which this contact happens, Ribeiro often quotes, in *Maíra*, passages from the previous book. In *Os Índios e a Civilização*, for instance, he describes the Indians he had met in his fieldwork as being usually more curious, more eager to learn about new things, than the non-Indian *sertanejos*: "We also often saw Indians we were studying oblige our Sertanejo companions to find answers for questions like:

"Where did the whites come from?"; "Who is the owner of metals?"; "Who makes matches?"; "How did salt originate?" (380). In *Maíra*, when the protagonist Isaías/Avá returns to his village, he is asked very similar questions by the other Mairuns:

> "Who is the owner of salt?
> "Who makes all the tools?
> "Who do all the matches belong to?
> "How do they make glass beads?"
> "Who is the Lord of the Mirrors?" (223)

Also in *Maíra*, the Mairum mestizo Juca describes himself as the son of a white man who brought several indigenous groups into contact with "civilization." But the Indians, according to Juca, "tell this story their own way. According to them, it was they who tamed my father, with great difficulty. Through him they got to know other whites who weren't coming to attack, shoot, and kill people" (116). The same process is described in *Os Índios e a Civilização*: "After the 'pacification' of some of the more warlike indigenous groups, it was discovered that they had made touching efforts to 'tame' the white. In many cases, the pacification undertaken by the SPI was interpreted in reverse, by the tribe" (184).

The dialogue between Alma and Isaías/Avá about the usage of *bá* (foreskin binding) and *uluri* (vagina cover) is almost identical to a dialogue reproduced by Ribeiro, in indirect speech, in *Os Índios e a Civilização*:

> "Come, Isaías, the water is delicious!"
> "I can't, I'm naked."
> "What are you talking about?"
> "I'm not wearing a bá."
> "Don't be ridiculous, do you think I have an uluri?" (*Maíra*, 227–28)

> A young Bororo once turned down my invitation to bathe in the river since, as he said, he was "naked under his pants." That is, he had no *bá*, the item of decorum which for him meant feeling "dressed." (327)

Still other passages could be cited as examples of Darcy Ribeiro's direct quoting of *Os Índios e a Civilização* in *Maíra*. But there are other ways in which he refers to the previous book: He also glosses in the novel several motifs taken from the study. In the latter, for instance, he describes the *regatão*, an Amazonian businessman, or

> the merchant who carries his wares in a small boat in which he lives and with which he plies each river, each stream where there is something to be

traded for alcohol, salt, matches, fish-hooks, needles, thread, ammunition, and a multitude of suchlike articles. A prompter of needs and the instrument of their satisfaction, the merchant is the king of the igarapé, and the boss and king of the river (26).

In *Maíra,* the institution *regatão* becomes a character: the *regatão* Juca, whose trajectory follows exactly the above description from *Os Índios e a Civilização*. A similar process happens with Juca's boatman, Boca, an Indian who receives a daily supply of marijuana in order to do his job. This is how Juca describes Boca to his employee Manelão: "Do you see, Manelão? Those half-breeds in their huts, Indians kidnapped from childhood, and never without grass. They smoke more than they eat, the rascals" (21). In *Os Índios e a Civilização,* the anthropologist Darcy Ribeiro tells us that

> As boatmen, the Tembé work nonstop for ten or even fourteen hours with only short breaks, bearing by oar and pole all that that moves on the river. Besides being crippling in itself, this work is the more exhausting since during each day of the journey there is generally only one stop, just long enough to prepare the always too meager food. And above all because in order to comply with the bosses' demands, the Indians are used to taking stimulants, like spirits and cannabis. (213)

The *nidjienigi,* the Kadiwéu shaman, who, according to Ribeiro in *Os Índios e a Civilização,* "albeit unconsciously will do everything to bring about his own assassination—for only this way can he indisputably confirm the power and terror he inspires in the group, as was always the case with the *nidjienigi*" (206), becomes one of the finest characters of *Maíra,* the *oxim,* who ends up, at the end of the novel, being torn to pieces by the other Mairuns.

Examples could be multiplied. Every important character in *Maíra,* with the exception of Alma and the federal agent Nonato, can be found as an agent of the contact between Indians and whites in *Os Índios e a Civilização*. Yet, as might be expected, the two books are quite different. One of the differences is the fact that, as a novel, *Maíra* creates individual characters, instead of simply discussing, as is the case in *Os Índios e a Civilização,* general categories such as the *aroe,* the mestizo, the Xokleng, the Tembé. Also, the author allows himself to be more playful with the language, and delegates the task of narrating to a number of voices—some Indian, some white, some mestizo.

But what distinguishes *Maíra* from *Os Índios e a Civilização* is, above all, the novel's intense use of indigenous texts. In *Os Índios e a Civilização,* we could already find references to those texts. In *Maíra,* they are quoted, and they affect the cosmogonic view of the novel and the way in which it is written.

A Tupi-Guarani Genesis

Though several of the cultures used in the composition of the Mairuns are not Tupi-Guarani, the basic cosmogony of this fictitious tribe is similar to that of the Urubu-Kaapor, a Tupi group from Maranhão among whom Darcy Ribeiro worked, the results of his research being published in the article "Uirá sai à procura de Maíra" (1957).[2] The article includes a summarized version, in Portuguese, of the Urubu-Kaapor creation stories. That he had available to him longer versions of these stories is made clear by the fact that they were included in his travelogue, published under the title *Diários Índios: Os Urubu-Kaapor* (1996).

Those stories bear many similarities, as we have seen, to the Tembé (Tupi) stories published by Nimuendaju in "Sagen der Tembé-Indianer." They also share many characteristics with other Tupi-Guarani texts. In fact, in *Maíra*, the chapter that tells the creation of the world begins with a quotation from the Apapokuva-Guarani texts published by Nimuendaju in "Die Sagen" (see chapter 4):

> *Ñanderuvuçu ou petei, pytu avytepy añoü ojucuaã*

> In the beginning, only the eternal bats flew in the infinite darkness. Then came our Creator, the Nameless One, who, alone, discovered himself as such and waited. (*Maíra*, 105)

In Nimuendaju, we read:

> Ñanderuvuçú oú peteí, pytú avytépy añoí okicuá.

> *Ñanderuvuçú* came alone; amid the darkness he discovered himself alone. The Eternal Bats fought among themselves in the darkness. (143)

The nameless creator of the Mairuns is later identified as Maírahú (Maíra-father), Maíra-Ambir (Maíra, the ancestor), or, as in Thevet, Maíra-Monan (Maíra of the Dead). He creates a son and sends him to the Earth to feel his creations: "One day, Ambir the Old wanted to experience his creations. He belched and hurled the belch into the world so it could become his son" (147). His son is Maíra-Coracir (Sun) or Maíraira (Maíra-son).

Maíra-father and Maíra-son appear, as we have seen, in the Urubu-Kaapor and Tembé stories. In Darcy Ribeiro's novel, they become central characters, along with Maíra-son's brother, Micura (skunk), the Moon.[3] In his wanderings around the Earth, Maíra-son discovers Mosaingar, an ancestor of the Mairuns. He enters this being and creates a place for himself in it. He can then enjoy the interior of the body, and, at the same time, see the world outside:

> There, seated, he perceived the symmetry of the right and left sides with everything duplicated but different, inverted, of that grandfather who would become his mother. He felt at first the strangeness of that body of smooth skin, devoid of hair but hairy in places . . . Through the eyes he saw the darkness of the world, the absence of color. Through the ears he heard and recognized the noise of the wind rustling in the forest. (121)

Like Maíra in the Urubu-Kaapor text, Kuaray in *Ayvu Rapyta*, and Ñandery-quey in Nimuendaju's "Die Sagen," this deity of Darcy Ribeiro's novel communicates with his mother before birth:

> Then Maíra begged Mosaingar to be his mother, who would be able to pick and taste all the fruit directly in front of her. Ambir the Old was annoyed. He said no, and beat his belly protesting:
> "A son still unborn does not speak." (121)

The possibility of seeing the world from inside the mother's body—a Tupi-Guarani motif—becomes one of the most original formal devices of *Maíra*. Maíra himself has the idea of repeating, much later, the experience of being in somebody else's body, of seeing the world from within a human being:

> Sometimes he [Maíra] also tires of his perpetual gyrations and wishes to descend just for a moment to his remade world. Once again he wants to see greens, reds, yellows. He wants to smell the odors he himself put into things. He wants to clothe the bodies of men; he wants to feel the pleasure of the women of his people, the Mairuns. He also wants to become emotional through sentiments of happiness and sadness, nostalgia and melancholy, disillusion and hope that enliven the Mairuns. (231)

He enters, then, several characters: the *aroe* (shaman) Remuí, the *oxim* Teidju, the young *tuxaua*-to-be Jaguar, and Isaías. Micura, jealous of those experiments, goes also to the Earth to "visit" Alma. Maíra's and Micura's experiments allow us to hear, in some cases for the first time, the point of view of those characters. But at the same time, Maíra and Micura give us their own impressions of those characters, commenting on their capacity to feel and see, their optimism or pessimism, their desire to enjoy the world, or their inability to do so. In the case of the old shaman, for instance, Maíra comments on his blindness and pessimism:

> Now I am going to visit once more my old guide of souls. He thinks he will be the last, the final one: the end of the series of so many guides that I have

known. He wants finality. It is sorrowful; my little light who still illumi-
nates the Mairun spirit. . . .

How can you continue living in that body, Remuí? It's worn out from
so much use. You can hardly see shadows. You can hardly hear voices and
the sound of your rattle. As to your sense of smell, perhaps you can still
catch the sweet stench of a human carcass. You could well eat grass thinking it was meat. My old guide of souls, I can't allow you to rest yet though
I understand how much you want to come to an end. (231)

Remuí's pessimism is compared with Jaguar's capacity to enjoy life:

Maíra-Coraci dives once again from the summit of the sky, this time to fall
into the innermost soul of Jaguar: his is certainly a Mairun body as it should
be. For him, the world is splendid, marvelous. That is how he sees it, magnificent under my light: technicolor, sparkling, luminous. Lights where it is
supposed to be clear, shade where it is suitable. (258)

Isaías's ambivalence, his difficulties readapting to the Mairum society after
having trained to be a Catholic missionary, are associated by Maíra with his
feeble and decayed body:

This shit of a body, worn out from such abuse. It is a tube: at one end, the
mouth through which it passes food inside, without enjoying its smell or
taste; at the other end, the ass-hole through which it shits, again without
enjoyment. Had I known they were going to be like this, I would have left
the people as my father made them. Speak, wretch. Speak, Avá. (275)

At first, Maíra's and Micura's "visits" to human beings could resemble
Christian possessions, also portrayed in the novel in the case of Perpetinha,
an evangelic young woman killed by her preacher, who believes she had
been possessed by the devil. Maíra's experiments, however, are just the opposite. In a Christian possession, the possessed being stops acting and feeling like himself. He/she becomes, for a time, another being. The possession
appeals, therefore, to the separation between body and spirit: A person's
body is temporarily home to a foreign spirit. In the case of Maíra's visits,
we are allowed to feel and see the guest body's sensations and impressions,
and, at the same time, have Maíra's impressions about them. There is no
separation, but simultaneity. And the guest body is not a mere instrument
for Maíra's actions, since its sensations are felt, enjoyed, and, as a matter of
fact, emphasized.

Through Maíra, we are allowed to see the novel's main characters simultaneously from within and from without. The key to this simultaneity
is given by the Tupi-Guarani creator-fetus, who is, at the same time, his

mother and himself. Maíra's visits to the other characters enhance, with rare concision, the novel's multiplicity of points of view. As an alternative to the omniscient narrator, Darcy Ribeiro uses in his novel a Native American non-omniscient god: a god who has to visit the bodies of his creatures in order to know what they think and feel.

The Tupi-Guarani creation story affects the novel even further. The adventures of the Mairum ancestor Mosaingar are going to be relived by Alma, the white woman who "goes native" among the Mairuns. Initially, this young woman from Rio, a former drug addict recently converted to Catholicism, comes to the Mairum village with the intention of becoming a missionary. But when she arrives at the mission near the village, she hears the protests of some old Mairum women, who convince her that the Mairum way of being was in fact healthier than that of the whites:

> The old women are right. They're healthy, mentally healthy. We are the sick ones, sick from indecency, from our repression of our humanity, from our rejection of what is natural. We are abominable. I've learned as much from the old women, now that you've explained what they said. Thank God for opening my eyes; I understand at last. The purity of God is not in the mortification of the flesh. The purity of God, if it exists, if God exists, is in life itself, in the capacity to fuck, to enjoy, to bring children into the world. (206)

Later, among the Mairuns, Alma maintains an active sexual life with several Indians, and gets pregnant. She does not know who the father of the child is, but the readers are informed that it could be Micura, who, during his "visit" to Alma, promised to leave a seed in her body: "I have a lot to do up there. Any night now I will return. And then, who knows, I may leave a seed" (292). Also, the *aroe* Remuí expresses his hope that Maíra-father could send a seed to another Mosaingar: "Who knows if perhaps the Old One, the Nameless One, will send another of his belches to enter some other Mosaingar? Then the twin sons of the Lord would be born for everything to start all over again"(233). And after her death, which happened as she tried, alone, to give birth to twins, the Mairuns started to refer to Alma as Mosaingar, their creation mother. Hence, in Darcy Ribeiro's novel, the white woman Alma is assigned the responsibility of giving birth to the new deities of the Mairuns—mixed blood deities, who could perhaps represent the beginning of a new era for the Mairuns: an era in which the whites' relationship with them could be epitomized by Alma's respect for their culture:

> I have adjusted perhaps as a result of the mutual respect with which I treat the Mairuns and they treat me. I don't want, I don't imagine, nor would I ever conceive or desire to make them my equals. I don't imitate them. I am I, they are they, and we understand each other. (322)

Also coming from Tupi-Guarani texts, the struggle between the Creator and his son is one of the novel's central themes. In Nimuendaju's "Die Sagen," for instance, this struggle is alluded to when the son of Ñanderuvuçú asks for his father's instruments in order to rule the world. In the case of the Urubu-Kaapor, the war between father (Maíra) and son (Maíra-mimi) is a permanent conflict:

> Since Maíra's son went up to the sky to stay with his brother, he has been continuously at war with his father: All these stones you see around in rivers, hills, ravines, levels, were houses of Maíra that Maíra-mimi wrecked.
>
> When there is lightning and thunder, it's because Maíra-mimi is fighting with his father.
>
> Maíra cannot stay for long in one place, he has to move on since Maíra-mimi is chasing him.
>
> Maíra is thin, his waist is like a tanajura ant's, because he can't eat, his son doesn't let him.
>
> Yet Maíra doesn't die, his son cannot win. When he destroys one house, Maíra turns into a caiman and slips into the water, he stays down there for days at a time, that's why he's thin. (1974, 21–22)

In the words of Darcy Ribeiro, the ethnologist:

> Still now, the hecatombs, the storms and the whole of life is conceived of as a struggle, and explained by the Urubu Indians through the allegory of an unending conflict between a father Maíra and a son Maíra in whom the hero is duplicated. Though they expect no help from Maíra nor could imagine appealing to or invoking him, his action is necessary and sufficient for maintaining the cosmic order, now as in the days of creation. (1974, 20)

In *Maíra*, too, that conflict permeates the whole novel. Maíra, with the help of his brother Micura, makes several changes to the world created by his father. He also castrates his father, whose penis, sprouting from the earth, was the instrument for the only sexual intercourse that humans were allowed to have (151). From then on the war between Maíra-Monan and Maíra-Coracir becomes a permanent process: "The war of the world had begun. It wasted all of the ancient times with ceaseless struggles and continues even today, without respite. It is a hard battle in which Maíra confronts Mairahú so that the world may remain as it is" (153).

The war between Maírahú (Maíra father) and Maíraíra (Máira son) is also reflected in the relationship between several characters in the novel. This is the case with Jaguar and his uncle Isaías/Avá. The Mairuns are described in the novel as a matrilinear society. In this kind of society the maternal uncle plays, in several aspects, the role of a father. The nephew is supposed to inherit the uncle's position as well as his qualities, and he has to pay that uncle a respect sometimes greater than what he owes his own carnal father. When Avá, who was supposed to be the tribe's next *tuxaua*, was still a boy, he was taken to the Catholic mission for treatment of small-pox. There, he was converted to Catholicism, baptized Isaías, and sent to Rome to become a priest. But cultural ambivalence became a heavy burden to him, and he was never able to take holy orders. Back in his village, he is not capable of becoming a Mairum again, either. He cannot have sex be-cause of Christian ideas about sin, he is too feeble and unskilled to hunt or fish, and often criticizes the Mairum way of being. He cannot become, as it was expected of him, a *tuxaua*.

The story of Isaías/Avá is based on a non-Tupi story: the biography of Akirio Boróro Keggeu, or Tiago Marques Apoburéu, described by Herbert Baldus (1937)[4]; the Bororos belong to a separate linguistic family, the Gê-Bororo, which otherwise affects *Maíra* (see below). Ribeiro himself met Apoburéu when he visited the Bororos, as he tells us in *Os Índios e a Civilização* and as he recalls in the central chapter of *Maíra*—a chapter that intrudes into the narrative to allow Darcy Ribeiro to speak directly as author:

> What is important here and now is to recall how I came to meet Avá, who was a Bororo and who called himself Tiago. That is how I know him. I saw him once, covering with feathers the tiny bones of his daughter who had died of smallpox. He was much comforted by reciting, with the appropriate cadences, the litany in Latin. (176)[5]

In the novel, Isaías/Avá's ambivalence is explained as "lack of soul" by the *aroe* (also a Bororo rather than a Tupi concept):

> But he came empty. He brought us nothing, not even himself. With him we have lost our chieftain-to-be who was to have become our chieftain. He returned empty, drained. It is as if he had been taken out of his skin. It is as if he had been turned inside out. But what they did was worse. They took away his spirit. He who is here is what remains of a man who has lost his soul. (232)

At one level, we can say that Isaías's soul was stolen during his stay among the Catholics, as the *aroe*, once again, explains: "He who has come is what remains of my son, Avá, after the most powerful false sorcerers of the Europeans robbed his soul"(232). At another level, however, it is Isaías's own nephew, Jaguar, who deprives him of his soul. Jaguar, like Isaías, belongs to the jaguar clan, and those who belong to that clan cannot kill jaguars: They can only receive dead jaguars as a gift from members of other clans. But the young man ignores the prohibition and kills a black jaguar during a hunt. Later, he is accused by the *aroe* for having killed, in that jaguar, his uncle's soul. Jaguar himself describes the conversation with the *aroe*:

> It took time for the guide of souls to start talking. He began by recalling the black puma, the one that I had brought, but he called it a jaguar. He said it was a perfect jaguar, mature and ferocious, that would heap glory on any hunter who brought it to the house of the clan of the Jaguar. "But it was you, Jaguar, a jaguar who killed your uncle." (260)

Not only does Jaguar "kill" his uncle, by depriving him of his soul, but he also kills his primeval ancestor, the jaguar. He repeats, in that gesture, the action of his literary ancestor, the protagonist of "My Uncle, the Iauaretê."

The Tupi-Guarani struggle between the creator and his son is associated by Darcy Ribeiro with the Greek (and Freudian) theme of Oedipus.[6] Hence, besides stealing his uncle's soul, Jaguar also takes away his women, Alma and Inimá. Alma came to the Mairum village with Isaías, and because of that she was initially thought to be his wife. Although they never become lovers and Isaías corrects the initial impression that she could be his wife by sending her to live in his clan's house, we find out, at the end of the novel, that he is, in fact, in love with her:

> *Lord, here I am once more, lacking Thee, lacking Alma. In vain I humiliated myself, supplicated, wept. The words froze in my throat. My eyes dried up. But my heart throbs, sighs, and keeps vigil. What will become of me without her?*
>
> *Lord, only Thou canst save me. My afflicted soul dies outside me, in agony. Inside me, how will I live without Thee, or her?* (327)

Alma is, therefore, Isaías's "alma," his soul, stolen by his nephew. And Inimá, Isaías's Mairum wife, becomes Jaguar's lover as well.

The same theme is repeated in connection with two other characters: Juca and Manelão. The *regatão* and Mairum mestizo Juca demonstrates for his young employee Manelão an affection that he has for no one else: He gives him advice, teaches him everything about the profession, and even entrusts him with secrets. For that reason we could say that Manelão occupies, in relation to Juca, the position of a son. Later, Manelão kills Juca and marries his widow, Nhá Coló.

By linking the Tupi-Guarani theme of the struggle between God-father and God-son to the Greek theme of Oedipus, Darcy Ribeiro gives emphasis to its tragic nature. Jaguar loves his uncle, and wants him to be the next *tuxaua*, among other reasons because that way he, Jaguar, could free himself from the heavy burden of being a *tuxaua*-to-be, that is, a *tuxauará*:

> Jaguar listens attentively, motionless. It is his uncle then, the true chief-to-be, who is returning. He himself will never have to assume chieftainship. What a blessing, he thinks, I will now live my life like the other young men. Maybe I will be able to travel upriver to become acquainted with the Mission, or down-river to Corrutela. Who knows, I might even end up in Brasilia or Belém? I will finally be free from everyone's tireless vigilance. Free from always being accompanied, no longer obliged to say where I am going, even when it's to the same place. (199–200)

But he cannot avoid his fate and becomes, by his own fault, a *tuxaua*. Jaguar's "tragic flaw," if he has one, is perhaps the lack of respect for his own cultural traditions: He breaks the rules of his society by hunting a forbidden animal and also by committing incest with his sister Mbiá before she had her first menstruation: "That jaguar was mine . . . even as my sister Mbía was mine before she began to menstruate" (260).

Isaías's fate in the novel is also tragic. He ends up being, among the Mairuns, what he could not be among the whites: a white himself. Not only that, but he becomes, at the end of the novel, an *oxim,* a dark shaman. Another word used by the Mairuns to refer to the *oxim* is *pajé-sacaca*—the same term they use to refer to the Catholic priest. In other words, Isaías escapes from becoming a *pajé-sacaca* among the whites only to become, at the end, a *pajé-sacaca* Mairum. The *oxim* is the most hated and feared person in the Mairum society. He lives completely isolated from the other people, and he knows that, like the Kadiwéu *nidjienigi,* he will be torn to pieces at the height of his glory, by the other Mairuns. Moreover, Isaías, as his biblical name reveals, is "the prophet who has his mouth burned by the words of God." In the words of Remuí, the *aroe,* he goes around the village with "his mouth speaking the words of another" (233). Isaías's words are also a self-fulfilling prophecy: He helps the Protestant missionary Gertrudes to translate the biblical apocalypse into the Mairum language. That is, he helps those Protestants to bring the Bible, itself an instrument of cultural destruction, to the Mairuns.

Tragedy, in *Maíra,* is always linked to the increasing pressure of the whites over the Indians' territory and culture. For the *aroe,* the reason for the whites' triumph can be attributed to Maíra-son himself, for his constant fights against his father:

> You yourself started all this, Maíra-Coraci. You wanted to be alone. There you are anew and renewed everyday, as you were yesterday as you always will be. Who will save us? What will become of the old Maíra-Monan, castrated by you? (233)

The same idea is present in the Urubu-Kaapor creation texts, according to which all the disasters that happen to them have, as an ultimate cause, the struggle between those two gods. Also, Maíra, for the Urubu-Kaapor, helped the whites (Karaíwa) from the beginning:

> Maíra wanted the Karaíwa to do things as well as he did, to be his equal. The Karaíwa know how to do things better because Maíra stayed longer with them teaching them everything.
>
> Maíra had no wish to teach the Kaapor how to make swords, knives, axes; he said the Karaíwa should make them and give them to the Kaapor. (1974, 21)

In the novel, Maíra's desire to help the whites becomes, in the opinion of the *aroe*, a form of betrayal:

> I am tired, the Earth is tired. Perhaps even the Sky is tired and wants to collapse. Only for you, Maíra is the bright clarity not a burden. Aren't there hours, though, when you also wish for eclipse? It surprises me that birds and children enter the world wanting to live life with joy and resolve. Why? I am tired. The Mairuns are tired, tired of living. And who knows, perhaps even the dead themsleves are tired of whirling about. Only the two of you, Maíra and Micura, in your bodies of fire and light, illuminating the new world, the world of the white people by day and by night, are not tired. (234)

The *aroe*'s cataclysmic view of the world can also be traced in Tupi-Guarani texts. In Nimuendaju's "Die Sagen," for instance, we read:

> These days the earth is already old, and our tribe no longer wants to multiply. We have to see the dead again; darkness will fall, the bat will descend and all those of us who are here on earth will have an end. The Blue Jaguar will descend to devour us. (150)[7]

As we have seen, the cataclysm for the Tupi-Guarani is linked to the search for *Ivy marã ey*, the place without ill. In *Maíra*, the journey to *Ivy marã ey* is contemplated by the *oxim* as a solution for Isaías's problem:

> In order to invigorate the Jaguar side, Avá would have to abandon everything and leave immediately, leave now, this instant, on his own two feet, in search of Ivimaraei, the Land without Evil. He would have to face the hardships of the struggle against Maíra-Monan to force him to acquiesce in his return to and integration in the world there below. But, for this, Avá does not have the necessary daring and strength. Does he? (318)

The search for *Ivy marã ey* is also connected to the Tupi-Guarani conception of the soul. For the Tupi-Guarani, the soul signifies, as we have seen, lack of ambivalence. It is true that they also see ambivalence as a condition of human existence—a condition that can be overcome only through the journey to *Ivy marã ey*. But for the Mbyá-Guarani, for instance, extreme cases of ambivalence cause serious diseases and disorder. This is the state of Isaías, as diagnosed by the *oxim*:

> His (the *oxim*'s) basic idea, defined at last, is that Isaías suffers from a fundamental ambiguity. Probably because his mother, Moitá, had fucked too much with too many men, mixing various semens. . . . The problem lies in separating these two psychic substances, making one of them die—that which lacks the strength to grow—and the other—that which has the greater possibilities—emerge vitalized. (318)

Other elements from the Tupi-Guarani creation stories also appear in *Maíra*, such as the blue jaguar, described in the Apapokuva-Guarani text as the guardian of Ñanderuvuçú's house: "And he [Ñanderuvuçú] went to stop the perdition of the world and only the blue jaguar is watching him"(Nimuendaju 1987, 150). In *Maíra*, the blue jaguar is also the guardian of Maíra-Monan's house, who sends him to attack his son in the beginning of their fight:

> Now he sent against his son what was most powerful: Jaguarinouí, the Great Blue Tiger, the size of the world. Maíra saw only, in the darkness of the nocturnal sky, that huge blue-black jaguar, growing, sparkling, furious, immense. It spiraled down, descending slowly on the light of the beams that were shooting from its eyes. It came to make an end of him, to make an end of everyone, to make an end of everything. (167–68)

The Gê-Bororo Ingredient and Its Consequences

In the central chapter of *Maíra*, Darcy Ribeiro introduced a non-Tupi-Guarani tradition in the form of Akirio, caught as this character was, like Isaías, between Catholicism and his own Gê-Bororo culture. This same culture in fact informs the novel in other ways, and determines the social organization imposed on the Mairuns. Isaías, for instance, describes his village as having "the form of an enormous cartwheel with its axis at the Great House. The spokes are the paths from the houses, and the studded rim, the two circular roads with the houses in between" (41). In *Os Índios e a Civilização*, we find a similar description of the Canela (Gê) village: "They live in round villages about three hundred yards across which seen from above look like an enormous cartwheel, thanks to the spoke-like paths which run from each house to the central patio" (364).

Also, the Mairum social organization is thus described by Isaías in the novel:

> An invisible line divides the village into two halves, that of the rising sun and that of the setting sun. Each has its clans that seek wives or husbands in the opposite band. This division of the village in halves reflects the divisions of the world as we know them, always divided into two: day and night; light and dark; the sun and the moon; fire and water; red and blue; and also male and female; good and bad; ugly and beautiful. (73)

This description is very similar to the description of the Canela made by Ribeiro in *Os Índios e a Civilização*:

> They have a highly complex social organization, based on a division into two exogamic phratries, each of which has seven matrilinear clans, whose positioning in the village follows directional patterns that correspond to the cardinal points. This structure is further complicated by the classificatory criterion which divides not just the tribe but the whole universe into two groups: to the one, belong sun, fire, wood, water, East and red; to the other, moon, night, wood, water, West and black. (364)

This social division, in inverted form, extends itself into the world of the dead (manon), as Isaías explains to Alma before they arrive in the village:

> [The dead Mairuns] haven't disappeared. According to our beliefs, they are still around here as spirits. Only they are transformed. That fat leaf we call mixu is a white deer to them, which they hunt. A white deer to them is our thick green leaf. Only an aroe, a guide of souls, like my father, can see and talk to them. (1985, 155)

In *Os Índios e a Civilização* we find a similar description of the Bororo division between the world of the dead and the world of the live beings:

> According to their view of things, the world of the living and of the dead forms a single whole, coexistent in the same space, yet what signifies something dead for the living is alive for the dead, and vice versa. Only the aroe-tawa-rari see and communicate with the two communities, that of the living and that of the dead. (393)

This division of the cosmos into binary opposites became a characteristic, in the writings of Claude Lévi-Strauss (himself a researcher of Bororo culture), of what he called "la pensée sauvage." Through Lévi-Strauss's structuralist theories, in the sixties, the Gê-Bororo binary division of the world was projected, by Lévi-Strauss himself and fellow anthropologists, philosophers, sociologists, and literary theorists, onto other indigenous cultures and onto several modalities of Western science as well. For Eduardo Viveiros de Castro, the abundance of studies about the Gê-Bororo in the sixties and seventies, which contrasted with the decline of interest in the Tupi-Guarani during the same period, is directly linked to the rise of structuralism as a theoretical approach:

> The declining influence of the German and American schools (Diffusionism, Culturalism) and the rise of Structural Functionalism (Britain) and Structuralism (France) are clearly linked to the shift from a "Tupi ethnology" to a "Gê ethnology." (1986, 95)

In the case of *Maíra*, binary oppositions affect not only the Mairum universe: They determine as well how the main characters are paired into opposite beings, who represent the inverted image of each other. Alma and Isaías, the two protagonists, for instance, can be considered binary opposites, on several accounts: She is a woman and he is a man; she is white and he is Indian; she has a carnal approach to life, while he emphasizes the spiritual side of things, and so on. But that relationship can also be inverted, at least in metaphorical terms. Alma is frequently referred to by the Mairuns as having masculine traits: Micura calls her "manly woman" and the Indians laugh because she pronounces several words like a man. Isaías, on the other hand, is called by the Mairuns a creature of Micura, that is, a lunar being, therefore associated with women, who are at every menstruation "shot by Micura's arrow." And in spite of being white, Alma adapts better to the Mairum world than Avá, a full-blooded Indian.[8]

Jaguar and Isaías are also opposites, as we have seen. So are the *aroe* and the *oxim*: the first, based on the Bororo *aroe-tawa-rari*, is the spiritual leader of the group, the bridge between the dead and the live beings; the second, inspired by the Kadiwéu *nidjienigi* and by the Bororo *bari*, is a "dark shaman," who cures and prepares the game for eating, but who can also cause death and is, for that reason, hated by the rest of society. The Bororo opposition between the *aroe* and the *bari* is described by Antonio Colbachini as "the two Bororo systems of religious beliefs" (119). The Catholic priests are opposed, in the novel, to the Protestant missionaries, and that opposition is considered by the *oxim* as equivalent to the opposition between himself and the *aroe*. The names of the Indian tribes Epexãs and Xãepes, neighbors of the Mairuns, are a syllabic inversion of each other. And they are, also, in opposite stages of contact with the whites: The Epexãs tried all they could to be assimilated by Brazilian society, but realizing that that was impossible, they "gave up, went back, and (they say) even forgot Portuguese" (173); the Xãepes, on the other hand, have not contacted any whites yet, although they often attack bypassing boats in order to acquire metal tools.[9]

Underlying the opposition between characters is the basic thematic division of the novel between father and son, life and death, Indian and white. The opposition between father and son is, as we have seen, a theme already present in Tupi-Guarani cosmogony, and it is projected onto several characters in the novel. It also represents the basic division between older and younger generations who are, in the case of the Mairuns, associated with lesser or greater desire for change. Thus, Maíra-Coraci is a transformer, who wants to change the world of his father:

> Maíra had always thought that the world of our Creator, the Nameless One, wasn't of much use. Without wanting to, he found himself imagining and inventing in his mind the world as it ought to be; a world good for his favorite people, the Mairuns, of the Iparanã. (150)

Isaías was, involuntarily, transformed by his contact with the whites, and Jaguar clearly represents a younger generation of Mairuns, less respectful of the tribe's beliefs. Juca, who represents a primitive form of capitalism, is, by the end of the novel, replaced by Manelão, who helps the Southern senator Andorinha bring cattle ranchers to the region. The old Catholic missionaries, whose life had been spent in trying to convert the Mairuns, are replaced by a new generation of Catholics, who will dedicate themselves to the conversion of the Xãepes.

The life-death binary is also a basic theme of the novel. From the death of Alma, discussed in the first chapter, we go, in the second chapter, to the death of the *tuxaua* Anacã. The complex funeral of Anacã (itself similar to the description given by Ribeiro in *Os Índios e a Civilização* of Bororo funerals) introduces us to several aspects of the Mairum universe, in the first part of the novel. The last "Mairum chapter" of *Maíra* is, conversely, the nomination of Jaguar as the new *tuxaua*. Maíra-Monan presides over the world of the dead, and Maíra-Coraci, the world of the live beings. Both worlds are in constant communication and can be understood by the *aroe*. Brasília, the capital (i.e., "navel") of Brazil, is considered by the Mairuns as the home of the evil spirits, a place of death, as Isaías explains:

> Brasilia returns me to the Mairuns, to our myths of creation. What is most sinister has a place here. Brasilia is the Mairun world transfigured. The worst of our world is here converted. Does it thrive? This region where the Iparanã rises is for us a kind of hell; it is the mouth of the subterranean world: the abode of Mairahú. Here the only residents are supposed to be enormous black dogs with gigantic mouths, guardians of Maíra-Monan, my Father-God—ingenuous, ferocious, capricious. It frightens me to think that the abode of Maíra-Monan is now exactly the navel of Brazil. Any

Mairun would have advised against the construction of a new capital in this place. (104)

But the main opposition in the novel is between Indians and whites. This opposition is already expressed in the title of Darcy Ribeiro's *Os Índios e a Civilização* (Indians and Civilization). Like the previous work, *Maíra* describes several stages of the contact between Indians and whites. And not only that: the opposition between these two sides of Brazilian society becomes, in this novel, a structuring device. Each of the novel's themes, the oppositions between father and son, life and death, and so on, is developed symmetrically in relation to both Indians and whites. Also, as one of the novel's most interesting formal techniques, we have, besides many Mairum and non-Mairum first-person narrators, a collective first person narrator who identifies with the Mairuns, but who is not identified with any character: "Whoever looks on this from outside, how will he understand? Only we, those from within, can know. Even so, only more or less. The Mairuns are a deep and secretive people." (1985, 40)

Hence, the Gê-Bororo binary social structure is also the organizing principle of *Maíra*. It constitutes, along with the Tupi-Guarani cosmogony, the strong indigenous substratum of this novel.[10] All this distinguishes it from the ethnographic argument and problematic binary of *Os Índios e a Civilização*. The words, thought, and logic of the "Indians" have intruded and shaped it so strongly as to threaten the neat coherence of the frame-story.

Part III

Confluence in the Rio Negro

It was she who thought about the future world,
about the future beings. After having appeared,
she started to think about how the world should be.
In her Room of White Quartz, she ate *ipadu*,
smoked the cigarette and began thinking
about how the world should be.

—*Antes o Mundo não Existia*

chapter 7

The Upper Rio Negro: Jurupari and the Big Snake

T HE FIRST NON-INDIAN ACCOUNTS of the rituals identified with Jurupari were published by Alfred Russel Wallace in his *Travels on the Amazon and Rio Negro* (1853).[1] What Wallace called the "Devil-music of the Indians" (241) is in fact a complex cultural phenomenon that permeates most aspects of life on the upper Rio Negro, whose tea-black waters, poor in fish, are dyed by roots. Indeed, Jurupari effectively defines this multilingual region, on the map and in history. As a phenomenon, the Jurupari rituals, narratives and songs are perhaps the most important markers of its striking coherence.

Lying along the borders of Brazil, Colombia, and Venezuela, the upper Rio Negro region is the home of more than 30 indigenous groups that speak roughly 20 languages from three linguistic families: Tukano (Eastern and Central), Arawakan (Maipuran variety), and Maku.[2] In spite of the large linguistic and cultural differences, celebrated in stories that tell the origin and characteristics of each, the intense interaction among these groups results in what has been called a "regional system," and a "regional network" (Neves, 132), which was already in place before the arrival of the Portuguese. Besides the Jurupari phenomenon, which highlights the specific role and use of musical instruments, the main characteristics of this system are the employment of *trocano* drums for communication; the use of several hallucinogenic and nonhallucinogenic drugs (tobacco, coca, *yagé*,

173

and *paricá*); exogamous marriages and patrilineal social organization; the ritual importance of the long-house or *maloca*; intense hierarchy among different groups and among sibs within each exogamous group; and shared aspects of cosmogony, such as the emphasis on ophidian history.

A key element in this system is undoubtedly the plurilingualism of most of these societies. Speaking two or three native languages, besides Spanish and Portuguese, is a common practice in the region, and often it is culturally enforced by rules that determine marriages between exogamous groups that speak different tongues (Neves, 142). Moreover, there is historical evidence of linguistic interaction. The Tariana, for instance, are generally believed to be an original Arawakan group that has become "Tukanized." And a few groups, such as the Baré and Warekena, have replaced their native languages with Nheengatu, the Tupian lingua franca widely used in the nineteenth century as the trade language in the region and still spoken today all along the Rio Negro (Neves, 136). Some Baniwa groups were described by Koch-Grünberg at the beginning of the twentieth century as being in the process of giving up their own (Arawakan) language and starting to speak Cubeo (a Tukanoan language). Less than twenty years later Nimuendaju observed the reverse process among the same groups.

Archaeologists still debate which groups arrived first in the region, but most agree that human presence in the Rio Negro goes back at least 3,200 years. The first European reference to Rio Negro appears in Fray Gaspar de Carvajal's account of Francisco de Orellana's 1541–42 expedition through the Amazon: "We saw the mouth of another large river, to the left, which flowed into our river. Its waters were inky black, thus we named it Rio Negro" (50). By the seventeenth century, the river and its tributaries had become the highway of the so-called *tropas de resgate* (rescue troops)—Portuguese slave hunters. Slaves soon became the major Portuguese enterprise in the region: "The Portuguese establishments in Rio Negro were founded to serve as concentration camps for the abundant trade in Indian slaves in the upper Rio Negro and upper Orinoco, using the Manao Indians as intermediaries" (Useche Losada, 87). In 1759, Father José de Moraes made the following observation about the slave trade in Rio Negro: "The abundance of people produced by this river and its neighboring territory is admirable. From the beginning until today the Portuguese continue to bring Indians from those backlands, and in my opinion 2000 souls must have been extracted from this river" (Meira, 8). In fact, the numbers were probably much larger. Around the same date, another Jesuit, Father João Daniel, declared that

from Rio Negro alone [there seem to have come] about 3 million Indian slaves, as we can see in the registration books. They were sold in the plazas and divided amongst the villagers. . . . because more than anywhere else these barbarian nations that ate one another were concentrated along this river. (quoted in Meira, 9)

The fact that the Indians, according to the priest, supposedly "ate one another," is a crucial part of the argument. Since enslavement of Indians was illegal, it was only allowed by both the Spanish and the Portuguese crowns under certain "just causes": intertribal warfare, the practice of cannibalism, and attacks against Europeans. False claims of cannibalism were therefore regularly used to justify European attacks and enslavement.

The Europeans also fostered ancient enmities in the region, provoking wars that once again justified their own attacks. Several Indian groups were involved in those wars, and many became intermediaries in the slave trade. The most often mentioned are the Manao, but other groups, like the Tariana, were also involved. The upper Rio Negro Indians still have narratives that tell the history of intertribal wars from those times, listing entire groups that disappeared as a result (Wright 1992, 264).

In the beginning of the eighteenth century, the Manao chief Ajuricaba, who was married to a Tariana woman, led a revolt against the Portuguese, and created a regional pan-Indian movement sometimes referred to as the first Indian Confederation in the Amazon (Reis, 79), which lasted from 1723 to 1728. As a response to the revolt, the Portuguese declared "just war" against the Manao, accusing them of alliances with the Dutch. The diplomat Joaquim Nabuco, himself hardly a lover of Indians, studied the documents of the period at the end of the nineteenth century, and strongly refuted those accusations: "This accusation was the best that the eager slave traders could use in order to receive authorization for their enslaving wars" (80).

After 1755, under the government of Marquis de Pombal, the enslaving of Indians was completely outlawed. The practice was replaced by a system of "directors" who managed the economic enterprises in the region. The directors were supposed to convince the Indians to "go down" *(descer)* to organized settlements, where they would be "protected" and would be expected to obey European laws. The objective of the *descimentos* was to control the frontier and also to provide labor for the economic activities developed by the directors: the gathering of spices and medicinal plants, production of manioc flour, cotton, indigo, coffee, etc. Several epidemics broke out as a result of those *descimentos* and the prolonged contact between Indians and military. Many thousands of people died, and many others fled the settlements and their own villages. By the end of the eighteenth century, the margins of the upper Rio Negro had experienced a great population decrease (Wright 1981, 139–59).

The fall of Marquis of Pombal and the failure of the *descimentos* system reduced Portuguese economic activities in the Amazon, allowing the Indians to enjoy a period of relative peace. The dramatic increase in the rubber commerce after the middle of the nineteenth century, however, brought further terrible changes. When Theodor Koch-Grünberg visited the region in 1903–5, he described how men and women from several communities would run in fear of any "civilized" man, completely terrorized by the rubber barons who dominated areas of both Colombia and Brazil. Trying to escape from violence and enslavement, the Indians in the upper Rio Negro often had to leave their ancestral land in search of other homes, creating, once again, territorial vacuums that were then occupied by other groups. This history of occupations and reoccupations of places is also detailed in recent narratives of the Baniwa and the Desana (Wright 1998, 233).

Missionary presence in the upper Rio Negro dates back to the late seventeenth century, when a letter from the Portuguese Crown assigned the task of conversion to the Carmelites, who were, from the beginning, directly and indirectly involved in the slave trade (Meira, 10). On the Spanish side, the Capuchinos of Andalucia and Cataluña were the first priests in the region; both were later replaced by the Franciscans, who proved more industrious and committed to conversion. And although missionary activity in the upper Rio Negro remained embryonic until the twentieth century, it left strong marks in the native populations. In the nineteenth century, several messianic movements led by Indians and mestizos mixed native elements with Christian influence. The most famous of these leaders was Venâncio Kamiko, the Içana Christ, still mentioned today in Baniwa and Tukano narratives.[3] In 1883, Franciscan missionaries, convinced that the word Jurupari meant devil, confiscated the Jurupari sacred instruments from the Indians, who rebelled and expelled the priests from the region.

Wallace's pioneer descriptions were followed by concentrated efforts to make the Jurupari phenomenon, and its corresponding narratives, better known. In fact, the very first full-length publications of native stories in Brazil have to do, one way or another, with the Jurupari. Such is the case with João Barbosa Rodrigues's *Poranduba Amazonense* and Ermanno Stradelli's *Leggenda dell' Jurupary,* both published in 1890. The first is a collection of stories (*poranduba* is a Nheengatu term for "tales of the imagination") from various regions of the Amazon, many of them from the upper Rio Negro, published bilingually in Portuguese and Nheengatu. The *Leggenda* is a long and complex Tariana version of the Jurupari narrative, published in Italian. It was collected by Maximiano José Roberto, a son of a Manao *tuxaua* and a Tariana woman who devoted a good deal of time to listening to indigenous stories from different groups and writing them down in Nheengatu. In fact, many of the stories he collected were also used by Antônio Brandão do Amorim in his posthumous *Lendas em Nheengatu e Português* (1928).

Jurupari (or Jurupary, Yuruparí) is a Nheengatu word whose meaning has been diversely explained. For Couto de Magalhães it meant "take from the mouth" (83). Batista Caetano translated it as "a being that comes to our hammock" (Couto de Magalhães, 83), and Stradelli, whose *Vocabulários* give the meaning of "juru" as "mouth," and "pari" as "a grid that protects the mouth of the river," claims to have been told by an Indian that Jurupari meant "born from the fruit." As a Nheengatu word, Jurupari is foreign to most groups in the region, and for that reason many anthropologists have objected to its use. In 1905, for instance, Paul Ehrenreich observed that:

> The constant use of words taken from *Língua Geral* side by side with other words from the language of the Tariana or other groups from the Uaupés is extremely disorienting. The name Yuruparí itself has created a lot of confusion, for this mythical character has nothing to do with the well-known Tupi forest spirit that missionaries identified with the Devil. It is, on the contrary, a solar hero, what is already explained by its name Izi, that means Sun in Tukano." (quoted in Schaden 1959, 150)

Schaden (1959) and Goldman (1963) also object to the use of the term. Employing it here, I follow Stephen Hugh-Jones's argument, that

> Leaving aside the confusions of the missionaries, there still exists a considerable body of myths about someone to whom those who recorded them rightly or wrongly assigned the name Yurupary. These myths are close variants of one another in spite of coming from societies widely separated in space. They are also close variants of other myths concerning characters whose names are given in the original language of the people who told them. All these myths come from a single geographic area and one in which the Indian cultures are, or were, strikingly similar to one another. In view of this, and leaving aside the Devil, I see no great objection to calling these myths Yurupary myths, nor to calling their heroes Yurupary, provided that it is understood that these heroes are not identical and that each has his own proper name. (7–9)

Some equivalent terms are *He* in Barasana, *Guelamun Yé* in Desana, *Koé* (Kowa) in Tariana, and *Waxti* in Tukano proper. It is important to note that the term Jurupari is often used by the Indians when talking to non-Indian visitors.

Jurupari and its equivalent terms are used to refer to the male initiation rituals that involve self-flagellation, ingestion of hallucinogenic drugs, eating, drinking, dancing, and playing instruments that must never be seen by women. The instruments themselves are called Jurupari (or its equivalent), and so is the cultural hero that taught men when and how to play them.

Despite the differences between various versions, most stories about the hero Jurupari include the birth of a male child (Jurupari) from a virgin (that is, prepubescent) mother who was, in most cases, impregnated by juice falling from a fruit. The child is taken away from the mother by the shaman and returns later as a powerful young adult who teaches the community the "new rules," i.e., the Jurupari rules. These rules are about general behavioral patterns, such as how to respect the exogamous marriage system, but above all, they tell men never to let women see the sacred Jurupari instruments, and never give in to innate female curiosity, licentiousness, and indiscretion. Women, on the other hand, are told by Jurupari that they are never to attempt to see the sacred instruments, under penalty of death if they disobey; and to be discreet, capable of keeping secrets, and free of curiosity and licentiousness.

Several versions also narrate an attempt on the part of the women to seize the Jurupari instruments. With varying degrees of success the women become, while in possession of the instruments, men's oppressors (in some cases men also start to menstruate). In some versions, the women's control of the sacred instruments represents the recovery of a power they once had.

Most versions also describe how Jurupari, as a powerful young man or a foolish elder, goes out to the forest with three youngsters, whom he tells not to pick fruit from a certain tree (or not to cook the fruit or burn the nuts from a tree). They disobey him and he then kills them by creating a storm that forces them to look for shelter in a cave that is actually his anus (or nose). The fathers of the deceased children decide to kill him, and he tells them that the only way to do that is by burning him in a fire. From his ashes grow different kinds of palm trees from whose wood the Jurupari instruments are carved.

Stradelli's *Leggenda*

To date, the longest published version of the Jurupari narrative is the one collected by Maximiano José Roberto among the Tariana and published in 1890 by Stradelli under the title *Leggenda dell' Jurupary*. To my knowledge, the first translation into Portuguese was done by Father Alcionílio Brüzzi Alves da Silva, and was published posthumously only in 1994. A new translation by Aurora Bernardini, edited by Sérgio Luiz Medeiros, has recently appeared (2002). In Spanish, the first translation came out in 1983 in a volume published by Victor Orjuela.

In the beginning of the *Leggenda,* most Tariana men had been killed by an epidemic, and the only ones left were a few elders, among whom there was a powerful shaman. Worried about the future of the Tariana, the women assembled and decided to abuse the old men sexually, and kill them if they failed to perform. The old shaman heard their plot, and furiously proclaimed that the women should keep away from any decision regarding the community. He also invited them to enter the lake with him, and without sexual intercourse he impregnated them all.

The most beautiful child conceived during this bathing event was a girl called Seucy from the Earth (later Seucy, the Pleiades), who later became pregnant from the juice of a fruit and gave birth to Jurupari. As in other versions, Jurupari was taken away from his mother after birth and raised in the forest. Years later, he came back as a powerful young man, who became the new *tuxaua,* and began to teach the Tariana a new set of rules. In order to explain those rules to the men, he called a meeting in which women were not allowed to participate. At the meeting, Jurupari told the men that no women should be allowed in men's festivals, and they should never see the Jurupari instruments. Any woman who disobeyed those rules should be killed, and so should any man who revealed the Jurupari secrets to them. Some women had been sent as spies to the meeting, but they were discovered and turned into stone. Still, the women did not give up, and continued to plot against Jurupari. In order to escape their hostility, Jurupari told five old men to build the Jurupari-house, a meeting place far to the west of the village. The old men finished their task early, and then wandered off to the neighboring Nunuiba village, where they were seduced by young women. Ualri, the anteater, the most foolish of these old men, revealed the Jurupari secret rules to a woman. Later, he followed three Nunuiba youngsters to the forest, where, at their request, he climbed a tree to gather some nuts. He told the young men not to burn the nuts because he would be blinded and suffocated by the smoke. They disobeyed him, and as a revenge, he caused a violent storm, told the youngsters to shelter in his nose, and killed them. Their fathers retaliated by burning Ualri to death.

Jurupari found out, through his magical powers, what had happened to Ualri. He took all his men to the Jurupari-house and publicly shamed the surviving old men. He then told them a story from the time of his ancestors. Inset into the main narrative, it goes as follows: In the old times, the Tariana could only dance with their own man or woman, and widows and widowers could not remarry. Since more women than men were born, women were forced to remain single. One young woman ran away, and married into the tribe of the jacami birds. She gave birth to two human beings, a boy named Pinon (snake in Tukano) and a girl named Meenspuin, names that denote the constellations Scorpio and Pleiades (Brotherston, 2000). After shooting, in ignorance, his own jacami relatives, Pinon took his mother and sister back to the land of their human ancestors. Upon arrival, in spite of his young age, he made several demonstrations of his power as a shaman, and forced the Tariana to change their strict marriage rules. We then find out that Pinon was the same powerful shaman that impregnated all the Tariana women in the beginning of the story. In other words, he was Jurupari's grandfather.

After telling this story, Jurupari taught the men the name of each instrument (wind and percussion), a repertoire remarkable for its linguistic federalism (Brotherston, 2000), and took them in several missions to preach the new rules to the neighboring tribes.

Stradelli's *Leggenda* has been plagued by polemics. In the same year that it was published (1890), the *Anais da Biblioteca Nacional, 1886–87*, which included Barbosa Rodrigues's *Poranduba Amazonense,* also appeared. In this volume, Barbosa Rodrigues published two Tariana narratives that are very similar to parts of the *Leggenda*. The first starts with the birth of Jurupari and goes through to his departure to the sky; the second tells a story similar to the narrative inset by Jurupari in Stradelli's *Leggenda,* the story of Pinon and Meenspuin. In Barbosa Rodrigues's version, the children have no names but are still identified with the constellations Pinon (Big Snake) and Seucy (Pleiades). According to his own testimony, Barbosa Rodrigues became even more interested in the Jurupari phenomenon when he was researching *A Muyraquytã e os Ídolos Simbólicos* (1898/99). In 1888 he had asked Maximiano José Roberto to provide him with a complete version of the narrative. According to him, he chose Maximiano because of his knowledge of Nheengatu and of the cultures in the region. But for reasons that remain unknown, Maximiano decided to give the text to Stradelli, who published it in Italy, without the Nheengatu version. Barbosa Rodrigues did not give up, and in the "very enhanced" second edition of the *Muyraquitã* (1899) he gave the following account of the episode:

> Many times I talked about the subject with Count Stradelli and Bento Aranha and, when I relied on receiving the manuscript (. . .) I learned that the Count was already in possession of it, and that he was going to translate it into Italian and take it to Europe. I then asked the Count if he would allow me to read it before he sent it to Europe, but he always managed to avoid doing so. (vii)[4]

He also reproduced, in the same "enhanced edition" of the *Muyraquitã* "another version" of the narrative which, he claimed, was collected prior to the one published by Stradelli. According to him, this version had remained unpublished because he "had to leave the Amazon." This version, still according to him, coincided with the one published by Stradelli. But as Héctor Orjuela has already observed, the reading of this "version" reveals that coincidence is not really the right term. One can say with almost absolute certainty that Barbosa Rodrigues's Jurupari is just a reproduction of the story published by Stradelli in 1890. There are not enough differences between the two versions for us to believe that they could have been told by two different narrators.

This is not the only difficulty that surrounds Stradelli's *Leggenda*. Since the text bears certain traits of the literary style of the time it was published, and since it is the longest known version of Jurupari's story, many have seen it as the creation, to a great degree, of Stradelli. This is, for instance, the opinion of an indisputable authority on the Jurupari phenomenon, Gerardo Reichel-Dolmatoff. For him, although Stradelli's narrative has received occasional attention from ethnologists, it has been used, most of the time, to feed the "imagination of certain *littérateurs*": "I have read Stradelli's 'legend' in Italian, Portuguese, and Spanish, and have formed my own conclusions about it. In my opinion, Amazonian Indians do not talk like that; they do not use florid images of immaculate maidens, wise law-givers, and purified spirits rising heavenward" (1989, 126).

On the other hand, Lévi-Strauss, in spite of being equally rude about the literariness of Stradelli's text, says that "It would seem that some early inquirers in the Amazonian basin, prominent among whom were Barbosa Rodrigues, Amorim, and Stradelli, were still able to find exoteric texts belonging to a learned tradition, and comparable in this connection to those discovered more recently by Nimuendaju and Cadogan among the southern Guarani" (1973, 271). Also, Stephen Hugh-Jones's excellent analysis of the Jurupari rituals in *The Palm and the Pleiades* gives a lot of importance to Stradelli's version of the narrative; and in Colombia, the *Leggenda* has been seen as a literary masterpiece (Orjuela) and even as the "origin of Colombian literature," as the subtitle of Cecilia Caicedo de Cajigas's book indicates.

The manuscript given by Maximiano to Stradelli has been lost, and since the latter spent the last years of his life fighting leprosy, there is a great probability that it will never be found. Thus, we cannot be sure about the extent to which the narratives collected by Maximiano José Roberto were changed by Stradelli. For his part, Stradelli himself claimed to have been completely faithful to the original manuscript, and described his translation as being "as straight-forward as possible" (1890, 453). On his writing style we have a comment by the folklorist Luiz da Câmara Cascudo, who was impressed by Stradelli's travel descriptions because, according to him, "they did not attempt to narrate exciting adventures, but simply told exactly what happened, no matter how boring that was" (33). Brandão do Amorim, who knew both Stradelli and Maximiano, describes the narrative as "the great legend collected by Max Roberto" (224).

There is no doubt that some stylistic devices allow us to hear Stradelli's voice in the *Leggenda*. When Jurupari, for instance, punishes the inquisitive women who had followed him by transforming them into stone (including his own mother), her statue is described as "having a malicious smile on her lips"—a description that resembles more Boccacio than other passages in the text. Yet, if we compare the *Leggenda* to other Jurupari narratives, there seem to be no major changes at the level of characters and plot. The following observation by Reichel-Dolmatoff about what Jurupari is not, which refers implicitly to Stradelli's narrative, could certainly be applied to many other versions of the narrative:

> Yuruparí is neither a "cult" nor a "religion"; it does not represent a "culture hero" or a "law giver"; in fact it is not a personalized concept at all. Yuruparí is not a "secret society" nor does it use "sacred paraphernalia." Yuruparí is not a legend except in the fantasy of some romantics; it is not an "epic poem" nor can it be compared, by any stretch of the imagination, with the Mayan *Popol Vuh,* the Germanic *Nibelungen Lied* or the Finnish *Kalevala.*" (1989, 97)

Against this, it must be pointed out that among the published Jurupari texts there are several that deal with a hero that can be described as a personalized ruler, as is the case with the examples analyzed by Jacqueline Bolens and quoted by Reichel-Dolmatoff himself in this same article. Among them, one could mention the narratives in Barbosa Rodrigues's *Poranduba,* and Brandão do Amorim's *Lendas.* In all of them, Jurupari, if not a lawgiver, is definitely a preacher and an enforcer of (often new) rules. These rules revolve around the idea of all-male secret rituals and instruments.

As for the structure, Stradelli said, in a very significant yet inexplicably ignored statement, that "[Maximiano] collected the legend from different narrators, compared and organized the various versions and then submitted them to the judgment of a group of Indians, so that he was able to make sure he could present the most faithful expression of the indigenous legend" (1890, 453). This report accords well with the remarkable coherence of the narrative, its intricate structure of plot and subplot, in particular of stories intercalated and of identities not immediately revealed in decidedly Native American fashion. Despite Stradelli's unequivocal statement, Câmara Cascudo later claimed, with apparently no evidence to support him, that the narratives collected by Maximiano were organized not by

Maximiano José Roberto but by Stradelli: "[Maximiano] simply kept the material he collected in its purity, without commenting on it or making any deductions about it. He then gave it to Stradelli, who translated it and adapted it to the narrative genre, articulating the different phases of the tale" (56). Cascudo's claim was accepted by both Reichel-Dolmatoff (1996, xxix) and Orjuela (129) yet seems less plausible than that made by Stradelli on Maximiano José Roberto's behalf.

Also, the fact that Lévi-Strauss compared Stradelli's text to such narratives as Nimuendaju's "Die Sagen," and León Cadogan *Ayvu-Rapyta* should not be ignored. First, because given Lévi-Strauss's long experience with South American indigenous texts, one would expect that had he had the slightest suspicion about the text published by Stradelli, he would not have included it in his list of the great South American sacred narratives. Second, because we learn from the publication of the Guarani texts mentioned above, and more recently, from Marc de Civrieux's publication of the So'to *Watunna*, that great cosmogonic narratives probably do exist in most lowland South American societies, but they are known only by initiates and revealed only to those who manage to obtain the community's complete trust. "Die Sagen," *Ayvu-Rapyta*, and *Watunna*, as we have seen, include phases of the world creation that up to the moment of their recording had been completely unknown to strangers. These phases antecede chronologically the actions of transformers or rulers whose adventures are also being told in those texts. Fragments of these adventures are usually known by all the population.

An episode of the *Leggenda* that is absent in most versions of the Jurupari narrative is the story of Pinon and Meenspuin, which chronologically antecedes Jurupari's birth. Barbosa Rodrigues's *Poranduba* includes it as a separate story, in the section dedicated to "Yurupary Myths." Significantly, the beginning of Barbosa Rodrigues's narrative situates it at the time when "young women tended Jurupari's instruments" (125). And the last sentence explains that what has just been told "happened in the beginning; it is the origin of our grandfathers" (127). The fact that Stradelli's version includes it as part of the Jurupari story could indicate that the *Leggenda*, like "Die Sagen," *Ayvu-Rapyta*, and *Watunna*, is a sacred text, acquired thanks to the trust that Maximiano José Roberto, as their descendant, enjoyed among the Tariana.

The sacredness of the *Leggenda* could explain as well the chronological ordering of further episodes that in other versions are parallel or completely disconnected from the Jurupari narrative. Ualri's story is a case in point. In other versions, Jurupari himself is portrayed as an old man who kills three youngsters who disobey him, and is then buried by the infuriated fathers of the children.[5] In Stradelli's *Leggenda,* the protagonist of the episode is not Jurupari himself, but Ualri, the anteater. Both characters, in all versions, have a crucial role to play in the Jurupari rituals: From their ashes, the pashiuba palm grows, providing wood for the Jurupari instruments.

On the chronology of apparently parallel episodes Hugh-Jones observed:

> Barasana myths are divided into a number of different cycles. Although not all the cycles are placed in a single, chronological order, stories about *Romi Kumu* and the other Sky People *(Umuari Masa)* are seen as older and earlier than stories about Manioc-stick Anaconda, which in turn are earlier and older than stories about *Yeba.* While the Barasana definitely recognize this chronology and also stress that the stories of each cycle are different, this does not prevent a certain degree of fusion from taking place. One of the most striking aspects of this fusion is that a person will often start telling a myth with one character as the main protagonist and then, half-way through the story, he will switch and start talking about another character. (168)

It is worth comparing these lines with Civrieux's explanations about the different *Watunna:*

> These popular versions which form an integral part of every Makiritare's daily life and recreation differ in fundamental ways from the *ademi* heard in the *Wanwanna.* The *ademi* are rigid and exact texts which cannot be altered in any way without losing their oral power. . . . But once outside the *Wanwanna,* everyone, including the women and children, is free to tell the stories in whatever form they like. These variations, altered and abbreviated, subject to personal interpretations and the teller's level of knowledge and memory, still fulfill the *Watunna's* essential role of teaching the tribe's history and spreading its ethical and social ideals. (16–17)

Like *Watunna,* Stradelli's *Leggenda* has the characteristics of the sacred and interconnected version of narratives that in everyday life are told in less ceremonious, ever-changing and disparate ways.

In general terms, the coherence between structure and plot in the *Leggenda* argues for an organization determined by the plot itself, which, as we have seen, is mostly about the birth and history of Jurupari and his efforts to impose his rules to the peoples of Uaupés. In other words, the *Leggenda* tells the story of an imperialist war, whose objective is not the acquisition of territory, but the imposition of a lifestyle. Unlike the tricksters analyzed in previous chapters, the hero Jurupari, master of this war, has no sense of humor. His only objective, if not obsession, is to impose his rules on the rest of the world. His powers, superhuman since his birth, become stronger throughout the narrative. As we have seen, Stradelli's Jurupari does not differ greatly from other Jurupari characters in the region, and although secret men's cults appear in other parts of lowland South America, Jurupari's imperative vocation seems quite extraordinary in the context of Amazonian literature. His exceptional behavior must be related to the peculiar history of the upper Rio Negro, where the practice of the rigid prohibitions related to the Jurupari ritual was adopted by various peoples otherwise separated by different languages and practices.

As we have noted, the exact trajectory of this history is still being debated by scholars. A good summary of these debates is given by Neves, who also formulates his own theory, based on archaeological and linguistic evidence, about the arrival of different groups in the Uaupés. In general terms, most scholars seem to agree with Nimuendaju's original thesis that both the Maku and the Arawak have been in the region longer than the Tukano (Nimuendaju 1950, 155). Neves, however, uses recently excavated evidence to show that the Arawakan Tariana migrated to the region after some Tukano groups had already begun to reside there (168). Reichel-Dolmatoff also believes that there were some Tukano groups already sharing the territory with the Arawak and the Maku when a new Tukano migration took place from the East. According to him, these new Tukanos were a patrilineal society who practiced exogamy, and since they lacked women, the local Arawaks allowed them to marry their women as long as they followed the Arawak matrilineal rules and endogamy. This caused great trauma to the Tukano, who, after much conflict, managed to impose their own rules about exogamy and patrilineal descent on the Arawaks. For Reichel-Dolmatoff, the phenomenon of Jurupari is linked to this imposition.

Neves does not offer a theory for the Jurupari phenomenon, but he questions Reichel-Dolmatoff's assumption that the Arawaks practiced endogamy and matrilineal descent:

> Another problem results from Reichel-Dolmatoff's presentation of Maipuran Arawakans as endogamous, matrilineal and uxorilocal societies. We have already seen that this is not the case (Hill, 1987; Wright, 1994) and, thus, there is no ground to support Reichel-Dolmatoff's claim. (169)

Be that as it may, the narrative emphasis on Jurupari's spreading of a new order in the region seems to go along with Reichel-Dolmatoff's idea that at some point in the upper Rio Negro history, new rules about the relationship between men and women were imposed on various groups. That could explain the region's extraordinary cultural unity.

Jurupari's imperialism is not limited to the neighboring groups. His is above all a war of men against women. The main objective of his rules is to teach men how to subjugate the female sex. In other words, one of the main themes of the *Leggenda* is power: the power of men against women and the power of Jurupari to impose his rules on other peoples. Jurupari's extraordinary power and his peculiar determination to rule, which does not allow him even to be touched by a woman, seem to be connected not only to the political situation of the upper Rio Negro, with its complex cultural wars and alliances, but also to his status as a powerful shaman, the successor of Pinon. Hugh Jones, for instance, says that the shamans "are also conceived of as sexually ambiguous. First, there is an ideal that they should remain celibate and unmarried as contact with women diminishes their power" (125).

Among Jurupari's shamanic instruments we find the magic stones that allow him to see what is happening or has happened in other places. Thanks to the use of these stones, the narrative plays with a series of revelations a priori and a posteriori which technically also afford Jurupari power over the narrative itself. This is one of the richest literary resources in the *Leggenda,* and the best demonstration of its structural coherence.

Such power does not come all at once. After Jurupari tells the old men to build the Jurupari-house, for instance, we switch to what is happening in the region of the Aiary river, away from the ruler's eyes. After Ualri's death, as we have seen, Jurupari again consults his magical stone in order to find out what had happened. As if he were watching a television screen, he "admired the beauty of the Nunuiba women, and laughed at the old men," but when he became aware of Ualri's stupidity, an access of anger made him throw the stone to the air. This scene allows us to see for the first time the power of Jurupari's magical stones, and at the same time, look through his eyes at the replay of an event that we had already seen. In other words, in spite of Jurupari's magical powers, at this point in the narrative we, the readers/listeners, know more than he. The stones are clearly linked to narrative reflexivity: They give Jurupari the power to know what happened in the past. But such reflexivity is also linked to the cosmic forces with which the shaman Jurupari interacts; the stones that allow him to know the stories, become, when thrown to the air, "little lights that have come to stain night's darkness" (28).

Then Jurupari goes to meet the foolish old men, who cannot find words to explain what happened to their companion Ualri. Jurupari, by contrast, knows exactly what to say, and tells them the story of Pinon and Meenspuin. As a narrative device, the insertion of such an episode in this position is impeccable. It is not merely a question of placing a story within a story, but of telling the Tariana creation story to old men who had been muted by their own foolishness. The most significant words of all—the cosmogonic narrative—are used against the old men's silence, turning Jurupari into the *owner of the word and of the world.* The creation story jus-

tifies Jurupari's deeds as well, since Pinon is his direct ancestor and the first
one to establish the rules now applied to all Tariana. Moreover, the revelation of who Pinon was makes explicit the narrative device of postponed
revelation, since Pinon can be identified with the anonymous shaman from
the beginning of the story.[6]

Pinon's episode is a turning point in the narrative. Before telling the
story, Jurupari seemed to doubt the effectiveness of his own rules, and
grew weepy and depressed after seeing how women and old men disobeyed
him. After he told the story, Jurupari became an implacable ruler, and the
narrative, with its multiple a posteriori revelations, acquires an almost fre-
netic rhythm. The process observed in relation to Ualri's story—we, the
readers/listeners knew, before Jurupari, what had happened—is inverted.
Now Jurupari, the owner of the narrative, tells, when he finds it convenient,
what has happened. This unconventional way of narrating seems to test,
as in the case of the Tariana women, the readers's patience and curiosity.
When Jurupari and his friends, for instance, arrived at the place where the
women had been converted to stone, they found only children's bones and
women's hair. We do not know what happened, and have to wait for them to
burn the bones, drink the ashes, and bury the corpses of their own mothers
to finally learn that the women had become desperate, not knowing what
had happened to their men (who had followed Jurupari in his proselytiz-
ing campaign), and had killed their male sons, cut their own hair (which
bore the smell of their husbands's lips), and tried, unsuccessfully, to take
the stone women with them. Where to? We don't know, because the narrative is interrupted once again when Jurupari puts his hand in the bag of
magical objects and finds out that he had been betrayed by the daughter of
the Ariana *tuxaua,* who had challenged his prohibition and seen the sacred
instruments. They return to the Ariana village and only then are we told
how the *tuxaua*'s daughter had betrayed them. After solving that problem
and preaching once again his rules to the Ariana women, Jurupari and his
friend Caryda go to the Jurupari-house in order to punish the foolish old
men. Then they go East, and arrive at a land where the position of *tuxaua*
was traditionally given to the most beautiful person, man or woman. The
tuxaua of the moment was Narumá, a woman, who asked to marry Date,
one of Jurupari's men. At this point the narrative is interrupted once
more, because Jurupari finally decides to tell his men—and his readers/
listeners—what had happened to the Tariana women: They had walked to
another village, where they were able to find new husbands. We then return
to the story of Date and Narumá, which ends in a war between men and
women, in which the latter, as might be expected, lose.

As we can see, the very rhythm of the narrative is determined by

Jurupari; in other words, it is intrinsically associated with the hero's extra-ordinary powers. The internal coherence of the text is inextricably based on a knowledge of the Jurupari phenomenon possible only for someone with a lifelong knowledge of Tariana culture. This all strengthens the idea that the *Leggenda* was not just collected but also arranged by Maximiano José Roberto, nephew of a *tuxaua,* rather than by Stradelli. After all, this much was said by Stradelli himself, who, as we have seen, claimed that his transla-tion of the manuscript was "as straightforward as possible."

Careful analysis of the narrative devices of the *Leggenda* not only helps us to understand the complex Jurupari phenomenon, it also confirms that Stradelli's translation should indeed be included among the great literary masterpieces of native South America. Such literariness does not threaten its role as the proclamation of social rules or as a possibly sacred text. Contrary to Reichel-Dolmatoff's claim, the *Leggenda* deserves compari-son with not only the *Popol Vuh,*[7] the *Nibelungen Lied,* and the *Kalevala,* but also the Bible and the *Theogony.* Like these texts, the *Leggenda* shows that the divorce between texts that are literary from those that are sacred, philosophical, or historical is a relatively recent creation of Western socie-ties, and it has been used to feed less the imagination of *littérateurs* than the prejudice of ethnographers.

Brandão do Amorim's *Lendas*

Jurupari and its taboos are a major theme in Brandão do Amorim's *Lendas em Nheengatú e em Português.* Amorim was born in Manaus and studied in Portugal. Before finishing his university degree in Coimbra he went back to his native city to work at the Botanical Museum, under the direction of Barbosa Rodrigues. Among his colleagues were Ermanno Stradelli and Maximiano José Roberto.

Lendas was a lifelong project whose publication was never witnessed by Amorim himself, who died in 1926. His brother sent the originals to *Revista do Instituto Histórico e Geográfico,* which published them two years later. The collection consists of thirty-three narratives, a few of which are different versions of the same story. The great majority of these narratives were collected in the upper Rio Negro region. All, except for two, have both Portuguese and Nheengatu versions, with numbered lines.

Before its publication, the manuscript of *Lendas* traveled from hand to hand and became, so to speak, a mandatory text for those interested in Amazonian culture. Mário de Andrade, Oswald de Andrade, Raul Bopp, Cassiano Ricardo, Plínio Salgado, and Menotti del Picchia—in other words, the *modernista* Pantheon—all read Amorim's *Lendas.* Such success has to be understood in terms not only of the narratives themselves, which are, in many cases, similar to the ones published by Barbosa Rodrigues's *Poranduba*, but also of their language. Unlike all collections of native narratives previously published, Amorim's uses, in the Portuguese translation, the colloquial discourse of the Amazon. Throughout the stories, he brings out the playfulness and freshness of the popular Amazonian version of Portuguese. His dialogues never sound "folkloric" or fossilized; on the contrary: they seem natural, intelligent, and alive. In fact, Amorim's careful working of the popular language can be matched, in Brazilian literary history before him, only by the works of the Simões Lopes Neto, who collected popular tales from his native Rio Grande do Sul. Yet Brandão do Amorim's *Lendas* have had a very different fate from those of his *gaúcho* counterpart: Although their language was celebrated and imitated by the best modernist writers, the legends themselves never managed to be included in literary histories, except as ethnographic sources—and even that very rarely.

The repetition of syllables within verbs of movement—an influence of Nheengatú—is one of the poetic traits of popular Amazonian speech that Amorim frequently employs, as we can see in the following examples: "a pele dos peixes brilhabrilhava" ("the skin of the fish shineshined," after Nheengatu "oueráuerá"); "elas nadanadavam" ("they swimswam," after Nheengatu "oytáuytá"); "as mulheres boiaboiavam perto dele" ("the women floatfloated near him," after Nheengatu "opuápuámo"), and so on. In all of these cases the repetitive, flickering nature of the movement in question is reinforced by the doubled syllables—a very effective and economical poetic device which will be used later by Raul Bopp in *Cobra Norato* (see next chapter), and by Guimarães Rosa.

While in regular Portuguese the diminutive *inho/inha* can only be used to modify adjectives, nouns and certain pronouns, in *Lendas* it is applied to verbs as well: "ela querzinho ir para o outro lado," and "Eles estão todos tristes, adoçazinho seu coração."[8] Onomatopoeia appears frequently: "soon the *pitiro* bird sang pitiro pitiro pitiro"; "he looked for her, his heart immediately went: *tike*," and so on. Regular Portuguese syntax is often replaced by a popular version of grammar that is closer to Nheengatú than to Portuguese itself. It is the case of *porção* (bunch, after Nheengatú "seyia"), which Amorim places directly after the noun—a totally unacceptable position from the point of view of standard Portuguese, but possible in Nheengatú: "ele viu gente porção" (he saw people bunch), and "viram n'uma árvore grande pássaro porção comendo a fruta dela" (they saw birds bunch on a big tree, eating her fruit).

Time is frequently described in metaphors that sound like Portuguese/Nheengatú versions of Homeric formulas: "before day prettied up"; "dawn began to pretty up"; "day was already blushing"; "before night tangled up our eyes"; "in the saddening of the afternoon," and so on. In general terms, *Lendas* are full of semantically unusual images, direct translations of Nheengatú that acquire in Portuguese dramatic poetic effect: "when he reached the dreadful of it [the waterfall], he disappeared"; "Pa, have you perhaps seen people run through this waterfall where death is boiling?"; "Three times our eyes have married," and so on.

Repetition is used in order to give the narratives a rhythm, keeping them closer to oral discourse. One of Amorim's most attractive techniques along this line is the constant use of *contam* (they say) interrupting sentences, as in the following example:

> A moment later, another young man saw the girl.
> His heart, they say, went: zih!
> Beautiful! beautiful, they say, he found her. (414)

Such interruptions also have the function of reminding the reader that these stories are not the creation of an individual, but belong to a collective body of knowledge.

The *modernistas'* enchantment with Amorim's collection is understandable: there was nothing in the Brazilian prose of the time to match his playful and sensitive rendition of popular, let alone Amazonian, language. For that reason, *Lendas* should be seen not simply as a "source text," but as one of the most significant *modernista* works.

Although Jurupari, as a character, appears only in the story "The origin of fire," his rules and Rio Negro's peculiar gender anxiety figure recurrently. In "The origin of fire," we are offered no information about Jurupari's birth or childhood. Instead, the "Sun's son" is preceded in the village by a young man who is fished from the river and teaches the community how to use the "mother of warmth" (fire) to cook. He then tells the *tuxaua* about the imminent arrival of the Sun's son, who will bring them the "new rules." This young man functions in the story as a helper and a spokesman for Jurupari, who stays in the village just a short time. It is he, the young man, who brings the sacred instruments from the water and who remains in the village to make sure the new rules are enforced.

Initially, he is confident of being able to resist the women, who become very interested in his good looks. He agrees to go to a dance with the *tuxaua* but vows he will not pay any attention to the women, because:

> Women's eyes disturb us.
> Their conversation make us go crazy.
> Not me.
> Women can make themselves sweet for me, they can even become affectionate. My eyes don't turn to look at them, they look to the other side. (352–53)

All the women in the village go and sit near the young man. They try to talk to him, but he falls asleep, so they attempt to wake him up:

> "Let's make his heart happy so that he isn't asleep. Let's give ourselves to him!"
>
> The young man felt something grabbing him, woke up, and knew immediately what it was. He jumped to the side, and said: "What do you want from me, crazy women?" (354)

Tired of being assaulted, he left the village, not before telling the *tuxaua* to protect the young men: "Keep a good eye on the young men. Notice what your women are like. They just about forced me" (354).

Women's capacity—and compulsion—to seduce is a common theme throughout the collection. In most stories, women are portrayed as sexually more active than men, causing, for that reason, a good amount of social disruption. "Piripiri," for instance, is the story of three young women who tried to force a deer-turned-young-man, Piripiri, to have sex with them. A shaman helped them by preparing a magic potion that would allow them to seduce Piripiri, but he warned the women not to touch the young man prematurely. But since women, according to the story, "don't know how to wait," they touched Piripiri's body too soon, and he turned into a star. The shaman lamented Piripiri's fate, putting the blame for it entirely on the women: "Poor Piripiri, poor guy! You were not even old enough to love and women's hands have already caused your disgrace" (117).

A story told within the story in "Moon Portrait Girl" explains how a handsome young man received constant sexual attacks from all the young women in the village, but always refused to give in to them. Tired of their insistence, he showed one of the women his secret: He had no genitalia, he was "neither woman nor man" (242). Since this young woman did not tell the secret to her friends, they continued to assault him, to the point of threatening his life if he did not concede. Desperate, the young man disappeared into the river. The character who tells the story is a young man who appears to be a young woman.

A similar story is told by the character Pacutinga, in the narrative "The daughters of Sufary." A beautiful young man appeared in a village during a solar eclipse. All the women in the village, who are described as being "hot as *coatis*," assaulted him. He complained to his mother, the moon, and told the women that he did not have the "flesh to make them pregnant" (326), that is, he did not have a penis. Again, the story is told by a woman who has no genitalia.

Women are repeatedly described as licentious, impatient, and indiscreet. Such a view corresponds to that in Stradelli's *Leggenda,* and seems to be related, more generally, to the Jurupari phenomenon. In *Leggenda* we are told about Jurupari's efforts to find the "perfect woman." Such a woman has no relation with the "immaculate maid" referred to, ironically, by Reichel-Dolmatoff. Perfection here is defined in very specific terms: a woman who is patient, knows how to keep secrets, and is not curious. In *Lendas*, Brandão do Amorim quotes a puberty chant in which the Tariana pray to the moon to make the young woman:

> (. . .) perfect so that we can offer her to the Sun!
> Make her as beautiful as you
> May she not enjoy knowing what happens among other people;
> May she know how to keep in her heart what others should not know;
> May she have a patient heart;
> That does not wish to try everything that appeals to her! (51–52)

A woman with such characteristics would not defy Jurupari's rules, or rather, for such a woman those rules would not be necessary.

In addition, it is women's licentiousness that causes men to lose their heads and reveal the secrets of Jurupari. In Amorim's collection, the story "The theft of the Jurupari instruments" deals with the common theme of women usurping the taboo instruments and then seducing the young men to teach them how to play them:

> They went home, painted their bodies with *carajuru*, and started to seduce the young men.
>
> Since the young men's heads, they say, were not ready yet to resist the seduction of their women, they immediately said yes. (430)

By learning how to play the sacred instruments, these women gained immediate access to power, and became men's oppressors:

> They started by telling men to replace them in the house chores. The men, they say, were sad because they had to dig manioc in order to make flour; weed the fallow and put their children to sleep as if they were women. (431)

The Jurupari instruments and the ability to play them are the concrete representation of the power that men have over women. Such power is not taken for granted nor is it considered men's natural gift; on the contrary, it is the result of the imposition of the "new rules" by Jurupari. And if men are not strong enough to resist women's attempts to seduce them, power will be again in the hands of women, as in the story we have just seen.

In these upper Rio Negro societies, men are apparently haunted by memories of a time when women ruled, which is sometimes described as prior to the adoption of Jurupari's rules, or as a temporary takeover by the women—possibilities that are not mutually exclusive. Whether this refers to an ancient matriarchy, as Cecilia Caicedo de Cajigas boldly proclaims; or to Reichel-Dolmatoff's theory of a change from a matrilineal to a patrilineal order—or indeed to neither—remains unsure.

In Stradelli's *Leggenda,* the power of women is undoubtedly related to the power that mothers have over their sons, as it is described in the following passage: "[Jurupari] smiled at the women's would-be cunning, since although the population included comprised a certain number of men, brothers of Seucy of the Earth [Jurupari's mother], they were not allowed a deliberative vote, being completely subject to their mothers' will" (18). The women in Stradelli's *Leggenda* are far from passive: They protest, boycott, and try to appeal to the communal principles that are being abandoned by the imposition of Jurupari's rules. When Jurupari excludes them from the meeting in the Canuké mountains, for instance,

> The women, who up to now were the only ones to decide about the activities in the village, were not glad to be excused from the planned meeting. They promised to depose the man who, at that moment, had been elected *tuxaua,* using the argument that he still did not have the ornament that would identify him as chief. (18)

Ultimately, when they cannot cope anymore, they run away.

Several of the war narratives included in Amorim's *Lendas* attribute the beginning of particular wars to women's disobedience of Jurupari's rules. Such is the case of the second story in the collection, "Buopé's War," which describes the war led by the eponymous Tariana *tuxaua,* who historically gave his name to the river known as Uaupés in Portuguese and Vaupés in Spanish: "Everybody still remembers how the Tarias made war against all the peoples in this river" (13). The war started because the wives of the Tarias, who had come from the Arara tribe,[9] decided to run away in protest of their husbands' behavior:

> As it was a habit of Buopé to dance the Jurupary every night in the Jurupary mountains, all men used to run away from their wives at dusk. These women, who were new in this place, among them Iauhi, daughter of Iauhixa, became immediately sad.
>
> The men, they say, did this everyday, they wouldn't miss one single night. Two moons later, Uauhi *[sic]* told the women they should all flee. (13)

Buopé sent his men after the women, who were brought back but refused to obey: "*Tuxaua,* we don't want to stay in a land where we, the women, cannot dance at parties with our husbands. For that reason, let the men go with us to our land where everything is more beautiful. Everything is ugly here"

(14). Buopé killed the women, by throwing them in the waterfall. In order to avenge the killing of his daughter, Iauhixa killed one of Buopé's sons. A bloody war started between the two nations, involving also the Uanana, allies of the Arara.

Lendas ethnographic notes, written by Brandão do Amorim himself, tell us the women were the ones who began the tradition of finding husbands in other groups. Couldn't this be another reason for male anxiety? In other words, if women started the rule of exogamy, there could be the danger of them spreading it beyond the accepted political alliances. In Stradelli's *Leggenda,* it is the mother of Pinon and Meenspuin who starts the practice of finding a husband in another group, since her people, who practiced endogamy, had arrived at serious problems due to the excess of women. The same happens in Barbosa Rodrigues's version of the story in *Poranduba.* But when the family returns to the mother's village, it is her son Pinon who, thanks to his extraordinary strength and magical powers, starts to impose new customs on his mother's people. In the *Leggenda,* this story is told by Jurupari, who adds that Pinon was an ancestor of the Tariana, and one of their first shamans. If the custom of searching for partners in other groups was implanted by women, it is men who take into their hands the task of imposing and controlling it.

If it is true that in Amorim's "Buopé's Wars" the idea of looking for wives in another tribe comes from Buopé himself, in the Uanana version of this war, included in the same collection, it was a Uanana woman, Pitiapo, who decided to find men somewhere else. It all happened because she was impressed by a young Tariana man who came to her village and was able to cross a dangerous waterfall without fear. She immediately told her father she wanted to marry this young man, and not her fiancé, Uatarampurá. The latter, however, decided to prove to Pitiapo that he was as brave as the Tariana young man. He tried to cross the waterfall, but died in the process. His father, once again, attributed his son's death to the fact that he was not capable of resisting women:

> Who could have said that Uatarampurá, because of a woman, would end up inside death's mouth?
>
> In truth, our hearts must not think as one because I, Uatarampurá's father, never cried for a woman. (64)

He then decided to avenge his son, swearing to kill the brave young man who had crossed the waterfall. In the meantime, Pitiapo went with some of her female friends to the Tariana village to look for the young man. His father, the *tuxaua* Buopé, claimed not to be afraid of Uatarampurá's father, and married Pitiapo to his son, and Pitiapo's friends to other young men in his village. But, once again:

> The men in this village went every night to the Jurupari mountains to dance the Jurupari.
>
> Pitiapo, they say, turned ugly because her husband didn't want to take her with him.
>
> One day, they say, Pitiapo told her friends:
>
> "It is better that we run away to our own village because our husbands will go after us, and then we will say to them: 'You are embittered hearts, you don't dance with your women, what do you want from us?'" (69)

They ran away and took Dassuen, one of Buopé's daughters, with them. This is the beginning of the war between the Tarianas and the Uananas, and all their allies.

Without denying the oppression of women implied by Jurupari's rules and confirmed by women's reactions to them in the stories above,[10] I tend to agree with Yolanda Murphy and Robert F. Murphy when they discuss the Karökö phenomenon among the Mundurucú (Tupi) Indians, which in some respects recalls Jurupari. They say that the idea that women once had power and could regain that power supports a less oppressive worldview for women than the assumption, prevalent in Judeo-Christian beliefs and Western intellectual traditions until mid-twentieth century, that men are "natural rulers": "Women, as people, are not inferior, for otherwise the rebellion of the males would have been unnecessary. Only their status is inferior, and this is so only because the men managed to shear them of their power in the remote past" (91).

Later Collections

The Jurupari phenomenon continued to dominate Rio Negro literature even after larger numbers of Christian missionaries had penetrated the region. The Salesians arrived in the upper Rio Negro in 1911, and by the forties they were the strongest Christian presence there. Like some religious orders before and after them, the Salesians helped to protect the Indians from economic exploitation and many forms of brutality, since the decay of the rubber commerce after 1910 had not done much to improve living conditions for the Indians, who continued to be used, more often than not as slaves, in the extracting of the kind of rubber known as balata (Wright 1998, 226). The SPI (Indian Protection Agency) established posts in the region only after 1921, and if sometimes it managed to control the atrocities committed against the Indians, its presence most of the time did little to intimidate the local barons. In fact, the bureau more often served as an intermediary in the decaying rubber trade. Nimuendaju's report on his 1927 journey talks again about a dramatic population decrease. In the 30s and 40s, rubber and balata were replaced by other extractive activities, but the violence and exploitation remained the same.

If the priests helped to shield the Indians from violent settlers, it was not without a price. Their strict Christian morality led to attacks on important aspects of the indigenous way of life. The long-houses, for instance (whose role in day-to-day and ritual life is described in detail by Stephen Hugh-Jones) were replaced by European-style family houses, and in Brazil they can no longer be found (Neves, 150). Shamans were persecuted and attacked, their artifacts were destroyed, and the use of beverages and drugs was prohibited (Moreira, 9).

The Salesians published important ethnographic works and many Rio Negro stories. Antonio Giacone's *Os Tucanos e Outras Tribos do Rio Uaupés* (1949) includes several animal narratives, and versions of the Jurupari (Waxti) story. Alcionílio Brüzzi da Silva, who, like Giacone, went to the Rio Negro in the forties, published the lengthy volume *A Civilização Indígena do Uaupés* (1962), which includes no narratives. The stories he collected throughout his life were published posthumously only in 1994 under the title *Crenças e Lendas do Uaupés,* along with narratives from other sources that he had translated and organized for publication.[11] The volume includes astronomical stories, stories about animals and spirits, and of course, Jurupari narratives.

Even when converted to Christianity, Rio Negro Indians continued, for the most part, to respect and practice the rituals of Jurupari. Egon Schaden narrated, in 1949, an episode that tellingly refines the limits of Christian conversion:

> A significant event that happened among the Tukano from Papuri (a tributary of the Uaupés): a converted Indian woman confessed to the missionary, before dying, that the worst sin of her life had been to see the Jurupari. "I was working near a creek and hiding under the sand I saw the Jurupari." (155)

In other words, she still believed fully in the taboo that banned women from seeing Jurupary and the musical instruments proper to this cult.

But the Salesians were not the only Christians to interfere in Rio Negro religious life. The arrival of American chewing gum companies in the 40s and the increase in United States military interests in the region (Wright 1992, 232) brought with it evangelical missionaries, detonating a war between Catholics and Protestants whose cultural victims were, once again, the Indians. New Indian messianic leaders started to appear, many inspired by the legendary chairman of the New Tribes Mission, Sophie Muller.

In the sixties and seventies, the fieldwork of scientists and ethnographers resulted in some of the most important renditions of the Jurupari phenomenon to date. Reichel-Dolmatoff's *Amazonian Cosmos* (first published in Spanish in 1968) included the Desâna creation story and a long analysis of it, while Stephen Hugh-Jones's *The Palm and the Pleiades: Initiation and Cosmology in Northwest Amazonia* (1979), transcribed and analyzed several Barasana Jurupari stories. Later, Reichel-Dolmatoff dedicated a whole volume to the Jurupari phenomenon: *Yurupary: Studies of an Amazon Foundation Myth* (1996). The Italian biologist Ettore Biocca also published, in his native language, an important study on upper Rio Negro groups, which includes several stories: *Viaggi tra gli Indi: Alto Rio Negro, Alto Orinoco—Appunti di un biólogo* (1965); and Manuel Nunes Pereira included Rio Negro narratives in his magnificent collection of stories from several Amazonian groups, *Morongueta: Um Decameron Indígena* (1967).

In the 1970s, the Brazilian military regime's attempts to bring what they defined as "economic development" to the Amazon did not spare the upper Rio Negro. Robin M. Wright, for instance, gives a dramatic description of how the construction of a military airstrip changed a Baniwa community in that same decade (1998). Also in the 1970s, Tukano Indians in the frontier region between Brazil and Colombia saw themselves involved in the drug traffic war by the guerrilla group M-19—a traumatic experience that brought, once again, many deaths to the Indians. In 1983, gold was found in the Traíra mountains, and the same Tukanos who had suffered with the involvement in the drug war saw their land invaded from night to day by more than 2,000 *garimpeiros* (Ramos, 209). In the beginning of the eighties, the Brazilian military, already under a transitional, democratic government, conceived a new security and economic plan for the Amazon: Projeto Calha Norte (North Trench Project), under which 14 percent of the national territory and 24 percent of legal Amazonia would come under their close scrutiny. The plan involved an improvement of airstrips and military installations in order to allow a more massive presence of military in the region; the construction of new highways, hydroelectric dams, more efficient means to control the frontier; and several agricultural projects. Its implementation has resulted in loss of land for several Amazonian Indians, including some upper Rio Negro groups.

Still, the Indians of upper Rio Negro go on, practicing their rituals and telling their stories as usual. Nowadays, most communities in the region will seem to an outsider, at first glance, quite Christianized. Many Indians are involved in such local economic activities as rubber-tapping, gold panning, and production of baskets for the tourist market in the cities. Yet when they return to their villages, they "have to provide their own subsistence in practically the same way it was provided by their ancestors five hundred or one thousand years ago" (B. Ribeiro, 12). Several communities speak their own language and practice many of their traditional rituals, which Christian missionaries now tend to regard simply as "folklore." Robin Wright's recent study of messianic movements among the Baniwa shows that structurally those religious movements are less Christian than had been supposed and closer to indigenous belief than to Christianity.

For Neves, the upper Rio Negro societies' unusual capacity for interaction and exchange, best demonstrated by their complex multicultural system, has been a crucial factor in their survival:

> It is this very flexibility within such social structure—the possibility of
> local groups reinventing or recreating themselves in face of historical
> changes without major structural ruptures—that allowed for the continu-
> ity of the upper Rio Negro regional system from pre-colonial times to the
> present, in the face of colonial and post-colonial transformations. (143)

Recently, Indian activism has brought more hopeful news to the upper Rio Negro communities. In 1987 the pan-Indian federation of Indigenous Organizations of Rio Negro (FOIRN) was founded. Its greatest accomplishment was the creation in 1996—after years of negotiation—of an Indian reserve. FOIRN has also been responsible for the opening of local museums and publication of a collection of volumes of native literature, "Indigenous Narrators of Rio Negro." Its first volume was *Antes o Mundo não Existia. Mitologia dos Antigos Desana-Kẽhíripõrã* (1995).

Before, the World Did Not Exist

Antes o Mundo não Existia (Before, the world did not exist) by Umusĩ Pãrõkumu (Firmiano Lana) and Tõrãmũ Kẽhíri (Luiz Gomes Lana), published in 1995, revised an earlier edition of 1980, in which Darcy Ribeiro's former wife Berta was involved. On various counts, it is the most significant collection of Rio Negro stories: the largest from the region and the first in Brazil ever to be signed by the Indians themselves. Umusĩ Pãrõkumu and Tõrãmũ Kẽhíri decided to publish it in order to correct what they saw as serious misinformation that was being passed around.[12] In the words of Tõrãmũ:

> At first I did not think to write these stories. But then I saw that even six-
> teen year old boys were recording and writing them. My cousin Feliciano
> Lana started to make some drawings in which he confused our group with
> others. Then I told my father: "everybody is going to think that our history
> is wrong, it is going to come out all mixed up." (B. Ribeiro, 10)

In a letter reproduced in the preface to Ribeiro's 1980 edition, Tōrāmü tells how he filled up a notebook with stories that he heard from his father; he then translated them into Portuguese and gave the originals to a priest, who sent them to the writer Márcio Souza. He was told by Souza to write to a publishing house saying he was an "authentic Indian." Then he met Berta Ribeiro, who became an intermediary in the process. In the 1995 edition published by FOIRN, Ribeiro's essay was eliminated, and the spelling of Desâna words followed the directives of a work group on Tukano languages, which made them, if more "correct," much more difficult to read.

Antes o Mundo não Existia is a long collection of narratives that tell the cosmogony of the Desâna—their origins and the transformations suffered by their society—along with the history of the authors' lineage. It begins with the creation of the world by Yebá Bıró, the "great-grandmother of the universe" who "appeared by herself" in "the middle of darkness." Female creators are rare in cosmogonies in general, so it should not be a surprise that one of the very few manifestations of such a phenomenon would appear in a cosmogony from the upper Rio Negro, a region where the idea (and fear) of female power is so pervasive.

Like the shamanistic trance, Yebá Bıró's creation of herself is an act of social imagination: For her to create herself, she had the help of six "mysterious things": "a bench made of white quartz, a fork-like cigarette holder, an *ipadu* [coca] gourd, the base of this *ipadu* gourd, a tapioca flour gourd and the base of this gourd" (19).[13] The objects described are at the center of Desâna life: the white quartz, used by the shaman during rituals, is an indicator of shamanistic power; coca and tobacco are also important tools in shamanistic rituals; and tapioca is their staple food. The coming into existence of the first Desâna is philosophically a definition of "Desânaness"; the first Desâna can exist once the objects that define Desâna life are in place. Moreover, during her act of self-creation, Yebá Bıró "covered herself with her ornaments," in other words, she defined herself, once again, through her (future) social existence.

After creating herself, Yebá Bıró went on to imagine the Five Thunders into life, giving them the task of creating humanity. But forgetful of Yebá Bıró's orders, they stayed leisurely in their houses, until the creator was forced to remind them of their task. As they started on the ritual preparations to create humanity, however, they got drunk, and became incapable of doing the job. Disappointed, the great-grandmother of the universe concluded that:

"Nothing is coming of this."

She thought, then, of creating another being that could follow her orders. She ate *ipadu,* smoked a cigarette and thought about how it should be. While she was thinking, a mysterious being that had no body was formed out of the smoke itself. It was a being that could not be touched or seen. Yebá Bʉró then got her skein for protection and wrapped it in it. She was acting as women do when they give birth. After she caught it with her skein, she greeted it, saying Ʉmukosurápanami, "Great-grandson of the World," to which he responded Ʉmukosuráñehkō, "Great-grandmother of the World." (22–23)

Ʉmukosurāpanami then visited the great Thunders, whose help and richness he used to create humanity. By now he had the company of his brother, Ʉmʉkomahsu Boreka. The two brothers embarked on the snake-boat that would take them to the different houses, or *malocas,* where various branches of humanity would soon be created. The snake-boat was the Third Thunder. According to the description: "The head of the snake looked like the stern of a boat. To them, it looked like a great steamboat that is called Pamurigahsiru, that is, "Canoe of the Future Humanity" or "Canoe of Transformation" (29).

At the head of the snake-boat, Ʉmukosurāpanami and Ʉmʉkomahsu Boreka started their long journey that led to the creation of humanity. Their first stops were on the margins of the Great Milk Lake, which, according to the authors, "must be the [Atlantic] ocean." Then they went up the Amazon, the Negro, and the Uaupés. At each stop they disembarked part of the treasure brought by the snake-boat/Third Thunder, and those riches became human beings. The snake-boat traveled under water, and the primordial beings that they created were, too, water-creatures: "The vessel came below the water, like a submarine. The huts are also below the waters. So much so that humanity came as Waimahsn, 'Fish People'" (31). The narrative describes and names each stop, in a monotonous repetition that goes on for pages, and whose objective is both ritualistic and foundational. Several locations are described, including places still inhabited by the different Desâna sibs, other Tukano groups, as well as modern cities and towns like Barcelos and Manaus.

Before arriving at the thirtieth stop, called Diábayabuwi'i or "Hut of the Songs," Ʉmukosurāpanami said: "Humanity is already formed. We find ourselves in the middle of the voyage and it is time to make them talk" (33). Boreka then gave each group their language:

> The Great-grandson of the World arrived after him. To communicate with him, he sent his invisible rod, which has the name "medicine man's bone."

The rod crossed the river, in front of Boreka. Seeing it, he went down to participate in the big ceremony that the Great-grandson of the World was going to have in order to give each one his own language: Desâna, Tukano, Pira-tapuyo, Tuyuka, Siriano, Barasano, Baniwa, White. Each one was going to receive their own language. (33)

As we can see, *Antes o Mundo não Existia* consciously affirms the linguistic plurality of the Rio Negro region which is celebrated in Stradelli's *Jurupari* when the hero Jurupari names each instrument in a different language.

Berta Ribeiro pointed to the analogy between

the growth of humanity and that of the fetus. Both develop in liquid envir-onment . . . and the several phases of this evolution are marked by the humanity's passage through 'transforming houses.' Their names indicate phases in human development: 'turn around house,' when the child starts to turn the head; 'crawling house,' etc; or they indicate the process of so-cialization: the houses, respectively, where young girls and young boys are initiated, becoming ready for reproductive functions. (39)

In other words, the journey of the snake-boat refers to the biological crea-tion of human beings as well as to their learning of the social processes that turn them into Desâna. At the same time, it is an account of the Desâna migration history and arrival in their present territory. Reichel-Dolmatoff saw no problem in interpreting this history of migration literally, so that the Tukano migration upriver, from the East, became a crucial element in his readings of Desâna texts. Other scholars, however, disagree. Neves, for instance, claims that there is no archaeological evidence to demonstrate this journey upriver.

As is so often the case with Native American cosmogony, the existence of the non-Indians is also explained in this creation story. When the snake-boat arrived at the fifty-sixth house (whose name, according to the authors, cannot be translated into Portuguese), humans emerged for the first time onto the surface of the Earth. The ancestors of different upper Rio Negro groups came out one by one: first, the Tukano proper; then the Desâna, fol-lowed by the Pira-Tapuyo, the Baniwa, and the Maku. To each of them, the Great-grandson of the World gave "well-being, and the wealth from which you were born"(39). Then it was the turn of the white man, to whom the Great-grandson of the world said:

You are the last one. I gave all the wealth I had to the other ones. Since you are the last one, you shall be a fearless person. You shall make war in order to expropriate other people's wealth. With that you will find money!

When he finished saying that, the first White man turned his back to
him, shot his rifle into the air, and went on towards the South. (40)

The violent behavior of whites is thus explained in humorous and tragic
terms.

The story of the big snake that travels upriver giving origin to humanity
is not exclusive to the Desâna: it is part of a more general Tukanoan cosmogony. The Cubeo, for instance, tell a very similar story: "According to
one version of the origin myth the sibs of a phratry are all descended from a
single water anaconda called *Pwénte ainkü* (Anaconda person), who divided himself into segments, the head becoming the leading sib of the phratry,
and each subsequent segment forming the remainder of the sib hierarchy"
(Goldman, 93). In *Relatos míticos cubeo* (1992), the anaconda is used by
the creators of humans, the Kwais, to give shape to the Amazonian rivers.

Even non-Tukano groups, like the Tariana, who do not see themselves as
descending from the traveling water anaconda,[14] reserve a special place in
their cosmogony for the Big Snake: In Stradelli's *Leggenda* their ancestor is
Pinon, that is, snake. In Barbosa Rodrigues's version of the Jurupari story,
it is the Big Snake who makes the women pregnant when the men who accompanied them could not procreate anymore because they were too old
(115), and as a child Pinon similarly bears the star markings of a snake.
Later, in the same story, the boy transforms his sister into the Pleiades; and
his mother, who had been swallowed by the Big Snake, is also transformed
into a star, the "Big Snake," or Pinon (127). In his comments about the "cosmogonic legends" of the Uaupés river, Brüzzi da Silva refers to a Big Snake
cycle, which is related to the origin of rivers (64). In general terms, the Big
Snake stories seem to refer to a much older cosmogonic and astronomical
history, while Jurupari, its direct descendant, is the transformer who comes
to teach new rules to the peoples from the upper Rio Negro.

The Big Snake and the snake-boat have become the protagonists of
many stories created and re-created by the mestizo population throughout
the Rio Negro and other Amazonian areas.[15] The Boiúna (big snake) as it
is called in Nheengatú, is the "Mother of the Rivers," a primordial being
that is linked to the very origins of humanity. As it is so often the case
with Native American narratives, the Boiúna is at the same time a creator and protector of water and all aquatic beings, and a cruel monster that
pursues and kills humans. For the riverine populations of the Amazon, the
monstrous Boiúna often takes the form of an attractive seducer/seductress
in order to deceive its victims. As in the Desâna narrative, it can also appear in the form of a big boat: "When the moon is waning and looks like a
silver boat, immediately after midnight, the Boiúna appears in the bizarre

shape of a ghost boat, high mast, sail up, sailing quietly through the bays" (Morais, 83).

To be sure, other traditions have emerged from this same area and doubtless will continue to do so. In 1983, for example, Eduardo Lagório published *100 Kixti (estórias) tukano,* which is enriched by autobiographical notes supplied by the native authors. Now we turn, however, to the resonance that the Jurupari and Anaconda stories have had on mainstream Brazilian literature.

chapter 8

Snake Norato (1931)

T HE AMAZONIAN BIG SNAKE made its way into one of the finest products of
the *Antropofagia* movement, Raul Bopp's *Snake Norato* (*Cobra Norato*
1931). A *gaúcho* southerner, Bopp is rarely associated by critics with
Antropofagia, a term that in Brazilian cultural studies has become inextricably linked to Oswald de Andrade and his 1928 "Manifesto" (see chapter 5), and has been reduced to being, at best, the invention of Oswald and
his then wife, the painter Tarsila do Amaral. In fact, the movement was far
broader than that. Manager of the first phase of *Revista de Antropofagia,*
and one of the editors of the second, Bopp later in life wrote the book *Vida e
Morte da Antropofagia* (1977), whose main purpose was to show how closely
he had been linked to this movement and to chide critics for their poor
memory.

Like the other *Antropófagos,* Bopp believed that the arrival of the Portuguese in America in 1500 had meant the interruption, for the people already living there, of a preferable way of life:

> The Indian was happy in his human dignity. "Sans roi et sans loi" (Mon-
> taigne). But the preachers of catechism arrived. They sent a question back
> to Rome: Is the Indian human, too?
>
> The Indian was forced to believe, to become devout, and to follow the
> liturgies of the Church. (Bopp 1966, 72)

He also engaged in the study of colonial chronicles and participated actively in the *Antropófagos'* discussion groups.

Invariably described by friends and biographers as a compulsive traveler, Bopp left his home state of Rio Grande do Sul and visited all regions of the country. After living in Recife, he moved to Belém in order to continue his law degree, and journeyed extensively throughout the Amazon.

It was during these trips that Bopp heard the language of the Amazonian people and their stories. It was also then that he came across Brandão do Amorim's collection, which, as we noted, was being passed from hand to hand in a still unpublished form. Mário de Andrade, for instance, read Amorim's *Lendas,* and its marks can be seen in the language of *Macunaíma.* The uncommon use of the verb *brincar* (to play, as in children's games) with the meaning of having sexual intercourse, which anyone familiar with *Macunaíma* will immediately associate with the novel, appears in Amorim: "We went to bathe and found this young man there. We were playing with him in the river" (279).[1] The repetition of syllables in verbs, a characteristic of Tupi very much used by Amorim in *Lendas* (see chapter 7) appears frequently in Mário's novel: "cantacantando"(singsinging); falafalando (speakspeaking), etc.

Amorim's collection also helped to feed the polemics between *Verde-amarelistas* and the *Antropófagos* (see chapter 4). The *Verdeamarelistas'* adoption of the tapir as their symbol was probably inspired by Amorim's texts. In the story "Buopé Wars," the *tuxaua* of the tapirs complained to the Tariana people about the large number of tapirs that were being killed for making shields. When asked by the Tariana to identify themselves, the tapir *tuxaua* proclaimed: "We are the tapir people," a sentence that echos strongly in the motto of the above-mentioned writers, who later identified themselves as Grupo Anta (the Tapir group). Oswald's engagements with the *Verdeamarelistas* in *Revista de Antropofagia* makes use, in turn, of a tapir killer: the trickster Poronominare, a character from Amorim's story of the same title. As we saw, Oswald published in 1929 a reply to the "Nheengaçú Verde-Amarelo Manifest" under the pseudonym "Poronominare."

An Ophidian Persona

In the case of Bopp, the effect that Amorim's narratives had on him is explicitly described in *Vida e Morte da Antropofagia*:

> One day [Alberto Andrade Queiroz] showed me some works by Antonio Brandão do Amorim, which had a strong indigenous flavor. It was a revelation. I had never read anything more delicious. It was a new idiom. The language at times had a Biblical grandiosity. . . . These readings took me to

a new state of sensitivity. I instinctively broadened the view I had of things. I got closer to rural speech, with its delicious syntax. (58–59)

The quote is strikingly similar to Mário's own view of the impact that reading Koch-Grünberg had on him (see chapter 2). In the case of Mário, fascination with indigenous texts led him, as we saw, to an intense process of intertextuality and re-creation that resulted in *Macunaíma*—so intense that we can have no doubts that Koch-Grünberg's narratives are the novel's most definitive source. Following Bopp, and along similar lines, some critics have wanted to see Brandão do Amorim's *Lendas* as the main source of *Snake Norato*. Lígia Averbuck, in the most important study of the poem, *Cobra Norato e a Revolução Caraíba* (1985) quotes Bopp's *Vida e Morte da Antropofagia* in order to conclude that:

> The native expression of *nheengatu* mythology, translated into its pure, concrete, and intuitive form, and revealing a perception of the world that is typical of the innocent forms of the myth, would be the seed of *Snake Norato*. (87)

And Jorge Tuffic, in his preface to the 1987 facsimile edition of Amorim's collection, adds:

> this work by Brandão do Amorim, which never appears in the bibliography of M.A. theses, is what gives us the exact measure of its great importance within the universe of *Snake Norato* (. . .) in an adaptation of the folk tale that agitates and moves through the forests of myth . . . (n/p)

Yet, when reading *Snake Norato* one finds very little evidence of "adaptations of folk tales" from Amorim's collection. *Lendas* includes, it is true, a Big Snake narrative ("The deaf or disobedient girls"), but this story bears no resemblance to the plot of *Snake Norato* beyond the fact that the Big Snake is, in both texts, a seducer of young girls—a common theme, as we will see, throughout the Amazon. At the level of plot, ways of narrating, and characters (if we exclude the Big Snake narrative just mentioned), *Snake Norato* does not draw on Amorim's *Lendas* at all. It is at the level of language that the influence can most be noticed. For Bopp, the narratives collected by Amorim had "a moving simplicity," and

> In their affectionate dialogues they used the diminutive of verbs, *estarzinho, dormezinho, esperazinho*. Certain stories, about human themes, were treated with an unusual lyric spice. For instance: "the young woman lit up her eyes to him," "the moonlight danced in her eyes," "the mother said to the daughter: don't look so *auch* at him." (1977, 59)

Indeed, one can point to certain similarities between the diction of the two works—*Snake Norato* and Amorim's *Lendas*. The diminutive of verbs, which so enchanted the poet when reading Amorim, is used a few times in *Snake Norato*, as in the following case: "Então esperazinho um pouco" (then "waitie" a bit). In fact, diminutives in general are profusely used by Bopp, as they are, too, by Brandão do Amorim. And the onomatopoeia, which, as we saw, is also common feature of Amorim's collection, appears frequently in *Snake Norato*: "Uei! Here a little river flows/ with his orphan waters escaping/ Ouch glu glu glu," and "Shaman got dizzy/ Squatted started disappearing/ whistling quietly fiu fiu fiu. (167; 181)

Snake Norato is divided into 33 small parts, some of them only a few lines long. In the first part, the unidentified poetic "I" strangles the snake Norato and enters his skin, in order to travel throughout the Amazon in search of his beloved, Queen Luzia's daughter. During this journey, he meets his travel companion, the dry-bum-armadillo. Together, they go to a party and see a shaman ritual. At the end of the poem, they find out that Queen Luzia's daughter has been abducted by Boiúna (Big Snake). They save her, and the poetic "I" is then able to marry her.

According to Cascudo, Snake Norato is:

> one of the best known legends in the further North of Brazil, Amazonas and Pará. An Indian woman was bathing in the Paraná waterfalls, between the Amazon and Trombeta rivers, in Óbidos, Pará, when she became pregnant by the Big Snake. The mother gave birth to a boy and a girl, and, following the shaman's advice, threw them in the river, where they grew up as water snakes. The boy, Honorato, and the girl, Maria Caninana were always together. Norato was good and Maria was bad. (1972, 271)

Snake Norato's protagonist is thus based on a popular Amazonian character who appears in many oral narratives throughout the region. Bopp probably heard it in his trips through the Amazon, although he could also have read it in any collection of popular Amazonian stories such as Inácio Batista de Moura's *De Belém a S. João de Araguaia* (1910), or José Carvalho's *O Matuto Cearense e o Caboclo do Pará* (1930). In many versions of the Snake Norato narrative, Norato disguises himself as an attractive man who goes to parties and seduces young women. The Norato of the popular narratives is therefore one of the many *encantados* (enchanted beings) that inhabit the Amazon, an animal or monster that can appear disguised as human. His origin is partly native: like Seucy, the mother of Jurupari, he was born from the intercourse between an Indian woman and Big Snake (Rodrigues, 115—see previous chapter). He belongs, therefore, to the Big Snake cycle mentioned by Barbosa Rodrigues in *Poranduba*.

But, as Cascudo observed (1983, 254), *encantados* themselves are not necessarily native.

In the poem, we are never told the origin of Snake Norato, nor do we know anything about his life. In fact, the poem is probably read quite differently depending on whether the reader is familiar or not with Amazonian popular stories. For a Paulista like me, *Snake Norato* was, for many years, the story of a man who impersonated a snake called Norato. An Amazonian probably reads it differently, as the story of a man who impersonated a well-known marvelous character, similar to the bad wolf or the Loch Ness monster.

Like other *encantados,* the Norato of the poem disguises as human in order to go to a party with his friend dry-bum-armadillo. At the party he wins the heart of a woman, Joaninha Vintém, but contradicting the usual behavior of *encantado* seducers, he remains faithful to his beloved, Queen Luzia's daughter. At the end of the poem, Norato fights against another well-known monster, Boiúna, or Big Snake. Once again, the monstrous Big Snake is a direct relative of the ophidian character from Rio Negro we saw in the last chapter—the monster who impregnated Seucy and swallowed the boy's mother in Barbosa Rodrigues's Jurupari narratives. Cascudo calls it "the most popular of Amazonian myths," and says that "Boiúna's prestige is limited to the panic caused by its voracity and its capacity to transform into various things in order to commit evil" (1972, 155). In Amorim's "The deaf and disobedient girls," some girls disobey their father and bathe in the river. Big Snake comes to them disguised as a handsome man. One of the girls has sex with him, and gives birth to snakes.

One of Big Snake's favorite disguises is a boat, as it appears in the poem:

> "Listen, brother, What you are seeing is not a ship. It is Big-Snake."

> "What about the silver hull? The sails full of wind?"

> "It is Big-Snake." (185)

Thus, *Snake Norato* tells the story of a conflict between two Amazonian marvelous creatures: the snake Norato, and his father (at least in some versions) Big Snake. It is, in other words, a conflict between two Indian characters who have become partly *caboclos,* or mestizos. However, to say that *Snake Norato* is the story of a conflict between these two creatures would probably be an overstatement, since the conflict itself takes place only at the end of the poem, in parts 29 through 31. Before that, and after the impersonation of the Snake by the poetic "I" in part 1, very little happens in the poem. The poetic "I" often gets lost. In part 9 he meets his travel companion, dry-bum-armadillo; in part 24 they go to a manioc flour mill in order to get some food, and to a party in part 25; in part 27 they see a shaman ritual.

This last is perhaps the most poetically agile passage in the poem. The shaman asks the jungle *(mato)* to send him a jaguar to help him perform his cure:

> "Jungle! I want my caruana-jaguar Maraca calls you"
> Jaguar arrived Jumped Entered the shaman's body
> "I want tafiá I want to smoke I want mimic-dance
> I don't like fire"
>
> Master *Paricá* calls in the ill
> of fever swells bad back
>
> "Only the Mother of the Lake can cure this"
> "The Tinga-vulture knows about swells" (181)

Communication between species seems most convincing in this episode, since the shaman depends on the jungle, the jaguar, and the *paricá* to do his work. Very much in agreement with the *modernista* practice, the shaman ritual is a culturally mixed event: The jaguar—an ally or double of the sha-man in many South American native narratives, as we saw in the analysis of "My Uncle, the Iauaretê" (see chapter 5)—takes possession of the shaman in a way that is rhythmically closer to African than to Native American rituals. This is reinforced by the fact that a *figa-de-angola* (an African amulet) is also used in the cure.

At the party, as we saw, the impersonated Norato behaves as a typical *encantado*, by attracting the interest of a woman and by not letting the people in the place know he is a snake. He and his friend armadillo play the guitar and sing popular songs. Popular poetry comes through in this passage (part 25) as quotation, in other words, as poetry inset in the larger poem. The same happens in part 24, when they go to the manioc-flour mill in order to get some food; the episode serves as an excuse for us to overhear two woman workers tell a *boto* story,[2] in which the dolphin appears dis-guised, as is fairly typical in these stories, as a handsome blond man.

The poetic "I"'s friendship with the dry-bum-armadillo reveals, once again, possibilities of an interspecies relationship that are reminiscent, to a certain degree, of those found in many native Amazonian stories. Norato is helped by and learns from the armadillo. It is the armadillo, for instance, who guides him out of the mud:

"Olelé. Who is there?"
"I am the dry-bum armadillo"

"Oh, brother Armadillo
How good you came here
I want you to teach me how to get out of this rotten throat"

"Then hold on to my tail
and I will pull you out" (158)

Except for this initial encounter, in which he uses his tail in order to save the poetic "I," the armadillo hardly behaves as a member of his species—he never goes into the earth, for instance, nor does he make use of his hard shell. As a helper of the poetic "I," the armadillo behaves and acts as a human being, and is closer, therefore, to human helpers of many European traditional stories than to native Amazonian stories like Amorim's.

In all aspects discussed—the presence of Snake Norato and Big Snake, the shaman ritual, the Amazonian stories told in the party, and, to a lesser degree, the friendship between the protagonist and the dry-bum armadillo—*Snake Norato* follows closely what we could call an Amazonian popular poetics, a poetics in which indigenous elements play an important, though not exclusive, role.

For Bosi, *Snake Norato* is, along with *Macunaíma*, one of the two "mythopoetic" products of *modernismo* (1970, 366). Wilson Martins goes even further, and claims that the two works

produce absolutely identical sounds and respond to an absolutely homogeneous mythology (mythology in a literal and literary sense). It is also a fact that both reproduce similar perspectives, fed by material that stems from common roots: the Amazonian mythical substrate. (195)

Yet is such a close identification fair? For, while the protagonist of Mário's novel never ceases to disconcert us for his trickster-like inconsistencies and his apparent lack of logic (which is, in fact, the logic of certain indigenous characters and narratives), the poetic "I" of *Snake Norato* never loses his white male consciousness, always maintaining the behavior of an impersonator. His perspective is that of someone alien to the Amazon. He is, in other words, a traveler.

Traveling inside the skin of Snake Norato, he is obsessed by his desire for Queen Luzia's daughter, and finding her is the main objective of his journey: "I am going to visit Queen Luzia / I want to marry her daughter" (86).

In part 2, we are told that in order to find her he has to go through several obstacles and tests:

> But before that you have to go through seven doors
> And see seven uninhabited-bellied women
> guarded by an alligator.

> —All I want to see is Queen Luzia's daughter.

> You have to give your shadow to the Beast of the Depth
> You have to do magic in the new moon
> You have to drink three drops of blood.

> —Ah, only if it is from the veins of Queen Luzia's daughter. (149)

Yet for all such warnings about tests and dangers of a would-be epic journey, and in spite of the clear-cut difference between the all-hero Norato and the all-villain Boiúna, the majority of the thirty-three parts that compose *Snake Norato* do not tell the epic tale of the defeat of Boiúna. Snake Norato expresses his desire to find Queen Luzia's daughter in part 1, and fights against the Big Snake only in part 31. Other than that, we see him getting sad and desperate; we accompany him through the events described (his encounter with the dry-bum-armadillo, their visit to the flour mill, the party, and the shaman ritual); and finally in part 28, the Boiúna appears disguised as a snake-boat.

The other parts of the poem that narrate the travels of the poetic "I" are for the most part taken up by descriptions of the Amazon at various times of day and night, and under various atmospheric conditions. Part 7, for instance, describes the brewing of a storm, which happens in part 8:

> Rain thuds down
> washing the vegetation

> Wind pillages the leafy trees
> arms in the air
> Big forest shakes

> Black clouds mound up
> Squatting monsters
> cover the fat-lipped horizons (157)

Part 11 describes night in the jungle:

I wake up
Moon showed up with bags under her eyes
Silence hurts inside the jungle

The stars opened up
The big waters shrank with sleep

Tired night stood still (160)

Part 11 describes dawn; part 14 noon; part 16 sunset, and so on.

In Native American literature landscape descriptions are not common, since they presuppose a gap between the subject and the world around him/her that does not tend to be part of the Native American world. For the most part, nature there plays the role of a subject, not a mere object of the human gaze. Furthermore, nature is a historical entity: it has a past and a present; it has gone through transformations that explain its present state and are mostly described in intricate narratives, not usually through metaphor. The etiological tales we saw in the analysis of Koch-Grünberg and *Macunaíma* fulfill precisely this function; they tell us how natural subjects came to be the way they are. Although often embedded in longer stories, etiological narratives are also autonomous tales; they fulfill functions (ritual, history, entertainment) that go much beyond the intent to describe. The Rio Negro narratives collected by Brandão do Amorim do not differ from those collected by Koch-Grünberg and many others in this respect. In them, the relationship between humans and animals is complex and varied, and can never be reduced to the Hegelian opposition between Culture and Nature. In *Vida e Morte da Antropofagia,* Bopp confessed his fascination with this aspect of Amorim's collection:

> In his [Amorim's] world the trees spoke. The sun walked from one place to the other. The children of Thunder took the Summer, once in a while, to the other side of the river. (59)

Although Amorim's narratives were analyzed in the previous chapter, it may be useful to recall some of them here, highlighting the communicative abilities of plants and animals that so much impressed Bopp. In the episode of Buopé's war, for instance, in which the tapirs demand their rights from the Tariana, the relationship between humans and animals takes the form of a contract between species that presupposes mutual respect. A similar contract is invoked, as we saw, in the Maya-Quiché *Popol Vuh* when the domestic animals rebel against maltreatment by the robot-people (see chapter 3).

Metamorphoses from one species to another occur frequently in Amorim's collection. For example, in "Piripiri" the deer Piripiri appears to young women as one transformed into a young man. And since the young women do not understand that, besides not being human, Piripiri is too young, their sexual advances towards him have fatal consequences for the animal; Piripiri ends up metamorphosed into the Piripirioca plant. In the story "The origin of the Uanana people," a group of women are impregnated by a swarm of bees, who came to them disguised, once again, as young men. The consequences are also fatal, but this time to the women, who end up having their blood sucked by the bees.

Like the humans, the animals in these stories also exist in previous, less perfected forms. In the story "Baré people," the trickster Poronominare encounters several animals (the tapir, the jararaca snake, and the armadillo) who, not knowing his identity, tell him they want to kill Poronominare because they heard he had raped and killed other men's wives and daughters. Poronominare kills each of the animals, leaving, in every case, a newer and better version of them.

As Bopp observed, the other creatures humans interact with in these narratives are by no means limited to animals. In the story "Macuxi people" (one of the very few Rio Branco narratives included in Amorim's collection), the first man was taught by a tree how to eat the fruit and spread the seeds:

—Look, your fruit fell from your body, what are you going to do with it now?
    The tree, they say, answered:
—As only you can walk from one place to the other, eat the flesh of the fruit, then put the seed under the earth. (Amorim, 205)

The Traveler "I"

In spite of Bopp's enthusiasm for the communicative abilities of animals and plants in Amorim's collection, we can hardly find examples of such behavior in his poem. It is true that *Snake Norato* is filled with rivers, trees and animals who speak, but something in their dialogues makes them noticeably different from the conversations in Amorim's collection. In part 2, for instance, the poetic "I," already disguised as Norato, starts his trip into the forest:

I disappear rudderless into the jungle
where old pregnant trees snooze

From every side they call me
—Where are you going, Snake Norato?
I have three young trees here waiting for you

I can't.
Tonight I am going to sleep with Queen Luzia's daughter. (150)

Not much later, in part 4, he is seen by a frog:

A froggy frog spies on me
I smell people
—Who are you?
—I am Snake Norato
I am the future lover of Queen Luzia's daughter. (152)

In both examples, Snake Norato's interaction with the other creatures is that of a passerby. Except for his travel companion dry-bum-armadillo, trees and animals do not play main character roles in the poem, which they do in several of the stories and substories in Amorim's collection, and in the novel *Macunaíma*. Their actions do not affect the poetic "I"'s life, or his journey. The dialogic and human-like behavior of nature in *Snake Norato* is almost always subordinated to an intent to describe the forest, so that the interaction between the poetic "I" and most nonhuman creatures in the poem obeys the logic of such descriptions.

The prevalence of Amazon descriptions in the poem is such that one could be justified in thinking that Norato's epic journey is just an excuse to present the reader with forest landscapes. The creatures he meets have, too, the main function of helping him describe the Amazon. For that reason, many times they are given a voice (or certain human characteristics) just so they can function as metaphors of certain Amazonian conditions. In part 5, for instance, the poetic "I" offers us a strikingly beautiful description of the geometric forms of the forest, and of the dominance of the rivers over the whole Amazonian environment:

Here is where the trees go to school
They are studying geometry

—You were born blind. You have to obey the river

—Alas, alas! We are slaves of the river
—You are condemned to work all the time
Your obligation is to produce leaves in order to cover the forest
—Alas, alas! We are slaves of the river (153)

In order to describe this specific situation more effectively, the poet gives voice to the trees, and makes them complain about being "slaves of the river." There is no story, no narrative: just a snapshot, a carefully constructed scene whose objective (to describe the dominance of the rivers) is still quite transparent.

Similarly, in part 17, the poetic "I" listens to the words of a stagnant lagoon:

> This lagoon has got fever It has swollen The water has stilled
> —Ouch, I was a bachelor river
> I was drinking my way through
> but the jungle [o mato] clogged me up
> Now my uterus hurts ouch ouch (168)

Once more, the effectiveness of the description is achieved through the humanization of the lagoon, who is given both a male and a female identity. What the poet wishes to describe is quite transparent: the impregnated river/lagoon stands for the Amazon's small, flooded, full-of-rotting-matter rivers.

The same technique is used again and again throughout the poem. In part 6, the poetic "I" gives the following description of the darkness of the rain forest: "I go under leafy arcades / Incognito bushes ask / —Is it day already?" (155); "skinned rivers forced to work" (152) brings to mind the constant movement of the rivers; "Squatting trees / wash uncombed branches in the current" (162) describes short, half-flooded trees; the tiny, occasional Amazonian creek about to be dried up by the sun is described in the following dialogue:

> Uei! Here a little creek passes by
> his orphan waters running away
> —Ouch glu-glu-glu
> Don't-tell-anybody
> If Sun appears he will swallow me up (167)

The poetic effectiveness of such descriptions is undeniable; yet, they are very distant from what critics refer to loosely as "Amazonian mythology." For if animals, plants, and natural phenomena are allowed to speak in the poem, it is because their words help the non-Amazonian poetic "I" to describe Amazonian nature. And who does he describe it to? Clearly to a non-Amazonian urban audience like himself. His choice of images is telling: The forest is most often described in terms that make it intelligible to urban audiences. Thus, the constant changes in its environment are compared to a factory:

> One hears whistles and a knock-knock
> They are welding sawing sawing
> It sounds as though they are producing earth . . .
> Gosh! They are really producing earth (155)

and the forest itself to a city: "Ventriloquist forest is playing city / Cubic bushes move around / under arcades of samaúma trees" (183). Through the eyes of this non-Amazonian traveler the forest is mostly described as a hostile environment ("the forest is an enemy of man"). Nature is cruel and exploitative: trees are slaves of the river, rivers are forced to work, birds cry because they are being punished, and so on. The images often resemble the green hell invoked by Rangel and the Spanish American jungle narratives contemporary to *Snake Norato* (see chapter 3); the forest is a place of death, bad smells, and decay:

> This is the forest of rotten breath
> giving birth to snakes
>
> Skinny rivers forced to work
> The current has goose-bumps
> pealing off the slimy banks
>
> Toothless roots chewing mud
>
> In a flooded stretch
> the swamp swallows the creek's water
>
> It stinks
> The wind changed places (152)

As in Rivera's *Vortex*, man cannot escape the forest. In order to destroy him, trees are told to produce shadow: "—You have to draw man into your shadow / The forest is an enemy of man" (153). The poetic "I" describes the forest as a labyrinth ("I slip through a labyrinth / with pregnant trees sitting in the dark / Hungry roots bite the ground"(156) just before being swallowed by it:

> Oh I am lost
> in a scared badly done depth of a jungle
>
> I got stuck in a uterus of mud
> The air became breathless (158)

After the "I" is rescued by the armadillo, the forest becomes sunnier and sometimes jollier ("Childish little sun / grew up greasy and gay," 163), but the predominant images are still afflictive:

> There are shouts and echoes hiding away
> breathless afflictions
> Starving hunched-back trees chewing cracking (167)

and the steps of the hero and his helper continue to be slowed down by the swamp:

> The swamp borrowed earth
> to build slimy landfills
>
> Starving roots fight
>
> Mud-stuffed water
> slowly slides on the soft bed
>
> The sour-faced swamp
> Has been walking with us from afar (171)

The implicit model for the poetic "I's" journey is offered by a travel-writing tradition made popular in the nineteenth century, thanks to Alexander von Humboldt's *Views of Nature*. As Mary Louise Pratt explains, Humboldt combined early nineteenth-century science with Romantic ideas about nature to reinvent a tradition that had already been established by the first European chroniclers who traveled to the Americas. Like sixteenth-century chroniclers, Humboldt "wrote America as a primal world of nature, an unclaimed and timeless space occupied by plants and creatures (some of them human), but not organized by societies and economies; a world whose only history was the one about to begin" (126). This is the world presented to us by Snake Norato: a world whose grandiose speaking-nature is closer to Humboldt's "harmonies" and "cycles" than to the creatures in Brandão do Amorim's collection. Commenting on Humboldt's descriptions, Pratt calls attention to their liveliness and movement:

> Here is a prose that fatigues not by flatness or tedium . . . , but by the
> dramatic and arhythmic ebb and flow that would have been intensified by
> oral delivery. An "ascent" of "less warm" air flashes to "wide extensions"
> at "icy poles"; a "broad ocean" to a continent's "flat shores"; cold water, like
> an unwelcome invader of the tropics, strikes, advances, suddenly turns;
> mountains abound, soar; rivers are enormous, abundant, aggressively seek-
> ing coasts; forests are impenetrable, and humming with invisible activity as
> they protect, radiate, cover, exhale, absorb, generate (123).

Humboldt himself refers to his own eyes as being always directed to "the combination of forces, to the influence of the inanimate creation on the animate world of animals and plants, to this harmony" (quoted in Pratt, 123–24). It is precisely this "harmony" that is made visible through Bopp's dialogic descriptions, where rivers enslave trees, and unidentified voices force plants and birds to work. As Pratt observed, "Humboldt's emphasis on harmonies and occult forces aligns him with the spiritual esthetics of Romanticism. It also aligns him with industrialism and the machine age, however, and with the developments in the sciences that were producing and being produced by that age" (124). Bopp's industrial metaphors operate in the same way, creating a world animated not so much by the Amazonian mythology referred to by critics, as by Brazil's industrial South. Mythology itself is left to the epic frame that opens and closes the poem: to Snake Norato, Boiúna, and the Currupira he meets when he is going to the Boiúna's house.

The context of travel writing also sheds further light on the poetic "I"'s relationship with the dry-bum-armadillo. For although, as we saw, this relationship has similarities to communication between species as it appears in native Amazonian stories, it is also very different from it. From their initial encounter, the armadillo remains with the poetic "I" until the end of the journey. He listens to his complaints about his desire to see Queen Luzia's daughter, and, as he knows his way around the forest (in spite of his *gaúcho* accent), he is able to tell the poetic "I," for instance, how far the sea is:

> —Is the sea far away, brother?
> —Yes
> It is ten leagues of forest and then ten leagues more
> —Let's go, then (166)

He also warns the poetic "I" about the need to travel faster, or about the dangers when they are approaching the Boiúna's house. It is at the armadillo's suggestion that they go to the manioc mill to steal some flour, and in order to find their way there, they are guided by the armadillo's brother-in-law, the tortoise. There is no question about the armadillo's important role in the poem, or about his knowledge of the Amazonian environment. Yet as we have seen, he rarely exhibits any armadillo-like behavior, nor do we learn anything about his past or present life. His role in the relationship with the poetic "I" seems not to differ a great deal from that of a human helper in traditional European stories. In fact, if we take the poem's epic frame seriously—that is, if we emphasize the poetic "I"'s search for Queen

Luzia's daughter and his fight against the Boiúna[3]—we will see the armadillo playing the role of the faithful helper of the epic hero, the one who saves him from danger and uses his local knowledge to help him achieve his task. On the other hand, the armadillo is also a confidant to the poetic "I," and in that role he supports those readings that emphasize *Snake Norato*'s lyric qualities.[4] He listens to the latter's yearnings for his beloved woman—yearnings that often take the form of sung poetry—and to his questioning about the mysteries of the world: "There are so many things we don't understand, brother / What is there behind the stars?" (174). He is, in other words, an interlocutor to the poetic "I"'s lyric self.

The context of travel writing helps us see the armadillo playing yet another role, as the native who guides and helps the foreign traveler, and is dispensed with once the journey is over. After saving Queen Luzia's daughter from the hands of the Boiúna, the poetic "I" tells the armadillo that they now should part: "This is it, brother / Follow your own way, now" (192).

While *Macunaíma* deconstructs travel writing by making its Amazonian hero write a letter back home describing the oddities and exoticism of life in the modern metropolis, *Snake Norato,* as we have just seen, reproduces and reinforces it. Needless to say, this does not detract from its poetic qualities. On the contrary: What makes *Snake Norato* a great poem is not any claim to authenticity on the part of its epic frame, but the beautiful artificiality of its descriptions, which rarely cease to betray the overpowering presence of the poetic "I." *Snake Norato* is in this sense less a poem about the Amazon than a poem about the shock caused by the Amazonian environment in a Southern man.

For all that, we can conclude that *Snake Norato* is perhaps closer to conceptual products of *Antropofagia* like the "Manifesto," in which native cultures contribute philosophically and ideologically but very little at the level of text, than it is to *Macunaíma*. If by reading Amorim, Bopp was able to recognize the existence of another sensitivity or even another "world" ("in his [Amorim's] world trees spoke"), he could not (or perhaps did not wish to) translate/cannibalize that world into poetry, except through the filter of an overpoweringly Southern poetic "I."

chapter 9

The Green Stage

I N THE 1970s the Amazon made world headlines thanks to the highest-ever rate of destruction of its natural habitat. Thousands of acres were being burned every day, while satellite images of interminable amounts of smoke and cleared forest areas invaded the homes of Europeans and North Americans, who were now obliged to add the term "rain forest" to their list of social preoccupations (Hecht and Cockburn). The generals who governed Brazil from 1964 to 1979 were responsible for this dramatic change in the rate of destruction of the world's largest forest, and their example has been followed by all the democratically elected governments that succeeded them.

Immediately after taking power in 1964, the generals established an economic plan for the region that included the construction of highways such as the Trans-Amazon and North Perimeter Road, fiscal incentives for entrepreneurs willing to invest in the Amazon, as well as incentives to help small and medium settlers to establish there. Cattle-ranching (and its immediate consequence: land speculation), mining, logging, and road-building became the main causes of destruction of the forest. In addition, the military created a duty-free zone in Manaus with the purpose of attracting foreign investors and tourists from the south of the country. Named for the Manao Indians of the region, Manaus was thrown into new prominence.

Located at the junction of the Negro and the Amazon rivers, the city of Manaus, capital of Amazonas state, was initially a product of late nineteenth-century rubber boom. While Belém, at the mouth of the Amazon, had been one of the largest Brazilian towns since the eighteenth century, Manaus was still a small village when rubber became one of the most desirable raw products in the world. In thirty years, the small village was changed into a bizarre European town in the middle of the jungle. Its most famous building, Teatro Amazonas (much featured in Werner Herzog's film *Fitzcarraldo*), was built entirely from materials brought directly from Europe, and at the beginning of the twentieth century it managed to attract famous opera singers. With the decline of the rubber trade after 1912, Manaus became again an isolated and provincial town.

It was this isolation that the generals were supposedly seeking to break when they created the duty-free zone. As at the time of the rubber boom, from night to day Manaus was again invaded from one day to the next by bureaucrats and businessmen from other parts of Brazil, and by stores and "maquiladoras" filled with electronic products to be consumed by tourists from the south. In its desire to "develop" the Amazon, the military was also eager to deny any cultural importance to the region. In 1974, the official secretary of culture of the Amazonas state was asked to report on artistic activities in the Amazon. His response was clear: "There was nothing there, our artistic production was zero" (M. Souza 1984, 31). On the other hand, the military had its official propaganda apparatus well in place. From television to popular music to theater, all media were under severe censorship and were often forced to include well and not-so-well disguised propaganda pieces.

In order to analyze this situation critically, the young members of a Manaus theater group, TESC,[1] decided to promote drama more concerned with their own region and its cultural production. This much is implicit in Márcio Souza's account of their aims and experience: *O Palco Verde* (1980), or "green stage." Their first play was "Zona Franca, Meu Amor" ("Duty-Free Zone, mon amour"), a comedy by Márcio Souza much influenced by Oswald de Andrade. The group received a big blow when they learned that military-regime censors would not allow the play to be staged. Although written by Souza, this and the other plays performed by TESC were effectively the result of group research and discussion (M. Souza 1984, 108–17).

The group then decided to stage "A Paixão de Ajuricaba" (1974), a piece based on the life of the Manao *tuxaua* Ajuricaba, the epitome of native Amazonian resistance to invasion. Their decision to reenact the life of Ajuricaba announced an attempt to rewrite the history of the Amazon. Set in the year of the hero's death, 1738, "Ajuricaba" is written in the "high language" of Portuguese translations of Greek plays. Its main characters are the hero Ajuricaba, his wife Inhambu, the Portuguese commander-in-chief, a priest, and an Indian prison guard. It also includes a chorus that echoes the questions asked by the tragic hero and his wife: Didn't he act out of love for his own people?; if so, why was he punished?; and why are we all subject to fear? At the end, these bigger-than-life questions succumb to the weight of history: Ajuricaba is killed by the guards who were taking him to trial in Belém.

The Greek tragedy framework allowed the group to bring Ajuricaba up (in Western terms) to the level of heroes more easily recognized by the West. The nobility of Ajuricaba thus becomes comparable to the nobility of well-known Greek characters; his importance for Amazonian history is also made equivalent to the importance that Oedipus and his tragic descendants had for Greek, and Western, history. Ajuricaba had not been, and continues not to be, recognized as a hero in Brazilian official history—an omission that the staging of the play tried to correct. At the same time, by focusing on ideas of justice and oppression, Souza and his group were able to use the eighteenth-century hero as a means to criticize the injustice and oppression committed by the military in the 1970s. Deliberate anachronisms were introduced to make these links clear. The Rio Negro region, for instance, is repeatedly called a "romantic country"—a curious appropriation of the epithet most frequently employed, in Western racist discourse, to deride sympathetic depictions of indigenous cultures. References to "filthy jails" echo common descriptions of the oppressive regime at the time; and constant references to future ecological disasters foreshadow the destruction of the forest about to be caused by the generals.

While "Ajuricaba"is based on accounts given mostly by the victorious non-Indian invaders, TESC's next plays, "Dessana, Dessana," and "Jurupari, a Guerra dos Sexos"[2] ("Jurupari, the War Between the Sexes") were the product of a deep engagement with indigenous texts from the upper Rio Negro region. In other words, rather than make up or reconstruct native discourse, as he had been obliged to do in "Ajuricaba," Souza now drew on it directly. As he explains in O Palco Verde (1980), even though members of TESC belonged to different social classes, most of them were, at least in the initial years of the group, middle-class university students who had hardly been in contact with the Amazonian forest, let alone the upper Rio Negro region. The knowledge of native literature allowed them to engage, for the first time, with the deeper geography and history of their own region.

Interestingly, this Manaus-based theater group was not the first to combine native Rio Negro literature and the political reality of the military regime. Antonio Callado's novel *Quarup* (1967) quoted the Big Snake narrative "How Night Was Created," transcribed in Couto de Magalhães's *O Selvagem*, in order to defend underground resistance to the military, which was still in its early (and not so violent) years. This story tells how the daughter and son-in-law of Big Snake let the night come out of a *tucum* nut. In *Quarup*, the convalescent protagonist Nando associates darkness with the underground fighting against the military regime. Such darkness has to be carefully maintained and cultivated until it forms a "lake of darkness, lake of honey immersed in its own waters, far from the murky river of mud. The *tucum* seeds were thousands of workers on the march, already damming the river below Manaus. The Big Snake" (537). The *tucum* nuts, hard to break, full of integrity, are associated by Nando with those people whom he considers the true revolutionaries—humble and brave people like the *sertanejo* Manuel Tropeiro: "A *tucum* coconut simply falls into the water from the trees along the bank, but everyone knows that what really holds back the commercial use of coconuts is that it costs so much time and money to crack them open" (535). And as in the native narrative, where the Big Snake's daughter and son-in-law prefer darkness because they want to make love, darkness represents for Nando at this moment a positive force, the opposite of enlightened literary or political images: "How to live in pitiless brightness such as this, Big Snake? And where shall the tapers of darkness be lit if your river ends?" (541).

In the children's play *The Big Snake Prophecy—or the Trans-Amazon*, by Zuleika Mello (1972), Big Snake is also politicized, yet to opposite ends, and far more crudely. Subtitled "a mythical play," *The Big Snake Prophecy* is a propaganda piece in favor or the military, and its aim is to convince children of the need to cut down the Amazon forest. Before the opening of the curtains an old Indian chief shares with the public the wise words of his deceased father: "My son, we are all brothers inside this big Mother-Nation called Brazil but we still live here, between the Amazon river and its fabulous subsidiaries, separated from our brothers from the North, Northwest, the Center and the South of our great country"(ix). Big Snake appears in it as a sorcerer who reveals, in a prophecy, that the Amazon, its animals and peoples will soon be "integrated" with the rest of the country. Later, she (Big Snake is feminine in the play) tries to convince the doubting alligator and a character called Amazonas (who represents the forest itself) that they shouldn't fear the felling of trees:

> AMAZONAS: See how I tremble. My body is hurt form all these terrible machines that make my green hair fall into the ground. Tell me, Big Snake, what is going to happen to us?

BIG SNAKE: Don't be afraid, Mother Forest. Nothing bad is going to
  happen to us. The white men came here to help us, to make us
  develop.

AMAZONAS: I can't understand.

BIG SNAKE: You need to understand. These machines will transform
  you into a line of asphalt that will extend from Ocean to Ocean,
  from the Atlantic to the Pacific, from the Pacific to Recife, from
  Recife to Peru.

AMAZONAS: Who told you those things, Big Snake? Who told you?

BIG SNAKE: Big Snake is a sorcerer . . . Men are going to plant luminous
  cities and green fields around you.

AMAZONAS: Go on. I want to know where this prophecy ends.

BIG SNAKE: Yes, and everybody will come here in search of gold, metals,
  and stones. And they will extract the black blood of the earth; the
  oil-blood that will feed the whole world. (18)

Indeed, the military's plan for the Amazon could hardly be expressed more
eloquently than in this play.

"Dessana, Dessana"

Signed by Márcio Souza and Aldísio Filgueiras, with music by the composer
Adelson Oliveira, "Dessana, Dessana" (1975) was TESC's closest experience
with ritual theater, a genre not frequently staged in Brazil. Once again, the
play or cantata was the result of prolonged research by the group. Their main
consultant was the Salesian priest Casimiro Beckstá, who had lived among
the Desâna for more than twenty years. During the preparation of the play,
he gave a seminar to the group, discussing Desâna ways of living. He also
introduced them to Feliciano Lana, a cousin of Luis Lana (Tōrāmũ Kēhíri)
and a nephew of Firmiano Lana (Umusī Pārōkumu), who were already in the
process of writing the major cosmogonical text *Antes o Mundo não Existia*
(see chapter 7). Feliciano showed them a version of Desâna cosmogony, and
this version became the group's basic text: "But it was Feliciano's version,
though incomplete, that worked as a point of departure for the cantata"
(M. Souza 1984, 38). A few days before opening night, Tōrāmũ Kēhíri visited
Manaus and attended some rehearsals of the play. In the words of Souza, "he
made some corrections to the libretto, taught us some dance routines, a bit
of Desâna etiquette and showed a great curiosity for the theater. He did not
imagine that whites could do things like that" (1984, 34).

Ideally, any analysis of a theater play should take into account elements
of performance that are not easily deducted from a published version. In
the case of a cantata like "Dessana, Dessana," even more so. All I have at

my disposal are different published versions of the play (including the most recent one, a luxurious volume that includes several photographs and the complete music scores) and a videotape of an orchestral performance of the music.[3] On this basis, I attempt an analysis of the text here, given its importance for the history of Brazilian theater and for accounts of intertextuality between native and non-native Brazilian literature.

"Dessana, Dessana" was performed by eighteen actors and actresses at the legendary Teatro Amazonas. Their public was mostly middle-class adults from Manaus who paid to see it. The exception was the evening of 20 July 1975, when the audience was made up of representatives of several Rio Negro tribes. The play is supposed to resemble a cantata, based, as Souza says, "a bit pretentiously on Monteverde"(1984, 33). The cast included several tenors, baritones, sopranos, and contraltos. The characters are Yebá-Beló, grandmother of the universe, who was played by three sopranos and one contralto; her grandsons the Four Thunders (two tenors, a bass, and a baritone); her other grandson Sulān-Panlāmin (a tenor); the transformer Boleka (a tenor), the people who traveled up the Amazon river and founded its different villages and towns; the daughter of the Thunder and mother of Bisiu (Jurupari) and a chorus.

The play tells us the cosmogony of the Desâna, in the compact version by Feliciano Lana. The link between the cosmogonic characters and the audience is made by the character Dessana, a Desâna Indian who starts the play dressed as a poor Brazilian in the middle of the pollution, heavy traffic, and rat-race of duty-free Manaus. Looking at the audience, he sings the biblical version of the creation of the world:

> The world
> was created
> in seven days.
> That's what they say, isn't it true?
> And on the last day
> the creator rested.
> That's what they say, isn't it true?
> In seven days everything started.
> That's what they say, isn't it true? (49)

Already in these first lines, the biblical truth is questioned by the insistent and anxious pleas for confirmation: "isn't it true?" In fact, although all published versions present the phrase as a question, in the sung version the intonation is ambiguous, making it sound both as "isn't it true?" and "it isn't true." The chorus tries to divert him from his questioning, confirming that the world was, indeed, created in seven days:

Yes, it is written,
in seven days everything started,
the sky, the earth, the rivers
and all of us,
and all of us. (49)

Dessana then clearly reveals his disbelief in the Bible:

But the right thing is that
the world needs to be created
everyday,
that is what the rock says
to the other rock.
That is what the birds say
to the clouds
And the creator
never rests
like the river and its flow. (49–50)

This establishes a conflict with the chorus, who continue to repeat the biblical version of the genesis. In other words, the play starts with a split between two worldviews: the Christian and the Desâna. But Dessana soon manages to convince the chorus of his creation story, at the same time that the city environment becomes more and more unreal, being replaced by a dark stage and a Desâna ceremonial stool. The group then starts singing the Desâna cosmogony.

The urbanized character Dessana serves as an intermediary between the cosmogonic text and present-day Manaus, where Indians look just like poor Brazilians and are discriminated against by the non-Indian population. At the end of the play, the stage goes back to the city environment, and Dessana is told by a policeman to move on. The presence of this character, at the beginning and end of the play, serves as an important reminder of the situation of detribalized Indians. At the same time, it establishes connections between these city Indians and their own cosmogonies, for it is precisely the apparently Christianized Dessana who provides the break in the rat-race of the city, tuning us in to deeper cosmogonic time.

Dessana also plays an important role in the cosmogonic text, as a narrator, and at times, as a commentator and even an instigator: in the beginning, for instance, he and the chorus try to convince Yebá-Beló, the grandmother of the universe, to create the world.

> Grandmother of the world,
> Thou who livest before everything.
> Grandmother of the world,
> Thou who livest before everything.
> Create, create, Yebá-Beló.
> Create, create, Yebá-Beló. (52)

The character Dessana brings the cosmogony to the present, rather than relegating it to a glorious past. The theatrical elements are extremely important here: visually, the audience can simultaneously see a de-tribalized, poor city Indian, and relate this familiar image to the beauty and grandiosity of the Desâna cosmogony that they are seeing performed.

If "Ajuricaba" tried to emphasize the dignity of the Indian character by making him similar to a Greek tragic hero, "Dessana, Dessana" performs the same operation through its music, which is entirely Western. Different musical styles are used: If some songs indeed approximate the play to a religious cantata, others bring it closer to popular rhythms such as *samba* and soft-rock ballads. Such musical choice follows the logic of the group, who did not want their middle-class urban public to see the Indians as ethnographic subjects. Thus, instead of performing a carefully studied ethnographic reproduction of a Desâna ritual, they opted for a balance between familiar and unfamiliar elements. The text remains reasonably faithful to the native source, while the music is intended to remind the audience of familiar rhythms, and in some cases of Christian sacred rituals—probably their closest experience in the realm of the "sacred." At the same time, the music allows the group room for repetition, an important ritual element, and for a multiplicity of voices.

Thus, Yebá-Beló is played by four women, three sopranos and one contralto. This is a striking theatrical choice, for on the one hand it accommodates a dispersal of the concept "creator," against an individualization that seems to be so inimical to Native American cultures[4]; and on the other it permits the multiplied character visually to represent the four elements associated with her physical being: the basket and its base, the sacred stool, the hallucinogenic *ipadu*, and the cigar.[5] As we saw, Yebá-Beló creates herself from elements that are central to Desâna life (more precisely, of Desâna shamanic life). Thus the creation of the world is (as in most cosmogonies we have read) the creation of the Desâna world—in other words, a cultural creation.

If the narrators of *Antes o Mundo não Existia* emphasized the invisibility of the objects that composed Yebá-Beló, in TESC's performance the ethereal aspect of the world-creator is expressed by the contrast between the dark stage and the extremely bright lights that illuminate the four singers. Also,

Yebá-Beló's discourse incorporates the description that in *Antes o Mundo não Existia* is given by the narrators:

> And there is nothing in the smoke
> I take my cigar and smoke,
> and there is nothing.
> In the smoke I look for a wandering signal,
> But I don't feel any breeze.
> And I am as lost as a traveler
> who became blind during the journey. (53)

In order to create the world, Yebá-Beló has to ask the help of the Four Thunders. In *Antes o Mundo não Existia*, she actually creates the Thunders, her brothers, so that they create the world. In this version, the Thunders are simply described as Yebá Beló's brothers. And while in *Antes o Mundo não Existia*, as we saw, the Thunders are not able to create the world because they are lazy or get drunk, here they refuse to do it, on the grounds that it is a project that surpasses their capacity, as the Thunder of the Southern House explains:

> We can't take the risk, sister.
> The world goes beyond, sister,
> our small powers, sister.
> Ask for something else, sister. (57)

By emphasizing the conflict between Yebá-Beló and the Thunders, "Dessana, Dessana" makes clear that the creation of the world, in the Desâna cosmogony, is not a guaranteed task, a job to be done in six days by one single creator, as in the biblical tradition. In *Antes o Mundo não Existia* and "Dessana, Dessana," there is always the risk that the world will not be created, for it depends on negotiations and agreements and on orders that have to be obeyed. And as in *Antes o Mundo não Existia*, the creation of the world ends up being performed not by the Thunders, but by a teenage boy, Sulãn-Panlãmin. But if in the first text this character is created from the cigar smoke and *ipadu* by Yebá-Beló herself, in the play he simply appears on the stage, and is called "the un-created" by Yebá-Beló:

> It is Sulãn, the un-created.
> It is Sulãn, the boy.
> He came.
> May he come, then, from the smoke,
> the boy.
> He who was not created

by anybody.
May he come then,
appear from the smoke. (59)

In both cases, as in the self-creation of Yebá-Beló, we can see the shamanic importance of smoke and *ipadu*.

In order to create the world, Sulán has to ask for the wealth that belongs to the Thunder Grandfather of the Sky (Thunder Third House in *Antes o Mundo não Existia*). In this case, unlike Kumu and Kēnhíri's text, the Thunder gives Sulán a choice: He can either create the world from *ipadu* (in which case the world would be unchanging and nothing would die), or from ornaments (in which case the world would be ever-changing and unstable). Sulán tries to get the *ipadu* but he is struck by lightning, and therefore he takes the ornaments, a result that is not seen as necessarily negative:

> Or a world
> of days and nights and later.
> A world of saying things in vain
> and forgetting.
> Believe me,
> I left the *ipadu* in the sky,
> so that women could exist.
> Believe me,
> I left the *ipadu* in the sky,
> so that men could exist,
> I left the *ipadu* in the sky
> so that things would change. (63)

Like the Pemon texts and *Macunaíma,* the play reinforces what in *Antes o Mundo não Existia* is taken for granted: a eulogy of the ever-changing nature of the world. As an enactment of a creation story to a middle-class urban population, the play is necessarily in dialogue with the Christian Bible, where instability and precariousness are always seen as negative.

Such eulogy continues, as the newly created people are described as "adults / but like children," and instead of being punished by the creator for eating the fruit of "forbidden tree of knowledge," as in the Bible, these first humans will be ready to inhabit the world only after they go through an education process:

> Thus, the boy decided
> that one day humans would go away,
> they would leave the underworld
> and intoxicate themselves with knowledge. (361–62)

A quest for knowledge: This is how the Desâna journey in the snake-boat is described in the play. To lead it, Sulān-Panlāmin wakes up Boleka, the first Desâna leader. But the journey will not be joined by all; the white man tries to convince the others not to go on the boat:

> Examine well
> What they want us to do:
> Leave this place
> where we are well,
> cross this milk lake,
> in order to arrive
> at the unknown.
> They say this
> will give us experience,
> we will know the secrets
> of the universe
> But why should we
> leave what is certain
> and go towards uncertainty? (70)

The behavior of whites was also accounted for in *Antes o Mundo não Existia*, where the white man was given the gun to make war because there were no other riches left. Here, the white man refuses to take part in the general trip, and is also left alone, "condemned / to live separate / from his brothers." Unlike the previous text, however, this is his own fault, the result of his determination to stay in the same place and

> build cities,
> invent machines
> that do the work for us.
> Let's stay here,
> and dominate nature,
> tame thunder,
> and submit the rivers.
> Generate wealth
> from forest leaves. (71)

At the others' uncertainties, he shows them his dominated thunder (the shotgun). Ultimately, the play presents the same argument as the cosmogonic Desâna text: The whites' violent behavior isolates them from other people. In "Dessana, Dessana," this leads to the climax of the play, when Dessana, Boleka, Sulān-Panlāmin, and the chorus respectively caution the others (and the audience) about the white man:

> Out, out, out,
>
> white skin,
>
> son of violence,
>
> Out, out, out,
>
> white skin,
>
> son of lying,
>
> Out, out, out,
>
> white skin,
>
> son of deceit. (72)

This climax is reached shortly before the end of the first act, when the trip in the snake-boat is announced.

The second act opens with the beginning of the journey, and goes on to describe the different houses where the snake-boat stops. While in *Antes o Mundo não Existia* we have the exhaustive list of all the houses—that is, ritual and potentially monotonous, the play describes fewer of them, but gives a longer explanation of their function. Thus, in the House of the White Rock, the first humans learn how to plant, fish, and hunt; in the Row of Stools House, they learn how to celebrate, dance, drink alcohol, live together; and so on. The last house is the Milk Lake House, or the house of sexual pleasures, which opens up the theme of the impregnation of a young woman by a fruit. As in the Rio Negro tradition in general, the young woman is the mother of Bissiu, or Jurupari. But no power issues are described here: The play treats the theme of Jurupari in exclusively sexual terms. The fruit that impregnates the young woman becomes then a metaphor for the greatness of sexual desire—a reading that is probably closer to the biblical tradition (by inversion) than it is to the theme of Jurupari as developed in *Antes o Mundo não Existia*. The story of the young woman ends the cosmogonic part of the play, with a celebration of sexual love by choruses of both men and women. But in a Brechtian interruption of catharsis, the play ends by bringing the audience again to modern Manaus. The final discourse by Dessana makes it clear that what was just heard by the audience happened "before the beginning," that is, in cosmogonic time: "Ah! But this was earlier / in the beginning before the beginning."

TESC's decision to stage a cosmogonic text cannot be isolated from the general movement of ritual theater as defended by such various twentieth-century figures as Antonin Artaud, Aimé Césaire, and Peter Brook, to mention just a few. A common argument of all of these authors and directors was the Nietzschean notion that theater originated in ritual, and that the only way for it to recover its meaningfulness in the contemporary world is by reviving its links with what Peter Brook calls the "holy" (42–64). Thus, although Souza never says so in his 1980 account of the movement, it seems clear that TESC's choice of text was a decision to break away from the bourgeois theater that ruled Manaus; in other words, it was aimed at "filling up the empty spaces" (as Brook's title has it) in Brazilian theater.

Indeed Brazilian theater was full of empty spaces, so to speak. Up to the late forties, the stage had been occupied exclusively by bourgeois comedies *(comédia de costumes)* in the style of late-nineteenth-century author Martins Pena (whose work was later staged by TESC). In the 1940s, the theater scene in Rio was shaken by the revolutionary works of the playwright Nelson Rodrigues, staged in nonrealistic performances by the director Ziembinski, a Polish immigrant much in tune with European trends of the time. Heavily influenced by Freud, Rodrigues's plays were a violent attack on traditional Catholic morality. Although his theater had followers in Abdias do Nascimento and the components of the Black Theater in Rio, and in spite of the vitality of the political theater of the early 1960s, few experiments with ritual theater per se were actually attempted on the Brazilian stage. Two exceptions were José Celso Martinez Correa's legendary performance of Oswald de Andrade's *O Rei da Vela* in 1968, cut short by censorship, and Chico Buarque de Hollanda's also legendary *Roda Viva*, attacked by a right wing militia in the same year. Both plays used Artaudian techniques, especially the "theater of cruelty," with its open assault on audience sensibility.[6]

It was only two years after the staging of "Dessana, Dessana" that the Brazilian stage would see its most successful performance ever in the genre of ritual theater: Antunes Filho's adaptation of Mário de Andrade's *Macunaíma*. Closer to the latter than to the previous experiments with the "theater of cruelty," TESC's performance of "Dessana, Dessana" saw ritual theater more in terms of an experience with the sacred—a sense that modern life and conventional religions had lost. Both performances relied heavily on visual elements, especially lighting and striking nonrealist sets, and while *Macunaíma* was highly dependent on choreography, "Dessana, Dessana," as we have seen, was centered on music. The two plays tried to involve their audiences through the use of what is conventionally called "magic": transformations, metamorphoses, disappearances, and so on. But while Antunes Filho's staging of *Macunaíma* before São Paulo and Rio audiences repeated the direction of Macunaíma's journey—i.e., bringing the Amazon to the South of Brazil—"Dessana, Dessana" had a distinct political objective: to make its Manaus audiences look differently at the Indians they saw every day as poor, displaced human beings. By comparing the Desâna creation story to the biblical Genesis, the character Dessana refuted the idea of one single genesis, that is, of one single version of history—quite a subversive gesture for those highly oppressive years. After all, the military was trying to impose on the Amazon the idea of one single, unidirectional, and inevitable version of history, which they called "development." Moreover, the play put this alternative genesis in the mouth of a detribalized Indian, thus forcing the audience to look at him and his culture with respect.

In other words, while it is true that TESC's performance of "Dessana, Dessana" was one of the most ambitious ritual stagings in the history of Brazilian theater (and the only one, to my knowledge, to attempt the performance of a native cosmogony), it is also true that the play cannot be explained exclusively through its connection with this genre. The presence of the character Dessana worked as a counterpoint to ritual theater, for he required a constant interruption in the involvement of the audience in the ritual process, by reminding them of a social, political, and racial situation that surrounded them in their everyday life.

"Jurupari, a Guerra dos Sexos"

TESC's next play, "Jurupari, a Guerra dos Sexos" attempted a continuation of the group's involvement in ritual theater. Once again, the source text was a cosmogonic narrative: Stradelli's *Leggenda*. The play, signed by Souza, was, like the other performances, the result of extensive research by the group. Originally, it was to have been staged in 1976, but authorization was denied by the censorship board then in power. For a few years, the project was abandoned, while the group gained local and national recognition with two satires whose main focus was the Manaus elite: "Folias do Látex" (1976) and the retitled version of "Zona Franca, Meu Amor," "Tem Piranha no Pirarucu," which had been let through by the censors. By this time, Souza himself had become a famous writer with the publication of his satirical novel, *Emperor of the Amazon* (1976), about the rubber boom.

In 1979, "Jurupari" was finally approved, with a few cuts, and the group took the project up again. In order to stage it, TESC had to go through a process of negotiation with the native communities. According to Souza, a group of what he calls "detribalized" Indians tried to stop the performance on the grounds that women would be allowed to see the sacred instruments of Jurupari. At the same time, still according to him, another group of "tribal Rio Negro Indians" celebrated the play, but demanded that no replicas of the sacred instruments should be shown (1984, 60).

Unlike other plays by the group, "Jurupari" never managed to attract large audiences. For Souza, this had to do with the fact that the public, who had gotten used to their satirical vein, found the play too hermetic (1984, 58). Yet other factors may have contributed to the popular failure of

"Jurupari." Unlike "Dessana, Dessana," this play relied solely on dialogue. There was no repetition, no music, no multiplication of voices, and in spite of Souza's description of the performance as ritual theater ("By recreating a myth on stage, it was as if we watched every night the birth of theater itself" [1984, 58]), the cosmogonic text was adapted into something closer to a bourgeois drama than to the previous experience of the group with "Dessana, Dessana." *But still, jurupari challenged western, w/ a point forever, descended the male/female dispute over power*

The play starts with a striking scene in which an old shaman pours some powder into a young shaman's nose. The young shaman goes into a trance, during which, in the words that describe the scene, "he is overtaken by all stories of the tribe." He then goes on to narrate the Jurupari story, which in the beginning, develops in a way close to Stradelli's version: The Tariana women lament the death of all men in the tribe and bathe in the forbidden lake. The old shaman (made even older in the play) admonishes them for having disobeyed the rules of the tribe, and without touching them, impregnates them all. As in Stradelli's *Leggenda,* the most beautiful of the children born from this act, Seucy of the Earth, in turn, gets pregnant from eating the "forbidden fruit" and gives birth to a beautiful child, Jurupari.

Now a change: On the stage the tribe is governed by a woman chief, the matriarch Naruna—the name of the woman *tuxaua* Date marries much later in the plot of the *Leggenda* (see chapter 7). The interest that men seem to show in the young Jurupari preoccupies Naruna and provokes the curiosity of the other women. Finally, the old shaman tells them who the child is:

OLD SHAMAN: Do you want to know who this child is?
NARUNA: Say, man, say it very loud.
OLD SHAMAN: It is Izi, woman. It is Jurupari.
NARUNA: Izi! We are lost. Let's get out of here. We will burn the *maloca.*
  We will escape to the Hook-of-the-Moon Mountains. We won't
  leave more than ashes in Tenui. (105)

In other words, the women already know about Jurupari, and the birth of the child seems to be the mere realization of a prophecy. The play therefore makes it inevitable that men should take over—so that their power is not the result of chance, as in Stradelli's text.

Moreover, the women, led by Naruna, go live in the Hook-of-the-Moon Mountains, and form their own community there, where men only go once a year in order to procreate, as in the well-known story of the Icamiabas, or the Amazon women. Once in a while, they send young emissaries to the village of the men in order to seduce them. One of these young emissaries, Diádue, is successful in seducing Uálri, as in Stradelli's text. But quite differently from that story, she is incapable of revealing any secrets to the women because she is completely marveled by her sexual experience with Uálri. The play then continues on this very distinct path: The function of Jurupari's teachings and rule becomes the mastering of perfect sexual techniques. Each of the sacred instruments, for instance (which in Stradelli's *Leggenda* were linked to the geographical distribution of the various cultural groups and languages in the Rio Negro), is described in the play in exclusively erotic terms:

> MAN: And this one, whose sound brushes the skin?
>
> JURUPARI: It is the jaguar-flute, of women's cunning and men's potency.
>
> MAN: This one explodes in fine tune.
>
> JURUPARI: It is drunkard, the flute of curiosity, which makes the boys touch, curious, the girls' nipples.
>
> MAN: This one sounds as though it could cut.
>
> JURUPARI: It is tintabri, the flute of the beautiful woman who, for being coquettish and punishing men by not giving herself, turned into an owl. (129)

If the core of Jurupari's teachings to men is how to give women sexual pleasure, it is inevitable that women should want to go back to live with their men, and that men, as a result, should have no problems in establishing their power over them. This is exactly what happens in the play. It seems that Souza and TESC, writing and performing in the decade of sexual liberation, wanted to appeal to their audience by making masculine power in the Tariana society dependent on sexual competence. So far, so good. Yet, in the longer view, the idea could seem to backfire. The play seems less liberating than Stradelli's *Leggenda* in the sense that it gives a justification for masculine power, and therefore makes women less capable of resisting it. The only issue that seems to interest women in the play is their sexual satisfaction: If they are satisfied, they will wish no power. Stradelli's *Leggenda*, as we saw, deals with power at a more complex level, and it is the very arbitrariness of masculine power that makes it vulnerable and gives women, at least conceptually, the possibility of change.

Moreover, Jurupari in the play is a character full of doubts and uncertainties. He flirts with Diádue and with Naruna, his own grandmother, whom he ends up killing with an arrow during a rather ambiguous courting scene. He also makes it clear that he likes to provoke women:

> I know you women desire me. You use all means to seduce me. For my part, I know I also provoke. Many times I cannot control myself and I walk through the village showing the signs of my desire. (133)

As a self-regarding seducer, Jurupari belongs more to bourgeois comedy than to the *Leggenda* that inspired the play.

But "Jurupari" also has many good moments, especially the visually striking first scene in which the widows lament the sexual loss of their husbands by standing over their corpses. The high degree of eroticism of this scene is merely an intensification of the eroticism already present in Stradelli's text. And although the play cannot be considered a comedy, it reveals at times the excellent comic vein that made Souza one of the best Brazilian writers of his generation. When Jurupari goes to see Naruna at the end of the play, for instance, he insists on using highly metaphoric language, which makes the matriarch respond as if he were drunk—a kind of exchange reminiscent of popular *autos*:

> JURUPARI: My sleep is flutes in the shadows.
> NARUNA: Flutes in the shadows? You must be drunk!
> JURUPARI: I haven't fallen asleep ever since I turned my head to this
>   meeting. I am looking at you and I avoid the meeting of my eyelids,
>   because the cold star demanded it.
> NARUNA: Cold star! Certainly you drank too much *caxiri*. (143)

Similarly, when Uálri explains to Jurupari why he was not able to resist Diádue, he says his sexual abstinence had been so prolonged that he started to dream women had no vaginas, that they were "lisas e saradas." The expression is a famous quote from Pero Vaz de Caminha's "Carta a el-rei Dom Manuel" (see chapter 4). Caminha used the term to describe the Indian women's intimate parts as being hairless and well-groomed, while Souza uses it, more literally, to mean "with no opening."

Uálri is one of the best-developed characters in the play. Souza was able to pick up the comic elements latent in Stradelli's text—above all Uálri's sexual incontinence, a characteristic related to the meaning of his name (anteater)—and turn them into brilliant popular comedy, as in the following lines:

> JURUPARI: How old are you, Uálri?
> UÁLRI: I am old enough to be many times a grandfather.
> JURUPARI: How have you lived? Well?
> UÁLRI: I have always stuck my nose where I shouldn't. This is to live,
>   isn't it? (119)

The same happens to Naruna, a character who was hardly present, as we saw, in Stradelli's text. Souza's portrayal of her as an oppressive matriarch who inverts expected gender roles also touches, at times, the realm of popular comic theater.

For all its limitations, Souza's exclusive concentration on the sexual aspects of the Jurupari narrative has undeniable dramatic advantages, especially at the comic level. And it is precisely as a comedy that the play, it seems, could become more effective.

In any case, TESC's attempts to bring Rio Negro cosmogonies to the stage have to be recognized as a remarkable feat: Rarely has Brazilian drama come so close to twentieth-century ritual theater. Even more significant, however, is the fact that these plays, especially "Dessana, Dessana," went beyond most ritual theater experiments by making Rio Negro cosmogonies politically significant in an Amazonian context. They brought native texts into the arena of current politics, connecting them directly to questions of performance, censorship, and warfare, both physical and ideological.

Part IV

The Arawak and the Uppermost Amazon

Once the sky was not high up as it is now
Once it all but brushed the trees
and the laughter of the *saangarite* could be
heard from here on earth
—*Santiago Manugari, Machiguenga Indian*

chapter 10

The Machiguenga and Their Heritage

L ARGELY UNNOTICED IN BRAZILIAN LITERATURE, the rain forest peoples of the uppermost Amazon have increasingly attracted attention in Spanish-speaking America. In the opening section of Galeano's *Genesis* (1982), the first part of his continental trilogy, *Memory of Fire,* the Huitoto, the Pano-speaking Cashinaua, the Arawak, and other groups from this part of the rain forest are prominent in telling the "true" story of Genesis: the flood, the finding of food (manioc, and the maize shared with the high-lands), and humankind's close kinship with the other animals (tapir, armadillo, monkey, jaguar).[1] In the highland countries of the Andes they have typically been seen as representatives of the "wild" beyond the frontier. This pattern was set up in nineteenth-century Ecuador by Juan León Mera, a student of Quechua, who in his influential novel *Cumandá: o un drama entre salvages* (1879), turned his attention to the eastern lowlands, where the heroine fights for her life among the "head-shrinking" Jivaro, a group today known and better understood as the Shuar. A similar di-chotomy between highland and lowland recurs in José Eustasio Rivera's classic Colombian novel *Vortex* (1924), while more recently in Peru several narratives have begun to deal in similar terms with the question of that country's "eastern territories" in the Amazonian lowlands: César Calvo's *Las tres mitades de Ino Moxo* (1981), Dante Castro Arrasco's *Otorongo y otros cuentos* (1986) and *Parte de combate* (1991), Thomas T. Büttner's *La*

rojez de anoche desde la cabaña (1989), and Róger Rumrrill's *El venado sagrado* (1992). In the novels of Vargas Llosa, especially *Green House* (1966), *Captain Pantoja and the Special Service* (1973), and *The Storyteller* (1987), these rain forest cultures have also been a recurrent point of reference. *The Storyteller* is in fact by far the most relevant to our purposes because of its persistent engagement with native texts, a distinctive feature that was initially overlooked (for example in Norbert Lentzen's wide-ranging survey of Vargas Llosa's "ethnic" writing). The native texts in question are those of the Machiguenga.

Only in the last quarter-century have texts in the Machiguenga language been published, and their literary impact has been limited to little other than *The Storyteller.* Here, however, they are of primary importance, in a novel that raises key questions about indigenist writing. As Arawak speakers, the Machiguenga are close to, and have indeed been identified with, the Campa (Ferrero, 35–37), with whom they share their homeland on the uppermost Amazon, at the gateway to and from Machu Pichu, Cuzco, and the Andes. Anti, the name given to them by the Inca, was transferred to Antisuyu, the northeastern quarter of the Inca empire Tahuantinsuyu, and later came to identify the whole cordillera of the "Andes."

Members of the Arawak family (which stretches the length of Amazonia, to emerge, ever entwined with Carib, into the Caribbean), the Machiguenga share rain forest cosmogony and beliefs and form part of the "Amazonian cosmos." At the same time, they have a history of their own as a result of living at the extreme western edge of the rain forest, where they have been for millennia, facing emissaries and intruders from the highlands. Their special version of rain forest culture is attested to in their literature, in cosmogonical narratives, shamanic chants, songs, and stories.

An early summary of the Machiguenga literary heritage was given, in Spanish, by José Pio Aza in 1927, in the *Revista de las Misiones Dominicanas.* A decade later, Secundino García published a series of articles in the same journal (1935–37), describing the Machiguenga belief system and giving Spanish versions of some stories. Further stories, still in Spanish, were published by the Machiguenga mestizo Fidel Pereira ("El dios cashire—el origen de la yuca y el de otras plantas" and "Chaingavane: el Pongo de Mainiqui y los petroglifos"); by Vicente de Cenitagoya (*Los machiguengas,* 1943); and by Andrés Ferrero, who repeats much of Secundino García's work (*Los machiguengas: Tribu selvática del sur-oriente peruano,* 1967). Then, in 1976, Harold Davis and Betty Elkins de Snell, from the Summer Institute of Linguistics (Peru), published a collection of fifteen stories in the Machiguenga language, with Spanish translations, a foundational statement which they entitled *Kenkitsatagantsi Matsigenka*. Subsequently, original-language Machiguenga texts have appeared in F. Pascual Alegre's *Tashorintsi: Tradición oral masiguenka* (1979), otherwise a highly prejudiced description of Machiguenga beliefs; and in Gerhard Baer's *Die Religion der Matsigenka: Ost-Peru* (1984), the most complete study of their society and religion, now available in Spanish, which includes some stunning shamanic songs, a war poem, as well as narratives and native maps. By far the best collection of Machiguenga stories to date is Joaquín Barriales's series "Mitos de la cultura machiguenga," published in the journal *Antisuyo* (without date, probably in the seventies).[2] This series of seventeen stories consistently provides source texts in the original language, and respects the styles of different narrators, who are named and briefly described at the end of each story. The same author published the study *Matsigenka,* in 1977, which includes a poem in the original language.

To these transcriptions of spoken and recited texts, France-Marie Casevitz's "Inscriptions: Un aspect du symbolisme matsiguenga" (1980), comes as a major corollary and underpinning. Relying on commentaries offered by Machiguenga shamans themselves, this article analyzes in admirable detail the visual language of inscriptions on stone and bone, which "write down" the voice of thunder and the jaguar, define territory, and affirm the social network. An example is the following description of the Upper Picha petroglyphs, given by the shaman Daniel:

> The one who makes *tiring* (the voice of thunder) is the true Master; he is master of a script similar in certain ways to that machine made for words (a tape-recorder). There's another script, that he has: It's the word he writes, a writing that he speaks . . . Once I lived on the Upper Picha and up there in the mountains, near the peaks where the rising sun appears, one can hear and see that writing. Its master calls us ooh . . . ooh . . . in the heart of the rocky slopes and we go to the place he calls from in order to see and hear what he is saying. Among the rocks we don't see him, we see his word and his writings. He is who also brings the jaguar of the rocks where one hears a voice saying ein'ein'ein . . . (that can only be the jaguar's); this is the way he announces his approach. (261)

Like the *timehri* and inscriptions of the Carib, this "writing" was said to have been brought to the Machiguenga by a culture hero—in this case Chaingavane—Makunaima-like and of possibly epic dimensions. Chaingavane later emigrated east and (according to Fidel Pereira) gave all his knowledge of tools and machines to the *viracochas,* or whites, not unlike the Tupi hero Maíra in the Urubu-Kaapor tradition.

Tasurinchi's Domain

In confirming Machiguenga culture as pan-Amazonian, wholly compa-rable to that of the Carib and the Tupi-Guarani, these texts tell first of the creator figure Tasurinchi, who breathes life into the beings of creation, the breath of life and speech celebrated explicitly in the Guarani title *Ayvu ra-pyta*. And as creator he is faced and dogged by a counterpart, Kientibakori, who is anxious to enslave and hold back the surge of creation, just as Odosha does in *Watunna*. In the scheme of world ages common to Native American cosmogony generally, this priviliged state or place corresponds to the time before the great catastrophes of flood and eclipse, when the earth was still linked to the sky by an umbilical cord *(omo'guto in'kite)*:

> The earth and sky were one, those who lived on earth often went to visit those who lived in the sky, and vice versa. One day, four men called 'Oxu (sloth), 'Katasari (the paucar or cacique bird), 'Tontori (porcupine) and 'Sani (wasp), wanted to go and visit the sky. A most mendacious man Ma'choeri prevented them. He told the sky dwellers that people were com-ing to kill them, and for that reason they decided to cut the sky's umbilical cord. The severed piece fell to earth. (Baer, 163)

From the start this whole cosmogonical arrangement has its celestial co-ordinate. As in the Amazonian myth system analyzed by Lévi-Strauss, there is incessant metamorphosis into and out of the main bodies of the sky: the Pleiades and fixed stars; sun, moon and the planets; comets that come and go; and meteors that plunge to earth. The principal pair, sun (Poreatsiri) and moon (Kashiri), are as usual both male, and histories of them give if anything prominence to the latter. The moon marries a Machiguenga woman and teaches her and her people how to cultivate manioc and other crops. In Benjamín Pereira's version of this narrative, collected by Barriales, Kashiri refuses to give manioc to another Machiguenga woman, who then reacts by throwing mud on him—an act that results in the blemish on Kashiri's face that is conveniently caught in the Spanish term "lunar." In the version published by Fidel Pereira, this blemish is the result of the moon's first sexual intercourse with his Machiguenga wife, who splashed the juice of the tree *Amanquerichi* on her husband's face. Kashiri's offsprings include the suns that light up the different levels of the Machiguenga cosmos, of which the one that warms up the Earth is the mildest version, his east-west trajectory having been determined by his father, Kashiri, at birth. But Kashiri's constant impregnation of his wife made her die when giving birth to her last twin children, causing the rage of her mother. The angry woman forced Kashiri to eat the flesh of her deceased daughter (F. Pereira, 1942),[3] and the moon from then on became a cannibal, collecting the bodies of the dead Machiguenga from the river in order to eat them in the sky. As with most Amazonian texts we have seen, Kashiri is at the same time a benevolent being, who brought agriculture to the Machiguenga, and the evil cannibal who devours their dead. What is more, manioc, also a daughter of the moon, is told that, if badly treated by planters, it may complain to Kashiri, according to the local doctrine of interspecies communication that includes not just animals but plants as well:

> Manioc, plantains, maize and sweet potatoes are the Moon's children.
> He (the moon) has gone up to the sky but there he is looking down on
> his daughters. He watches the people to see that they do not neglect their
> crops, and notices if they complain about his daughters. Moon knows that
> his daughter is happy to be eaten and says: I am most pleased. Manioc
> likes being chewed and fermented. Moon grows angry (if his daughters are
> not well treated), and may take them up again to the sky. The Matsigenka
> would then again eat roasted earth. (Barriales, n.d.: 3, 168–69)

Manioc is a sacred plant among the Machiguenga: only those who eat it are true people (Baer, 193). During communal gatherings, the women sing to Kashiri asking him not to take the manioc back to the sky (Baer, 194).

As a set of core beliefs, this cosmogony is variously expressed and elaborated in Machiguenga life, not least in the range of oral and inscribed texts which constitute their literature. The narratives that tell the creation story as such suggest a larger frame, an intricate interlinking pattern of episodes, determined not so much by linear chronology as by greater or lesser time depths (world catastrophes like the flood, and human endeavor), and by the several intertwining threads of genealogy and kinship. The rhythm and pace of certain episodes are notable and rely also on strong onomatopoeic effects. A good example is the story of the deer-hunter who himself is hunted by the deer:

> Then the sorcerer [malagüero] sang
> and was afraid in the night;
> more came and they all shook his trap,
> between them they made it collapse,
> and he shouted: ee! ee!
> All the deer run after him, terok, terok
> his wife heard him when he shouted ee! ee!
> she tried to follow him but the people told her:
> the deer have already got him.
> Again they heard his shout, and the deer
> went on bothering him:
> down there he would be heard still shouting: ee! ee! (Barriales, n.d.: 3, 170)

For their part, the shamanic songs and chants exquisitely condense the vision of the earth without ill (which the Guarani called *Ivy mará ey*), the paradise that preceded the severing of earth from sky, but which is always immanent and recoverable to heightened senses, or by enhanced perception and consciousness altered by *ayahuasca* and other hallucinogens, in a deeper awareness of the world around and within the human body:

> I'm off to a place that is very lovely,
> to the horizon of trees that are of even height
> where the trees flourish tenderly.
> Sickness has alarmed me,
> has made me flee.
> I'm off to a very lovely place,
> to the horizon of trees that are of even height.
> I'm suffering
> as I take ayahuasca,
> I'm suffering as I go on
> taking sweet ayahuasca.
> Sickness has alarmed me,
> I'm going to that place,
> tiny and neat are the new leaves of those trees.
> I'm going to where the wind blows,
> to the horizon of trees that are of even height. (Baer, 130)

Following the model of *Watunna, Antes o Mundo não Existia,* and for that matter, the *Popol Vuh* of the Maya, the cosmogony of the Machiguenga then leads out into history proper. First, it establishes these people in their own place, specifying landmarks like the mount of salt into which Pareni (Yagontoro's wife and Pachakama's sister) was transformed; and Pongo de Mainique, where the ancestors were born—the mighty rapids and whirlpool of the Urubamba whose inscribed rocks affirm the navel of the Machiguenga territory. Exactly parallel to that in the narratives of the Tucano, Desâna, and Orinoco Carib, this moment of birth never ceases to give coherence to the time and space of the Machiguenga world. Here the long strands of their social network converge. Averse to village life, the Machiguenga, like the Pemon, form small groups, a factor that has caused some outsiders to remark on their being "scattered" or "dispersed," often with the ulterior intention of denying them cultural unity and therefore the right to their land. But the fact that their society is spread out does not indicate a lack of coherence, for all the reasons given here. As Barriales points out:

> The similarities between narratives, in areas far distant from one another,
> shows us a significant dimension of the unity of the apparently fragmented

tribe; and on collating family and kinship data we often find lines of connection that we should never have imagined. And this affords the idea of a unity forged not just in language but through other stronger bonds, which give consistency and character to neighbourhoods. (1977, 12)

Songs performed at parties often make fun of the distant neighbors, showing how conscious the Machiguengas are of those who live far away. An example is "Canción de Masato de Eva" reproduced by Gerhard Baer:

> Ay, ay, ay
> I come from far away,
> Something I heard: what is it?
> What are they talking about?
> I say to my mother's son-in-law
> what does it mean?
> ay, ay, ay.
> He told, my mother's son-in-law,
> the women who live downstream
> are just like birds,
> like little white *chonpite* birds,
> they're *chonpite* birds,
> ay, ay, ay. (Baer, 196)

The Machiguenga resistance to the formation of villages, which so bothered the earlier Dominican priests, reveals an idea of community essentially distinct from the European model. In the words of Barriales:

> The concept of settlement *(poblado)*, for the Machiguenga, is none other than a firm togetherness with their ancestors. Settlement is any place one of them lives, where a neighbor lives and where he may go whenever he wants. Settlement is any habitat he identifies with and not simply a specific place where he has a roof over his head. Settlement is house, field, river, forest, because in all these places the Machiguenga live, those of today and those of yesterday. Hence the concept of settlement includes the sky and the sub-soil since hundreds of kin dwell there. Their whole cosmogonic thinking coincides with the term settlement, and is very far from our terminology of houses, streets, squares and crowds. (1977, 27)

The Andean Frontier

As for their specific history as a frontier people, hard against the Andean cordillera, the Machiguenga match their close kin and neighbors the Campa in recording a long series of invasions that goes back to pre-Spanish and even to pre-Incan times. The Inca campaigns are remembered, along with the names of the emperors that launched them, general terms for high-lander being the Quechua "viracocha" or "punaruna." Like the Campa and the Shipibo, the Machiguenga conserve a detailed record from centuries past, and although they have typically resisted the military incursion of the highlanders, they have also recognized the positive social values of the Tahuantinsuyu system; they even keep up a version of the Inkarri legend analyzed with great perception by the Quechua scholar José María Arguedas in "Puquio, una cultura en proceso de cambio" (1956), remembering the Inca whose head will one day be restored to its body. Their narratives tell of "friendly relations with the lords of Cuzco, consecrated through myths and legends like that of Pachakama; the barter of maize seeds, sweet potato, and coca, in return for jaguar skins, seeds for adornment, and feathers" (Barriales 1977, 8). An imperial Quechua name was adopted by the Machiguenga hero Juan Santos Atahualpa, who led the resistance to eighteenth-century attempts by the Spaniards (1742–52) to cross and erase the ancient Anti frontier, in order to reduce to slavery and *reductions* the rain forest peoples who lived (and live) beyond it.

In the Machiguenga narratives, the role of Inca creator deity and "earth maker" Pachacamac (Pachakama, Pachakamue) is of special interest. On the one hand, this figure is almighty: His crown signifies the power of the earthquake (pachacuti); he brings maize and is recognized as the bearer of the imperial voice, whose words alone can reduce the rain forest peoples to the condition of animals and mere jungle creatures (monkey, tapir). Yet in contest with the Machiguenga creator deity Yagontoro (whose name means armadillo), he has a fatal flaw. His very power leaves him open to drunkenness, and it is by this means that the local people contrive to imprison him in a ravine, frustrate his attempts to dam and divert the rivers that flow from the highlands through their territory, and finally kill him.

On the other side of the frontier, this history is corroborated in indigenous texts from the highlands. The Huarochiri Manuscript (1608) tells, in Quechua, how the first "tahuantinsuyu" was set up in Ayacucho, long before the Inca, as a result of the securing of the eastern frontier towards the Amazon and the rain forest. In his *Nueva corónica* (1613), Guaman Poma writes at length about the Anti, the people of this frontier; he admires their courage and their sophisticated knowledge of their environment in matters of agriculture, poison, dress, worship, and music, as well as their intelligence of other species, like the jaguar and the monkey, whose languages and worldviews they can interpret. Just these themes are then reworked in the Quechua kingship drama *Apu Ollantay,* whose eponymous hero is from Antisuyu and has a non-Quechua name (Brotherston 1992, 33, 207–8, 251).

Although there can be no doubt about the great age and significance of the frontier that has divided the Machiguenga and other lowlands peoples from the highlanders, this native evidence shows us that it was typically a site of interchange between cultures each rich in itself in tradition and resources. This understanding certainly modifies received Western notions of an absolute divide between "high" and "low" cultures and in particular helps to correct the view of Inca subjects (first propagated by Alexander von Humboldt and endlessly repeated since) as mere machines, mindless pawns of despotic power.

After the arrival of Pizarro, European and then Peruvian dealings with the Machiguenga tended to follow the patterns established in encounters with the earlier *viracochas,* yet with certain key differences. Chief among these were the overwhelming Christian need to proselytize an imported state ideology, which over time became less patient towards the very "primitives" it was anxious to exploit, and hence employed ever more vicious modes of economic intrusion. In the late nineteenth century, after years of relative peace, the "rubber fever" brought great waves of violence, "abuse, the selling of people and death" (Barriales 1977, 8), which decimated the Machiguenga and their neighbors. Yet they resisted it all, and even if reduced in number, they have been able to hold on to a frontier territory so deeply defined for them in cosmogony and history. Nowadays, they are the largest Amazonian group in the region. In the words of Joaquín Barriales:

> For those who have tried to deny the existence of Indians, or think that
> they will shortly be absorbed into the overpowering society of the nation,
> as many continue to be, there they are, telling us "Naro Matsigenka" (I am
> Matsigenka). (Barriales 1977, 11)

In short, the literature of the Machiguenga, recently published, reveals all the imaginative vigor and philosophical sophistication of other Amazonian and rain forest cosmogonies, with which parallels may repeatedly be drawn. In establishing a particular place of emergence and birth, this literature also serves as a charter, literally inscribing territory at the very margin between rain forest and cordillera. Machiguenga texts—known, recited, written, sung, taught, and exchanged between generation and generation, gender and gender—give coherence and anchor resistance in times of crisis, of which this last decade has provided the most severe and menacing case.

chapter 11
The Storyteller (1987)

N 1996, the German Book Trade presented a peace prize to Mario Vargas Llosa, thus provoking a worldwide wave of protest.[1] The reasons for the protest become patent in Vargas Llosa's essay "Questions of Conquest," published in *Harper's Magazine* in 1990 and reworked as "El Nacimiento del Peru" in *Hispania*'s 1992 commemorative issue:

> Indian peasants live in such a primitive way that communication is practically impossible. It is only when they move to the cities that they have the opportunity to mingle with the other Peru. The price they must pay for integration is high—renunciation of their culture, their language, their beliefs, their traditions and customs, and the adoption of the culture of their ancient masters. After one generation they become mestizos. They are no longer Indians.
>
> Perhaps there is no realistic way to integrate our societies other than by asking the Indians to pay that price. Perhaps the ideal—that is, the preservation of the primitive cultures of America—is a utopia incompatible with this other and more urgent goal—the establishment of societies in which social and economic inequalities among citizens be reduced to human, reasonable limits and where everybody can enjoy at least a decent and free life. (Vargas Llosa 1990, 52)

Vargas Llosa's developmentalist argument is well known: It has been used by both right and left as an excuse for exterminating indigenous cultures since at least the middle of nineteenth century, Domingo Faustino Sarmiento's *Life in the Argentine Republic in the Days of the Tyrants* (1845) being a salient case. Yet, one-time candidate for the presidency of Peru, Vargas Llosa distances himself from Sarmiento (in his day, president of Argentina), criticizing him precisely for having defended the destruction of the Indian cultures of his native Argentina:

> The case of Domingo F. Sarmiento is particularly sad to me, for I admire him very much. He was a great writer and also a great idealist. He was totally convinced that the only way in which Argentina could become modern was through Westernization; that is, with the elimination of everything that was non-Western. He considered the Indian tradition, which was still present in the countryside of Argentina, a major obstacle for the progress and modernization of the country. He gave the moral and intellectual arguments in favor of what proved to be the decimation of the native population. (53)

For his part, Vargas Llosa speaks in terms of "request and choice" ("asking the Indians to pay that price"). Yet even if the verb "ask" distinguishes his argument from Sarmiento's open defense of genocide, his proposition is not actually that different from his Argentinian predecessor's. Though he recognizes that the "price" to be paid by the Indians is high, he still sees it as payable, and the survival of the culture in which they were born becomes consequently an "option." Should the Indians "decide" not to renounce their culture, they will still be held responsible for the nonestablishment of a just society in Peru, so that whatever happens to them as a result (lack of respect, violent racism, land dispossession, even death) can then be regarded as their own fault. The violence implicit in Vargas Llosa's argument would be easier to see were we not so numbed by the scale of genocide perpetrated against indigenous cultures throughout the Americas during the last five hundred years. One has only to imagine the reaction it would provoke if used to refer to a minority European culture; or to ask the Jewish people or the Muslims, to abandon their culture, their religion, their tradition in the name of an "integrated society."

Yet in 1987 Vargas Llosa had published *The Storyteller,* which can be considered, on at least two accounts, an indigenist novel: it relies strongly on intertextuality with indigenous works and denounces the violence of the whites against the Indians during certain periods of Peruvian history, especially the years of the "rubber boom." Within the oeuvre of the Peruvian writer, this novel is quite distinctive; it is the author's first intertextual dialogue with Indians and, up to the present, his most lyrical work.

Structurally, *The Storyteller* is divided into eight chapters. The first and last set up the frame from which the text is being written: In Florence, the "I," a Peruvian writer, sees a photographic exhibition of Machiguenga Indians, which reminds him of his own travels in the Amazon and of his old friend Saúl Zuratas, or Mascarita, whom he has not seen in years and who was the first person to tell him about the Machiguengas. The internal chapters alternate between the story of this Florentine "I" and his relationship with Mascarita (chapters 2, 4, and 6) and stories told by the other "I" narrator of the text: the storyteller (chapters 3, 5, and 7), whose identity is gradually linked to that of Mascarita.

The Florentine narrator's biography bears several similarities to Vargas Llosa's own life: the first trip to the Amazon, the studies at Universidad de San Marcos, a long stay in Europe, his career as a writer and as the host of a TV program, all lead us to associate this first-person narrator with the author himself. The similarities are such that several critics have assumed, rather unproblematically, that author and narrator are one and the same.[2]

This "I" narrator also has views about the future of the Indian cultures that have been expressed by Mario Vargas Llosa. The following lines, for instance, pronounced by the Florentine "I" to Mascarita during a discussion, are strikingly similar to the author's statements in "Questions of Conquest," quoted above:

> What did he suggest, when all was said and done? That, in order not to change the way of life and the beliefs of a handful of tribes still living, many of them in the Stone Age, the rest of Peru abstain from developing the Amazon region? Should sixteen million Peruvians renounce the natural resources of three-quarters of their national territory so that seventy or eighty thousand Indians could quietly go on shooting at each other with bows and arrows, shrinking heads and worshipping boa constrictors? Should we forgo the agricultural, cattle-raising, and commercial potential of the region so that the world's ethnologists could enjoy studying first hand kinship ties, potlatches, the rites of puberty, marriage and death that these human oddities had been practicing, virtually unchanged, for hundreds of years? No, Mascarita, the country had to move forward. Hadn't Marx said that progress would come dripping blood? Sad though it was, it had to be accepted. We had no alternative. If the price to be paid for development and industrialization meant that those few thousand naked Indians would have to cut their hair, wash off their tattoos, and become mestizos—or, to use the ethnologists' most detested word, become acculturated—well, there was no way round it. (21–22)

Yet the novel as a whole immerses the reader deeply in precisely this "doomed" culture. Nearly half of the text rehearses Machiguenga cosmogony, brilliantly retelling narratives such as the ones about the male moon and the rebellious deer, and even quoting a song in Machiguenga language. Moreover, the book itself is dedicated to the *kenkitsatatsirira*—the Machiguenga word for "people who tell stories." For those reasons, several critics refer to Vargas Llosa as a "defender of the indigenous cultures" in *The Storyteller*. The title of Jill Courtney Everart's thesis, for instance, is eloquent in this respect: *Mario Vargas Llosa's The Storyteller: Cultural Understanding and Respect Through the Art of Storytelling* (1993). Catherine Poupeney Hart, similarly, sees in *The Storyteller*

> beyond possible compensatory factors, amid the chaos in Peru that inheres in the evocation of the (relative) Arcadia of the Machiguenga, the novel shows the way towards someone who can recognize it, can hear the voice of 'the man who talks,' the voice of the other. (535)

Sara Castro-Klarén also thinks that in this novel Vargas Llosa "continues the tradition established by Miguel Angel Astúrias, Alejo Carpentier, and José María Arguedas" and shares "their anthropological aspiration" (222). And Emil Volek describes *The Storyteller* as "the fruit of love, of a deep immersion in the mythological world of the Machiguenga and of a masterly, inspired artistic *creation from within and as if for an authentic indigenous public*" (40).

Should we conclude from these statements that *The Storyteller* represents an ideological lapse in the work of Vargas Llosa? Or are they proof that an author's ideology may not only be absent from his creative work, but may appear in it completely inverted? Emil Volek asks a similar question about the novel with respect to the author's political role, and decides that this supposedly new position can only represent a literary game:

> This new social transcendence that is claimed for the artist, does it equal a new aesthetic and political stance on Vargas Llosa's part, or is it just part of an inconsequential literary game? The little voyeurist divertissement *In Praise of the Stepmother* (1988), which chronologically followed *The Storyteller,* and the collapse of political involvement after his defeat in the elections, would seem to support the second option. (39)

The "Authentic Indian" and José María Arguedas

In order to understand Vargas Llosa's ideological use of Machiguenga literature in *The Storyteller,* we need to understand the changes in the way he has seen the Indians over the years and to make a careful reading of his Machiguenga sources, comparing them with his text in order to see what purpose they serve in it. Above all, we need first to establish the whole context of his engagement with native literature, by examining his enduring concern, if not obsession, with his immediate predecessor and one-time mentor, the great Peruvian indigenist writer José María Arguedas.[3]

In 1964, Vargas Llosa published an article titled "José María Arguedas descubre al indio auténtico," in which he compares certain *modernista* authors, as well as the *indigenistas* who followed them, with Arguedas. He concludes that "The first to overcome these contradictions, and break the vicious circle that Peruvian literature moved in, were César Vallejo, in poetry, and José María Arguedas, in prose narrative" (4).

For Vargas Llosa the *modernistas,* who belonged to the coastal bourgeois Peruvian culture, could not have written good texts about the Indians for the simple reason that they did not know them (3). Moreover, *modernismo* coincided in Peru, as he says, "with the high point of *Hispanismo,*" which "consisted, in part, in the systematic justification of the conquest and the mindless, indiscriminate defense of the Spanish contribution to Peru's history" (4). One of its main representatives, Riva Agüeros, is, in the opinion of the novelist, "Always ready to forgive the killings and plundering of the conquest, and to explain away the cultural lethargy of the colony, Riva Agüeros is implacable when pinpointing the defects of victims" (4).

The racism of the *modernistas,* in his opinion, led the *indigenistas* to the contrary view, though with dubious results: "The indigenists, who loathed modernist 'formalism,' reacted by concentrating all their attention on 'content,' on subject matter, and they neglected problems of procedure and creative method to the extent of writing with their feet" (4). With the works of José María Arguedas, on the other hand, "the Indian really enters Peruvian literature" because "unlike his predecessors, Arguedas speaks about Indians not from hearsay or on precarious information: he knows them from within and understandably so since, culturally speaking, he has been an Indian" (6). Evidently, as he points out, such knowledge has to be complemented by the fact that Arguedas "is a great creator, one of the purest and most original to have been born in America" (6).

What distinguishes Arguedas's works is the fact that he is

> an objective writer, though on the basis of a primary and radical commitment to the Indian. This commitment springs from his love for the Indian, from the fascination that Quechua culture has for him. It should not be forgotten that a good part of his intellectual input has consisted of gathering native folklore and translating it into Spanish. (6)

For Vargas Llosa, Arguedas "is the first in Latin America to succeed in replacing the abstract and subjective Indians invented by *modernistas* and *indigenistas* with *real characters*: that is, solid, objective beings, present in society and history" (6). And he does that through "translating the Indians' own language," which allows him to "recreate in Spanish the inner world of the Indian, his feelings, his psychology, his myths" (6). Such "translation" is done through several formal devices, such as "the systematic rupture of traditional syntax, words in sentences following not a logical but an intuitive and emotional order" (6).

The result, for Vargas Llosa, is that

> Arguedas's testimony is definitive: the Indian is not obsequious, servile, mendacious, or hypocritical, rather his behavior may be, in specific circumstances, and out of necessity. These masks are in fact shields against fresh aggression and attack. The Indian presents himself thus knowingly before those who steal his land and his flocks, who imprison him and rape his wife and daughters. But in the inner life of the community the Indian never bows, he hates falsehood and religiously keeps to given moral norms. (7)

According still to Vargas Llosa, Arguedas does not limit his texts to the relationship between Indians and whites: "he also shows the phenomenon of transculturation that arises from the clash between the two communities, the exchange it promotes, and the Indians' adopting and adapting customs and habits from the Whites, in line with their own psychology and value system" (7). And he sees in the works of Arguedas not only the transculturation of the Indians, but the processes of "Indianization" of the whites as well: "These brutal and racist bosses, proud as they are of being White, in fact no longer really are: without their knowing or suspecting it, the community that they enslave has won them over bit by bit, colonizing them imperceptibly" (7). Finally, Vargas Llosa points out the lack of individual characters in Arguedas, which is related, in his opinion, to "the collectivist spirit of the Indians" (7).

Thirteen years later, Mario Vargas Llosa's position with respect to the Indians had gone through severe changes, and so had his views on Arguedas's work. In 1977, eight years after Arguedas's suicide, he signalled these changes in his inaugural speech to the Peruvian Academy: Here, he strongly denied any ties that could link Arguedas's texts to the indigenous cultures, pointing to the dangers of taking an author's opinions about his/her own work too seriously, as he himself had done before:

> Taking literally what José María Arguedas said about what he wrote has led many—including me, at one stage—to think that the virtue of his books was to have shown Indian reality more truthfully than other writers. That is, the documentary nature of his fiction. (25)

Instead, Vargas Llosa now sees Arguedas's work as a *distortion* of reality: "from knowing the Sierra more directly and immediately, Arguedas did not distort Andean reality the less. His work, insofar as it is literature, amounts to a radical denial of the world that inspired it: a pretty lie" (27).

He regards Arguedas's texts as the result not of the writer's profound involvement with the Andean culture, but of

> his unhappy and heightened childhood, his early orphanhood, abuse by his
> stepmother and stepbrother, the orgies that the latter forced him to witness
> and which doubtless ruined his sex life, his being someone halfway between
> two cultures, and the need to exorcize bitterness, nostalgia, and hatred
> from his memory. (26)

Based on these personal experiences, Arguedas's greatest achievement now lies in the fact that "while he was seeming to 'describe' the Sierra, he worked a bold magic: he *invented* his own Sierra" (30).

If in the 1964 critique a great importance had been placed on Arguedas's changes of the Spanish language through the use of Quechua vocabulary and syntax, the 1977 speech begins with the expression of Vargas Llosa's own desire to "affirm the pride that every Peruvian must feel in speaking Castilian and in being, thanks to Spain, a full member of one of the world's most dynamic cultural provinces" (24). Arguedas's linguistic experiments, which he had described before as "dyslexic Castilian," he now sees as minor when compared with the author's "dyslexia in things and people" (30).

Thus, Arguedas's portrayal of the injustices suffered by the Indians "is not exactly realistic" because it is, in Vargas Llosa's opinion, exaggerated, and based on the author's childhood traumas (30). Violence, according to him, appears amplified in Arguedas's fiction because the victims are usually children or marginalized creatures; and the conjunctural violence of Peruvian society becomes "congenital with life," universal:

> These marginals are, in the reality of fiction, the center of the world, the
> axis around which the stories are born. Chief witnesses to the violence
> that is congenital with life, their most pitiful examples are simultaneously
> minds lucidly aware of their tragic condition, who bemoan their fate. (33)

The violent power relationship between Indians and *principales* seem to him now to be "a relationship more magico-religious than socio-economic" (32). And the defense of the powerless, in Arguedas's works, demonstrates "a tendency to self-pity and even a latent masochism: people enjoy suffering so as to feel sorry for themselves" (33).

As evidence of Vargas Llosa's political shift after 1970, these texts need no comment; they speak for themselves. Less clear, perhaps, is the writer's modification of the term "realist," less conventional in the first text than in the second. There, he criticized the *indigenistas* for their naive aspiration to realism, and praised Arguedas because, owing to his profound involvement with the Andean culture, he was able to open the Spanish language and the form of his narrative to modifications operated by non-European, indigenous elements. Arguedas was a "realist" not because he tried to portray Andean culture faithfully, but because he could portray different aspects of that culture and, at the same time, bring it into his work, let it influence his writing.

The crude division between "realism" and "nonrealism" in the 1977 speech, on the other hand, permits Vargas Llosa a curious sleight of hand. First, he rules out connections between literature and historical, or social, reality ("Literature expresses a truth that is not history, sociology, nor ethnology" [27]), but strangely enough maintains its strong dependence on personal history, or biography. Second, by classifying Arguedas's works simplistically as nonrealist, he inexplicably breaks the ties between those works and indigenous culture, as if the only way that tie could be kept were in a conventionally realistic portrayal of the Andes. Nothing is said about the intertextual relationship between Arguedas's and Andean texts, nor about the decisive influence of Quechua and Andean cultural elements on Arguedas's works.

Thus, the presence of collective characters, which in the 1964 article was seen as "both a feature of the community he is invoking and a formal device," becomes in the 1977 speech a Bakhtinian carnivalization (7), and a nonrealistic, original "addition" of Arguedas's to the world of the Andes. Along the same lines, the role of music in Arguedas's writings is seen as result of a "a childhood demon of the author's that has been universally projected in his fiction" (41), no reference being made to the importance of music in the Andean society.

In 1977, the year of his inaugural speech to the Peruvian Academy, Vargas Llosa discussed the condition of the writer in Latin America in a lecture given at the University of Cambridge ("La utopía arcaica"). In his opinion, Latin American narrators and poets suffered constant pressures to become socially and politically engaged, more so than their European colleagues. José María Arguedas was, according to him, an example of a writer who had been acutely sensitive to those pressures, and his attempts to reconcile the fight against social injustice with the desire to conserve the indigenous cultures was a major contributing factor to his suicide:

> There can be no doubt, for me, that this contradiction, which worried
> Arguedas his life long and made him at once pro and contra "modernity,"

together with socio-political forces that exerted huge moral and psychological pressure on him, were a major factor in that long crisis which ended
in a bullet one noon in December 1969. That shot still echoes, as a warning
of the thralldom that being a writer in Latin America involves. (Vargas
Llosa 1977, 28–29)

Such conflict finds its clearest expression, according to Vargas Llosa, in
Arguedas's last book, *The Fox from Up Above and the Fox from Down Below*
(a title derived from the Huarochiri Manuscript) in which

It is the very notion of "development," modernization, and technological
advance which is devilishly represented and exorcized in the book. The
secret reason for this rejection is the intuition, which never left Arguedas,
that such a society (even under another ideological banner) can arise only
on the ashes of that other society, archaic, rural, traditional, magic (folkloric in the best sense of the word), in which Arguedas—maybe rightly, maybe
wrongly: I couldn't say—saw the best of Peru. For him this was intolerable
at the same time as politically inarticulable. (28)

Vargas Llosa's doubt ("I couldn't say") about whether Arguedas was or
was not right in considering the indigenous cultures "the best of Peru" is
actually rhetorical: the answer is given in the title of the lecture, "La utopía
arcaica"—utopia being the "no place" of the indigenous societies of Peru,
archaically detached from the present.

The expression "utopía arcaica" is repeated, as we will see, in *The
Storyteller,* and it also provides the title of one of the writer's most recent
work of criticism. In an interview about this book, given in October 1996,
Vargas Llosa once more defended a developmentalist position, while criticizing the first world's "excessive concern with the environmental question
in the Third World" (Grillo). For the writer, "This is a new form of discrimination. You cannot stop progress, and a way of harmonizing it with
environmental protection has yet to be found" (Grillo).

Mario Vargas Llosa's general view of the American indigenous cultures,
his belief that these cultures should be sacrificed in the name of economic
development, has to be taken into account when we read *The Storyteller.* It
permeates the Florentine "I"'s opinions on the subject, the construction of
the character Mascarita, portrayed in it as a defender of Amazonian cultures, and the author's rewriting of Machiguenga texts.

Reproducing Tasurinchi's Narratives

In *The Storyteller,* especially in those chapters narrated by the eponymous
character (3, 5, 7), Vargas Llosa draws deeply on Machiguenga texts. The

stories collected by Barriales, along with García's articles, and Andre Ferrero's and Cenitagoya's books (see chapter 10), were Vargas Llosa's main sources for writing these "native" chapters of the novel—the core chapters, in which Machiguenga cosmogony is recounted by the storyteller. In a note at the end of the book, the writer explicitly thanks Joaquín Barriales for his translations of "many Machiguenga songs and myths that appear in my book" (1989, 247), though without naming the published source in *Antisuyo*. And all the other authors who compiled Machiguenga texts and/ or studied their way of living are explicitly named in the novel.

Such an appeal to sources is the remarkable feature of *The Storyteller*: it establishes a close link between fiction and scholarship and between fiction and the Machiguenga themselves. And not only are all of the sources explicitly mentioned in the novel, but nearly half of the text consists of a rewriting of them. Vargas Llosa's creation process can be seen in the way he carefully incorporates those texts into his prose, comparing versions, and paying attention even to small details.

The storyteller's description of his arrival at the house of the first Tasurinchi, for instance, was closely inspired by Andres Ferrero's chapter on the "cortesía machiguenga," with a small inversion in the order of speaking:

> At last Tasurinchi arrived. "I'm here," I said to him. "Are you there?" "Here I am," he answered, pleased to see me, and my parrot repeated: "I am, I am."[4] Then his wife rose to her feet and unrolled two mats for us to sit on. She brought a pot of freshly roasted cassava that she emptied out onto plantain leaves, and a little jar of masato. (1989, 46)

> Upon arrival, it is not the newcomer who speaks first but the person receiving the visit. *¿Pukhaibi?* = Are you there?, he says. To which the other replies: *ehe* = so it is. That is all. There is no embracing, smacking of hands, or ceremonious greetings.
> The owner of the house gets up, takes some mats and unrolls them at his feet and withdraws saying not a word. This is the sign that hospitality is granted.
> They sit. With men, there is a silent pause, to see who will open fire.
> Meanwhile, the owner of the house brings a pot of cassava, and empties it on to plaintain leaves or pamuco. Banana and other food will be offered, when there is some. Finally comes the masato. (Ferrero, 176)

The same process can be observed in the following description of the demon kasibarenini: "Among all the many different kaamgarinis that Kientibakori breathed out, the worst little devil is kasibarenini, it seems. Small as a child, if he turns up somewhere in his earth-colored cushma it is because somebody's sick there" (Vargas Llosa 1989, 66). Secundino García describes this demon in very similar words: "These devils whistle as well, and that is why they are called whistlers . . . They are like children, and they wear an earth-colored cushma" ([91, 225]; according to García, the demon who visits the ill is kaseribarérini rather than kasibarenini, as Mascarita says).

One of the novel's descriptions of Morenanchiite, lord of the thunder, is made by Mascarita in the form of questions:

> The first time I heard the story of Morenanchiite, the lord of thunder, it made a great impression on me. I asked everyone about it. I made them tell it one, many times. Does the lord of thunder have a bow? Yes, he has a bow. But in-stead of loosing arrows he looses thunder. And does he go about acompanied by jaguars? Yes. By pumas too, it seems. And although he's not a Viracocha, does he have a beard? Yes, he has a beard. (210)

Once again, the description follows the information given in García and Ferrero:

> They are the lords of thunder. They have a small weapon called *ibégaro,* which shoots hundreds of missiles. When these strike an object, even an invisible one, it thunders . . . A singular feature of the Morenanchiite is that they have thick beards. (Ferrero, 336)

A story told by García, and repeated in very similar words by Ferrero, is transformed by Vargas Llosa into an experience narrated by one of the Tasurinchis visited by Mascarita. After losing a son, this Tasurinchi and his wife tell a *seripigari* that they would like to see the boy once more. The *seripigari* goes to the world of the spirits and finds the boy, who comes to visit his parents, not as a child anymore, but as a young man. Just as in Ferrero (320), the young man walks up to his mother and sucks her breasts (Vargas Llosa 1989, 57–58).

The revenge of the deer, as part of an interspecies contract, is taken from the traditional Machiguenga story reproduced by Barriales in *Antisuyo,* and quoted above (see chapter 10). The re-creation, quoted below, is also very close to the original:

> Tasurinchi now had a second arrow ready. Troc, troc. Then he saw another stag arriving, pushing through the branches, making the leaves rustle. It took its place next to the first one and began drinking. They seemed content, both of them, drinking water. Shh, shh, shh. Tasurinchi loosed his arrow. It missed this time, too. What was happening? . . . His world had gone dark. And there he was, shooting. He shot all his arrrows. Troc, troc. Troc, troc.

The deer kept on coming. More and more, so many, so very many. The drumbeat of their hoofs echoed and reechoed in Tasurinchi's ears. Troc, troc. (Vargas Llosa 1989, 194)

The appearance of Inaenka, smallpox, is present in several sources, including Ferrero and Barriales, and Vargas Llosa re-creates it in very similar terms in his novel. The same happens with the story of Pareni and her brother Pachakamue, clearly taken from Cenitagoya's book. The journey of Katsiborerini, the comet, comes straight from Barriales, with a few modifications.

Several other details of such intertextuality could be mentioned, like the reproduction of an entire song in Machiguenga and Spanish from Barriales's *Matsigenka*. But the examples given can offer an idea of the importance of Machiguenga texts in the novel. They are interwoven with the narration of Machiguenga history since the invasion of the whites, told in a style similar to the Machiguenga stories themselves, and with elements from Mascarita's life, which will be discussed later.

In the all-important matter of Machiguenga writing there is a further parallel. The following description of the incised bone given by Mascarita to the Florentine "I"—the first contact he ever had with the Machiguengas—can be associated with a drawing reproduced by France-Marie Casevitz:

It was a small white bone, shaped liked a diamond and engraved with a geometric design in a yellowish-brick color. The design represented two parallel mazes made up of bars of different sizes, separated by identical distances, the smaller ones seemingly nestled inside the larger ones.
. . . The bone is from a tapir and the drawing is not the awkward scrawl it appears to be—just a few primitive strikes—but a symbolic inscription. . . .
If you think these symbols are whirlpools in the river or two coiled boa constrictors taking a nap, you may be right. (14)

This corresponds to the drawing from the upper Picha described by a Machiguenga shaman as *Oipuuitakara nia*: "When the water traces foamy whirlpools. Tapir bone. The foamy whirlpools are the places of passage or oblivion where one goes to be purified, to forget an unhappy past, to enhance luck" (275).

These engraved bones, whose pattern is passed from father to son, are designed and engraved by a man and given to a woman—usually his wife—who uses it to decorate the baby-carrier, and protect the baby from any harm. Casevitz also explains that:

The sacred nocturnal diamond . . . is engraved with signs dictated by the lord of thunder and by his creature, the jaguar. It illustrates this different writing: hieroglyphs which articulate the message of the shaman appealing to his jaguar allies to help him in his struggles against the powers of evil. (295)

The explanation obviously inspired Mascarita's text: "Morenanchiite, the lord of thunder, dictated it to a jaguar, who dictated it to a witch-doctor friend of mine from the forests of the Alto Picha" (14). But Mascarita goes even further, saying that the lines "are, mainly, the order that reigns in the world" (17).

Even though played down by Vargas Llosa, this particular bone design can be seen as a key to the very structure of the novel. The two parallel labyrinths, connected by a line, could be said to represent its two narrating voices: The storyteller's chapters, for instance, have a clear labyrinthic organization in the way in which the *storyteller/Tasurinchi* often tells a Tasurinchi (man, in the novel) a story about another Tasurinchi who had been told a story by a fourth Tasurinchi and so on. The chapters narrated by the Florentine "I," on the other hand, have also a concentric approximation to the figure of Mascarita/storyteller. Each labyrinth mirrors the other: the mysteries proposed by the Florentine "I" (what happened to Mascarita and who are these mysterious storytellers) are solved in the storyteller chapters by Mascarita himself. But the solution of those mysteries can also be seen as a construct of the Florentine "I," who confesses that the identification of the storyteller in the picture with Mascarita is a decision of his: "I have decided that it is he who is the storyteller in Malfatti's photograph. A personal decision, since objectively I have no way of knowing" (240).[5]

The comments by the Machiguenga shaman Daniel about the petroglyphs as transcriptions, quoted in the previous chapter, take this connection even further, by defining the language of the Lord of Thunder simultaneously as *word that writes writing that speaks*—another possible description of the novel in its interplay between speaker and writer, spoken and written words.

Also, as Emil Volek observes, the style of the core chapters betrays native influence by catching "some dialect features of Amazonian and indigenous Spanish in general. Among these features there stand out special uses of the gerund" (212). In all these respects—narrative events, characters, style, and structure—there can be no doubt about the importance of the Machiguenga texts, even written texts, in *The Storyteller*. This represents a step never taken by Vargas Llosa before: the rethinking of rigid Western distinctions between life and death, humans and the rest of nature, spiritual and material worlds, and so on.

Perverse Tribute

For all that, yet more significant is the degree to which Vargas Llosa not so much follows as subverts his Machiguenga originals, a feature not emphasized by critics.[6] He makes significant changes to the Machiguenga cosmogony, which affect quite drastically the way we regard this Amazonian community as we read the book. Of course any author of fiction is free to adapt his sources at will. But Vargas Llosa's specific reference to sources, and to data taken from his own life, expresses his desire to give the novel essayistic and autobiographic qualities, to create the illusion that what we are reading actually happened to the author, and that the information about the Machiguenga corresponds to ethnographic information, or to field work observation. It is precisely this essayistic tone, along with the importance that the Machiguenga texts really have in the novel, that makes any changes to the Machiguenga cosmogony even more significant. In other words: Within the novel's close interplay between fiction and reality, and between the indigenous sources and the rewriting of them, some elements are maintained, while others are changed, added, or eliminated. What can those modifications tell us about the author's position with regard to the indigenous culture?

In his careful rewriting of the Kashiri story, for instance, Vargas Llosa even compares two different versions of it. The first one, closer to Barriales's, Ferrero's, and Pereira's, tells us that the moon married a young Machiguenga girl and taught her family how to cultivate manioc and other plants. But another girl (in fact a little devil disguised as a girl) was also interested in the moon, and because of his lack of interest, she defecated and "dug her hand into the filth and waited, storing up fury. When she saw him coming, she threw herself at him from among the trees. And before the moon could escape, she'd rubbed his face with the shit she'd just shat" (114).

In the other version, closer to Cenitagoya's, Kashiri's spots are caused by parts of the corpse of his dead wife, whom his mother-in-law obliged him to eat. In both cases, however, the storyteller emphasizes how unhappy the moon was, ever since, for having his face spotted:

> Kashiri knew at once that those stains could never be washed away. Marked by such shame, what was he going to do in this world? Sadly, he went back to Inkite, the sky above. There he has remained. Because of his stains, his light was dimmed. (114)

The emphasis is related to the storyteller/Mascarita's feeling of marginality caused by his physical deformity, a maroon spot that covers half of his face. In fact, the moon's spots are going to be mentioned several times throughout the novel, approximating Kashiri to Mascarita himself: "What had to happen would not happen while the sun was in Inkite, but later, when Kashiri rose. Kashiri, the resentful, the stained one" (195); and "During the night, dazed by the false light of Kashiri, the stained one, he fell asleep" (199). Mascarita's *lunar* (skin spot) brings him close to Kashiri, *la luna* (moon).

The obsession with physical deformity makes Mascarita place the moon in a position of marginality, which is not found in the Machiguenga's texts. In those texts, as noted in the previous chapter, Kashiri is not only the one who taught the Machiguenga how to plant the yucca, but also somebody to whom the Machiguengas owe continuous fear and respect, for if they do not treat the yucca well, Kashiri will be upset and claim revenge (Barriales n.d. 3: 168; F. Pereira 1942, 244). Moreover, Kashiri is responsible for collecting and eating the corpses of those who died, an indispensible social role.

The same obsession with physical deformity was added by Vargas Llosa to the story of Inaenka, or smallpox. In *The Storyteller*, the woman's evilness is caused by the fact that she limps, a characteristic absent in the Machiguenga texts. In order to drive her away from the Machiguengas, her disguised son offers to take her to a place where her limping foot can become normal:

> "If anyone sets foot there and bathes in the rivers, it's enough to straighten anything that's crooked, and any limbs that anyone has lost grow back again. I'll take you there. You'll lose your limp. You'll be happy, Inaenka. Follow me."
>
> He spoke with such conviction that Inaenka, astounded by this odd-colored boy who was not afraid of her and promised her what she most wanted—normal feet—followed him. (200–1)

By approximating Mascarita to Kashiri and Inaenka, Vargas Llosa habilitates him as his kind of Machiguenga character, grooming him for the role of the storyteller: Like the marginal and resentful Kashiri, Mascarita can have a place in the Machiguenga society that allows him to perform his creative activity—to tell stories. The *creative role* of Mascarita is emphasized by the fact that he calls himself and the Machiguenga men in general *Tasurinchi*—the name of the Machiguenga creator, who, as we have seen, blew the world into existence. This is another important modification introduced by Vargas Llosa into the Machiguenga world, since among the Machiguenga themselves the term *Tasurinchi* ("the one who blows") is reserved for the creator of their people, or to demigods from their cosmogony, like Pareni and Pachakamue.[7]

On the other hand, Mascarita's obsession with his own physical defect compromises his reliability as a narrator. As Sara Castro-Klarén observes in her article, the discovery of the storyteller's identity at the end of the novel forces the reader to go back, so to speak, to the beginning, and reevaluate this narrator's discourse. Hence, even if we do not follow Vargas Llosa's frequent invitations to check the sources of his novel, we are made to suspect the storyteller's stories on the grounds that he is not a Machiguenga, but an outsider; that suspicion is only confirmed by the storyteller's constant references to physical deformity. Hence, Mascarita's *creativity* can also be read as a profanation of Tasurinchi's creation. And as an act of profanation, Mascarita's false identification with Tasurinchi brings him close to Kientibakori, the evil principle and creator of all bad things, who, in order to deceive the Machiguenga, also pretended to be Tasurinchi himself.

By constructing Mascarita/storyteller as an unreliable narrator, Vargas Llosa brilliantly deconstructs what is perhaps the most emotionally charged passage in the novel: the moment in which the Floretine "I" confesses that what makes him so fascinated with Mascarita's fate is his friend's capacity to become a true Machiguenga; the fact that Mascarita had been able, in other words, to become "other":

> That my friend Saul gave up being all that he was and might have become so as to roam through the Amazonian jungle, for more than twenty years now, perpetuating against wind and tide—and, above all, against the very concepts of modernity and progress—the tradition of that invisible line of wandering storytellers, is something that memory now and again brings back to me, and, as on that day when I first heard of it, in the starlit darkness of the village of New Light, it opens my heart more forcefully than fear or love has ever done. (244–45)

But Mascarita never became a Machiguenga: As his final speech demonstrates, he continued to be as immersed as ever in his Jewishness and in his personal obsessions. Like the missionaries that he so fiercely criticized in the beginning of the novel, in this speech he combines Tasurinchi with Jehovah, and, later, with Jesus Christ and himself:

> Jehovah-Tasurinchi, that was who he was. He protected them, it seems. He had taught them what they must do and also taught them taboos. So they knew their obligation. They lived quietly, it's said. Content and without anger, perhaps.
>
> Until one day, in a remote little ravine, a child was born. He was different. A seregórompi? Yes, perhaps. He started by saying: "I am the breath of Tasurinchi, I am the son of Tasurinchi, I am Tasurinchi. I am all three things at once." That's what he said. And that he'd come down from Inkite

to this world, sent by his father, who was himself, to change the customs because the people had become corrupt and no longer knew how to walk. They must have listened to him in astonishment. Saying: "He must be a storyteller." Saying: "Those must be stories he's telling." He went from one place to another, the way I do. (215)

As María Isabel Acosta Cruz puts it, "Saúl's last narrative is a clear violation of the role of the storyteller" (140). Moreover, Mascarita's changes to the Machiguenga cosmogony are accompanied by discourse features that indicate his insecurities and doubts, his self-conscious role as an outsider: "Everything was going very well, perhaps. They seemed happy, perhaps" (63).[8] Also, Mascarita actively tries to make changes in the Machiguenga culture by questioning, for instance, their custom of killing the babies with physical deformities right after birth (211). He poses similar questions about the role of women in the Machiguenga society. In the words of Acosta Cruz:

> His text questions the role of women in the tribe by portraying them as silent second-class citizens who are either ignored or openly abused and brutalized by the men and thus are more marginal. . . . In Saúl's stories the most striking feature of the women is that they don't have any name, and while it is true that the men do not have proper names either, they at least share the common name "Tasurinchi." The women only have a description, they are the wife of Tasurinchi (possession in a communal sense). . . .
>
> Saúl's stories continually display odd, off-centered women who do not fit any tribal behavioral pattern. (140)

But if it is true that Machiguenga women cannot participate in some ritual ceremonies reserved for men and that several of the Machiguenga everyday activities are gender-defined, women in their society could by no means be considered "second-class citizens," or marginal. In fact, Machiguenga society is both matrilinear and matrilocal: The lineage of the mother determines the patterns of marriage, and the husband-to-be has to move close to this mother-in-law and pay her several services before he can marry (Casevitz-Renard, 229). An adult man can only consider himself fulfilled as long as he is married; and the Machiguenga women know contraceptive and abortive herbs that grant them the exclusive decision of how many children the couple is going to have.

Mascarita's active attempts to change the Machiguenga way of being follow the behavior of the ethnographers and missionaries whom he so strongly condemns. The irony is that he decided to become a Machiguenga exactly because he did not want to be an ethnographer—that is, because he did not wish to interfere with their world.

Framed as the result of the Florentine "I"'s admiration for his friend's capacity to "go native," *The Storyteller* presents Mascarita precisely as a proof that "going native" is impossible. In that sense, Mascarita allows Vargas Llosa not only to make a critique of radical ethnography, but also to meta-criticize indigenist literature as a whole; or as Rowe puts it, to "ridicule the indigenists" (102). In fact, Mascarita's speeches to and about the Machiguenga could be described with Vargas Llosa's own words about Arguedas in "Entre sapos y halcones": "Discreet hecatomb, daring contraband, successful fiction destroys actual reality and replaces it with another whose elements have been named, ordered, and moved in such a way that they essentially betray what they claim to recreate" (27). Like Arguedas and, in the opinion of Vargas Llosa, all of those who try to "re-create" indigenous cultures (including himself), Mascarita cannot avoid "betraying" the Machiguenga. Otherness, to put it in more fashionable terms, cannot be achieved. Thus, although Mascarita is presented in the novel as having no sympathy for the Andean Indians, it seems to be Vargas Llosa's lifelong obsession with Arguedas that is behind the construction of this character. It is no coincidence, therefore, that the expression "utopía arcaica," often used to describe Arguedas's project, is also employed in the novel to refer to Mascarita's views: "Thinking it over—in the light of the years that have since gone by, and from the vantage point of this broiling-hot Florence—we were as unrealistic and romantic as Mascarita with his archaic, antihistorical utopia" (78).

But Mascarita is not the only one to operate changes in the Machiguenga cosmogony in *The Storyteller*. His constant re-creation of the Machiguenga world is granted extraordinary importance in the novel because the storyteller is responsible in it for giving the Machiguenga a cultural coherence that otherwise they would not have:

> ... those storytellers who—by occupation, out of necessity, to satisfy a human whim—using the simplest, most time-hallowed of expedients, the telling of stories, were the living sap that circulated and made the Machiguengas into a society, a people of interconnected and interdependent beings. It still moves me to think of them ... (93)

Mario Vargas Llosa's Machiguengas need the storyteller because the novel shows them as a dispersed group. This fact is evident in the storyteller chapters: The people whom Mascarita visits live in extremely small groups, mostly of disintegrated nuclear families, and they are often uninformed about the other Machiguengas as well as about their own history and cosmogony. Such dispersion is confirmed by the Florentine narrator, who uses the "scientific evidence" of the Schneil couple to show that the

Machiguengas were a "diaspora—little groups scattered here and there with virtually no contact between them, each one fighting desperately for survival" (161).

Machiguenga social organization, rather than being the simple, almost casual gathering of a few people that the novel shows us, is extremely complex; and, as among the Pemon, the habit of living far from friends and relatives does not presuppose a lack of knowledge about them: the satirical poem "Canción de masato de Eva," quoted in the previous chapter, is a demonstration of the Machiguenga's constant interest in and knowledge about their distant neighbors. In fact, only in a highly structured society, with very defined rules about marriage and kinship and a very clear idea of who they are and what makes them distinctive from other people, could individuals withstand the sophisticated habit of living far from neighbors and relatives, and yet feel part of a group.

Not only are the Machiguenga portrayed as dispersed in the novel, they are made nomadic as well. In what the Florentine "I" calls "the most persistent of their myths" (212), the Machiguenga are referred to as "the people that walk" because, according to the novel, the creator Tasurinchi told his people that if they stopped walking, the sun would fall from the sky: "Then why, if they were so pure, did the men of earth begin walking? Because one day the sun started falling. They walked so that it wouldn't fall any further, to help it rise. So Tasurinchi says" (38).

In other words, it is the Machiguenga's own cosmogony that justifies their nomadism in *The Storyteller.* But no references to such an aspect of the Machiguenga cosmogony can be encountered in the Machiguenga narratives, or in the literature about the group. In fact, as we have seen, the sun has relatively little importance in the Machiguenga worldview when compared to his father, Kashiri, the moon. Moreover, as discussed in the previous chapter, the Machiguenga are not nomadic: like many other peoples in the Amazon, they have a complex system of all-year and winter houses, hunting shacks, and collective ritual houses.[9] They move to a different location every two to three years, but always within their traditional territory; that habit, also common to many peoples in the Amazon, has been associated in recent studies of the forest with the double necessity of preserving the resources and, at the same time, making changes in the environment. Far from being a tragic and suicidal strategy, this movement has, for thousands of years, helped hundreds of Amazonian cultures adapt the environment to their needs while still preserving it.

The consequences of the changes made by Vargas Llosa to the Machiguenga cosmogony are very clear: by defining the Machiguenga as a nomadic tribe, he denies them, as is so often the case, their right to the land.

And if it is true that, as the novel tells us, the *viracochas* intensified the group's need to look for refuge in the least populous areas of the forest, the novel also presents such movement as not entirely negative, since it helps keep the Machiguenga faithful to their cosmogonic essence of wandering people. As Tasurinchi, the herb man, puts it:

> They'll come and I'll go. Is that a bad thing? No, that's a good thing. It must be our destiny, Tasurinchi. Aren't we the ones who walk? So, then, we should thank the Mashcos and the Punarunas. The Viracochas too. Do they invade the places where we live? They force us to fulfill our obligation. Without them, we'd become corrupt. The sun would fall, perhaps. The world would be darkness, the earth belong to Kashiri. There would be no men, and surely much cold. (138)

This argument resembles one that has often justified the dispossession of indigenous lands in the Americas: The natives are driven away because of us, and because they run away, they cannot be considered legitimate owners of their land. Putting it in yet other words, the argument goes like this: We impoverish the Indians, take away their lands, and decimate their population, and because they are poor, have no land, and are so few, they have to disappear. This circularity becomes explicit in Vargas Llosa's 1990 "Questions of Conquest":

> If forced to choose between the preservation of Indian cultures and their complete assimilation, with great sadness I would choose modernization of the Indian population, because there are priorities; and the first priority is, of course, to fight hunger and misery. My novel *The Storyteller* is about a very small tribe in the Amazon called the Machiguengas. Their culture is alive in spite of the fact that it has been repressed and persecuted since Inca times. It should be respected. The Machiguengas are still resisting change, but their world is now so fragile that they cannot resist much longer. They have been reduced to practically nothing. It is tragic to destroy what is still living, still a driving cultural possibility, even if it is archaic; *but I am afraid we shall have to make a choice.* For I know of no case in which it has been possible to have both things at the same time, except in those countries in which two different cultures have evolved more or less simultaneously. (53, my emphasis)

The victims are the ones to be blamed: Vargas Llosa's ironic comments about the Peruvian *modernistas* in 1964 could now be applied to his own discourse. And the Florentine narrator's divided opinions about the changes brought about in the Machiguenga society, as a result of Protestant missionaries relocating the Machiguengas through the creation of villages, do not disguise the fact that the tribe's disappearance would be, according to him, their own fault:[10]

> They were no longer that handful of tragic, indomitable beings, that society broken up into tiny families, fleeing, always fleeing, from the whites, from the mestizos, from the mountain people and from other tribes, awaiting and stoically accepting their inevitable extinction as individuals and as a group, yet never giving up their language, their gods, their customs. (163–64)

By changing Machiguenga cosmogony in order to explain their nomadism, Vargas Llosa is able to justify the presence of an outsider like Mascarita, and hence his novel's most dramatic addition to the Machiguenga world: the invention of the storyteller figure in the first place.

Nowhere in the texts about the Machiguenga or in their own narratives is there an allusion to an institution or a character minimally similar to Vargas Llosa's. The only concrete reference mentioned in the novel is Paul Marcoy, the author of *Travels in South America: From the Pacific Ocean to the Atlantic Ocean* (1875): "One of the first references occurs in the book written by Paul Marcoy, the explorer. On the banks of the Urubamba he came across an 'orateur,' whom the French traveler witnessed literally hypnotizing an audience of Antis for hours on end" (157). But Marcoy's *orateur* is actually nothing more than a Machiguenga boatman who decides to tell the travellers (and not an audience of Antis) some stories (Marcoy, 436). The only other scholars who are quoted with respect to the existence of the storyteller are the Schneil couple. This Summer Institute husband and wife were obviously inspired by Betty and Wayne Snell, Summer Institute scholars whose work may have been used as source of information and material for the novel itself. It is significant that the Snells were the only scholars to have had their names changed in the novel.

Vargas Llosa's invention of the role of storyteller does not make his novel any worse, or better, but it does change the way we see the relationship of *The Storyteller* with the Machiguenga culture. Attributing the only possible cultural cohesion of the Machiguenga to an individual like the storyteller is another way of dispossessing them: If they are hardly a group anymore, how can we respect them culturally? How can we wish to keep them alive?

Several critics, however, without looking at the sources, have assumed, unproblematically, that the storytelleres are, for instance "traditional taletellers of a people in Peruvian Amazonia, the Machiguenga, and the only bond between the wandering and dispersed families that they entertain" (Hart, 521); or that Vargas Llosa's "initial intention of showing Machiguenga mentality and culture 'in the most authentic possible manner' obviously implies representing the discourse of their orators" (Marcone, 138). As we have seen, such (mis)understandings have allowed *The Storyteller* to be regarded as a defense of the Machiguenga Indians and a celebration of their culture.

But if Vargas Llosa's exploited Machiguenga deserve some sympathy from the reader, the novel allows little more than that. As a dispersed, no-madic group, whose "own" cosmogony defines them as fugitive and passive, and whose lack of cultural cohesion makes questionable even their status as a group, the Machiguenga created in *The Storyteller* can only occupy a place reserved for marginal people, for pariahs like Mascarita. As Jean Franco puts it:

> For Vargas Llosa there is neither struggle nor resistance; in order to survive the Machiguengas have no weapon other than passivity. They have to do without anger and resentment. That is, Vargas Llosa creates a space for differ-ence (as does Apartheid) but not for antagonism; he allows the Machiguenga to survive via myth and narrative, but not via organization. The political message of non-violence is presented as if it were tribal wisdom despite the fact that these tribes are currently immersed in the political struggle. (18)

Nothing could be more distant from Vargas-Llosa's view than the fol-lowing words of a Machiguenga about their reputation of "savages" in the seventies:

> They call us assassins because we have killed those who were killing us and stealing our wives, but we simply say "Naro notimakye aka, kameti notimakye, Ogari naro iragashinetakyena naro arío nompugatanakyempa" (I live here, and live well, but the one who comes and causes problems I'll kill). (Barriales 1977, 9)

The complete identification between the Florentine "I" and Vargas Llosa has driven some critics to read the novel as the result of the author's "twenty-five year obsession with the figure of the storyteller": "In the sixth part of this novel Vargas Llosa confesses that 'Since my frustrated attempts in the early 1960s to write a story about the Machiguenga storytellers, the theme has gone on haunting me'" (Rivas, 191). But such identifica-tion can lead us to a paradox. Vargas Llosa's obsession with the storyteller, if taken seriously, is in fact an obsession with his own invention. Hence, like Mascarita, Vargas Llosa and his Florentine persona perversely betray the Machiguenga that they claim to celebrate. Such betrayal coincides with Vargas Llosa's view of novel-writing as

> a form of personal exorcism and a modified representation of the world. The novelist sheds his 'demons' or obsessions and at the same time transforms harmless reality or truth into a living lie, that is creative and spawns a reality or truth of another, superior order: the work of fiction. (Rotella, 93–94)

By now, I could appear to have arrived at the same conclusions as those who see *The Storyteller* mainly as a postmodern, metalinguistic statement. But Vargas Llosa's metalanguage can hardly be seen as an end in itself, since it serves the double purpose of undermining the possibility of indigenous political resistance in the Americas, and delegitimizing intertextuality between indigenous and Latin American literatures.

Yet the intertextual dialogue of *The Storyteller* with the Machiguenga texts is the novel's greatest achievement; what makes it, in other words, worth reading. Against the author's political will, that alone is a proof that those Indians should have the right to continue to be what they are and the right to remain on their land and resist—or change—as they please.

Epilogue

O F ALL THE TEXTS STUDIED HERE, Vargas Llosa's *The Storyteller* is the only one that meticulously modifies indigenous sources in order to deny native cultures the right to remain as they are. Yet his fatalistic view that the contact between Indians and non-Indians will necessarily result in a complete cultural suppression of the former is shared by the great majority of the nonnative authors whom we have read, whatever their ideological positions may be. Most notable is the case of Darcy Ribeiro, whose novel *Maíra,* for all its sympathetic depiction of indigenous knowledge and ways of life, ends with an overwhelmingly pessimistic view of the future of his invented tribe, the Mairuns. We see in the last chapter that the whites have perfected their forms of exploitation, which are now much more efficient, and that the region will succumb to what they call "progress." Isaías, who gave up his life among the Catholic priests in order to be Mairum again, becomes an employee of the insensitive and arrogant woman who acts as missionary to a small evangelical church. Even more striking is the god Maíra's recognition that he has been defeated by the Christian god, when he asks, in his poignant final question: "What kind of God am I? A mortal God?" (310). Ribeiro himself said that his novel told "the end of an ethnic group" (Sá, 1993)—an unambiguous reading of its agonic predictions. It is true that such a pessimistic view of the Mairuns' future is grounded, at least partially, in indigenous texts, in the Tupi-Guarani counterposing of intense joy in life with the menace of destruction and cataclysm. Moreover, the novel's multiple points of view allow the Indians to express feelings and opinions that do not necessarily agree with the author's claims—a possibility foreclosed in *The Storyteller* by the Chinese-box structure that Vargas Llosa imposes on his narrative. Thus, if the old *aroe* does not see any future for the Mairuns, Jaguar has the opposite opinion, and throughout the novel, the collective Indian narrator voice emphasizes the Mairuns' joy of living. All the same, the general feeling we are left by the end is lack of hope.

Guimarães Rosa's "My Uncle, the Jaguar" differs little in this respect. The mestizo protagonist tried to live among and work for non-Indians, only to realize that they despised him. Isolated, he returned to the culture of his deceased Indian mother, present now only in the form of their totem, the jaguar. The only kind of relationship he can have with non-Indians at this point is one of violence, and he ends up being killed by his interlocutor—a projection of ourselves, the readers. If this is the fate of Indians in texts where their culture is seen as philosophically antagonistic to the West, in those where they appear as national heroes their future is not much brighter. Gonçalves Dias's warriors, for instance, are definitely heroes of the past. As for Macunaíma, the trickster deconstruction of the national hero, we saw that he became the last of his tribe, overcome by loneliness, isolation, and longing for the time he had spent in São Paulo.

Whether or not the demise of indigenous cultures is lamented as unjust and genocidal (as in *Maíra*, "My Uncle, the Jaguar," and Gonçalves Dias's poems), and whether or not it is presented more positively, as an inevitable step along the path towards modernity (as in Vargas Llosa's *The Storyteller*), neither Romantic nor Modernist appropriations of native texts, genres, and ways of seeing the world seem to leave much room for cultural survival. Yet, if it is true that throughout the Americas native peoples share a history of dispossession, abuse, and extermination perpetrated by the Europeans and their creole successors, and that many cultural groups and millions of individuals have perished and are still perishing as a direct result of such behavior, it is also true that those who survive attest to the great capacity of indigenous cultures to re-create and reinvent themselves amidst the worst adversities. The philosophical basis for such adaptability and ability to resist can be found in the literature of the four rain forest traditions studied here—Carib, Tupi-Guarani, Tukano-Arawak (Rio-Negro), and Machiguenga. Each shows coherence in time and place, through a shared genesis in which the world is not created perfect by an omnipotent god and destroyed, ever since, by humans, but depends rather on a process of catastrophes, changes, and negotiations that is still taking place. The role of the human species in this process is not one of rulership: Humans learn from other species, whose existence and needs they must always be aware of. The same emphasis on learning and change can be observed in the shaman heroes' epic feats, coherent as they are throughout the different cultural groups: They bring seeds and plants to humans, teach them how to work the land, make poisons, provide cures, play musical instruments, and so on. As a whole, this shared genesis celebrates agriculture, cure, change, chance, and the will to go on living life on earth with other humans and with other species.

Perhaps nowhere is native capacity to reinvent itself put to such severe tests as in the modern city, hostile as it is in principle to rain forest ways of life. Yet, paradoxically, the only nonnative text studied in this book that seems not to evince a generally pessimistic view of the indigenous future is set precisely in a big city. Márcio Souza's play "Dessana, Dessana" presents us with a detribalized Desâna protagonist who lives among other poor Brazilians in the Manaus of the 1970s, a city then suffering under the deadly Amazonian directive of the military dictatorship (1964–78). Visually, the character Dessana appears to the audience as an Indian who has lost his culture (reminiscent, perhaps, of the Mairun future foreseen in Ribeiro's novel). Yet he is able to confront the biblical genesis with the Desâna cosmogony. He finds sustenance in his own roots and can go on to imagine alternatives to the developmentalist discourse that the military were then dictating in the region.

Souza's urban Desâna raises questions of evident concern to fellow Indians living today. An exemplary case is Kaká Werá Jecupé, whose autobiography is entitled, in Portuguese and Guarani, *Oré awé roiru'a ma: Todas as Vezes que Dissemos Adeus.* ("All the times we said goodbye." The Guarani puts initial emphasis on the "we" [oré] while saying goodbye is more like having repeatedly to move on).

Published in São Paulo in the early 1990s, Jecupé's story begins with the fact of dispossession thirty or so years before. Txucarramãe Indians living in the state of Bahia, his family was driven from their land by non-Indians. Homeless migrants, they journey far to find shelter among the Guarani living in Krucutu, and then Morro da Saudade, a community which, in turn, is being gradually encroached upon by the sprawling mass of São Paulo. Here, the newborn Jecupé learns the language of his Guarani hosts, only to become painfully aware of the non-Indian menace surrounding the community. Determined not just to give up, he revisits his family's former home in Bahia, though to little effect, and travels south to Florianópolis and other parts, eventually deciding to become an activist. In September 1992, he helps organize Anhangabaú-Opá, a major act of reconciliation that drew together, in the very heart of São Paulo, Guarani, Xavante and Quechua Indians, along with priests of African-Brazilian religions, Hindus, Arabs, Yoga gurus, Zen Buddhists, and members of the New Age Rainbow Order. In the same spirit, he performed rituals together with the Liberation Theologian Cardeal Arns, in the *Catedral da Sé*, throwing his spears to the ground in the act of becoming a *menonomure,* or true Guarani warrior. On the pages of newspapers he was featured as the guru who would help cure the city of its many undeniable ills.

In practice, this public exposure lent him and his book high credibility in the eyes of a whole gamut of alternative groups, ecologist and New Age, whose ideas indeed he has come to adopt to some degree. Throughout the book we find, for instance, references to various New Age notions, such as "Mother Earth," "the four elements," and "spirit-guides." Gike, a New Age friend from Florianópolis, explained to him: "There are some traditions I like, although I practice them in my own way. I really like your traditions. They are sincere and in communion with the soul of the Earth. I also like the Yoruba traditions. After all, I am a daughter of the Yoruba goddess Iansã, am I not?" (37). However their philosophy may be perceived, from Jecupé's point of view his New Age friends had a definite social attraction. Among them he is able to live out his Guarani identity in ways that are usually unacceptable to non-Indians, just as he can find allies in his political cause.

At the same time, he has been viewed with suspicion if not hostility by many intellectuals and academics. None of them has cared to deny that he was born and raised an Indian or that he writes, just that the combination of the two factors has proved highly problematic. On the cover of his book he is identified by his Indian face, and the statement that "Together with Daniel Munduruku, Olívio Tupã, and Roman Quetchua, Kaká Werá Jecupé is a coordinator of NAÊ (Intertribal Association for Solidarity and Defense of Indigenous Citizenship)." Yet his critics harbor doubts about whether he has the right, in their view, to be classified or categorized as a "genuine Indian." An anthropologist friend confided that Jecupé was no longer an Indian, and that his book was a hodgepodge of ideas, only a few of which were native. Another friend, a historian, confessed to his difficulty in reconciling traditional commonality with the fact of authorship by a named individual.

As a native Brazilian writer, Jecupé has clear antecedents in intellectuals like Akuli (Pemon) and Maximiano (Taria), who were so concerned to transcribe, translate, edit, and in this sense author(ize) tribal texts, a tendency that materializes fully in the publication of Pārōkumu and Kēhíri's version of the Desâna cosmogony, *Antes o Mundo não Existia*. And the questions his book raises relate just as well, in one way or another, to many similar examples of contemporary native authorship elsewhere in the Americas—by Elicura Chihuailaf (Mapuche) in Chile, Victor Montejo (Maya-Quiché) in Guatemala, Victor de la Cruz (Zapotec) in Mexico, Leslie Marmon Silko (Laguna Pueblo) in the United States, to name only a few. In Jecupé's case, it is worth noting that not only is his book the first major statement of its kind in Brazil but that the hostility it has provoked there exposes an especially deep and long-standing prejudice, whereby Indians can be Indians only insofar as they conform to the stereotype of tribal, scantily clad, and illiterate.

Technically, Jecupé's text is genial for the way it masters and plays with language, in the first place that of the colonizing Portuguese, at the same time as it gives space and resonance, from the title on, to words and terms proper to the prior "general language" (língua geral) of lowland South America, Tupi-Guarani, his own first tongue. Moreover, his text does all this with a fine matter-of-fact irony and a sophisticated sense of self and self-representation. Indeed, looking closely at Jecupé's modes of dealing with concepts of identity, especially with regard to "soul loss" and contexts of memory, may help review the propositions in this book, as it were through his eyes and from the platform of his authority. As he tells it, his life story negotiates just the dilemmas faced by the main characters in this reading of Amazonian literatures, crossing and recrossing the notional boundary between fiction and life, and opening into the future.

The story starts even before his birth, in Bahia: "When I was music in my mother's belly, our village was attacked. Men holding small steel thunders created a huge storm; they threw themselves against us from all sides, making a rain of flames" (16). According to Indian norms, awareness precedes birth, as it does, for example, in Tupi-Guarani cosmogony and Ribeiro's reworking of it in *Maíra,* when from the womb the first Twin converses with his mother. For Jecupé, entry in consciousness, already here in the womb, stems from a loud violence that threatens inherited harmony. The intrusive guns are defined in appropriately child-like terms, which of course cannot but remind us of how amused Europeans were by the first reactions to the firearms they brought to America. By this means, the invasion then, in the sixteenth century is directly connected with the continuing invasion in Jecupé's day, a centuries-long tale of dispossession on which every Native American life has come to be predicated, and which is the first fact of his own life. As a consequence, on the road to São Paulo from the northeast, the landless family becomes "nomadic," entering the category that for writers like Vargas Llosa is the one to which Indians have always in principle belonged.

Once incorporated into the communities of their Guarani hosts in São Paulo, the family faces further dispossession, not just through the physical precariousness of those communities engulfed in the urban sprawl, but because of the strategies used by the "city" to control and deploy its populations. The very fact of existence comes to depend on the ability to register it in the alien system:

> When we arrived and settled among the Guarani in São Paulo, the city ended up demanding my father's name and the names of all the Guarani in exchange for survival. They told us that without a civilized name and number one did not exist. So, what were we? We just were, we did not exist. And we remained a long time without existing until water and resources ran short and we were forced to exchange means of survival with the civilized people. One of the things we exchanged was our names. Thus Gwirá, the bird, became José. Taí, beauty, became Esperança. Tupã-mirim, the small god, became Zé Ninguém (Joe Nobody). And I became the son of Miguel, formerly Mecaron-tié." (16–17)

The detail of the name exchanges itself implies an economy and its tenets: the resplendent American bird for Jesus' compliant father, beauty for long-suffering Christian hope (in the consumer market, this beauty Taí had already served to name a product of Coca Cola Brazil), and god-like spirit for nothing at all. Refining the argument, when it comes to the individual case of the first-person narrator, the shift is multiple yet incomplete and opaque. His father has become Miguel, yet the meaning of his original name is left unstated, while the son records no name at all for himself. A fundamental factor in Native American culture, the question of proper names and identity likewise persistently concerns the literary heroes in this book. As we saw, from the first moments of encounter, Europeans were especially impressed by the Guarani articulation of concepts whose nearest Western equivalents are soul, name, and word.

For Jecupé, this public reduction through naming is understood as the beginning of what he calls "soul loss," a process that intensifies when he is made to go to school. School means a cluster of decisive experiences, relating to dress, photographic image, writing, and the whole idea of education, which have exercised the great minds of the West in the line of Rousseau, though most often with scant regard for the kind of urgent political consequences foregrounded by Jecupé. The school itself invitingly bears the name of one of Brazil's most notorious Indian-killers, the *bandeirante* Borba Gato, and Jecupé agrees to attend only upon the insistence of his father, who, in turn, had been persuaded he should by a woman from the city. His reluctance stemmed from an acute sense of what he was learning already from life around him, perceived as it was through the filter of Guarani culture and custom:

> There were fish to catch, good hearts-of-palm, blue butterflies that we fol-
> lowed in order to find the magic gourd-head where they dyed their wings.
> Many important things to learn! To weave, carve, understand the right
> space and time to gather the leaves or plant seeds, and paint. (21)

Traditional indigenous education—learning to weave, paint, carve, and to know the environment—precedes and sharply contrasts with nonindigenous education in school.

In school, the outer sign of soul loss is not just Western dress but uniform, the formal reduction to number: "In the beginning they did not mind me walking around the school barefoot and with no shirt on. But then they started to demand that I wore a uniform: navy-blue shorts, white socks, black shoes, white shirt, and a little tie with a white band on it which indicated first grade" (22). Worse was to come, in the form of his photographed face stuck on to a school document:

> When Mother realized it, they had stolen my soul. It had gotten stuck to
> the piece of paper, cut up, black and white and without sun, in a document
> called student ID. I told her they made me stand up before a machine that
> exploded a light on my face. "Anguery, mi tã je jucá anguery," chief Capitão
> Branco said, "Spirit thieves, they stole the boy's soul in order to kill it." (22)

The black-and-white snapshot, representing only the boy's face, is the image of a lifeless cut-up creature, in other words, a creature without a soul. Not just that, it is the result of active theft, even murder (*jucá*, the deadly shot), which vividly epitomizes the process of reduction and containment that began with the whole community's changes of name. Moreover, as if this were not enough, the young Kaká has to confess to his mother that the teacher also had taken him to obtain a birth certificate on which, instead of his own name, she had put the name of her own son, who had died newborn.

> Mother got me off the school and beat my dad with one of those clubs that
> are used for hunting caitetu (wild boar), and she made him go and ask for
> my spirit back. The teacher cried, but those documents remained forever
> marked with the soul of the name of her son, who had died new-born. (22)

Apart from the humor implicit in his father's being treated like a boar (for having allowed his son to become so vulnerable in the first place), this passage is notable for the precise articulation of mark with soul and with name, on a document which belongs to another individual.

The other thing Jecupé learns at school is alphabetic writing, "to draw on paper the things that are said" (22). This is the phenomenon long diagnosed in the West as responsible for separating humans from "nature," and for legitimizing the colonizers' dominance over the colonized; for Jecupé it undoubtedly is part of the process of soul loss. As he puts it, the process means "translating from the red painted writing of my body to the white body of this written painting" (8). Yet as this highly poetic phrase indicates, from the start it is more complex, not least because at no point does he forget that we know all this precisely because he has written it down for us to read in his book. Indeed, as the thread in an enhanced idea of education, writing became part of his way back to the community, after his lonely years on the road.

For, paradoxically in Lévi-Strauss's terms, writing is key to the process of recovery which begins when Jecupé returns to Morro da Saudade and sees the old chief teaching the children of the community how to read and write in Portuguese and Guarani:

> The tribal council had arrived at the conclusion that in that place which used to be Atlantic rain forest and was now a poor suburb of São Paulo, the path to resistance had to go through a deeper understanding of other cultures, particularly of so-called civilization. The village hadn't escaped *Anhan*, Evil's teeth, on the contrary, it was falling straight into its mouth. (40)

It is, after all, sheer ability as a writer that enabled him to complete his autobiography and to present it to his readers in terms that lack nothing in literary sophistication and political challenge.

Styling himself as a traveler, he is no less adept than Mário de Andrade's character Macunaíma in parodying notions of America as the "New World" discovered by Europeans, and he has the same recourse to classic chronicles like Pero Vaz de Caminha's *Carta a el-rei Dom Manuel*:

> With time I started to wander through the wide trails of the city, called avenues. I walked through its steel jungles and ate its artificial fruit in order to discover the Brazils. On the asphalts where I walked, whatever one plants won't grow. I tried the good and the bad. I met a sort of chief who wears ties like I did in my school days, and who is, as a certain ancient and historic scribe might have said, far too shameless. (27)

"Whatever one plants won't grow" is the inversion of a famous sentence in Caminha's letter, according to which whatever one planted [in Brazilian soil] would grow. And the expression "far too shameless" was used by Caminha (the "ancient and historic scribe" alluded to here) to describe the naked Indians on the coast of Brazil.

This parody of received Western discourse, from a resolutely native perspective, in turn issues into a project that directly parallels Oswald de Andrade's anthropophagy—a literary and cultural link that Jecupé is clearly aware of when he says:

> My mentor spirits (the *tamaí*) pushed me into the jaguar's mouth, this
> *yauaretê* called metropolis, as a test, so that I would learn and eat from your
> language and culture, should I survive. That's how I ate the bread kneaded
> by civilization. I survived. For that reason, I devoured the brain of your
> knowledge. (8)

Being pushed into the jaguar's mouth is precisely what most elicits reliance on his own speech: the *tamaí* guardians who do the pushing, and the *yauaretê* itself, savage yet kin in Guimarães's story, and the dynamic principle that manifests itself as the city's automobiles in Macunaíma's eyes.

In Jecupé's text, the question of self-representation, soul loss, and memory is perhaps nowhere more finely cast than in the chapter "The river of Peri and Ceci," which tells of his and his community's encounter with the mass medium of television. This happened as a result of Manchete TV wanting to include live Guarani in their soap opera version of Alencar's novel *O Guarani*. Over the century and a half since it was published, this Romantic work is remarkable for how often and variously it has been reworked: as Carlos Gomes's opera *Il Guarani*, recently revised by Werner Herzog and performed in Washington, D.C., as well as in more than one film; of all these versions, the Manchete soap would clearly reach the widest public while having to respond most closely to the demands of that public.

The ironies in Jecupé's narrative are so intricately layered as to defy easy analysis. For a start, in the chapter title he plays between proper and common nouns, the "river" being both Rio and that which features in the lives of the lovers Peri and Ceci. The thirty Guarani leave for Rio from São Paulo under little illusion about the dangers the sortie implies:

> We were getting acquainted with the place of the *iksos,* where the evil
> *anguery* live, up on the huge cement tree—inside the tree—the place of the
> soul-thieves. We saw what they do after they steal them: they lock them up
> in small rectangular boxes and put these boxes inside bigger boxes, very
> orderly, and then they take them out and put them in big electronic boxes
> and multiply them, and cut them, and chop them, and stick them together
> again. The sunny morning was chopped up many times and placed behind
> the bird multiplied by the factor of a thousand in order to disguise the
> opaque tone of its locked-up soul. (48)

Upon arrival their concern was such that the Guarani council asked for a meeting, worried about the soul-thieves (the kind denounced already by Capitão Branco) and what might happen to them if they got too involved in this technology of the box. The director of the soul-thieves, Marcos Schettman, managed to convince Jecupé that his people, the Jews, had also been oppressed, and that they were recording the soap opera in order to defend the indigenous peoples. The recordings proceeded, allowing the Guaranis from São Paulo, twentieth-century Guaranis, to participate in the creation of a seventeenth-century native identity, partly invented by Alencar and Schettman:

> I, an Aymoré warrior. Adventurers from the other side of the ocean came in search of gold and land, destroyed a Guarani village and are now about to attack us. Young women bathing in the light of the river. Young children playing and rolling on the ground. Firearms are cocked.—Cut!, said the direcor Marcos Schettman. (49)

These Guarani Indians who act out a native identity written by white men constitute a mirror-image of Jecupé's own procedure as a writer. He acts out his Guarani identity before us, simulating a dialogue around the fire:

> Now, according to the tradition, I make the fire, I throw aromatic herbs and sticks in it; and I invite you to sit by it. Sit down, please. I must ask you to make yourself comfortable: this ritual will help you listen to the *ne'porã*, the beautiful words, the elders' sacred words that will pass through these stories, filled with old lessons from the Guarani people. And I invent this fire in order to follow the tradition correctly, for everything else comes from what already happened, and is retold here. (17)

By using expressions such as "act out" and "simulate" I do not intend to deny the veracity of Jecupé's Guarani identity, but rather to stress his own insistence on representation and performance—an insistence that alerts us to the complex layering of multiple identities in the text. Of course the Guarani identity Jecupé constructs was not invented by whites, and here native notions of how beautiful words *(ne'porã)* rather than characters pass through the story are used to stunning effect (one arguably reflected in Borges); but it is re-presented in the language and writing system that the whites have imposed on the native populations. This process is thoroughly discussed in the text through the many subtleties and ironies with which the very subject of identity is treated. It is true that the "civilized" indeed stole the souls of the native peoples with the help of mechanisms of representation and reproduction such as printing, documenting, and photography. In the meantime, urban Indians like Jecupé use these same mechanisms to reaffirm and re-create their own identities. Thus, the Guarani who enact the soap-opera version of a Romantic Indianist novel may indeed be taking part in what most cultural historians would discard as a third-hand version (the soap opera) of what in any case is seen as a fake representation of Indian-ness (Alencar's romantic novel). Yet the Guaranis *are* Indians, and their enacting of this supposedly fake Indian identity becomes, for that reason, quite complex: first, because it necessarily reestablishes continuities between Alencar's sources and the contemporary Indians, and second, because the scene recorded by the Guarani in the television studio is the representation of a violent history that is indeed shared by Alencar's seventeenth-century Indians and the contemporary Guarani, if not by all native peoples of the Americas. The Rio soap opera allows the Guarani to call attention to this history, at the same time that it shows to an unprecedentedly wide audience that they, the Guaranis, are still alive as a culture, and can appear in the most unexpected places, such as soap operas and the center of huge cities. My intention is not to celebrate soap operas, or to ignore the mechanisms of exploitation that may be implied by the hiring of Guarani Indians as actors (Jecupé is silent on this point). Neither do I wish to deny the great imbalance of power between those who control forms of representation like television, films, and book publishing, and those who appropriate them as supposed tools for resistance. All such issues are important, and more often than not they have been overlooked in many recent analyses of the subalterns' power to resist oppression by appropriating and changing the tools of the oppressors (as these have been understood, for example, by Nestor García Canclini, Jesús Martín-Barbero, and Homi Bhabha).

In fact, Jecupé's book emphasizes that the Guarani are oppressed by the city people, who pollute their water, cut their trees, steal their land, and treat them like dirty beggars. Yet, like all of us, the Guarani are capable of negotiating and re-creating their identity for their own benefit, without necessarily becoming, for that reason, less Indian. Jecupé's text is acutely aware of those processes of negotiation, to the point that it becomes almost impossible for his readers to peel off all the multiple layers of identities that compose his discourse.

Complexities of this order certainly continue to inform Jecupé's role in and account of the Anhangabaú-Opá in 1992. As he readily admits, this "a mega-event," all-inclusive in a New Age fashion, also appeals to the idea of reconciliation, even forgiveness, between Indians and their dispossessors. But in this case, of whom, by whom? In his text, possible New Age lack of discrimination is sharply curtailed by the arrows that reaffirm him as a Guarani warrior (the *menononure*) in the *Catedral da Sé*, a process that culminates in the revelation, by an elder, of his Guarani name, Werá Jecupé, used to sign the book we are reading. That, he claims, is his real name, the last of the layers he is going to peel off. Yet, given his earlier account of name exchange and his emphasis on performance and negotiation, one cannot help suspecting that this is but another layer, a name that hides other names which non-Indians will never know: As he says, among the Guarani "names are good, because they protect the name" (20). Names may also be relational and depend on the stage of life of a human being and those who surround her/him: One may be a hero, but also someone's husband, someone's mother, etc.; such names are chosen by the community and only become effective through rituals. At heart, everyone has yet another name, known only to members of the tribe, or of the clan, which remains close to essence and soul, and is protected by all of these other names. The task of shielding this innermost name from danger is not simple, nor can it be neglected. Jecupé's New Age Indian-ness could be understood to have the function of name in this sense.

In any case, this reading of his participation in Anhangabaú-Opá is supported by Jecupé's forceful reminder of how the process of dispossession, 500 years on, was by no means over, and of how it was being monstrously obscured, every day, in modern media. Paraphrasing TV "news" (not least the Brazilian global network *Globo*), he couches in biblical discourse an account of the massacre of 300 Yanomami at the hands of gold-hungry prospectors who had illegally entered their territory. Governing and permeating the whole is the initial Guarani term *anguery*:

> The *anguery,* soul-thieves, promoted the confusion. On the first day, the television spoke of more than two hundred Yanomami dead in the extreme north of the country, in Haximu [in the Roraima region]. On the second day it said there hadn't been that many deaths. On the third day, almost nobody had died. On the fourth day they made an English anthropologist translate a Yanomami Indian who said in good Portuguese that the Yanomami had said that what happened a few days before had not happened. On the fifth day the news changed the location of Haximu, it wasn't in Brazil anymore, it was in Venezuela. On the sixth day they put American troops into Venezuela, who had accidentally killed some Yanomami. On the seventh day, the global god rested. (78)

Not least, by virtue of its very name, Anhangabaú-Opá meant the recovery, momentary but physical, of a place in the heart of South America's biggest city. Degraded by European settlers as the "devil's creek," and the source of diseases like typhus (Bueno, 47), the toponym Anhangabaú points rather in Guarani to a place imbued with spiritual danger. In Jecupé's text, a similar reading is made of Moema and other Guarani place-names that the city uses to identify and correlate its inhabitants; the result is to revive the proper name, to de-reify it, and restore it to its linguistic owner.

A deceptively brief and unpretentious work, Jecupé's autobiography engages fully with the ideological and philosophical questions raised by the texts to which this reading of the rain forest literatures is devoted. In doing so, it is less decidedly pessimistic, and nurses the thought that Indians and the oppressors identified in their history might work together to fight the violence and exploitation that threaten imminently to destroy the planet we share. Using the same alphabetical writing system that has served imperial ends, Jecupé attempts to teach his readers native cultural practices and ways of thought; thus, his written words reverse, at least textually, the process of colonization: "I came so that we can undress ourselves. So that we can discover the Brazils" (8). Now it is the native authors who are choosing their own modes of dialogue with established literary traditions, setting out ways of understanding the world that draw on their own memory and intelligence, and stating a political will and commitment that eagerly reimagines the boundaries between literature and life.

Notes

1. Pacaraima Texts

1. Schomburgk already observed that fact among the So'to: "They looked upon every printed or written word as something supernatural and followed the eyes of the person reading with the keenest tension, they being firmly convinced that the page betrays their own most hidden thoughts to the reader" (1: 360).

2. In *Watunna,* Iureke and his twin also save themselves from a flood by climbing on twin palm trees that turn, like Marahuaka, into stone.

3. *Watunna* was made into a hypnotically intelligent film by Stacey Steers in 1989, with narration by Stan Brackage.

4. Neil Whitehead suggests that maize "may have been of greater significance in Carib diet than modern ethnography has suggested" (1988, 48). The story told by Mayuluaípu may be a historical evidence of this importance.

5. João Barbosa Rodrigues (1899) also draws on the importance of jade to make explicit comparisons between Amazonian and Meso-American cultures.

2. *Macunaíma (1928)*

1. For that reason, some critics, especially in recent years, refer to the movement initiated in that famous week as *modernismo paulista* (São Paulo modernism).

2. This is how Mário de Andrade is referred to in Brazilian literary criticism and history.

3. The letter to Alceu Amoroso Lima, as well as other letters that include some important references to *Macunaíma,* and the two unpublished prefaces to the novel were reproduced by Telê Porto Ancona Lopez (1974). Parts of that material were republished by the critic in her superb critical edition of *Macunaíma* (which I refer to as Lopez 1988) as well.

4. For a detailed analysis of the letter to Raimundo de Morais, see Eneida Maria de Souza.

5. The spelling of the Pemon names was adapted by Mário de Andrade. *Makunaíma* becomes *Macunaíma Zigé* becomes *Jiguê,* and so on. I have respected those differences: *Makunaíma,* in this study, refers to Akuli and Mayuluaípu's character, while *Macunaíma* refers to Mário de Andrade's.

6. Unless otherwise stated, all the emphases in quotations are by the authors.

7. The same argument is developed, as we saw, in Koch-Grünberg's original narrative.

8. Walter Roth describes the practice, among Amazonian Indians, of group challenges to see who can provide the best explanation about specific characteristics of plants and animals (483).

9. See, for instance, Alfredo Bosi (1988, 171) and Silviano Santiago (1988, 192).

10. This is how Schomburgk describes the *muiraquitãs*: "Extremely remarkable things at all events are the green Amazon-stones (Lapis nephriticus), the Piedras hijadas of the Spaniards, about which all Indian accounts agree that they come from the Amazons. Alexander von Humboldt found these stones among the Indians of the Rio Negro where they were carried on the neck as amulets for protection against fever, and the bites of poisonous snakes: Von Martius saw them on the rio Negro among the residents at Sylves, while I came across them in Georgetown.

"It was through the Caribs along the Guiana coast that these stones were brought into Georgetown where they are known as *Macuaba* or *Calicot* stones. On the Orinoco they are called *Macagua,* apparently the same term as the former. Formerly the Caribs brought them to the capital in considerable quantities, but very rarely nowadays. I only once had the opportunity of seeing a specimen which was in the possession of a merchant there. It corresponded accurately enough not only in shape but also in color with the description given by Alexander von Humboldt. From what the people told me, these stones were formerly often brought to town in the shape of fish and other animals, as well as with figures carved on their surfaces.

"According to Barrere the Caribs treasured them more than gold: such a stone was the price of a slave" (2: 263).

Barbosa Rodrigues has also a lengthy study on the subject (1899).

11. Uiara is a water goddess in the Tupi-Guarani tradition.

12. For the presence of Tupi in "Carta pras Icamiabas," see Maria Augusta Fonseca's "A Carta pras Icamiabas."

13. The Pemon origin of the term and its meaning are pointed out by Proença (177). "Pú'yito, der After," translates Koch-Grünberg in the German edition of the narratives. A form of *puíto (pú:yi)* also appears in Koch-Grünberg's glossary (1928) under the meaning *anus.* (In Armellada's dictionary (1948) it has the meaning of *vagina.* In the same dictionary one can see that the particle *-to* follows nouns and means "our.")

14. Thus, Eneida Maria de Souza's observations about the differences between this episode of the novel and what she calls simply "folktales" cannot be accepted: "The listeners realize that the whole story is false and unmask the narrator. If in the context of folktales the idea of illusion and sustained fiction within reality is always preserved, fiction, in *Macunaíma,* is a strategic move to deceive others" (117). The difference between the "fictional" and the "real" is already present in the Pemon sources.

15. Literally "commodity exchange" (parallel to "stock exchange").

16. In the English translation of the novel, the Arekuna phrase was replaced by a sentence in Welsh!

17. *Lingua do pê* is a children's game in which an extra syllable, starting with the consonant "p," is added before or after every syllable of spoken words. The result is a cryptic language understood only by those who dominate the game.

18. *Watunna* has a similar story.

19. Walter Roth mentions a Carib (Cariña) version of the Makunaíma story in which the trickster has his leg cut off, and becomes the Pleiades.

20. Although the novel incorporates no plots of African origin, there is a definite black presence, above all in dialogue and in the ceremony in the "Macumba" chapter.

3. Penetrating the Dark Interior

1. Although as a Cuban Alejo Carpentier is not strictly a South American writer, *The Lost Steps* was written during his stay in Venezuela and reflects the writer's profound involvement with the region at the time.

2. A recent example is Marcone 1996, which focuses on "la novela de la selva" (*The Lost Steps, The Storyteller,* and others) yet avoids the concept of a resident "escritura de la selva."

3. Tieko Myiazaki inexplicably calls it a novel (75).

4. I owe this information to María Helena Rueda.

5. The translations of *Canaima* that I cite are, for the most part, a combination of both existing translations, listed in the bibliography.

6. See, for instance, Irlemar Chiampi, 1989.

7. Carpentier observed about Villa-Lobos in 1952: "But there is in that quartet, a kind of assimilation of landscape, of songs, of nature, of popular music, of such a nature—being so total—that when Villa-Lobos makes the instruments of his quartet perform, they make a music that can only be Brazilian" (quoted in González Echevarría 1977, 188).

8. It is important to note that the Schomburgk brothers' journey is directly linked to Great Britain's territorial interests at the time and its disputes with Brazil over the Guyana territory. In fact, the 1840 line that resulted from an agreement between the two countries was named "Schomburgk line." Although other historical accounts indicate that Schomburgk's claims about the violence of the Brazilians are basically correct, his political involvement in the question has to be acknowledged. For more on the subject, see Nabuco.

4. Tupi-Guarani Texts

1. The dates of those migrations are still being discussed. The main argument in favor of a recent dispersal of the Tupi-Guarani groups is the similarity between all Tupi-Guarani languages. For a good perspective on the debate about the migration of Tupi-Guarani groups, see the articles by Noelli and by Heckenberger, et al.

2. For an excellent study on Pombal's edict and its censorial role, see Mariani.

3. For an excellent study on Caminha's Letter, see Greene.

4. Cannibalism among native South Americans has been the subject of heated debates between those who consider it an invention of European travelers, and those who believe it was indeed practiced. See, for instance, Arens; Barker, et al; and Whitehead 2000.

5. All quotes are from the Brazilian edition (Staden, 1974).

6. Thirty years before, at the famous Rouen Festival of 1550, a group of fifty Tupinambá took part in a ceremony for Henry II and his wife Catherine de Médici (and, of course, the king's lover, Diana de Poitiers). Surrounded by Brazilian birds, monkeys, and a sumptuous "jungle decoration," the fifty Indians and an equal number of European sailors staged everyday Tupinambá activities and, at the end, war games, including Tupi exhortation songs—traditionally sung by the elders of the community to motivate the younger ones to fight. Even though the specific songs sung for the occasion were not recorded, the Festival is a demonstration of the European interest in and contact with Tupinambá culture and texts. For a detailed description of the festival, see Ferdinand Dénis 1850.

7. Gonçalves Dias, for instance, in *O Brasil e a Oceania,* asks the reader to forgive him for using Thevet (117). Manuela Carneiro da Cunha calls the traveller "the hateful, pedantic, condescending—and according to the Huguenot Léry—lying Franciscan André Thevet, who claims to have seen what he never saw, to have been where he never was, and who fills lacunas with boring and rambling classical references for each one of the institutions he describes" (1993, 158). Whatever is said about Thevet, he was a major source of texts from South America as well as an enthusiast of Mexican codices. The Mendoza Codex, once in his possession and now in the Bodleian Library, bears the inscription, "André Thevet cosmographe."

8. There is no agreement among specialists about the number of Guarani who lived in the Guairá before the arrival of the Europeans. Statistics seem to vary between 30,000 and "millions." Fifty thousand is a number accepted by Monteiro and Meliá.

9. See, for instance, Lugon.

10. This opinion is shared by Meliá, 96.

11. According to Paulo Prado, who commented on the speech in the 1922 facsimile edition of Abbeville's work, the Tupi text has bad mistakes and incomprehensible parts, and the French translation that accompanies it does not correspond to the original.

12. All quotations are from the Brazilian edition.

13. All quotations are from the Brazilian edition.

14. In the second edition, posthumously organized by Couto de Magalhães's nephew, the Tupi originals were omitted, in order to be published in a separate volume as part of Ollendorf's course of Nheengatú.

15. Although *O Selvagem* was published in 1876, a year after Machado de Assis's poems (included in the collection "Americanas"), its second part (where we find the texts quoted by Machado de Assis) was presented in 1874 to the Instituto Histórico e Geográfico, according to the preface (written by the author's nephew)

to the second edition of the book (1913): "The second part of the original edition of *O Selvagem* reproduces a paper that the author read, in 1874, in the Instituto Histórico e Geográfico Brasileiro, entitled 'Region and Savage races,' which sold out in little more than three months" (no page number).

16. A Portuguese version of those stories was included in "Contribuições para a ethnologia do valle do Amazonas," 1885.

17. Curupira is a Tupi spirit of the forest, who has a deformed body.

18. There was a previous edition of this work, in German, published in São Leopoldo (Rio Grande do Sul), and called *Mythen, Sagen und Märchen brasilischer Indianer, zusammengestellt und eingeleitet* (no date; the date of the introduction is 1919).

19. All quotations are from the Brazilian edition.

20. The Guarani villages on the coast of São Paulo are Itariri, Rio Branco, Bananal, Rio Silveira, and Boa Vista (Promirim); in Santa Catarina there is the village Biguaçu.

21. For an excellent work on suicide among the Kaiowá, see Meihy.

5. Romanticism and After

1. Those readers interested in a comprehensive and masterful study of Brazilian *Indianismo* should read David Treece's *Victims, Allies, Rebels* (2000). In this work, Treece arrived, quite independently, at some of the same conclusions about Gonçalves Dias's poetry that I reached in my 1997 doctoral thesis. Our focus, however, is quite different: Treece makes a thorough analysis of Gonçalves Dias's work in terms of the poet's political and personal position in the Brazilian society of the time. My interest is more narrowly defined by Dias's use of sources.

2. Such distinctions between the Tupi and Botocudos (or Tapuias) resemble the comparisons made in the Caribbean context between Arawaks and Caribs (Treece, 34).

3. See Treece for a detailed analysis of "Meditação."

4. All translations of Gonçalves Dias's poetry are by Gordon Brotherston.

5. Coutinho, 190.

6. The experiment was described by the author in 1931, in a book entitled *Experiência No. 2*.

7. For obvious reasons, this is not the place to discuss the *modernistas'* relation to African-Brazilian cultures. For the most part, the *modernistas* have been accused of not including African-Brazilian cultures in their works. In terms of scale, the accusation is certainly fair. But the modernists did not ignore Afro-Brazilians entirely: One has only to look at Bopp's *Poemas Negros*; at Mário's own contributions on slave culture to *Revista de Antropofagia*, and his "Macumba" chapter in *Macunaíma* (what other Brazilian novel of the time had dealt so openly with the theme?) and to the several references throughout the *Revista de Antropofagia* to similar works from other parts of the country.

8. This is the same poem quoted by Machado de Assis.

9. Although all quotes are from David Treece's magnificent translation of the

short story, "The Jaguar," I prefer to retain a literal translation of the title ("My Uncle, the Iauaretê"), since it is more in line with my argument.

10. Koch-Grünberg also refers to the Pemon shamans' capacity to turn into jaguars.

11. Nunes Pereira, for instance, published a biography of Nimuendaju in 1946 entitled *Curt Nimuendajú: Síntese de uma Vida e de uma Obra*.

12. Subsequently, other novels dealing with Tupi culture have been published in Brazil (apart from Darcy Ribeiro's *Maíra*: see below). Antonio Callado's *A Expedição Montaigne* (1982), and Darcy Ribeiro's *A Utopia Selvagem* (1982), can hardly be said to engage in intertextual dialogue with indigenous literature. They satirically analyze, once again, the romantic legacy with respect to the indigenous cultures of Brazil.

6. *Maíra* (1976)

1. For Ribeiro, the term *civilization* has no necessarily positive connotations.

2. The article was republished in 1974 in the book *Uirá sai à Procura de Deus* and was made into a film, *Uirá*, in 1970, directed by Gustavo Dahl.

3. It is in the Mbyá creation story, *Ayvu Rapyta*, that the brothers are more directly associated with Sun and Moon.

4. Akirio Boróro Keggeu's life is also analysed in Fernandes (1960).

5. Tiago Marques Apoburéu was the major force behind the monumental *Enciclopédia Bororo* published by the Salesians Albisetti and Venturelli (1960). He also wrote most of the stories included by Antonio Colbacchini and Albisetti in *Os Bororos Ocidentais*. In the words of Darcy Ribeiro: "this book should not have been signed [by Colbacchini and Albisetti], it should have the name of Tiago Marques Apoburéu, who wrote it. But this has been the normal practice, up to now: to pillage Native knowledge like that" (Sá 1993, 84).

6. The theme of Oedipus and the importance of Sigmund Freud's theories for the novel are further developed in Sá 1990.

7. The same passage from Nimuendaju's collection is quoted by Darcy Ribeiro in *Os Índios e a Civilização*

8. For a more complete reading on oppositions in *Maíra*, see Sá 1990.

9. The Epexãs correspond to the Guajaras from *Os Índios e a Civilização*, and the Xãepes to the Xokleng.

10. The choice of these two macrolinguistic groups is itself interesting. Eduardo Viveiros de Castro (1986) uses the Gê-Bororo as a constant term with which to contrast the Tupi-Guarani. He explains his choice as follows: "Taking advantage of the fact . . . that these societies are among the best described, ethnographically and theoretically, in South American ethnology, we shall use them as a bench mark when constructing and defining the model of Person and society among the Arawcté (Tupi-Guarani). As we shall see, the Gê and the Tupi-Guarani societies appear to be diametrically opposed, in a virtual continuum of the socio-cultural formations of South American peoples" (29).

7. The Upper Rio Negro

1. Alexander von Humboldt described a similar ritual among the Arawak from the upper Orinoco region (Schaden 1959, 155).

2. The Tukano groups include the Desâna, Barasana, Tukano proper, Pira-Tapuya, Uanano, Karapana, Tuyúca, Mirití-Tapuyo, and Cubeo. The Arawakans include the Baniwa, Tariana, Curripaco, Wakuenai, Warekena, Baré, and Piapoco. The Maku include the Bara, Hupdu, Yöhup, Nadëb, Dôw, and Kaburi.

3. For an excellent study on messianic movements in the upper Rio Negro, see Wright 1998.

4. For further discussion of this polemic, see Orjuela.

5. See, for instance, Mendoza and Correa.

6. For readings of the cosmogonic dimensions of the *Leggenda* and its connections with deeper levels of time and astronomical phenomena, see Brotherston (2000) and Hugh-Jones.

7. For an explicit comparison with the *Popol Vuh,* see Brotherston 2000.

8. Not translatable—something like: "She wantie to go to the other side" and "They are all sad, why don't you sweetie their heart?"

9. According to Neves, "there is no group in the Uaupés today known as 'Arara.' Amorim states that the Arara used to be brothers-in-law of the Uanana. He also reports (17) about the Uanana calling for help among the Arapaço, Desâna, Cubeo, and Tukano. Could the Arara be a sib of one of these groups?" (185).

10. As for recent testimonies on women's reactions to Jurupari rules, we have Christine Hugh-Jones's observations of women's seclusion during a Jurupari ritual among the Barasana, described by her husband Stephen Hugh-Jones: "According to my wife, who remained with the women during the *He* rites . . . young Barasana women are indeed afraid of the *He* instruments and it is they in particular who rush out from the house when they are brought to the outside from the river and when they are brought inside early the next day. But this fear is actively induced by a kind of mock hysteria from the elder women. To say that all Barasana women were afraid of the *He* would be to confuse ideal with practice. In fact, most Barasana women know in precise detail what the *He* look like and know more or less exactly what is going on on the other side of the palm-leaf screen that separates them from men during the rites, even to the extent of being able to say which particular named instruments are being played by which individuals" (29).

11. Including Stradelli's "Jurupari" and narratives already published by Giacone, Biocca, and Saake.

12. A probable reference to the version of the Desâna creation story published by Reichel-Dolmatoff (1971).

13. All the translations of *Antes o Mundo não Existia* into English quoted here were made by Jessi Aaron, based on the 1995 edition of the book.

14. Rather, the Tariana came into the world through a hole in a big rock in the Arara waterfall (see, for instance, Moreira, 13).

15. See, for instance, the recent volumes of oral narratives organized by Maria

do Socorro Simões and Christophe Golder, which include several versions of the Big Snake story.

8. *Snake Norato* (1931)

1. According to Cavalcanti Proença, the expression also appears in Portuguese romances (66).

2. *Boto* is the pink freshwater dolphin of the Amazon, about whom many popular stories are told. Like Norato, the *boto* appears in parties disguised as a good-looking man (more rarely as a woman) and seduces young women. For an excellent study of *boto* narratives, see Slater.

3. Othon Moacyr Garcia, for instance, considers it the only epic poem in Brazilian literature.

4. Angel Crespo in his introduction to the Spanish edition of *Snake Norato,* calls it a "lyric poem."

9. The Green Stage

1. TESC (Teatro Experimental do SESC) ceased to exist in 1980. TESC was sponsored by SESC (Social Services for Commerce Employees), which continues to support many activities and plays throughout the country.

2. Both plays, plus "A Paixão de Ajuricaba" were included in the first volume of Márcio Souza's *Teatro.*

3. The videotape was given to me by Márcio Souza, who also very generously talked about the 1975 performances.

4. The trickster Makunaíma, for instance, performs several different roles in the Pemon stories and in the curing formulas, as we saw. Moreover, in later versions, he appears multiplied as Makunaímas. The Mbyá-Guarani creator shares his task with the hummingbird, and so on.

5. In *Antes o Mundo não Existia,* Yebá Buró creates herself from six elements, not four: a quartz stool, a fork to hold the cigarette, a bowl of *ipadu,* the support for this bowl, a bowl of manioc flour, and the support for this bowl.

6. The actors of *Roda Viva,* for instance, threw pieces of raw liver at the audience.

10. The Machiguenga and Their Heritage

1. See, for instance, Marcel D'Ans.

2. I would like to thank Professor Gerhard Baer, from the University of Basel, Switzerland, for kindly sending me a copy of these works.

3. In Cenitagoya's version of the Kashiri narrative, the spots on the moon are the uneaten remains of his wife's body.

11. *The Storyteller* (1987)

1. A computer version of these protests circulated on the Internet, generated by the Gruppe Hamburg, by the Deutsch-Chilenisches Kulturzentrum, the Sur Buchvertrieb and the Referat Kirchlicher Weltdienst des nordelbischen Missions-

zentrums und kirchlichen Weltdienstes. I would like to thank James Park for sending it to me.

2. Sara Castro-Klarén, for instance, describes the novel in the following way: "The novel will alternate chapters in which the author/narrator Vargas Llosa evokes his friendship with Zurata and their common interest in the Machiguengas" (206). And José Andres Rivas repeatedly calls the Florentine narrator "the character that represents Vargas Llosa."

3. See William Rowe for a further view of Vargas Llosa's complex relationship with the figure of José María Arguedas.

4. These welcoming formulas are strikingly similar to the Tupi ones transcribed by European chroniclers (see chapter 4).

5. Margaret Snook also pointed to the two labyrinths as an image of the structure of the novel, without referring to Casevitz: "The contrastive, parallel structure of the novel, which permits a view of the storyteller from within and from without, is echoed in one of the novel's striking images. While at the university, Saúl presents the narrator with a gift, a Machiguenga artifact which is engraved with the figures of two parallel labyrinths" (68).

6. Efraín Kristal (1998, 156–69) summarizes Vargas Llosa's rewriting of Machiguenga. He notes specifically that the storyteller figure was invented and that the Machiguenga are not nomadic. Yet he draws no conclusions, ideological or otherwise, from this recasting, and does take into account precisely the native narratives which Vargas Llosa drew most heavily on in his novel, those published by Barriales in *Antisuyo*. The argument I present here was previously set out in my doctoral dissertation (1997, 301–65) and in my article "Perverse Tribute" (1998).

7. The usage of the term *Tasurinchi* as the equivalent of a male proper name is thus explained by Elisa Calabrese: "Other data, however, complete the set of convergences and divergences; this happens when [the Schneil couple] explain that proper names, in Machiguenga, are provisional, relative and temporary (83), which enables the reader to get over the perplexity initially caused by the valency of the term, in which the proper name *Tasurinchi* indicates various subjects" (58). Wayne Snell tells us that the Machiguenga have no proper names (283); Casevitz-Renard, on the other hand, explains that naming among them is a complicated and lifelong activity: Names are given immediately after birth, not to be pronounced until the children can walk, and they are modified according to the bearer's important feats. Gerhard Baer adds that the Machiguenga avoid revealing their names to strangers (47).

8. See Emil Volek for further comments on this subject.

9. For the traditional housing habits of the Machiguenga, see Casevitz-Renard.

10. In fact, as Jean Franco puts it, although this narrator tries to present a reasonable and impartial image with respect to the Protestants and their Summer Institute of Linguistics, his sympathy for the changes they operate in the Machiguenga society is quite obvious: "This reasonable guise allows the author to make political and ideological judgements, passing them off as common sense. The most notorious example of this may be found in his references to the missionaries of the

Summer Institute of Linguistics, which sponsored his first visit to the Amazon for-est. Although Vargas Llosa does not negate the polemics around the Institute, he presents a basically benign image of the missionaries and carefully avoids entering into the shadier aspects of its relationship with national governments and indige-nous groups" (15).

Works Cited

Abbeville, Claude d'. 1963. *Histoire de la mission des pères capucins en l'isle de Maragnan et terres circunvoisines.* Graz: Akademische Druck- und Verlagsanstalt.

———. 1975. *História da Missão dos Padres Capuchinhos na Ilha do Maranhão e Terras Circunvizinhas.* Translated by Sérgio Milliet. Belo Horizonte: Itatiaia.

Achebe, Chinua. 1975. "Colonialist Criticism." In *Morning Yet on Creation Day.* New York: Double Day.

Acosta Cruz, María Isabel. 1990. "Writer-Speaker? Speaker-Writer? Narrative and Cultural Intervention in Mario Vargas Llosa's *El hablador.*" *Inti* 29–30: 133–45.

Alegre, Florencio Pascual. 1979. *Tashorintsi: tradición oral machiguenga.* Lima: Centro amazónico de antropología y aplicación práctica.

Alencar, José Martiniano de. 1962. *Ubirajara. Lenda Tupi.* São Paulo: Melhoramentos.

———. 1965. "Benção Paterna." *Obra Completa.* Vol. 1. Rio: Aguilar, 1965.

———. 2000. *Iracema.* 1865. Translated by Clifford E. Landers. Oxford: Oxford University Press.

———. n.d. *O Guarani.* Rio: Garnier.

Allen, Paula Gunn. 1983. "The Sacred Hoop: A Contemporary Indian Perspective on American Indian Literature." In *Symposium on the Whole: A Range of Discourse toward an Ethnopoetics.* Edited by Jerome Rothenberg and Diane Rothenberg. Berkeley: University of California Press.

Amorim, Antônio Brandão do. 1987. *Lendas em Nheengatú e em Português.* Manaus: Fundo Editorial-ACA.

Anchieta, José de. 1946. *Arte de Gramática da Língua Mais Usada na Costa do Brasil.* 1595. Reprint, São Paulo: Anchieta.

Andrade, Mário de. 1984. *Macunaíma.* Translated by E. A. Goodland. New York: Random House.

Andrade, Oswald de. 1998. "Anthropophagite Manifesto." Translated by Adriano Pedrosa and Veronica Cordeiro. In *XXIV Bienal de São Paulo: Núcleo Histórico: Antropofagia e Histórias de Canibalismo.* Vol. 1. São Paulo: Fundação Bienal.

Antelo, Raúl. 1988. "Macunaíma: Apropriação e Originalidade." In *Macunaíma. O Herói sem Nenhum Caráter,* edited by Telê Ancona Lopez. Paris: Association Archives de la Littérature Latino-Américaine, des Caraibes et Africaine du XXe Siècle. Brasilia: CNPQ.

Arens, William. 1979. *The Man-Eating Myth: Anthropology and Anthropophagy.* Oxford: Oxford University Press.

Arguedas, José María. 1975. "Puquio, una cultura nacional en proceso de cambio." In *Formación de una cultura nacional indoamericana.* Mexico City: Siglo XXI.

Armellada, Cesareo. 1948. *Gramática y diccionario de la lengua pemón.* 2 vols. Caracas: C. A. Artes Gráficas.

———. 1964. *Tauron Panton: cuentos y leyendas de los indios pemon.* Caracas: Ediciones del Ministerio de Educación.

———. 1972. *Pemontón Taremuru.* Caracas: Universidad Católica Andrés Bello.

———. 1973. *Tauron Panton II: así dice el cuento.* Caracas: Universidad Católica Andres Bello.

Arvello-Jiménez, Nelly, and Horacio Biord. 1994. "The Impact of Conquest on Contemporary Indigenous Peoples of the Guiana Shield." In *Amazonian Indians: From Prehistory to the Present,* edited by Anna Roosevelt. Tucson: The University of Arizona Press.

Averbuck, Lígia Morrone. 1985. *Cobra Norato e a Revolução Caraíba.* Rio: José Olympio.

Aza, José Pío. 1927. "Folklore de los salvajes machiguengas." *Revista de las Misiones Dominicanas* 43: 237–45.

Baer, Gerhard. 1994. *Cosmología y shamanismo de los matsiguenga (Perú oriental).* Quito: Abya-Yala.

Bakhtin, Mikhail. 1984. *Rabelais and His World.* Translated by Helene Iswolsky. Bloomington: Indiana University Press.

Baldus, Herbert. 1937. "O Professor Tiago Marques e o Caçador Apoburéu." In *Ensaios de Etnologia Brasileira.* São Paulo: Nacional.

Barcelo Sifontes, Lyll. 1982. *Pemonton wanamari: to maimu, to eseruk, to patasek—el espejo de los pemonton: su palabra, sus costumbres, su mundo.* Caracas: Monte Avila.

Barco Centenera, Martín del. 1965. *The Argentine and the Conquest of the River Plate.* Translated by Walter Owen. Buenos Aires: Insituto Cultural Walter Owen.

Bareiro Saguier, Rubén, ed. 1980. *Literatura guarani del Paraguay.* Caracas: Biblioteca Ayacucho.

———. 1990. *De nuestras lenguas y otros discursos.* Asunción: Universidad Católica Nuestra Señora de la Asuncíon.

Barker, Francis, Peter Hulme, and Margaret Iversen. 1998. *Cannibalism and the Colonial World.* Cambridge: Cambridge University Press.

Barreto, Afonso Henriques de Lima. 1978. *The Patriot.* Translated by Robert Scott-Buccleuch. London: Collins.

Barriales, Joaquín. 1977. *Matsigenka.* Lima: Misiones Dominicanas.

———. n.d. "Mitos de la cultura machiguenga." *Antisuyo* 3:163–181; 5:111–134; 6:138–159.

Basso, Ellen. 1987. *In Favor of Deceit. A Study of Tricksters in an Amazonian Society.* Tucson: University of Arizona Press.

Bhabha, Homi. 1994. *The Location of Culture.* London: Routledge.

Biocca, Ettore. 1965. *Viaggi tra gli indi: Alto Rio Negro, Alto Orinoco—appunti di un biólogo.* 4 vols. Roma: Consiglio Nazionale delle Ricerche.

Bolens, Jacqueline. 1967. "Mythe de Jurupari. Introduction a une analyse." *L'Homme. Revue française d'anthropologie* 7, no. 1: 50–66.

Bopp, Raul. 1966. *Movimentos Modernistas no Brasil. 1922–1928:* Rio: São José.

———. 1977. *Vida e Morte da Antropofagia.* Rio: Civilização Brasileira; Brasília: INL.

———. 1998. "Cobra Norato." In *Poesia Completa.* Edited by Augusto Massi. São Paulo: EDUSP/José Olympio. 125–193.

Bosi, Alfredo. 1970. *História Concisa da Literatura Brasileira.* São Paulo: Cultrix.

———. 1988. "Situação de *Macunaíma.*" In *Macunaíma. O Herói sem Nenhum Caráter,* edited by Telê Ancona Lopez. Paris: Association Archives de la Littérature Latino-American, des Caraibes et Africaine du XXe Siècle; Brasilia: CPNQ.

Brandenburger, Clemens. 1931. *Lendas dos Nossos Índios.* Rio: Francisco Alves.

Brook, Peter. 1996. *The Empty Space.* New York: Touchstone.

Brotherston, Gordon. 1979. *Image of the New World: The American Continent Portrayed in Native Texts.* London: Thames and Hudson.

———. 1987. "The Latin American Novel and Its Indigenous Sources." In *Modern Latin American Fiction: A Survey,* edited by John King. London: Faber and Faber.

———. 1992a. *Book of the Fourth World: Reading the Native Americas through Their Literature.* Cambridge: Cambridge University Press.

———. 1992b. "Gaspar Ilóm en su tierra." In *Hombres de maíz,* by Miguel Astúrias, edited by Gerald Martin. 2nd ed. Vol. 21 of Colección Archivos. Paris: ALLCA XX.

———. 1993. "Pacaraima as Destination in Carpentier's *Los Pasos Perdidos.*" *Indiana Journal of Hispanic Literatures* 1 no. 2: 161–83.

———. 1999. "Jurupary Articula o Espaço dos Tária e a Ciência da América Tropical." *Revista do Museu de Arqueologia e Etnologia da Universidade de São Paulo* 9: 259–67.

Bueno, Francisco da Silveira. 1998. *Vocabulário Tupi-Guarani-Português.* 6th ed. São Paulo: Brasilivros.

Büttner, Thomas T. 1989. *La rojez de anoche desde la cabaña.* Lima: Colmillo Blanco.

Cadogan, León. 1959. *Ayvu Rapyta: textos míticos de los mbyá-guarani del Guairá.* Vol. 227 of *Boletim da Faculdade de Filosofia, Ciências e Letras.* São Paulo: Universidade de São Paulo.

Caicedo de Cajigas, Cecilia. 1990. *Origen de la literatura colombiana: el yurupary.* Pereira: Universidad Tecnológica.

Calabrese, Elisa. 1993. "*El hablador* de Vargas Llosa o la imposibilidad de la utopía." *Discurso* 10 no. 2: 53–62.

Callado, Antonio. 1978. "As Três Viagens de Escritores Latino-Americanos." *Ensaios de Opinião* 6: 94–98.

———. 1982. *A Expedição Montaigne.* Rio: Nova Fronteira.

————. 1984. *Quarup*. Rio: Nova Fronteira.

Calvo, César. 1981. *Las tres mitades de Ino Moxo y otros brujos de la Amazonía*. Iquitos, Peru: Proceso.

Camargo, Suzana. 1977. *Macunaíma: Ruptura e Tradição*. São Paulo: Massao Ohno; João Farkas.

Caminha, Pero Vaz de. 1974. *Carta a el-rei dom Manuel sobre o achamento do Brasil. 1º de maio de 1500*. Lisboa: Imprensa Nacional; Casa da Moeda.

Campbell, Alan Tormaid. 1989. *To Square with Genesis: Causal Statements and Shamanic Ideas in Wayapí*. Iowa City: University of Iowa Press.

Campos, Augusto de. 1975. "Revistas Re-vistas: os Antropófagos." In *Revista de Antropofagia. Reedição da Revista Literária Publicada em São Paulo. 1a e 2a "Dentições." 1928–1929*. São Paulo: Abril.

Campos, Augusto de, and Haroldo de Campos. 1982. *ReVisão de Sousândrade: Textos Críticos, Antologia, Glossário e Biobibliografia*. Rio: Nova Fronteira.

Campos, Haroldo de. 1973. *Morfologia do Macunaíma*. São Paulo: Perspectiva.

————. 1983. A Linguagem do Iauaretê. In *Guimarães Rosa*, edited by Eduardo F. Coutinho. Rio: Civilização Brasileira.

Cardim, Fernão. 1939. *Tratados da Terra e da Gente do Brasil*. São Paulo: Nacional.

Carpentier, Alejo. 1956. *The Lost Steps*. Translated by Harriet de Onís. New York: Alfred Knopf.

————. 1990. "Visión de América." In *Obra Completa* 13. México: Siglo XXI.

Carroll, Michael P. 1984. "The Trickster as Selfish Buffoon and Culture Hero." *Ethos* 12 no. 2: 105–31.

Carvalho, Flávio de. 2001. *Experiência N º 2 realizada sobre uma procissão de corpus christi. Uma possível teoria e uma experiência*. Rio: Nau.

Carvajal, Fray Gaspar de. 1992. *Relación del nuevo descubrimiento del Rio Grande de las amazonas*. Quito: Comisión Nacional Permanente de Conmemoraciones Cívicas; Museo Antropológico del Banco Central de Guayaquil.

Cascudo, Luiz da Câmara. 1936. *Em Memória de Stradelli*. Manaus: Livraria clássica.

————. 1972. *Dicionário do Folclore Brasileiro*. Vol. 1. Brasília: Instituto Nacional do Livro/ MEC.

————. 1983. *Geografia dos Mitos Brasileiros*. Belo Horizonte: Itatiaia; São Paulo: EDUSP.

Casevitz, France-Marie. 1980–81. "Inscriptions. Un aspect du symbolisme matsiguenga." *Journal de la Societé des Americanistes* 68: 261–95.

Casevitz-Renard, F.M. 1972. "Les Matsiguenga." *Journal de la Societé des Américanistes* 61: 215–53.

Castello, José Aderaldo. 1953. *A Polêmica sôbre a Confederação dos Tamoios*. São Paulo: FFCL-USP.

Castro, Eduardo B. Viveiros de. 1986. *Araweté: os deuses canibais*. Rio: Jorge Zahar.

————. 1987. "Nimuendaju e os Guarani." In *As Lendas da Criação e Destruição do Mundo como Fundamentos da Religião dos Apapocúva-Guarani*, by Curt Nimuendaju, translated by Charlotte Emmerich and Eduardo B. Viveiros de Castro. São Paulo: Hucitec/Edusp.

Castro Arrasco, Dante. 1986. *Otorongo y otros cuentos*. Lima: Lluvia.

———. 1991. *Parte de combate*. N.p.: Manguaré.

Castro-Klarén, Sara. 1990. "Myth, Ideology, and Revolution: From Mayta to Tasurinchi." In *Understanding Mario Vargas Llosa*. Columbia, SC: University of South Carolina Press.

Cenitagoya, Fr. Vicente de. 1943. *Los machiguengas*. Lima: Sanmarti.

Chateaubriand, François-René. 1978. *The Natchez*. 3 vols. New York: H. Fertig.

———.1963. *Atala and René*. Translated by Rayner Heppenstall. London: Oxford University Press.

Chiampi, Irlemar. 1989. "Sobre la teoría de la creación artística en *Los pasos perdidos*, de Alejo Carpentier." *Cuadernos Americanos* 3 no. 14: 101–16.

Civrieux, Marc de. 1980. *Watunna: An Orinoco Creation Cycle*. Edited and translated by David Guss. San Francisco: North Point.

Clastres, Hélène. 1995. *The Land without Evil : Tupi-Guarani prophetism*. Translated by Jacqueline Grenez Brovender. Urbana: University of Illinois Press.

Colbacchini, Antonio, and Cesar Albisetti. 1942. *Os Boróros Orientais: Orarimogodogue do Planalto Oriental de Mato Grosso*. São Paulo: Nacional.

Cooper, James Fenimore. 1985. *The Leatherstocking Tales*. 2 vols. New York: Viking Press.

Coutinho, Afrânio, ed. 1965. *A Polêmica Alencar-Nabuco*. Rio: Tempo Brasileiro.

Cowell, Adrian. 1961. *The Heart of the Forest*. New York: Alfred Knopf.

Cunha, Euclides da. 1944. *Rebellion in the Backlands*. Translated by Samuel Putnum. Chicago: University of Chicago Press.

Cunha, Manuela Carneiro da, ed. 1992. *História dos Índios no Brasil*. São Paulo: FAPESP; Companhia das Letras; SMC.

———. 1993. "Imagens de Índios do Brasil: o século XVI." In *Palavra, Literatura e Cultura*, edited by Ana Pizarro. São Paulo: Unicamp; Fundação Memorial da América Latina.

D'Ans, Marcel. 1975. *La verdadera Bíblia de los cashinaua*. Lima: Mosca Azul.

Davis, Harold, and Betty Elkins de Snell. 1976. *Kenkitsatagantsi matsigenka: Cuentos folkloricos de los machiguega*. Yarinacocha, Peru: Instituto Lingüístico de Verano.

Dénis, Ferdinand. 1850. *Une Fête Brésilienne Célébrée a Rouen en 1550*. Paris: J. Techener.

———. 1968. *Resumo da História Literária do Brasil*. Translated by Guilhermino César. Porto Alegre: Lima.

———. *Os Maxacalis*. 1979. Translated by Maria Cecília de Moraes Pinto. São Paulo: SCCT.

Dias, Antonio Gonçalves. 1965. "Americanas." In *Poesias Completas de Gonçalves Dias*. Vol. 2. Rio: Científica.

———. n.d. "O Brasil e a Oceania." *Obras Posthumas de Gonçalves Dias*. Rio: Garnier.

———. n.d. "Meditação." *Obras Posthumas de Gonçalves Dias*. Rio: Garnier.

Dundes, Alan. 1962. "The Morphology of North American Indian Folktales." Ph.D. diss., Indiana University.

Durbin, Marshall. 1985. "A Survey of the Carib Language Family." In *South American*

Indian Languages, edited by Harriet E. Manelis Klein and Louisa R. Stark. Austin: University of Texas Press.

Everhart, Jill Courtney. 1993. "Mario Vargas Llosa's *El Hablador*: Cultural Understanding and Respect through the Art of Storytelling." Master's thesis, University of Virginia.

Évreux, Yves d'. 1864. *Voyage dans le nord du Brésil fait durant les années 1613 et 1614 par le père Yves d'Évreux.* Edition de Ferdinand Dénis. Leipzig; Paris: A. Franck.

Fabre, Alain. 1998. *Manual de las lenguas indígenas sudamericanas.* 2 vols. München: Lincom Europa.

Farage, Nádia. 1991. *Muralhas dos sertões. Os indígenas no rio Branco e a colonização.* SP: Paz & Terra; ANPOCS.

Fausto, Carlos. 1992. "Fragmentos de História e Cultura Tupinambá. Da etnologia como instrumento crítico de conhecimento etno-histórico." In *História dos Índios no Brasil,* edited by Manuela Carneiro da Cunha. São Paulo: FAPESP; Companhia das Letras; SMC.

Fernandes, Florestan. 1960. "Tiago Marques Apoburéu: um Bororo Marginal." In *Mudanças Sociais no Brasil.* São Paulo: Difusão Européia.

———. 1970. *A Função Social da Guerra na Sociedade Tupinambá.* 2d ed. São Paulo: Pioneira; EDUSP.

Ferreira de Castro, José Maria. 1930. *A Selva.* Lisboa: Guimarães.

Ferrero, Andres. 1967. *Los machiguengas: tribu selvática del sur-oriente peruano.* Villava-Pamplona, Peru: OPE.

Fonseca, Maria Augusta. 1988. "A Carta pras Icamiabas." In *Macunaíma. O Herói sem Nenhum Caráter,* by Mário de Andrade, edited by Telê Porto Ancona Lopez. Paris: Association Archives de la Littérature Latino-Américaine, des Caraibes et Africaine du XXe Siècle; Brasilia: CNPQ.

Franco, Affonso Arinos de Melo. 1937. *O Índio Brasileiro e a Revolução Francesa.* Rio: José Olympio.

Franco, Jean. 1991. "¿La historia de quien? La piratería postmoderna." *Revista de crítica literaria latinoamericana* 33: 11–20.

Galeano, Eduardo. 1987. *Genesis.* Vol. 1, *Memory of Fire.* Translated by Cedric Belfrage. New York: Pantheon.

Gallegos, Rómulo. 1948. *Doña Bárbara.* Translated by Robert Malloy. New York: P. Smith.

———. 1984. *Canaima.* Translated by Jaime Tello. Norman: University of Oklahoma Press.

———. 1996. *Canaima.* Edited by Michael Doudoroff, and translated by Will Kirkland. Paris: ALLCA XXᵉ/UNESCO; Pittsburgh: University of Pittsburgh Press.

Galvão, Eduardo. 1959. "Aculturação Indígena no Rio Negro." *Boletim do Museu Paraense Emílio Goeldi. Antropologia* 7: 37–52.

Galvão, Walnice Nogueira. 1979. "Indianismo Revisitado." *Cadernos de Opinião* 13: 36–43.

Gandavo, Pero de Magalhães. 1964. *História da Província de Santa Cruz. Tratado da Terrado Brasil.* 1576. São Paulo: Obelisco.

Garcia, Othon Moacyr. 1962. *Cobra Norato. O Poema e o Mito.* Rio: São José.

García, Secundino. 1935. "Mitología machiguenga." *Misiones dominicanas del Perú* 17: 95–99, 170–79, 220–28.

———. 1936. "Mitología machiguenga." *Misiones dominicanas del Perú* 18: 2–13, 86–97, 131–39, 166–76, 212–19.

———. 1937. "Mitología machiguenga." *Misiones dominicanas del Perú* 19: 11–17.

García-Canclini, Néstor. 1995. *Hybrid Cultures: Strategies for Entering and Leaving Modernity.* Translated by Christopher L. Chippari and Silvia L. López. Minneapolis: University of Minnesota Press.

Gilii, Filippo Salvatore. 1780–1784. *Saggio di storia americana, o sia storia naturalle, civile, e sacra du regni e delle provincie spagnuole di terra-ferma nell'America meridionale.* 4 vols. Roma: Per Luigi Perego.

Giorgi, Diógenes de. 1989. *Martín del Barco Centenera. Cronista fundamental del Río de la Plata.* Montevideo: Nuevo Mundo.

Goldman, Irving. 1963. *The Cubeo: Indians of the Northwest Amazon.* Vol. 2 of *Illinois Studies in Anthropology.* Urbana: Illinois University Press.

González, Natalício. 1958. *Ideología guaraní.* Vol. 37, Ediciones Especiales. México City: Instituto Indigenista Interamericano.

González Echevarría, Roberto. 1990a. *Alejo Carpentier: The Pilgrim at Home.* Austin: University of Texas Press.

———. 1990b. *Myth and Archive. A Theory of Latin American Narrative.* Cambridge: Cambridge University Press.

———. 1996. "Canaima and the Jungle Books." In *Canaima,* by Rómulo Gallegos, edited by Michael Doudoroff and translated by Will Kirkland. Paris: ALLCA XXᵉ/UNESCO; Pittsburgh: University of Pittsburgh Press.

Greene, Roland. 1999. *Unrequited Conquests. Love and Empire in the Colonial Americas.* Chicago: University of Chicago Press.

Grenand, Françoise, et. al. 1987. *Contes amérindiens de Guayane.* Paris: Conseil international de la langue française.

Grillo, Cristina. 1996. "Vargas Llosa afirma literatura engajada." *Folha de São Paulo,* 7 October.

Guaman Poma de Ayala, Felipe. 1980. *El primer nueva corónica y buen gobierno.* Edited by J. V. Murra and R. Adorno, 3 vols. Mexico City: Siglo XXI.

Güiraldes, Ricardo. 1995. *Don Segundo Sombra.* Edited by Gwen Kirkpatrick and translated by Patricia Owen Steiner. Pittsburgh: University of Pittsburgh Press.

Guss, David. 1985. *The Language of the Birds.* San Francisco: North Point.

———. 1986. Keeping It Oral: A Yekuana Ethnology. *American Ethnologist* 13 no. 3: 413–29.

———. 1989. *To Weave and Sing: Art, Symbol and Narrative in the South American Rain Forest.* Berkeley: University of California Press.

Gutiérrez, Juan María. 1945. *Poesías.* Buenos Aires: Estrada.

Harris, Wilson. 1968. *Palace of the Peacock.* London: Faber and Faber.

Hart, Catherine Poupeney. 1990. "Le rejet de la chronique ou la construction de l'utopie archaïque dans *L'homme qui parle* de Mario Vargas Llosa." In *Parole exclusive, parole exclue, parole transgressive: Marginalisation et marginalité dans les pratiques discursives,* edited by Antonio Gomez-Moriana and Catherine Poupeney Hart. Longueuil, Québec: Préambule.

Hartt, Charles Frederick. 1875. *Amazon Tortoise Myths.* Rio de Janeiro: n.p.

Hecht, Susanna B., and Alexander Cockburn. 1989. *The Fate of the Forest: Developers, Destroyers, and Defenders of the Amazon.* London: Verso.

Heckenberger, Michael, Eduardo G. Neves, and James Petersen. 1998. "De onde surgem os modelos? As origens e expansões Tupi na Amazônia Central." *Revista de Antropologia (USP)* 41 no. 1: 69–96.

Hill, Jonathan D. 1990. "Poetic Transformations of Narrative Discourse in an Amazonian Society." *Journal of Folklore Research* 27 no. 1–2: 115–31.

Hudson, William Henry. 1998. *Green Mansions.* Edited by Ian Duncan. Oxford; New York: Oxford University Press.

Hugh-Jones, Stephen. 1979. *The Palm and the Pleiades: Initiation and Cosmology in Northwest Amazonia.* Cambridge: Cambridge University Press.

Huxley, Francis. 1956. *The Affable Savages.* London: Rupert Hart-Davis.

Ibáñez, Sara de. 1960. *Canto a Montevideo.* Buenos Aires: Losada.

Jackson, Michael. 1996. *Things As They Are: New Directions in Phenomenological Anthropology.* Bloomington: Indiana University Press.

Jecupé, Kaká Werá. n.d. *Oré Awé Roiru'a Ma. Todas as Vezes que Dissemos Adeus.* São Paulo: Fundação Phytoervas.

Jung, Carl G. 1993. "On the Psychology of the Trickster Figure." In *Symposium of the Whole: A Range of Discourse Toward an Ethnopoetics,* edited by Jerome Rothenberg and Diane Rothenberg. Berkeley: University of California Press.

Kempen, Michiel van. 1989. *Surinaamse Schrijvers en Dichters.* Amsterdam: De Arbeiderpers.

Koch-Grünberg, Theodor. 1928. *Vom Roroima zum Orinoco. Ergebnisse einer Reise in Nordbrasilien und Venezuela in den Jahren 1911–1913.* 4 vols. Berlin: D. Reimer.

———. 1967. *Zwei Jahre unter den Indianern. Reisen in Nordwest–Brasilien 1903/ 1905.* Graz: Akademische Druck.

———. 1984. *Del Roraima al Orinoco.* Translated by Federica de Ritter. 3 vols. Caracas: Banco Central de Venezuela.

Kristal, Efraín. 1998. *Temptation of the Word. The Novels of Mario Vargas Llosa.* Nashville: Vanderbilt University Press.

Ladeira, Maria Inês, and Gilberto Azanha. 1988. *Os Índios da Serra do Mar. A Presença Mbyá-Guarani em São Paulo.* São Paulo: Centro de Trabalho Indigenista; Stella.

Lagório, Eduardo. 1983. *100 Kixti (Estórias) Tukano.* Brasília: Funai.

Lentzen, Norbert. 1996. *Literatur und Gesellschaft: Studien zum Verhältnis zwischen Realität und Fiktion in den Romanen Mario Vargas Llosas.* Bonn: Romanistischer Verlag.

León Mera, Juan. 1976. *Cumandá: o un drama entre salvajes.* 1879. Madrid: Espasa-Calpe.

Léry, Jean de. 1990. *History of a Voyage to the Land of Brazil, Otherwise Called America*. Translated by Janet Whatley. Berkeley: University of California Press.

Lévi-Strauss, Claude. 1973. *From Honey to Ashes*. Vol. 2, *Introduction to a Science of Mythology*. Translated by John and Doreen Weightman. London: Jonathan Cape.

———. 1990a. *The Naked Man*. Translated by John and Doreen Weightman. Chicago: University of Chicago Press, 1990.

———. 1990b. *The Origin of Table Manners*. Translated by John and Doreen Weightman. Chicago: University of Chicago Press.

———. 1990c. *The Raw and the Cooked*. Translated by John and Doreen Weightman. Chicago: University of Chicago Press.

Lienhard, Martin. 1978. "Apuntes sobre los desdoblamientos, la mitología americana y la escritura en *Yo el Supremo*." *Hispamérica* 7: 3–12.

———. 1992. *La voz y su huella*. Lima: Horizonte.

Lopez, Telê Porto Ancona. 1974. *Macunaíma: A Margem e o Texto*. São Paulo: Hucitec; SCET.

Lopez, Telê Porto Ancona, ed. 1988. *Macunaíma. O Herói sem Nenhum Caráter*, by Mário de Andrade. Critical Edition. Vol. 6 of Coleção Archivos. Paris: Association Archives de la Littérature latino-américaine, des Caraibes et africaine du XXe Siècle; Brasilia: CNPQ.

Lugon, Clovis. 1977. *A República "Comunista" Cristã dos Guaranis. 1610/1768*. Translated by Álvaro Cabral. Rio: Paz e Terra.

Machado de Assis, Joaquim Maria. 1924. "Americanas." In *Poesias Completas: Chrysalidas, Phalenas, Americanas, Occidentaes*. Rio: Garnier.

Maestri, Mário. 1994. *Os Senhores do Litoral. Conquista Portuguesa e Agonia Tupinambá no Litoral Brasileiro*. Porto Alegre: Editora da Universidade.

Magalhães, José Vieira Couto de. 1913. *O Selvagem*. Rio: Magalhães.

Magalhães, José Gonçalves de. 1864. *A Confederação dos Tamoyos: Poema*. Coimbra: Imprensa Literária.

Marcone, Jorge. 1993. "*El Hablador* de Mario Vargas Llosa y la Imagen de la Amazonía en el Perú Contemporáneo." *La Chispa 93. Selected Proceedings*, edited by Gilbert Paolini. New Orleans: Tulane University Press.

Marcoy, Paul. 1875. *Travels in South America: From the Pacific Ocean to the Atlantic Ocean*. Translated by Elihu Rich. Vol. 1. New York: Scribner, Armstrong.

Mariani, Bethania S.C. 1998. "L'Institutionnalisation de la langue, de la mémoire et de la citoyenneté au Brésil durant le XVIIᵉ siècle: Le rôle des académies littéraires et de la politique du Marquis de Pombal." *Langages* 130: 84–96.

Martin, Gerald. 1989. *Journeys through the Labyrinth: Latin American Fiction in the Twentieth Century*. London: Verso.

Martín-Barbero, Jesús. 1993. *Communication, Culture, and Hegemony: From Media to Mediations*. London: Sage.

Martins, Heitor. 1973. "Canibais Europeus e Antropófagos Brasileiros." In *Oswald de Andrade e Outros*. São Paulo: Conselho Estadual de Cultura.

Martins, Wilson. 1965. *O Modernismo*. Vol. 6 of *Literatura Brasileira*. São Paulo: Cultrix.

Matos, Cláudia Neiva de. 1988. *Gentis Guerreiros*. São Paulo: Atual.

Medeiros, Sérgio Luiz Rodrigues. 1991. *O Dono dos Sonhos*. São Paulo: Razão Social.

Meihy, José Carlos Sebe Bom. 1991. *Canto de Morte Kaiowá: História Oral de Vida*. São Paulo: Edições Loyola.

Meira, Márcio. 1993. *Livro das Canoas. Documentos para a História Indígena da Amazônia*. São Paulo: Fapesp and Núcleo de História Indígena e do Indigenismo.

Meliá, Bartolomeu, S.J. 1986. *El guaraní conquistado y reducido. Ensayos de etnohistória*. Asunción: Universidad Católica.

Mello, Zuleika. 1972. *A Profecia da Cobra Grande ou a Transamazônica*. Rio: Serviço Nacional de Teatro.

Mendoza, José and François Correa. 1992. *Relatos míticos cubeo*. Santafé de Bogotá: Servicio Colombiano de Documentación.

Métraux, Alfred de. 1950a. "Jaguar-Man." In *Funk & Wagnalls Standard Dictionary of Folklore, Mythology, and Legend*, edited by Maria Leach. Vol. 2. New York: Funk and Wagnalls.

———. 1950b. *A Religião dos Tupinambás e suas Relações com as Demais Tribos Tupi-Guarani*. Translated by Estevão Pinto. São Paulo: Editora Nacional.

Migliazza, Ernest C. 1985. "Languages of the Orinoco-Amazon Region: Current Status." In *South American Indian Languages*, edited by Harriet E. Manelis Klein and Louisa R. Stark. Austin: University of Texas Press.

Mindlin, Betty, and Suruí Indians. 1995. *Unwritten Stories of the Suruí Indians of Rondonia*. Translated by Sonia Nussenzweig Hotimsky. Austin: University of Texas Press.

Miyazaki, Tieko Yamaguchi. 1980. "*Canaima* no Contexto dos Romances sobre a Selva." *Revista de Letras* 20: 75–87.

Montaigne, Michel de. 1993. "On the Cannibals." In *Essays*. Translated by M. A. Screech. London: Penguin.

Monteiro, John Manuel. 1994. *Os Negros da Terra. Índios e Bandeirantes nas Origens de São Paulo*. São Paulo: Companhia das Letras.

Moraes, Raimundo de. 1936. *Na Planície Amazônica*. 4th ed. São Paulo: Companhia Editora Nacional.

Moran, Emilio F. 1993. *Through Amazonian Eyes. The Human Ecology of Amazonian Populations*. Iowa City: University of Iowa Press.

Moreira, Ismael Pedrosa, and Ângelo Barra Moreira. 1994. *Mitologia Tariana*. Manaus: Instituto Brasileiro de Patrimônio Cultural.

Murphy, Yolanda, and Robert F. Murphy. 1974. *Women of the Forest*. New York: Columbia University Press.

Nabuco, Joaquim. 1941. *O Direito no Brasil*. São Paulo: Nacional.

Nery, F. J. de Santa-Anna. 1889. *Folk-lore brésilien*. Paris: Perrin.

Neves, Eduardo Góes. 1998. "Paths in Dark Waters: Archaeology as Indigenous History in the Upper Rio Negro Basin, Northwest Amazon." Ph.D. diss., Indiana University.

Nimuendaju, Curt. 1914. "Die Sagen von der Erschaffung und Vernichtung der Welt als Grundlagen der Religion der Apapocuva-Guaraní." *Zeitschrift für Ethnologie* 46: 284–403.

———. 1915. "Die Sagen der Tembé-Indianer (Pará und Maranhão)." *Zeitchrift für Ethnologie* 47: 281–301.

———. 1950–55. "Reconhecimento dos Rios Içana, Ayari e Uaupés." *Journal de la Sociétè des Américanistes* 39 no. 44: 149–78

———. 1987. *As Lendas da Criação e Destruição do Mundo como Fundamentos da Religião dos Apapocúva-Guarani.* Translated by Charlotte Emmerich and Eduardo B. Viveiros de Castro. São Paulo: Hucitec/Edusp.

Nóbrega, Manuel da, S.J. 1959. "Diálogo sobre a Conversão dos Gentios." In *A Conversão do Gentio,* by Mecenas Dourado. Rio: São José.

Noelli, Francisco da Silva. 1996. "As Hipóteses sobre o Centro de Origem e Rotas de Expansão dos Tupi." *Revista de Antropologia (USP)* 39 no. 2: 7–53.

Noronha, Ramiro. 1952. *Exploração e Levantamento do Rio Culuene, Principal Formador do Rio Xingu. Reconhecimento de Verificação ao Divisor Arinos-Paranatinga. Fundação dum Posto de Proteção aos Índios, Medição e Demarcação de Terras para os Bacairi.* Rio: Departamento de Imprensa Nacional.

Nunes, Benedito. 1972. "A Antropofagia ao Alcance de Todos." In *Do Pau Brasil à Antropofagia e às Utopias,* by Oswald de Andrade. Vol. 6 of *Obras Completas.* Rio: Civilização Brasileira.

———. 1979. *Oswald Canibal.* São Paulo: Perspectiva.

Oliveira-Cézar, Filiberto. 1892. *Leyendas de los indios guaraníes.* Buenos Aires: Penser.

Orjuela, Héctor H. 1983. *Yurupary: mito, leyenda y epopeya del Vaupés.* Bogotá: Instituto Caro y Cuervo.

Pagden, Anthony. 1982. *Fall of Natural Man: The American Indian and the Origins of Comparative Ethnology.* Cambridge: Cambridge University Press.

Pārōkumu, Umusĩ and Tōrāmũ Kēhíri. 1995. *Antes o Mundo não Existia. Mitologia dos Antigos Desana-Kēhíripōrã.* São João Batista do Rio Tiquié: UNIRT/FOIRN.

Paula, Eunice Dias de, Luiz Gouvea de Paula, and Elizabeth Aracy Rondon Amarante, eds. 1984. *Confederação dos Tamoios: a união que nasceu do sofrimento.* Brasília: CIMI; Petrópolis: Vozes.

Pereira, Fidel. 1942. "Leyendas machiguengas." *Revista del Museo Nacional (Lima)* 11 no. 2: 240–44.

———. 1944. "Chaingavane: el Pongo del Mainiqui y los petroglifos." *Revista del Museo Nacional (Lima)* 13: 84–88.

Pereira, Lúcia Miguel. 1943. *A Vida de Gonçalves Dias.* Rio: José Olympio.

Pereira, Manuel Nunes. 1940. *Bahíra e suas experiências: etnologia amazônica.* Belém do Pará: Martins.

———. 1946. *Curt Nimuendaju: Síntese de uma vida e de uma obra.* Belém: n.p.

———. 1954. *Os Índios Maués.* Rio: Organização Simões.

———. 1967. *Moronguetá: Um Decameron Indígena.* 2 vols. Rio: Civilização Brasileira.

Pinto, Ernesto. 1964. "De nuestros abuelos y de los piaches." In *Tauron Panton*, by Cesáreo Armellada. Caracas: Ediciones del Ministerio de Educación.

Posse, Abel. 1989. *Daimón*. Buenos Aires: Emecé.

Prado, Paulo. 1922. "Glossário das palavras e frases da língua tupí, contidas na *Histoire de la mission des pères capucins en l'isle de Maragnan et terres circonvoisines*, do Padre Claude d'Abbeville." *Revista do Instituto Histórico e Geográfico Brasileiro* 148: 5–100.

Pratt, Mary Louise. 1992. *Imperial Eyes. Travel Writing and Transculturation*. London: Routledge.

Proença, M. Cavalcanti. 1987. *Roteiro de Macunaíma*. Rio: Civilização Brasileira.

Propp, Vladimir. 1971. *Morphology of the Folktale*. Translated by Laurence Scott. Austin: University of Texas Press.

Quiroga, Horacio.1967. *Cuentos de la selva*. Buenos Aires: Losada.

———. 1968. *Obras inéditas y desconocidas*. Vols. 4–5. Montevideo: Arca.

Radin, Paul. 1956. *The Trickster: A Study in American Indian Mythology*. London: Routledge.

Rama, Angel. 1982. *Transculturación narrativa en América Latina*. México City: Siglo XXI.

Ramos, Alcida. 1988. "Indian Voices: Contact Experienced and Expressed." In *Rethinking History and Myth: Indigenous South American Perspectives on the Past*, edited by Jonathan Hill. Urbana: University of Illinois Press.

———. 1998. "Development Does not Rhyme with Indian, or Does It?" In *Indigenism: Ethnic Politics in Brazil*. Madison: University of Wisconsin Press.

Rangel, Alberto. 1927. *Inferno Verde. Scenas e Scenarios do Amazonas*. Rio: Arrault.

Reichel-Dolmatoff, Gerardo. 1971. *Amazonian Cosmos. The Sexual and Religious Symbolism of the Tukano Indians*. Chicago: University of Chicago Press.

———. 1989. "Biological and Social Aspects of the Yuruparí Complex of the Colombian Vaupés Territory." *Journal of Latin American Lore* 15 no. 1: 95–135.

———. 1996. *Yuruparí. Studies of an Amazon Foundation Myth*. Cambridge, Massachusetts: Harvard University Center for Study of World Religions.

Reis, Arthur Cézar Ferreira. 1931. *História do Amazonas*. Manaus: n.p.

Renard-Casevitz, France-Marie. 1992. "História Kampa, Memória Ashaninca." In *História dos Índios no Brasil*, edited by Manuela Carneiro da Cunha. São Paulo: FAPESP; Companhia das Letras; SMC.

Ribeiro, Berta. 1980. "Os Índios das Águas Pretas." In *Antes o Mundo não Existia: A Mitologia Heróica dos Índios Desâna*, by Umúsin Panlõn Kumu. 1st ed. São Paulo: Livraria Cultura Editora.

Ribeiro, Darcy. 1970. *Os Índios e a Civilização*. Rio: Civilização Brasileira.

———. 1974. "Uirá vai ao Encontro de Maíra—as Experiências de um Índio que saiu à Procura de Deus." In *Uirá sai à Procura de Deus: Ensaios de Etnologia e Indigenismo*. Rio: Paz e Terra.

———. 1982. *A Utopia Selvagem*. Rio: Paz e Terra.

———. 1984. *Maíra*. Translated by E. H. Goodland and Thomas Colchie. New York: Aventura.

———. 1996. *Diários Índios: os Urubus-Kaapor.* São Paulo: Companhia das Letras.

Riester, Jürgen. 1984. *Textos sagrados de los Guaraníes en Bolivia.* La Paz: Los Amigos del Libro.

Rivas, José Andres. 1988. "*El hablador*: metáfora de una autobiografía nostálgica." *Antípodas* 1: 190–200.

Rivera, José Eustasio. 1935. *Vortex.* Translated by Earle K. James. London: Putnam.

Roa Bastos, Augusto. 1960. *El naranjal ardiente: nocturno paraguayo.* Asunción: Diálogo.

———. 1986. *I, the Supreme.* Translated by Helen Lane. New York: Knopf.

———. 1988. *Son of Man.* Translated by Rachel Caffyn. New York: Monthly Review.

Rodó, José Enrique. 1967. "Rubén Darío." *Obras Completas.* Madrid: Aguilar.

Rodrigues, João Barbosa. 1881. "Lendas, Crenças e superstições." *Revista Brasileira* 10: 24–47.

———. 1890. *Poranduba Amazonense ou Kochiyma Uara Porandub: 1872–1887.* Rio: Leuzinger.

———. 1899. *Muyrakytã e os Ídolos Symbólicos: Estudo da Origem Asiática da Civilização do Amazonas nos Tempos Prehistóricos.* 2nd ed. Muito Aumentada. Rio: Imprensa Nacional.

Roe, Peter. 1982. *The Cosmic Zygote: Cosmology in the Amazon Basin.* New Brunswick: Rutgers University Press.

Romero, Sílvio. 1943. *História da Literatura Brasileira.* Vol. 3. Rio: José Olympio.

———. 1977. *Estudos Sobre a Poesia Popular do Brasil.* Petrópolis: Vozes.

Rosa, João Guimarães. 1963. *The Devil to Pay in the Backlands.* Translated by James Taylor and Harriet de Onis.

———. 2001. "The Jaguar." In *The Jaguar and Other Stories,* edited and translated by David Treece. Oxford: Boulevard.

Rotella, Pilar V. 1994. "Hablador, escribidor, escritor: Mario Vargas Llosa y el poder de la Palabra." In *Mario Vargas Llosa: Opera omnia,* edited by Ana María Hernández de López. Madrid: Pliegos.

Roth, Walter. 1915. "An Inquiry into the Animism and Folk-Lore of the Guiana Indians." In *Thirtieth Annual Report of the Bureau of American Ethnology.* Washington, D.C.: Smithsonian Institution.

Rowe, William. 1996. *Hacia una poética radical. Ensayos de hermenéutica cultural.* Lima: Mosca Azul; Beatriz Viberbo.

Ruiz de Montoya, Antonio. 1989. *Conquista espiritual hecha por los religiosos de la Compañia de Jesus en las provincias de Paraguay, Paraná, Uruguay y Tape.* Rosario: Equipo difusor de estudios de historia iberoamericana.

Rumrrill, Róger. 1992. *El venado sagrado: relatos de la Amazonía.* N.p.: Centro de Estudios Regionales de Cultura Amazónica.

Sá, Lúcia. 1990. "A Literatura entre a Antropologia e a História: uma leitura de *Maíra* e *Quarup.*" Master's thesis, Universidade de São Paulo.

———. 1993. "A Dor e o Gozo de ser Índio. Interview with Darcy Ribeiro." *Indiana Journal of Hispanic Literatures* 1 no. 2: 161–83.

Salgado, Plínio, Menotti del Picchia, and Cassiano Ricardo. 1972. "Manifesto

Nheengaçu Verde Amarelo." In *Vanguarda Européia e Modernismo Brasileiro. Apresentação Crítica dos Principais Manifestos, Prefácios e Conferências Vanguardistas, de 1857 até Hoje*, edited by Gilberto Mendonça Teles. Rio: Vozes.

Santiago, Silviano. 1988. "A Trajetória de um Livro." In *Macunaíma. O Herói sem Nenhum Caráter*, by Mário de Andrade, edited by Telê Porto Ancona Lopez. Paris: ALLCA XX; Brasilia: CNPQ.

Santilli, Paulo. 1994. *Fronteiras da República. História e Política Entre os Macuxi no Vale do Rio Branco*. São Paulo: Fapesp & Núcleo de História Indígena e do Indigenismo.

Sarmiento, Domingo Faustino. 1961. *Life in the Argentine Republic in the Days of the Tyrants; or Civilization and Barbarism*. New York: Collier.

Schaden, Egon. 1959. *A Mitologia Heróica de Tribos Indígenas do Brasil. Ensaio Etno-sociológico*. Rio: Serviço de Documentação do Ministério da Educação e Cultura.

———. 1962. *Aspectos Fundamentais da Cultura Guarani*. São Paulo: Difusão Européia.

Schomburgk, Richard. 1848. *Travels in British Guiana During the Years 1840–1844*. 2 vols. Translated by Walter E. Roth. Georgetown, Guyana: Daily Chronicle.

Silva, P. Alcionílio Brüzzi da. 1962. *A Civilização Indígena do Uaupés*. São Paulo: Missão Salesiana.

———. 1994. *Crenças e Lendas do Uaupés*. Quito: Ediciones Abya-Yala; Manaus: Inspetoria Salesiana Missionária da Amazônia; Centro de Documentação Etnográfica e Missionária.

Simões, Maria do Socorro, and Christophe Golder, eds. 1995. *Abaetetuba conta*. Belém: Universidade Federal do Pará.

Siqueira, Priscila. 1984. *Genocídio dos Caiçaras*. São Paulo: Massao Ohno.

Slater, Candace. 1994. *Dance of the Dolphin: Transformation and Disenchantment in the Amazonian Imagination*. Chicago: University of Chicago Press.

Snell, Wayne. 1972. "El Sistema de Parentesco Entre los Machiguengas." *Historia y cultura* 6: 277–92.

Snook, Margaret L. 1991. "Reading and Writing for Meaning: Narrative and Biography in *El Hablador*." *Mester* 20 no. 1: 63–71.

Sommer, Doris. 1991. *Foundational Fictions: The National Romances of Latin America*. Berkeley: California University Press.

Sousa, Gabriel Soares de. 1971. *Tratado Descritivo do Brasil em 1587*. São Paulo: Nacional; Edusp.

Sousândrade, Joaquim de. 1979. *O Guesa*. Edited by Jomar Moraes. São Luís, Maranhão: Sioge.

Souza, Antônio Cândido de Mello e. 1971. *Formação da Literatura Brasileira*. Vol. 2. São Paulo: Martins.

Souza, Eneida Maria de. 1988. *"Macunaíma": A Pedra Mágica do Discurso*. Belo Horizonte: Editora UFMG.

Souza, Gilda de Mello e. 1979. *O Tupi e o Alaúde: Uma Interpretação de "Macunaíma."* São Paulo: Duas Cidades.

Souza, Inglez de. 1946. *O Missionário*. Rio: José Olympio.

Souza, Márcio. 1977. *The Emperor of the Amazon*. Translated by Thomas Colchie. New York: Avon.

———. 1984. *O Palco Verde*. Rio: Marco Zero.

———. 1987. *Teatro I*. Rio: Marco Zero.

Spix, Johann Baptist von, and Karl Friedsrich P. Martius. n.d. *Viagem pelo Brasil. 1817–1820*. Translated by Lúcia Furquim Lahmeyer. Vol. 3. São Paulo: Melhoramentos.

Staden, Hans. 1974. *Duas Viagens ao Brasil*. Translated by Guiomar de Carvalho Franco. São Paulo: EDUSP; Belo Horizonte: Itatiaia.

Stradelli, Ermanno. 1890. "L'Uaupés e gli Uapés." *Bollettino de la Società Geogràphica Italiana* III, vol. 3, 425–53.

———. 1929. "Vocabulários da Língua geral Português-Nheengatú e Nheengatú-Português, Precedidos de um Esboço de Gramática Nheênga-Umbuê-Sáua Miri e Seguidos de Contos em Língua Geral Nheeêngatu Poranduua." *Revista do Instituto Histórico e Geográfico Brasileiro* 104. No. 158: 5–768.

———. 1964. *La Leggenda dell' Jurupary e Outras Lendas Amazónicas*. Caderno 4. São Paulo: Instituto Cultural Italo-Brasileiro.

Thomas, David John. 1982. *Order without Government: The Society of the Pemon Indians of Venezuela*. Vol. 13 of *Illinois Studies in Anthropology*. Urbana: University of Illinois Press.

Treece, David. 2000. *Exiles, Allies, Rebels. Brazil's Indianist Movement, Indigenist Politics, and the Imperial Nation-State*. Westport; London: Greenwood Press.

Tufic, Jorge. 1987. "Brandão de Amorim e a Literatura Nacional." In *Lendas em Nheengatú e em Português* by Antônio Brandão do Amorim. Manaus: Fundo Editorial.

Turner, Terence. 1988. "History, Myth, and Social Consciousness among the Kayapó of Central Brasil." In *Rethinking History and Myth: Indigenous South American Perspectives on the Past,* edited by Jonathan Hill. Urbana: Illinois University Press.

Useche Losada, Mariano. 1987. *El proceso colonial en el Alto Orinoco-Rio Negro (Siglos XVI a XVIII)*. Bogota: Fundación de Investigaciones Arqueológicas Nacionales; Banco de la República.

Vargas, Dora del Carmen. 1990. "El guaranítico como expresión de identidad en Escritores de Corrientes, Argentina." Ph.D. diss., University of Tennessee.

Vargas Llosa, Mario. 1964. "José María Arguedas descubre al indio auténtico." *Visión del Peru* 1: 3–7.

———. 1977. *La utopía arcaica*. Working Papers no. 33. Cambridge: Center of Latin American Studies, University of Cambridge.

———. 1978. *José María Arguedas, entre sapos y halcones*. Madrid: Centro Americano de Cooperación.

———. 1989. *The Storyteller*. Translated by Helen Lane. New York: Farrar, Straus, Giroux.

———. 1990. "Questions of Conquest." *Harper's Magazine*, December, 45–53.

———. 1996. *La utopía arcaica: José María Arguedas y las ficciones del indigenismo*. Mexico City: Fondo de Cultura Económica.

Vittori, José Luis. 1991. *Del Barco Centenera y "La Argentina."* Santa Fe: Colmegna.

Volek, Emil. 1994. *"El hablador* de Mario Vargas Llosa: Utopías y distopías post-modernas." In *Literatura hispanoamericana entre la modernidad y la post-modernidad.* Bogotá: Universidad Nacional.

Wallace, Alfred Russel. 1889. *Travels on the Amazon and Rio Negro. With an Account of the Native Tribes, and Observations on the Climate, Geology, and Natural History of the Amazon Valley.* London: Ward, Lock, and Co.

Walty, Ivete Camargos. 1991. "Narrativa e Imaginário Social: Uma Leitura das Histórias de Maloca Antigamente, de Pichuvy Cinta Larga." Ph.D. diss., Universidade de São Paulo.

Wasserman, Renata R. Mautner. 1984. "Preguiça and Power: Mário de Andrade's *Macunaíma." Luso-Brasilian Review* 21 no. 1: 99–116.

Whitehead, Neil. 1988. *Lords of the Tiger Spirit: A History of the Caribs in Colonial Venezuela and Guyana, 1498–1820.* Dordrecht: Foris.

———. 2000. "Hans Staden and the Cultural Politics of Cannibalism." *Hispanic American Historical Review* 80 no. 4: 721–51.

———. 2002. *Dark Shamans. Kanaima and the Poetics of Violent Death.* Durham: Duke University Press.

Wolf, Eric. 1959. *Sons of the Shaking Earth.* Chicago: Chicago University Press.

Wright, Robin M. 1981. "History and Religion of the Baniwa Peoples of the Upper Rio Negro Valley." Ph.D. diss., Stanford University.

———. 1992. "História Indígena do Noroeste da Amazônia." In *História dos Índios no Brasil,* edited by Manuela Carneiro da Cunha. São Paulo: FAPESP; Companhia das Letras; SMC.

———. 1998. *Cosmos, Self, and History in Baniwa Religion. For Those Unborn.* Austin: University of Texas Press.

Zorrilla de San Martín, Juan. 1973. *Tabaré.* Mexico City: Porrúa.

Index

Lúcia Sá is assistant professor at Stanford University. She teaches Brazilian and Spanish American literatures and has published several articles on Brazilian poetry and fiction, Peruvian fiction, censorship in Brazil, and Brazilian popular culture. Her research interests include the intertextual relationships between indigenous narratives and twentieth-century literature in Brazil and Spanish America, discourses of identity in Latin America, Brazilian avant-garde poetry, and Brazilian popular culture.